Lecture Notes in Computer Science 9000

Commenced Publication in 1973
Founding and Former Series Editors:
Gerhard Goos, Juris Hartmanis, and Jan van Leeuwen

T0212842

Mikhail Kovalev   Silvia M. Müller
Wolfgang J. Paul

A Pipelined Multi-core MIPS Machine

Hardware Implementation and Correctness Proof

 Springer

Authors

Mikhail Kovalev
Sirrix AG
Im Stadtwald D3 2, 66123 Saarbrücken, Germany
E-mail: m.kovalev@sirrix.com

Wolfgang J. Paul
Saarland University
Department of Computer Science
66123 Saarbrücken, Germany
E-mail: wjp@cs.uni-saarland.de

Silvia M. Müller
IBM Germany Research and Development GmbH
Schönaicher Str. 220, 71032 Böblingen, Germany
E-mail: smm@de.ibm.com

ISSN 0302-9743   e-ISSN 1611-3349
ISBN 978-3-319-13905-0   e-ISBN 978-3-319-13906-7
DOI 10.1007/978-3-319-13906-7
Springer Cham Heidelberg New York Dordrecht London

Library of Congress Control Number: 2014956104

LNCS Sublibrary: SL 1 – Theoretical Computer Science and General Issues

Typesetting: Camera-ready by author, data conversion by Markus Richter, Heidelberg

Printed on acid-free paper

Springer is part of Springer Science+Business Media (www.springer.com)

Preface

This book is based on the third author's lectures on computer architecture, as given in the summer semester of 2013 at Saarland University. It contains a gate level construction of a multi-core machine with pipelined MIPS processor cores and a sequentially consistent shared memory. This opens the way to the formal verification of synthesizable hardware for multi-core processors in the future.

We proceed in three steps: i) we review pipelined single core processor constructions and their correctness proofs, ii) we present a construction of a cache-based shared memory which is kept consistent by the MOESI protocol and show that it is sequentially consistent, and iii) we integrate the pipelined processor cores into the shared memory and show that the resulting hardware simulates the steps of an abstract multi-core MIPS machine in some order. In the last step the reference machine consists of MIPS cores and a single memory, where the cores, together with the shared memory, execute instructions in a nondeterministic order.

In the correctness proofs of the last two steps a new issue arises. Constructions are in a gate level hardware model and thus deterministic. In contrast the reference models against which correctness is shown are nondeterministic. The development of the additional machinery for these proofs and the correctness proof of the shared memory at the gate level are the main technical contributions of this work.

October 2014

Mikhail Kovalev
Silvia M. Müller
Wolfgang J. Paul

Contents

1

Introduction

Building on [12] and [6], we present at the gate level the construction of a multi-core MIPS machine with "basic" pipelined processors and prove that it works. "Basic" means that the processors only implement the part of the instruction set architecture (ISA) that is visible in *user mode*; we call it ISA-u. Extending it to the full architecture ISA-sp, that is visible in *system programmers mode*, we would have to add among other things the following mechanisms: i) local and inter processor interrupts, ii) store buffers, and iii) memory management units (MMUs). We plan to do this as future work. In Sect. 1.1 we present reasons why we think the results might be of interest. In Sect. 1.2 we give a short overview of the book.

1.1 Motivation

The are several reasons why we wrote this book and which might motivate other scientists to read it.

Lecture Notes

The book contains the *lecture notes* of the third author's lectures on Computer Architecture 1 as given in the summer semester 2013 at Saarland University. The purpose of ordinary architecture lectures is to enable students to draw the building plans of houses, bridges, etc., and hopefully, also to explain why they won't collapse. Similarly, we try in our lectures on computer architecture to enable students to draw the building plans of processors and to explain why they work. We do this by presenting in the classroom a complete gate level design of a RISC processor. We present correctness proofs because, for nontrivial designs, they are the fastest way we know to explain why the designs work. Because we live in the age of multi-core computing we attempted to treat the design of such a processor in the classroom within a single semester. With the help of written lecture notes this happened to work out. Indeed, a

M. Kovalev et al.: A Pipelined Multi-core MIPS Machine, LNCS 9000, pp. 1–6, 2014.
© Springer International Publishing Switzerland 2014

student who had only 6 weeks of previous experience with hardware design succeeded to implement the processor presented here on a field programmable gate array (FPGA) within 6 weeks after the end of the lectures [8].

Multi-core Processor Correctness

To the best of our knowledge, this book contains the first correctness proof for the gate level implementation of a multi-core processor.

Shared Memory Correctness

As a building block for the processor design, the book contains a gate level implementation of a cache consistent shared memory system and a proof that it is sequentially consistent. That such shared memory systems can be implemented is in a sense *the* fundamental folklore theorem of multi-core computing: i) everybody believes it; experimental evidence given by the computers on our desk is indeed overwhelming, ii) proofs are widely believed to exist, but iii) apparently nobody has seen the entire proof; for an explanation why the usual model checked results for cache coherence protocols fail to prove the whole theorem see the introduction of Chap. 8. To the best of our knowledge, this book contains the first complete correctness proof for a gate level implementation of a cache based sequentially consistent shared memory.

Building Plans for Formal Verification

Proofs in this book are presented on paper; such proofs are often called "paper-and-pencil proofs". Because they are the work of humans they can contain errors and gaps, which are hopefully small and easily repaired. With the help of computers one can debug proofs produced by humans: one enters them in computer readable form into so called *computer aided verification systems* (CAV systems) and then lets the computer check the correctness and completeness of the proof. Technically, this reduces to a syntax check in a formal language of what the system accepts as a proof. This process is called *formal verification*. Formal, i.e., machine readable proofs, are engineering objects. Like any other engineering objects, it makes a lot of sense to construct them from a building plan. Sufficiently precise paper and pencil proofs serve this purpose extremely well. Proofs published in [12] led, for instance, very quickly to the formal verification of single core processors of industrial complexity [1,3]. The proofs in this book are, therefore, also meant as blueprints for later formal verification work of shared memory systems and multi-core processors. This explains, why we have included some lengthy proofs of the bookkeeping type in this text. They are only meant as help for verification engineers. At the beginning of chapters, we give hints to these proofs: they can be skipped at a first reading and should not be presented in the classroom. There is, however, a benefit of going through these proofs: afterwards you feel more comfortable when you skip them in the classroom.

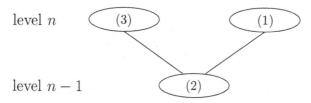

level n

level $n - 1$

Fig. 1. Functional correctness (1) is shown on level n. Proof obligation (3) is not necessary for the proof of (1) but has to be discharged on level n in order to guarantee implementation (2) at level $n - 1$. If level n is considered in isolation it drops out of the blue

"Obscure" Proof Obligations

In recent research we have encountered a general and quite hideous source of gaps in formal verification work. Systems are composed of successive layers, where on each layer n the user sees a certain computational model, and the model on layer n is implemented in the simplest case simply in the model of layer $n - 1$. Typical layers are i) digital gates and registers, ii) instruction set architecture (ISA), iii) assembly language, iv) high level language (+ maybe assembly), and v) operating system kernel. These models often are *very well* established and are successfully used for such a long time that one does not worry about their completeness in places where one should. This can lead to the situation established in Fig. 1. Imagine we want to prove a property of a system component specified and implemented on level n. We successfully finish the proof (1) that the implementation meets the specification on level n, both on paper and in the formal verification work. We overlook the fact that level n is implemented (2) in level $n - 1$ and that certain not so well published implementation details lead to proof obligations (3) on the higher level n. If we restrict attention to the single level n, these proof obligations are completely obscure and drop out of the blue; their absence does not show up in the proof of the desired correctness property (1). Of course, in mathematics, there are no obscure proof obligations, and proof obligation (3) is only overlooked on level n if we disregard the fact that simulation of level n by lower levels has to be established. We give two examples of this effect and remedy one of them in this book:

- The documentation of instruction set architectures tends to hide the processor pipeline from the user. This does not always work. Between certain operations (like the write of an instruction during page fault handling and a subsequent fetch), one better waits long enough (which exposes the pipe depth) or drains the pipe (which is a meaningless operation in a usual ISA model where instruction execution is sequential). The same pipe drain should occur between an update of a page table and its subsequent use by the memory management unit (MMU). In the scenario studied here, these problems do not occur: there is no MMU yet and – as in early work on sequential processor verification – we assume for the time being that code is not self modifying. Identifying for a multi-core processor *all* such implementation dependent proof obligations, which are obscure at the ISA level alone, is a major research project and part of the future work outlined below.

- Digital hardware is *not* the lowest system layer one has to consider in hardware design. If one studies hardware with different clock domains, one has to consider the more detailed hardware model from the data sheets of hardware vendors; within each clock domain one can use timing analysis to establish a simulation theorem justifying the use of digital design rules for gates and registers except at the borders of the clock domain. This approach was sketched in [10] and is worked out in Chap. 3 here. But even in a single clock domain it turns out that for the drivers, the buses, and the main memory components considered here, the digital model does not suffice to derive all proof obligations for the digital control circuits of the units. Additional proof obligations that arise from the detailed hardware model have to be discharged by the digital control logic. This explains our treatment of the detailed hardware model here. Note, by the way, that in [12] and subsequent formal verification work only the digital hardware model was considered. As a result, the control for the main memory as published in [12] violates the obligations coming from the detailed model. That the formally verified hardware did not crash (indeed it ran immediately without ever crashing) was luck: the hardware implementer had secretly changed the verified design in a single place which happened to fix the problem. For details see the introduction of Chap. 3.

Basis for Future Work

In the preceding paragraph, we have pointed out the existence of software conditions which have to be met by ISA programs and which stem from implementation details of the processor hardware. We have given examples for such conditions even in the context of single core processors. It is of paramount importance to identify *all* such software conditions at the ISA level, because without such knowledge it is simply impossible to guarantee that any program (written directly in ISA or compiled or assembled into ISA) performs as specified: any software conditions we have overlooked and which are not met by our software might bring the system down. For multi-core processors operating in system mode this appears now as a quite nontrivial task. As outlined in [2, 15] we intend to proceed in the following way:

- Define without software conditions the full ISA-sp visible by system programmers for a multi-core machine which is at the same time sufficiently realistic and sufficiently small to permit gate level implementation by a group working in an academic environment. In [15] this has been done for a machine called MIPS-86. It has an x86-like memory system and a MIPS instruction set. In addition to the machine considered here it has store buffers, MMUs, advanced programmable interrupt controllers (APICs) and mechanisms for inter processor interrupts. The model still has to be augmented to permit multiple memory modes.

- Augment the design of this book by the missing units. Augment the proofs of this book to show that the machine built this way implements the specified ISA-sp. *Identify the software conditions which make the proof work.*

1.2 Overview

Chapter 2 contains some very basic material about number formats and Boolean algebra. In the section on congruences we establish simple lemmas which we use in Chap. 5 to prove the remarkable fact that binary numbers and two's complement numbers are correctly added and subtracted (modulo 2^n) by the very same hardware.

In Chap. 3, we define the digital and the physical hardware model and show that, in common situations, the digital model is an abstraction of the detailed model. For the operation of drivers, buses, and main memory components we construct circuits which are controlled completely by digital signals, and show in the detailed model that the control circuits operate the buses without contention and the main memory without glitches. We show that these considerations are crucial by constructing a bus control which i) has no bus contention in the (incomplete) digital model and ii) has bus contention for roughly 1/3 of the time in the detailed model. In the physical world, such a circuit destroys itself due to short circuits.

Chapter 4 contains a collection of various RAM constructions that we need later. Arithmetic logic units, shifters, etc. are treated in Chap. 5.

In Chap. 6, the basic MIPS instruction set architecture is defined and a sequential reference implementation is given. We make the memory of this machine as wide as the cache line size we use later. Thus, shifters have to be provided for the implementation of load and store operations. Intuitively, it is obvious that these shifters work correctly. Thus, in [12], where we did not aim at formal verification, a proof that loads and stores were correctly implemented with the help of these shifters was omitted. Subsequent formal verification work only considered loads and stores of words and double words; this reduced the shifters to trivial hardware which was easy to deal with. As this text is also meant as a help for verification engineers, we included the correctness proof for the full shifters. These proofs argue, in the end, about the absence of carries in address computations across cache line boundaries for aligned accesses. Writing these arguments down turned out slightly more tricky than anticipated.

With the exception of the digital hardware model and the shifters for load and store operations, the book until this point basically contains updated and revised material from the first few chapters in [12]. In Chap. 7, we obtain a pipelined machine from the reference implementation by a fairly simple transformation. However, in contrast to the old pipelined construction from [12], we incorporate improvements from [6]. As a result, both the transformation and the correctness proof are simpler. A small gap in the corresponding proof in [12] is closed. The improved stall engine controlling pipeline stalls from [6] is used. Liveness is treated in greater detail than in [12].

The main new technical material is in the last two chapters. In Chap. 8, we construct a shared memory system whose caches are kept consistent by the MOESI protocol [16] and we prove that it is sequentially consistent.

In Chap. 9, we extend the specification of the basic MIPS ISA to the multi-core case. We construct the multi-core machine by hooking the pipelined processors from Chap. 7 into the shared memory system from Chap. 8. This construction is fairly straightforward. Then, we combine previous correctness proofs into an overall functional correctness proof of the multi-core machine. Intuitively, it is quite clear why this works. Still, making this intuition precise required the introduction of a modest amount of new proof machinery. We conclude Chap. 9 by proving liveness of the multi-core machine.

2

Number Formats and Boolean Algebra

We begin in Sect. 2.1 with very basic definitions of intervals of integers. Because this book is meant as a building plan for formal proofs, we cannot make definitions like $[1 : 10] = \{1, 2, \ldots, 10\}$ because CAV systems don't understand such definitions. So we replace them by fairly obvious inductive definitions. We also have to deal with the minor technical nuisance that, usually, sequence elements are numbered from left to right, but in number representations, it is much nicer to number them from right to left.

Section 2.2 on modulo arithmetic was included for several reasons. i) The notation *mod k* is overloaded: it is used to denote both the congruence *relation* modulo a number k or the *operation* of taking the remainder of an integer division by k. We prefer our readers to clearly understand this. ii) Fixed point arithmetic is modulo arithmetic, so we will clearly have to make use of it. The most important reason, however, is that iii) addition/subtraction of binary numbers and of two's complement numbers is done by exactly the same hardware[1]. When we get to this topic this will look completely intuitive and, therefore, there should be a very simple proof justifying this fact. Such a proof can be found in Sect. 5.1; it hinges on a simple lemma about the solution of congruence equations from this section.

The very short Sect. 2.3 on geometric sums is simply there to remind the reader of the proof of the formula for the computation of geometric sums, which is much easier to memorize than the formula itself.

Section 2.4 introduces the binary number format, presents the school method for binary addition, and proves that it works. Although this looks simple and familiar and the correctness proof of the addition algorithms is only a few lines long, the reader should treat this result with deep respect: it is probably the first time that he or she sees a proof of the fact that the addition algorithm he learned at school always works. The Old Romans, who were fabulous engineers in spite of their clumsy number systems, would have *loved* to see this proof.

---

[1] Except for the computation of overflow and negative signals.

M. Kovalev et al.: A Pipelined Multi-core MIPS Machine, LNCS 9000, pp. 7–27, 2014.
© Springer International Publishing Switzerland 2014

Integers are represented in computers as two's complement numbers. In Sect. 2.5, we introduce this number format and derive a small number of basic identities for such numbers. From this we derive a subtraction algorithms for binary numbers, which is quite different from the school method, and show that it works. Sections 2.2, 2.3, and 2.5 are the basis of our construction of an arithmetic unit later.

Finally, in Sect. 2.6 on Boolean Algebra, we provide a very short proof of the fundamental result that Boolean functions can be computed using Boolean expressions in disjunctive normal form. This result can serve to construct all small circuits – e.g., in the control logic – where we only specify their functionality and do not bother to specify a concrete realization. The proof is intuitive and looks simple, but it will give us the occasion to explain formally the difference between what is often called "two kinds of equations": i) identities[2] $e(x) = e'(x)$ which hold for all x and ii) equations $e(x) = e'(x)$ that we want to solve by determining the set of all x such that the equation holds[3]. The reader will notice that this might be slightly subtle, because both kinds of equations have exactly the same form.

2.1 Basics

2.1.1 Numbers, Sets, and Logical Connectives

We denote by

$$\mathbb{N} = \{0, 1, 2, \ldots\}$$

the set of natural numbers including zero, by

$$\mathbb{N}^+ = \{1, 2, \ldots\}$$

the set of natural numbers excluding zero, by

$$\mathbb{Z} = \{\ldots, -2, -1, 0, 1, 2, \ldots\}$$

the set of integers, and by

$$\mathbb{B} = \{0, 1\}$$

the set of Boolean values.

For integers i, j with $i < j$, we define the interval of integers from i to j by

$$[i : j] = \{i, i+1, \ldots, j\} \ .$$

Strictly speaking, definitions using three dots are never precise; they resemble intelligence tests, where the author hopes that all readers who are forced to take the test arrive at the same solution. Usually, one can easily find a

---

[2] In German: Identitäten.
[3] In German: Bestimmungsgleichung.

Table 1. Logical connectives and quantifiers

$x \wedge y$	and
$x \vee y$	or
$\neg x$, $\bar{x}$	not
$x \oplus y$	exclusive or, $+$ modulo 2
$x \rightarrow y$	implies
$x \leftrightarrow y$	if and only if
$\forall x$	for all
$\exists x$	exists

corresponding and completely precise recursive definition (without three dots) in such a situation. Thus, we define the interval $[i : j]$ in a rigorous way as

$$[i : i] = \{i\}$$
$$[i : j + 1] = [i : j] \cup \{j + 1\} .$$

The Hilbert $\in$-Operator $\in A$ picks an element from a set A. Applied to a singleton set, it returns the unique element of the set:

$$\in\{x\} = x .$$

For finite sets A, we denote by $\#A$ the *cardinality*, i.e., the number of elements in A.

Given a function f operating on a set A and a set $A_1 \subseteq A$, we denote by $f(A_1)$ the image of set A_1 under function f, i.e.,

$$f(A_1) = \{f(a) \mid a \in A_1\} .$$

In statements and predicates we use the logical connectives and quantifiers from Table 1. For the negation of x we can write $\neg x$ as well as $\bar{x}$.

In computer science literature, logarithms are to the base of two, unless explicitly stated otherwise. This text is no exception.

2.1.2 Sequences and Bit-Strings

A sequence a of n many elements $a_i = a[i] = a(i)$ from set A, where $n \in \mathbb{N}^+$ and $i \in [0 : n - 1]$, can come in many flavors. In this book we use three of them.

1. A sequence numbered from left to right starting with 0 is written as

$$a = (a^i) = (a_0, \ldots, a_{n-1}) = a[0 : n - 1]$$

and is formalized without the dots as a mapping

$$a : [0 : n - 1] \rightarrow A .$$

With this formalization the set A^n of sequences of length n with elements from A is defined as

$$A^n = \{a \mid a : [0 : n - 1] \to A\} \ .$$

2. A sequence numbered from left to right starting with 1 is written as

$$a = (a_1, \ldots, a_n) = a[1 : n]$$

and is defined as

$$a : [1 : n] \to A \ .$$

The set A^n of such sequences is then formalized as

$$A^n = \{a \mid a : [1 : n] \to A\} \ .$$

3. We can also number the elements in a sequence a from right to left starting with 0. Then we write

$$a = (a_{n-1}, \ldots, a_0) = a[n - 1 : 0] \ ,$$

which, surprisingly, has the same formalization as a sequence starting with 0 and numbered from left to right:

$$a : [0 : n - 1] \to A \ .$$

The set A^n is again defined as

$$A^n = \{a \mid a : [0 : n - 1] \to A\} \ .$$

Thus, the direction of ordering does not show up in the formalization *yet*. The reason is, that the interval $[0 : n - 1]$ is a set, and elements of sets are unordered. The difference, however, will show up when we formalize operations on sequences.

The concatenation operator $\circ$ is defined for sequences $a[n - 1 : 0]$, $b[m - 1 : 0]$ numbered from right to left and starting with 0 as

$$\forall i \in [n + m - 1 : 0] : (a \circ b)[i] = \begin{cases} b[i] & i < m \\ a[i - m] & i \geq m \ , \end{cases}$$

or, respectively, for sequences $a[0 : n - 1]$, $b[0 : m - 1]$ numbered from left to right as

$$\forall i \in [0 : n + m - 1] : (a \circ b)[i] = \begin{cases} a[i] & i < n \\ b[i - n] & i \geq n \ . \end{cases}$$

For sequences $a[1 : n]$ and $b[1 : m]$ numbered from left to right, concatenation is defined as

$$\forall i \in [1 : n + m] : (a \circ b)[i] = \begin{cases} a[i] & i \leq n \\ b[i - n] & i > n . \end{cases}$$

Concatenation of sequences a with single symbols $b \in A$ is handled by treating elements b as sequences with one element $b = b[0]$.

Let $i \leq j$ and $j \leq n - 1$. Then for sequences $a[0 : n - 1]$ we define a subsequence $a[i : j]$ as

$$a[i : j] = c[0 : j - i] \quad \text{with} \quad c[k] = a[i + k]$$

and for sequences $a[n - 1 : 0]$ a subsequence $a[j : i]$ is defined as

$$a[j : i] = c[j - i : 0] \quad \text{with} \quad c[k] = a[i + k] .$$

For sequences $a[1 : n]$ and indices $i \leq j$, where $1 \leq i$ and $j \leq n$, subsequence $a[i : j]$ is defined as

$$a[i : j] = c[1 : j - i + 1] \quad \text{with} \quad c[k] = a[i + k - 1] .$$

A single element $x \in \mathbb{B}$ is called a *bit*. A sequence $a \in \mathbb{B}^n$ is called a *bit-string*. For bits $x \in \mathbb{B}$ and natural numbers $n \in \mathbb{N}^+$, a bit-string obtained by repeating x exactly n times is defined in the format of an intelligence test by

$$x^n = \underbrace{x \ldots x}_{n \text{ times}} .$$

and formally by

$$x^1 = x$$
$$x^{n+1} = x \circ x^n .$$

Examples of such strings are

$$1^2 = 11$$
$$0^4 = 0000 .$$

In these examples and later in the book, we often omit $\circ$ when denoting the concatenation of bit-strings x_1 and x_2:

$$x_1 x_2 = x_1 \circ x_2 .$$

When dealing with the construction of RAMs and memory systems, it is sometimes convenient to talk about bytes rather than individual bits. Function $byte(i, x)$ is used to extract the i-th byte from a bit-string $x \in \mathbb{B}^{8k}$, where $i \in [0 : k - 1]$:

$$byte(i, x) = x[8 \cdot i + 7 : 8 \cdot i] .$$

Complement $\bar{a}$ of a bit-string $a \in \mathbb{B}^n$ is defined in an obvious way:

$$\bar{a} = (\overline{a_{n-1}}, \ldots, \overline{a_0}) .$$

For logical connectives $\circ \in \{\wedge, \vee, \oplus\}$, bit-strings $a, b \in \mathbb{B}^n$, and a bit $c \in \mathbb{B}$, we borrow the notation from vector calculus to define the corresponding bit-operations on bit-strings[4]:

$$a[n-1:0] \circ b[n-1:0] = (a_{n-1} \circ b_{n-1}, \ldots, a_0 \circ b_0)$$
$$c \circ b[n-1:0] = (c \circ b_{n-1}, \ldots, c \circ b_0) .$$

2.2 Modulo Computation

There are infinitely many integers and every computer can only store finitely many numbers. Thus, computer arithmetic cannot possibly work like ordinary arithmetic. Fixed point arithmetic[5] is usually performed modulo 2^n for some n. We review basics about modulo computation.

For integers $a, b \in \mathbb{Z}$ and natural numbers $k \in \mathbb{N}^+$, one defines a and b to be *congruent mod k* or *equivalent mod k* iff they differ by an integer multiple of k:

$$a \equiv b \bmod k \leftrightarrow \exists z \in \mathbb{Z} : a - b = z \cdot k .$$

Congruence mod k has a number of important properties which we formalize below.

Let R be a relation between elements of a set A. We say that R is *reflexive* if we have aRa for all $a \in A$. We say that R is *symmetric* if aRb implies bRa. We say that R is *transitive* if aRb and bRc imply aRc. If all three properties hold, R is called an *equivalence relation* on A.

Lemma 2.1 (congruence properties). Congruence mod k is an equivalence relation.

Proof. We show that the properties of an equivalence relation are satisfied:

- Reflexivity: For all $a \in \mathbb{Z}$ we have $a - a = 0 \cdot k$. Thus, $a \equiv a \bmod k$ and congruence mod k is reflexive.
- Symmetry: Let $a \equiv b \bmod k$ with $a - b = z \cdot k$. Then, $b - a = -z \cdot k$. Thus, $b \equiv a \bmod k$.
- Transitivity: Let $a \equiv b \bmod k$ with $a - b = z \cdot k$ and $b \equiv c \bmod k$ with $b - c = u \cdot k$. Then, $a - c = (z + u) \cdot k$, and thus, $a \equiv c \bmod k$.

□

---

[4] Note that here $\circ$ is not to be confused with the concatenation operator.

[5] The only arithmetic considered in this book. For the construction of floating point units see [12].

Lemma 2.2 (plus, minus equivalence). Let $a, b \in \mathbb{Z}$ and $k \in \mathbb{N}^+$ with $a \equiv a'$ mod k and $b \equiv b'$ mod k. Then,

$$a + b \equiv a' + b' \bmod k$$
$$a - b \equiv a' - b' \bmod k \ .$$

Proof. Let $a - a' = u \cdot k$ and $b - b' = v \cdot k$, then we have

$$a + b - (a' + b') = a - a' + b - b'$$
$$= (u + v) \cdot k$$
$$a - b - (a' - b') = a - a' - (b - b')$$
$$= (u - v) \cdot k \ ,$$

which imply the desired congruences. □

Two numbers r and s in an interval of the form $[i : i + k - 1]$ that are both equivalent to a mod k are identical.

Lemma 2.3 (equality from equivalence). Let $i \in \mathbb{Z}$, $k \in \mathbb{N}^+$, and let $r, s \in [i : i + k - 1]$, then

$$a \equiv r \bmod k \wedge a \equiv s \bmod k \rightarrow r = s \ .$$

Proof. By symmetry we have $s \equiv a$ mod k and by transitivity we get $s \equiv r$ mod k. Thus, $r - s = z \cdot k$ for an integer z. We conclude $z = 0$ because $|r - s| < k$. □

Let R be an equivalence relation on A. A subset $B \subset A$ is called a *system of representatives* if and only if for every $a \in A$ there is exactly one $r \in B$ with aRr. The unique $r \in B$ satisfying aRr is called the *representative* of a in B.

Lemma 2.4 (system of representatives). For $i \in \mathbb{Z}$ and $k \in \mathbb{N}^+$, the interval of integers $[i : i + k - 1]$ is a system of representatives for equivalence mod k.

Proof. Let $a \in \mathbb{Z}$. We define the representative $r(a)$ by

$$f(a) = max\{j \in \mathbb{Z} \mid a - k \cdot j \geq i\}$$
$$r(a) = a - f(a) \cdot k.$$

Then $r(a) \equiv a$ mod k and $r(a) \in [i : i + k - 1]$. Uniqueness follows from Lemma 2.3.

Note that in case $i = 0$, $f(a)$ is the result of the integer division of a by k:

$$f(a) = \lfloor a/k \rfloor \ ,$$

and

$$r(a) = a - \lfloor a/k \rfloor \cdot k$$

is the remainder of this division. □

We have to point out that in mathematics the three letter word "mod" is not only used for the *relation* defined above. It is also used as a *binary operator* in which case $(a \bmod k)$ denotes the representative of a in $[0 : k-1]$. Let $a, b \in \mathbb{Z}$ and $k \in \mathbb{N}^+$. Then,

$$(a \bmod k) = \in\{b \mid a \equiv b \bmod k \wedge b \in [0 : k-1]\} \,.$$

Thus, $(a \bmod k)$ is the remainder of the integer division of a by k for $a \geq 0$. In order to stress when mod is used as a binary operator, we *always* write $(a \bmod k)$ in brackets. For later use in the theory of two's complement numbers, we define another modulo operator. Let $a, b \in \mathbb{Z}$ and $k = 2 \cdot k'$ be an *even* number with $k' \in \mathbb{N}^+$. Then,

$$(a \text{ tmod } k) = \in\{b \mid a \equiv b \bmod k \wedge b \in [-k/2 : k/2 - 1]\} \,.$$

From Lemma 2.3 we infer a simple but useful lemma about the solution of equivalences mod k.

Lemma 2.5 (solution of equivalences). Let k be even and $x \equiv y \bmod k$, then

1. $x \in [0 : k-1] \rightarrow x = (y \bmod k)$,
2. $x \in [-k/2 : k/2 - 1] \rightarrow x = (y \text{ tmod } k)$.

2.3 Geometric Sums

For $q \neq 1$ we consider

$$S = \sum_{i=0}^{n-1} q^i$$

the geometric sum over q. Then,

$$q \cdot S = \sum_{i=1}^{n} q^i$$
$$q \cdot S - S = q^n - 1$$
$$S = \frac{q^n - 1}{q - 1} \,.$$

For $q = 2$ we state this in the following lemma.

Lemma 2.6 (geometric sum). For $n \in \mathbb{N}^+$,

$$\sum_{i=0}^{n-1} 2^i = 2^n - 1 \,.$$

We will use this lemma in the next section.

2.4 Binary Numbers

For bit-strings $a = a[n - 1 : 0] \in \mathbb{B}^n$ we denote by

$$\langle a \rangle = \sum_{i=0}^{n-1} a_i \cdot 2^i$$

the interpretation of bit-string a as a *binary number*. We call a the *binary representation* of length n of the natural number $\langle a \rangle$. Examples of bit-strings interpreted as binary numbers are given below:

$$\langle 100 \rangle = 4$$
$$\langle 111 \rangle = 7$$
$$\langle 10^n \rangle = 2^n .$$

Applying Lemma 2.6, we get

$$\langle 1^n \rangle = \sum_{i=0}^{n-1} 2^i = 2^n - 1 ,$$

i.e., the largest binary number representable with n bits corresponds to the natural number $2^n - 1$.

Note that binary number interpretation is an injective function.

Lemma 2.7 (binary representation injective). Let $a, b \in \mathbb{B}^n$. Then,

$$a \neq b \rightarrow \langle a \rangle \neq \langle b \rangle .$$

Proof. Let $j = \max\{i \mid a_i \neq b_i\}$ be the largest index where strings a and b differ. Without loss of generality assume $a_j = 1$ and $b_j = 0$. Then,

$$\langle a \rangle - \langle b \rangle = \sum_{i=0}^{j} a_i \cdot 2^i - \sum_{i=0}^{j} b_i \cdot 2^i$$
$$\geq 2^j - \sum_{i=0}^{j-1} 2^i$$
$$= 1$$

by Lemma 2.6. $\qquad\qquad\square$

Let $n \in \mathbb{N}^+$. We denote by

$$B_n = \{\langle a \rangle \mid a \in \mathbb{B}^n\}$$

the set of natural numbers that have a binary representation of length n. Since

$$0 \leq \langle a \rangle \leq \sum_{i=0}^{n-1} 2^i = 2^n - 1 \, ,$$

we deduce

$$B_n \subseteq [0 : 2^n - 1] \, .$$

As $\langle \cdot \rangle$ is injective and

$$\#B_n = \#\mathbb{B}^n = 2^n = \#[0 : 2^n - 1] \, ,$$

we observe that $\langle \cdot \rangle$ is bijective and get the following lemma.

Lemma 2.8 (natural numbers with binary representation). For $n \in \mathbb{N}^+$ we have

$$B_n = [0 : 2^n - 1] \, .$$

For $x \in B_n$ we denote the binary representation of x of length n by $bin_n(x)$:

$$bin_n(x) = \in\{a \mid a \in \mathbb{B}^n \wedge \langle a \rangle = x\} \, .$$

To shorten notation even further, we write x_n instead of $bin_n(x)$:

$$x_n = bin_n(x) \, .$$

It is often useful to decompose n bit binary representations $a[n-1:0]$ into an upper part $a[n-1:m]$ and a lower part $a[m-1:0]$. The connection between the numbers represented is stated in Lemma 2.9.

Lemma 2.9 (decomposition). Let $a \in \mathbb{B}^n$ and $n \geq m$. Then,

$$\langle a[n-1:0] \rangle = \langle a[n-1:m] \rangle \cdot 2^m + \langle a[m-1:0] \rangle \, .$$

Proof.

$$\begin{aligned}
\langle a[n-1:0] \rangle &= \sum_{i=m}^{n-1} a_i \cdot 2^i + \sum_{i=0}^{m-1} a_i \cdot 2^i \\
&= \sum_{j=0}^{n-1-m} a_{m+j} \cdot 2^{m+j} + \langle a[m-1:0] \rangle \\
&= 2^m \cdot \sum_{j=0}^{n-1-m} a_{m+j} \cdot 2^j + \langle a[m-1:0] \rangle \\
&= 2^m \cdot \langle a[n-1:m] \rangle + \langle a[m-1:0] \rangle
\end{aligned}$$

$\square$

We obviously have

$$\langle a[n-1:0] \rangle \equiv \langle a[m-1:0] \rangle \bmod 2^m \, .$$

Using Lemma 2.5, we infer the following lemma.

Table 2. Binary addition of 1-bit numbers a, b with carry c

a	b	c	c'	s
0	0	0	0	0
0	0	1	0	1
0	1	0	0	1
0	1	1	1	0
1	0	0	0	1
1	0	1	1	0
1	1	0	1	0
1	1	1	1	1

Lemma 2.10 (decomposition mod equality). For $a \in \mathbb{B}^n$ and $m \leq n$,

$$\langle a[m - 1 : 0] \rangle = (\langle a[n - 1 : 0] \rangle \bmod 2^m) .$$

Intuitively speaking, taking a binary number modulo 2^m means "throwing away" the bits with position m or higher.

Table 2 specifies the addition algorithm for binary numbers a, b of length 1 and a carry-bit c. The binary representation $(c', s) \in \mathbb{B}^2$ of the sum of bits $a, b, c \in \mathbb{B}$ is computed as

$$\langle c' s \rangle = a + b + c .$$

For the addition of n-bit numbers $a[n - 1 : 0]$ and $b[n - 1 : 0]$ with carry in c_0, we first observe for the sum S:

$$\begin{aligned} S &= \langle a[n - 1 : 0] \rangle + \langle b[n - 1 : 0] \rangle + c_0 \\ &\leq 2^n - 1 + 2^n - 1 + 1 \\ &= 2^{n+1} - 1 . \end{aligned}$$

Thus, the sum $S \in \mathbb{B}^{n+1}$ can be represented as a binary number $\langle s[n : 0] \rangle$ with $n + 1$ bits. For the computation of the sum bits we use the method for long addition that we learn in elementary school for decimal numbers. We denote by c_i the carry from position $i - 1$ to position i and compute (c_{i+1}, s_i) using the basic binary addition of Table 2:

$$\begin{aligned} \langle c_{i+1}, s_i \rangle &= a_i + b_i + c_i \\ s_n &= c_n . \end{aligned} \tag{1}$$

That this algorithm indeed computes the sum of the input numbers is asserted in Lemma 2.11.

Lemma 2.11 (correctness of binary addition). Let $a, b \in \mathbb{B}^n$ and let $c \in \mathbb{B}$. Further, let $c_n \in \mathbb{B}$ and $s \in \mathbb{B}^n$ be computed according to the addition algorithm described above. Then,

$$\langle c_n, s[n - 1 : 0] \rangle = \langle a[n - 1 : 0] \rangle + \langle b[n - 1 : 0] \rangle + c_0 .$$

Proof. By induction on n. For $n = 0$ this follows directly from (1). For the induction step we conclude from $n - 1$ to n:

$$\langle a[n-1:0]\rangle + \langle b[n-1:0]\rangle + c_0$$
$$= (a_{n-1} + b_{n-1}) \cdot 2^{n-1} + \langle a[n-2:0]\rangle + \langle b[n-2:0]\rangle + c_0$$
$$= (a_{n-1} + b_{n-1}) \cdot 2^{n-1} + \langle c_{n-1}, s[n-2:0]\rangle \qquad \text{(induction hypothesis)}$$
$$= (a_{n-1} + b_{n-1} + c_{n-1}) \cdot 2^{n-1} + \langle s[n-2:0]\rangle$$
$$= \langle c_n, s_{n-1}\rangle \cdot 2^{n-1} + \langle s[n-2:0]\rangle \qquad (1)$$
$$= \langle c_n, s[n-1:0]\rangle . \qquad \text{(Lemma 2.9)}$$

$\square$

The following simple lemma allows breaking the addition of two long numbers into two additions of shorter numbers. It is useful, among other things, for proving the correctness of recursive addition algorithms (as applied in recursive hardware constructions of adders and incrementers).

Lemma 2.12 (decomposition of binary addition). For $a, b \in \mathbb{B}^n$, for $d, e \in \mathbb{B}^m$, and for $c_0, c', c'' \in \mathbb{B}$, let

$$\langle d\rangle + \langle e\rangle + c_0 = \langle c't[m-1:0]\rangle$$
$$\langle a\rangle + \langle b\rangle + c' = \langle c''s[n-1:0]\rangle ,$$

then

$$\langle ad\rangle + \langle be\rangle + c_0 = \langle c''st\rangle .$$

Repeatedly using Lemma 2.9, we have

$$\langle ad\rangle + \langle be\rangle + c_0 = \langle a\rangle \cdot 2^m + \langle d\rangle + \langle b\rangle \cdot 2^m + \langle e\rangle + c_0$$
$$= (\langle a\rangle + \langle b\rangle) \cdot 2^m + \langle c't\rangle$$
$$= (\langle a\rangle + \langle b\rangle + c') \cdot 2^m + \langle t\rangle$$
$$= \langle c''s\rangle \cdot 2^m + \langle t\rangle$$
$$= \langle c''st\rangle .$$

2.5 Two's Complement Numbers

For bit-strings $a[n-1:0] \in \mathbb{B}^n$, we denote by

$$[a] = -a_{n-1} \cdot 2^{n-1} + \langle a[n-2:0]\rangle$$

the interpretation of a as a *two's complement number*. We refer to a as the *two's complement representation* of $[a]$.

For $n \in \mathbb{N}^+$, we denote by

$$T_n = \{[a] \mid a \in \mathbb{B}^n\}$$

the set of integers that have a two's complement representation of length n. Since

$$T_n = \{[0b] \mid b \in \mathbb{B}^{n-1}\} \cup \{[1b] \mid b \in \mathbb{B}^{n-1}\}$$
$$= B_{n-1} \cup \{-2^{n-1} + x \mid x \in B_{n-1}\}$$
$$= [0 : 2^{n-1} - 1] \cup \{-2^{n-1} + x \mid x \in [0 : 2^{n-1} - 1], \} \qquad \text{(Lemma 2.8)}$$

we have the following lemma.

Lemma 2.13 (integers with two's complement representation). Let $n \in \mathbb{N}^+$. Then,
$$T_n = [-2^{n-1} : 2^{n-1} - 1] \ .$$

By $twoc_n(x)$ we denote the two's complement representation of $x \in T_n$:

$$twoc_n(x) = \in\{a \mid a \in \mathbb{B}^n \wedge [a] = x\} \ .$$

We summarize basic properties of two's complement numbers.

Lemma 2.14 (properties of two's complement numbers). Let $a \in \mathbb{B}^n$. Then, the following holds:

$$[0a] = \langle a \rangle \quad \text{(embedding)}$$
$$[a] \equiv \langle a \rangle \bmod 2^n$$
$$[a] < 0 \leftrightarrow a_{n-1} = 1 \quad \text{(sign bit)}$$
$$[a_{n-1}a] = [a] \quad \text{(sign extension)}$$
$$-[a] = [\bar{a}] + 1 \ .$$

Proof. The first line is trivial. The second line follows from

$$[a] - \langle a \rangle = -a_{n-1} \cdot 2^{n-1} + \langle a[n-2 : 0] \rangle - (a_{n-1} \cdot 2^{n-1} + \langle a[n-2 : 0] \rangle)$$
$$= -a_{n-1} \cdot 2^n \ .$$

If $a_{n-1} = 0$ we have $[a] = \langle a[n-2 : 0] \rangle \geq 0$. If $a_{n-1} = 1$ we have

$$[a] = -2^{n-1} + \langle a[n-2 : 0] \rangle$$
$$\leq -2^{n-1} + 2^{n-1} - 1 \quad \text{(Lemma 2.8)}$$
$$= -1 \ .$$

This shows the third line. The fourth line follows from

$$[a_{n-1}a] = -a_{n-1} \cdot 2^n + \langle a[n-1 : 0] \rangle$$
$$= -a_{n-1} \cdot 2^n + a_{n-1} \cdot 2^{n-1} + \langle a[n-2 : 0] \rangle$$
$$= -a_{n-1} \cdot 2^{n-1} + \langle a[n-2 : 0] \rangle$$
$$= [a] \ .$$

For the last line we observe that $\overline{x} = 1 - x$ for $x \in \mathbb{B}$. Then,

$$[\overline{a}] = -\overline{a_{n-1}} \cdot 2^{n-1} + \sum_{i=0}^{n-2} \overline{a_i} \cdot 2^i$$

$$= -(1 - a_{n-1}) \cdot 2^{n-1} + \sum_{i=0}^{n-2} (1 - a_i) \cdot 2^i$$

$$= -2^{n-1} + \sum_{i=0}^{n-2} 2^i + a_{n-1} \cdot 2^{n-1} - \sum_{i=0}^{n-2} a_i \cdot 2^i$$

$$= -1 - [a] . \quad \text{(Lemma 2.6)}$$

$\square$

We conclude the discussion of binary numbers and two's complement numbers with a lemma that provides a subtraction algorithm for binary numbers.

Lemma 2.15 (subtraction for binary numbers). Let $a, b \in \mathbb{B}^n$. Then,

$$\langle a \rangle - \langle b \rangle \equiv \langle a \rangle + \langle \overline{b} \rangle + 1 \bmod 2^n .$$

If additionally $\langle a \rangle - \langle b \rangle \geq 0$, we have

$$\langle a \rangle - \langle b \rangle = (\langle a \rangle + \langle \overline{b} \rangle + 1 \bmod 2^n) .$$

Proof. By Lemma 2.14 we have

$$\langle a \rangle - \langle b \rangle = \langle a \rangle - [0b]$$
$$= \langle a \rangle + [1\overline{b}] + 1$$
$$= \langle a \rangle - 2^n + \langle \overline{b} \rangle + 1$$
$$\equiv \langle a \rangle + \langle \overline{b} \rangle + 1 \bmod 2^n .$$

The extra hypothesis $\langle a \rangle - \langle b \rangle \geq 0$ implies

$$\langle a \rangle - \langle b \rangle \in B_n .$$

The second claim now follows from Lemma 2.5. $\square$

2.6 Boolean Algebra

We consider Boolean expressions with constants 0 and 1, variables $x_0, x_1, \ldots$, $a, b, \ldots$, and function symbols $^-, \wedge, \vee, \oplus, f(\ldots), g(\ldots), \ldots$. Four of the function symbols have predefined semantics as specified in Table 3.

For a more formal definition one collects the constants, Boolean variables, and Boolean function symbols allowed into sets

Table 3. Boolean operators

x	y	$\overline{x}$	$x \wedge y$	$x \vee y$	$x \oplus y$
0	0	1	0	0	0
0	1	1	0	1	1
1	0	0	0	1	1
1	1	0	1	1	0

$$C = \{0, 1\}$$
$$V = \{x_0, x_1, \ldots\}$$
$$F = \{f_0, f_1, \ldots\} \ .$$

and denotes the number of arguments for function f_i with n_i. Now we can define the set BE of Boolean expressions by the following rules:

1. Constants and variables are Boolean expressions:

$$C \cup V \subset BE \ .$$

2. If e is a Boolean expression, then $(\overline{e})$ is also a Boolean expression:

$$e \in BE \rightarrow (\overline{e}) \in BE \ .$$

3. If e and e' are boolean expressions then so is $(e \circ e')$, where $\circ$ is a binary connector:

$$e, e' \in BE \wedge \circ \in \{\wedge, \vee, \oplus\} \rightarrow (e \circ e') \in BE \ .$$

4. If f_i is a symbol for a function with n_i arguments, then we can obtain a Boolean expression $f_i(e_1, \ldots, e_{n_i})$ by substituting the function arguments with Boolean expressions e_j:

$$(\forall j \in [1 : n_i] : e_j \in BE) \rightarrow f_i(e_1, \ldots, e_{n_i}) \in BE \ .$$

5. All Boolean expressions are formed by the above rules.

We call a Boolean expression *pure* if it uses only the predefined connectives and doesn't use any other function symbols.

In order to save brackets, one uses the convention that $^-$ binds stronger than $\wedge$ and that $\wedge$ binds stronger than $\vee$. Thus, $\overline{x_1} \wedge x_2 \vee x_3$ is an abbreviation for

$$\overline{x_1} \wedge x_2 \vee x_3 = ((\overline{x_1}) \wedge x_2) \vee x_3 \ .$$

We denote expressions e depending on variables $x = x[1 : n]$ by $e(x)$. Variables x_i can take values in $\mathbb{B}$. Thus, $x = x[1 : n]$ can take values in $\mathbb{B}^n$. We denote the result of evaluation of expression $e \in BE$ with a bit-string $a \in \mathbb{B}^n$ of inputs by $e(a)$ and get a straightforward set of rules for evaluating expressions:

1. Substitute a_i for x_i:
$$x_i = a_i .$$

2. If $e = (\overline{e'})$, then evaluate $e(a)$ by evaluating $e'(a)$ and negating the result according to the predefined meaning of negation in Table 3:
$$(\overline{e'})(a) = \overline{e'(a)} .$$

3. If $e = (e' \circ e'')$, then evaluate $e(a)$ by evaluating $e'(a)$ and $e''(a)$ and then combining the results according to the predefined meaning of $\circ$ in Table 3:
$$(e' \circ e'')(a) = e'(a) \circ e''(a) .$$

4. Expressions of the form $e = f_i(e_1, \ldots, e_{n_i})$ can only be evaluated if the symbol f_i has an interpretation as a function
$$f_i : \mathbb{B}^{n_i} \to \mathbb{B} .$$

In this case evaluate $f_i(e_1, \ldots, e_{n_i})(a)$ by evaluating arguments $e_j(a)$, substituting the result into f and evaluating f:
$$f_i(e_1, \ldots, e_{n_i})(a) = f_i(e_1(a), \ldots, e_{n_i}(a)) .$$

The following small example shows that this very formal and detailed set of rules captures our usual way of evaluating expressions:
$$(x_1 \wedge x_2)(0, 1) = x_1(0, 1) \wedge x_2(0, 1)$$
$$= 0 \wedge 1$$
$$= 0 .$$

Boolean equations, therefore, are written as
$$e = e' ,$$

where e and e' are expressions involving variables $x = x[1 : n]$. They come in two flavors:

- Identities. An equation $e = e'$ is an *identity* iff for any substitution of the variables $a = a[1 : n] \in \mathbb{B}^n$, expressions e and e' evaluate to the same value in $\mathbb{B}$:
$$\forall a \in \mathbb{B}^n : e(a) = e'(a) .$$

- Equations which one wants to solve. A substitution $a = a[1 : n] \in \mathbb{B}^n$ solves equation $e = e'$ if $e(a) = e'(a)$.

We observe that identities and equations we want to solve **do** differ formally in the *implicit quantification*. If not stated otherwise, we usually assume equations to be of the first type, i.e., to be implicitly quantified over all free variables. This is also the case with *definitions* of functions, where the left-hand side of an equation represents an entity being defined. For instance, the following definition of the function

$$f(x_1, x_2) = x_1 \wedge x_2$$

is the same as

$$\forall a, b \in \mathbb{B} : f(a, b) = a \wedge b .$$

We may also write

$$e \equiv e'$$

to stress that a given equation is an identity or to avoid brackets in case if this equation is a definition and the right-hand side itself contains an equality sign.

In case we talk about several equations in a single statement (this is often the case when we solve equations), we assume implicit quantification over the whole statement rather than over every single equation. For instance,

$$e_1 = e_2 \leftrightarrow e_3 = 0$$

is the same as

$$\forall a \in \mathbb{B}^n : e_1(a) = e_2(a) \leftrightarrow e_3(a) = 0$$

and means that, for any given substitution a, equations e_1 and e_2 evaluate to the same value if and only if equation e_3 evaluates to 0. In other words, equations $e_1 = e_2$ and $e_3 = 0$ have the same set of solutions.

In Boolean algebra there is a very simple connection between the solution of equations and identities. An identity $e \equiv e'$ holds iff equations $e = 1$ and $e' = 1$ have the same set of solutions.

Lemma 2.16 (identity from solving equations). Given Boolean expressions e and e' with inputs $x[1 : n]$, we have

$$e \equiv e' \leftrightarrow \forall a \in \mathbb{B}^n : (e(a) = 1 \leftrightarrow e'(a) = 1) .$$

Proof. The direction from left to right is trivial. For the other direction we distinguish cases:

- $e(a) = 1$. Then $e'(a) = 1$ by hypothesis.
- $e(a) = 0$. Then $e'(a) = 1$ would by hypothesis imply the contradiction $e(a) = 1$. Because in Boolean algebra $e'(a) \in \mathbb{B}$ we conclude $e'(a) = 0$.

Thus, we have $e(a) = e'(a)$ for all $a \in \mathbb{B}^n$.   □

2.6.1 Identities

In this section we provide a list of useful identities of Boolean algebra.

- Commutativity:

$$x_1 \wedge x_2 \equiv x_2 \wedge x_1$$
$$x_1 \vee x_2 \equiv x_2 \vee x_1$$
$$x_1 \oplus x_2 \equiv x_2 \oplus x_1$$

- Associativity:

$$(x_1 \wedge x_2) \wedge x_3 \equiv x_1 \wedge (x_2 \wedge x_3)$$
$$(x_1 \vee x_2) \vee x_3 \equiv x_1 \vee (x_2 \vee x_3)$$
$$(x_1 \oplus x_2) \oplus x_3 \equiv x_1 \oplus (x_2 \oplus x_3)$$

- Distributivity:

$$x_1 \wedge (x_2 \vee x_3) \equiv (x_1 \wedge x_2) \vee (x_1 \wedge x_3)$$
$$x_1 \vee (x_2 \wedge x_3) \equiv (x_1 \vee x_2) \wedge (x_1 \vee x_3)$$

- Identity:

$$x_1 \wedge 1 \equiv x_1$$
$$x_1 \vee 0 \equiv x_1$$

- Idempotence:

$$x_1 \wedge x_1 \equiv x_1$$
$$x_1 \vee x_1 \equiv x_1$$

- Annihilation:

$$x_1 \wedge 0 \equiv 0$$
$$x_1 \vee 1 \equiv 1$$

- Absorption:

$$x_1 \vee (x_1 \wedge x_2) \equiv x_1$$
$$x_1 \wedge (x_1 \vee x_2) \equiv x_1$$

- Complement:

$$x_1 \wedge \overline{x_1} \equiv 0$$
$$x_1 \vee \overline{x_1} \equiv 1$$

- Double negation:

$$\overline{\overline{x_1}} \equiv x_1$$

Table 4. Verifying the first of de Morgan's laws

x_1	x_2	$x_1 \wedge x_2$	$\overline{x_1 \wedge x_2}$	$\overline{x_1}$	$\overline{x_2}$	$\overline{x_1} \vee \overline{x_2}$
0	0	0	1	1	1	1
0	1	0	1	1	0	1
1	0	0	1	0	1	1
1	1	1	0	0	0	0

- De Morgan's laws:

$$\overline{x_1 \wedge x_2} \equiv \overline{x_1} \vee \overline{x_2}$$

$$\overline{x_1 \vee x_2} \equiv \overline{x_1} \wedge \overline{x_2}$$

Each of these identities can be proven in a simple brute force way: if the identity has n variables, then for each of the 2^n possible substitutions of the variables the left and right hand sides of the identities are evaluated with the help of Table 3. If for each substitution the left hand side and the right hand side evaluate to the same value, then the identity holds. For the first of de Morgan's laws this is illustrated in Table 4.

2.6.2 Solving Equations

We consider expressions e and e_i (where $1 \leq i \leq n$), involving a vector of variables x. We derive three basic lemmas about the solution of Boolean equations. For $a \in \mathbb{B}$ we define

$$e^a = \begin{cases} e & a = 1 \\ \overline{e} & a = 0 \end{cases}.$$

Inspection of the semantics of $^-$ in Table 3 immediately gives the rule for solving negation.

Lemma 2.17 (solving negation). Given a Boolean expression $e(x)$ and $a \in \mathbb{B}$, we have

$$e^a = 1 \leftrightarrow e = a .$$

Inspection of the semantics of $\wedge$ in Table 3 gives

$$(e_1 \wedge e_2) = 1 \leftrightarrow e_1 = 1 \wedge e_2 = 1 .$$

Induction on n results in the rule for solving conjunction.

Lemma 2.18 (solving conjunction). Given Boolean expressions $e_i(x)$, where $1 \leq i \leq n$, we have

$$\left(\bigwedge_{i=1}^{n} e_i \right) = 1 \leftrightarrow \forall i \in [1 : n] : e_i = 1 .$$

From the semantics of $\vee$ in Table 3, we have

$$(e_1 \vee e_2) = 1 \leftrightarrow e_1 = 1 \vee e_2 = 1 .$$

Induction on n yields the rule for solving disjunction.

Lemma 2.19 (solving disjunction). Given Boolean expressions e_i, where $1 \leq i \leq n$, we have

$$(\bigvee_{i=1}^{n} e_i) = 1 \leftrightarrow \exists i \in [1:n] : e_i = 1 .$$

2.6.3 Disjunctive Normal Form

Let $f : \mathbb{B}^n \to \mathbb{B}$ be a switching function[6] and let e be a Boolean expression with variables x. We say that e *computes* f iff the identity $f(x) \equiv e$ holds.

Lemma 2.20 (computing switching function by Boolean expression). Every switching function is computed by some Boolean expression:

$$\forall f : \mathbb{B}^n \to \mathbb{B} \ : \exists e : f(x) \equiv e .$$

Moreover, expression e is pure.

Proof. Let $b \in \mathbb{B}$ and let x_i be a variable. We define the *literal*

$$x_i^b = \begin{cases} x_i & b = 1 \\ \overline{x_i} & b = 0 . \end{cases}$$

Then by Lemma 2.17,

$$x_i^b = 1 \leftrightarrow x_i = b . \tag{2}$$

Let $a = a[1:n] \in \mathbb{B}^n$ and let $x = x[1:n]$ be a vector of variables. We define the *monomial*

$$m(a) = \bigwedge_{i=1}^{n} x_i^{a_i} .$$

Then,

$$m(a) = 1 \leftrightarrow \forall i \in [1:n] : x_i^{a_i} = 1 \quad \text{(Lemma 2.18)}$$
$$\leftrightarrow \forall i \in [1:n] : x_i = a_i \quad \text{(2)}$$
$$\leftrightarrow x = a .$$

Thus, we have

$$m(a) = 1 \leftrightarrow x = a . \tag{3}$$

---

[6] The term *switching function* comes from electrical engineering and stands for a Boolean function.

We define the *support* $S(f)$ of f as the set of arguments a, where f takes the value $f(a) = 1$:

$$S(f) = \{a \mid a \in \mathbb{B}^n \wedge f(a)\} \ .$$

If the support is empty, then $e = 0$ computes f. Otherwise we set

$$e = \bigvee_{a \in S(f)} m(a) \ .$$

Then,

$$\begin{aligned}
e = 1 &\leftrightarrow \exists a \in S(f) : m(a) = 1 \quad \text{(Lemma 2.19)} \\
&\leftrightarrow \exists a \in S(f) : a = x \quad \text{(3)} \\
&\leftrightarrow x \in S(f) \\
&\leftrightarrow f(x) = 1 \ .
\end{aligned}$$

Thus, equations $e = 1$ and $f(x) = 1$ have the same solutions. By Lemma 2.16 we conclude

$$e \equiv f(x) \ .$$

$\square$

The expression e constructed in the proof of Lemma 2.20 is called the *complete disjunctive normal form* of f. As an example, we consider the complete disjunctive normal forms of the sum and carry functions c' defined in Table 2:

$$c'(a, b, c) \equiv \bar{a} \wedge b \wedge c \vee a \wedge \bar{b} \wedge c \vee a \wedge b \wedge \bar{c} \vee a \wedge b \wedge c \tag{4}$$

$$s(a, b, c) \equiv \bar{a} \wedge \bar{b} \wedge c \vee \bar{a} \wedge b \wedge \bar{c} \vee a \wedge \bar{b} \wedge \bar{c} \vee a \wedge b \wedge c \ . \tag{5}$$

Simplified Boolean expressions for the same functions are

$$c'(a, b, c) \equiv a \wedge b \vee b \wedge c \vee a \wedge c$$

$$s(a, b, c) \equiv a \oplus b \oplus c \ .$$

The correctness can be checked in the usual brute force way by trying all 8 assignments of values in $\mathbb{B}^3$ to the variables of the expressions, or by applying the identities listed in Sect. 2.6.1.

In the remainder of this book, we return to the usual mathematical notation, using the equality sign for both identities and equations to be solved. We will only use the equivalence sign when defining predicates with the equality sign in the right-hand side. Whether we deal with identities or whether we solve equations will (hopefully) be clear from the context.

3

Hardware

In Sect. 3.1 we introduce the classical model of *digital circuits*. This includes the classical definition of the *depth* $d(g)$ of a gate g in a circuit as the length of a longest path from an input of the circuit to the gate. For the purpose of timing analysis in a later section, we also introduce the function $sp(g)$ measuring the length of a *shortest* path from an input of the circuit to gate g. We present the classical proof by pigeon hole principle that the depth of gates is well defined. By induction on the depth of gates we then conclude the classical result that the semantics of switching circuits is well defined.

A few basic digital circuits are presented for later use in Sect. 3.2. This is basically the same collection of circuits as presented in [12].

In Sect. 3.3 we introduce *two hardware models*: i) the usual digital model consisting of digital circuits and 1-bit registers as presented in [11, 12] and ii) a detailed model involving *propagation delays, set up* and *hold* times as presented, e.g., in [10,14]. Working out the proof sketch from [10], we formalize timing analysis and show by induction on depth that, with proper timing analysis, the detailed model is simulated by the digital model. This justifies the use of the digital model *as long as we use only gates and registers*.

In the very simple Sect. 3.4 we define n-bit registers which are composed of 1-bit registers in order to use them as *single* components $h.R$ of hardware configurations h.

As we aim at the construction of memory systems, we extend in Sect. 3.5 both circuit models with open collector drivers, tristate drivers, buses, and a model of main memory. As new parameters we have to consider in the detailed model the *enable* and *disable times* of drivers. Also – as main memory is quite slow – we have to postulate that, during accesses to main memory, its input signals should be stable *in the detailed model*, i.e., there should be no *glitches* on the input signals to the memory. We proceed to construct digital interface circuitry for controlling buses and main memory and show in the detailed model that, with that circuitry, buses and main memory are properly operated. These results permit to abstract buses, main memory *and their interface circuitry* to the digital model. So in later constructions, we only

M. Kovalev et al.: A Pipelined Multi-core MIPS Machine, LNCS 9000, pp. 29–82, 2014.
© Springer International Publishing Switzerland 2014

have to worry about proper operation of the interface circuitry in the digital world, and we do not have to reconsider the detailed model.

For readers who suspect that we might be paranoid, we also prove that the proof obligations for the interface circuitry which we impose on the digital model cannot be derived from the digital model itself. Indeed, we construct a bus control that i) is provably free of contention in the digital model and which ii) has – for common technology parameters – bus contention for about 1/3 of the time. As "bus contention" translates in the real world to "short circuit", such circuits destroy themselves.

Thus, the introduction of the detailed hardware model solves a very real problem which is usually ignored in previous work, such as [12]. One would suspect that the absence of such an argument leads to constructions that malfunction in one way or another. In [12], buses are replaced by multiplexers, so bus control is not an issue. But the processor constructed there has caches for data and instructions, which *are* backed up by a main memory. Moreover, the interface circuitry for the instruction cache as presented in [12] *might* produce glitches[1]. On the other hand, the (digital) design in [12] was formally verified in subsequent work [1,3]; it was also put on a field programmable gate array (FPGA) and ran correctly *immediately* after the first power up without ever producing an error. If there are no malfunctions where one would worry about them in view of later insights, one looks for explanations. It turned out that the hardware engineer who transferred the design to the FPGA had made a single change to the design (without telling anybody about it): he had put a register stage in front of the main memory. In the physical design, this register served as interface circuitry to the main memory and happened to conform to all conditions presented in Sect. 3.5. Thus, although the digital portion of the processor was completely verified, the design in the book still contained a bug, which is only visible in the detailed model. The bug was fixed without proof (indeed without being recognized) by the introduction of the register stage in front of the memory. In retrospect, in 2001 the design was *not* completely verified; that it ran immediately after power up involved luck.

A few constructions for control automata are presented for later use in Sect. 3.6. This is basically the same collection of automata as presented in [12].

3.1 Digital Gates and Circuits

In a nutshell, we can think of hardware as consisting of three kinds of components which are interconnected by wires: gates, storage elements, and drivers. Gates are: AND-gates, OR-gates, $\oplus$-gates, and inverters. In circuit schematics we use the symbols from Fig. 2.

---

[1] In the design from [12] the glitches can be produced on the instruction memory address by the multiplexer between pc and dpc as described in Chap. 7.

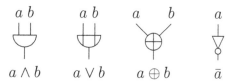

Fig. 2. Symbols for gates in circuit schematics

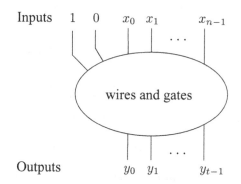

Fig. 3. Illustration of inputs and outputs of a circuit C

A circuit C consists of a finite set G of gates[2], a sequence of input signals $x[n-1:0]$, a set N of wires that connect them, as well as a sequence of output signals $y[t-1:0] \subseteq Sig(C)$ chosen from all signals of circuit C (as illustrated in Fig. 3). Special inputs 0 and 1 are always available to be used in a circuit.

The *signals* $Sig(C)$ of the circuit consist of the inputs

$$In = \{x_{n-1}, \ldots, x_0, 0, 1\}$$

and of (the outputs of) the gates

$$Sig(C) = In \cup G .$$

Depending on its type, every gate has one or two inputs which are connected to signals of the circuit. We denote the input signals connected to a gate $g \in G$ of a circuit C by $in1(g), in2(g)$ for gates with two inputs (AND, OR, $\oplus$) and by $in1(g)$ for gates with a single input (inverter). Note that we denote the output signal of a gate $g \in G$ simply by g.

At first glance it is very easy to define how a circuit should work. For a circuit C, we define the values $s(a)$ of signals $s \in Sig(C)$ for a given substitution $a = a[n-1:0] \in \mathbb{B}^n$ of the input signals:

---

[2] Intuitively, the reader may think of $g \in G$ consisting of two parts, one that uniquely identifies the particular gate of the circuit (e.g., a name) and another that specifies the type of the gate (AND, OR, $\oplus$, inverter).

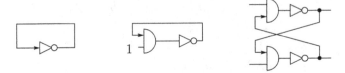

Fig. 4. Examples of cycles in circuits

1. If $s = x_i$ is an input, then

$$\forall i \in [n - 1 : 0] : x_i(a) = a_i .$$

2. If s is an inverter, then

$$s(a) = \overline{in1(s)(a)} .$$

3. If s is a $\circ$-gate with $\circ \in \{\wedge, \vee, \oplus\}$, then

$$s(a) = in1(s)(a) \circ in2(s)(a) .$$

Unfortunately, this is not always a definition. For counterexamples, see Fig. 4. Due to the cycles, one cannot find an order in which the above definition can be applied. Fortunately, defining and then forbidding cycles solves the problem.

A *path* from s_0 to s_m in C is a sequence of signals $(s[0 : m])$ such that for all $i < m$ we have

$$s_i = in1(s_{i+1}) \vee s_i = in2(s_{i+1}) .$$

The length $\ell(s[0 : m])$ of this path is

$$\ell(s[0 : m]) = m .$$

The path is a *cycle* if $s_0 = s_m$. One requires circuits to be free of cycles.

Lemma 3.1 (length of a path in a circuit). Every path (without cycles) in a circuit with set G of gates has length at most $\#G$.

Proof. By contradiction. Assume a path $s[0 : k]$ with $k > \#G$ exists in the circuit. All s_i are gates except possibly s_0 which might be an input. Thus, a gate must be (at least) twice on the path:

$$\exists i, j : \ i < j \wedge s_i = s_j .$$

Then $s[i : j]$ is a cycle[3].   □

---

[3] This proof uses the so called *pigeonhole principle*. If $k + 1$ pigeons are sitting in k holes, then one hole must have at least two pigeons.

Since every path in a circuit has finite length, one can define for each signal s the *depth* $d(s)$ of s as the number of gates on a longest path from an input to s:

$$d(s) = \max\{m \mid \exists \text{ path } s[0:m] : \ s_0 \in In \wedge s_m = s\} .$$

For later use we also define the length $sp(s)$ of a shortest such path as

$$sp(s) = \min\{m \mid \exists \text{ path } s[0:m] : \ s_0 \in In \wedge s_m = s\} .$$

The definitions imply that d and sp satisfy

$$d(s) = \begin{cases} 0 & s \in In \\ d(in1(s)) + 1 & s \text{ is an inverter} \\ \max\{d(in1(s)), d(in2(s))\} + 1 & \text{otherwise} \end{cases}$$

$$sp(s) = \begin{cases} 0 & s \in In \\ sp(in1(s)) + 1 & s \text{ is an inverter} \\ \min\{sp(in1(s)), sp(in2(s))\} + 1 & \text{otherwise} . \end{cases}$$

By straightforward induction, we show that the output of a circuit is well-defined.

Lemma 3.2 (well-defined circuit output). Let $d(s) = n$, then output $s(a)$ of the circuit is well defined.

Proof. By induction on n. If $n = 0$, then s is an input and $s(a)$ is clearly well defined by the first rule. If $n > 0$, then we have $d(in1(s)) < n$. If s is not an inverter, we also have $d(in2(s)) < n$. By induction hypothesis $in1(s)(a)$ and $in2(s)(a)$ (for the case if s is not an inverter) are well defined. We now conclude that $s(a)$ is well defined by the second and third rules.   □

3.2 Some Basic Circuits

Boolean expressions can be translated into circuits in a very intuitive way. In Fig. 5(b) we have translated the simple formulas from (4) for $c'(a, b, c)$ and $s(a, b, c)$ into a circuit. With inputs (a, b, c) and outputs (c', s) this circuit satisfies

$$\langle c', s \rangle = a + b + c .$$

A circuit satisfying this condition is called a *full adder*. We use the symbol from Fig. 5(a) to represent this circuit in subsequent constructions. When the b-input of a full adder is known to be zero, the specification simplifies to

$$\langle c', s \rangle = a + c .$$

The resulting circuit is called a *half adder*. Symbol and implementation are shown in Fig. 6. The circuit in Fig. 7(b) is called a *multiplexer* or short *mux*.

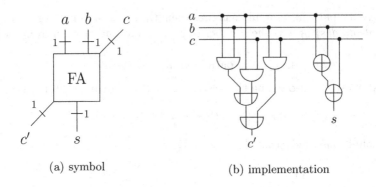

(a) symbol   (b) implementation

Fig. 5. Full adder

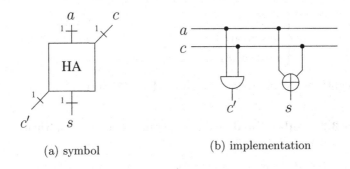

(a) symbol   (b) implementation

Fig. 6. Half adder

Its inputs and outputs satisfy

$$z = \begin{cases} x & s = 0 \\ y & s = 1 \,. \end{cases}$$

For multiplexers we use the symbol from Fig. 7(a). The n-bit multiplexer or short n-mux in Fig. 8(b) consists of n multiplexers with a common select signal s. Its inputs and outputs satisfy

$$z[n-1:0] = \begin{cases} x[n-1:0] & s = 0 \\ y[n-1:0] & s = 1 \,. \end{cases}$$

For n-muxes we use the symbol from Fig. 8(a). Figure 9(a) shows the symbol for an n-bit inverter. Its inputs and outputs satisfy

$$y[n-1:0] = \overline{x[n-1:0]} \,.$$

n-bit inverters are simply realized by n separate inverters as shown in Fig. 9(b). For $\circ \in \{\wedge, \vee, \oplus\}$, Fig. 10(a) shows symbols for n-bit $\circ$-gates. Their

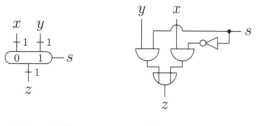

(a) symbol   (b) implementation

Fig. 7. Multiplexer

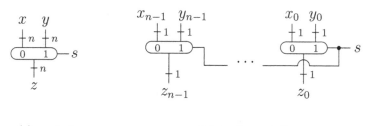

(a) symbol   (b) implementation

Fig. 8. n-bit multiplexer

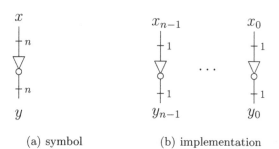

(a) symbol   (b) implementation

Fig. 9. n-bit inverter

inputs and outputs satisfy

$$z[n-1:0] = x[n-1:0] \circ y[n-1:0]$$
$$u[n-1:0] = v \circ y[n-1:0] \, .$$

n-bit $\circ$-gates are simply realized in the first case by n separate $\circ$-gates as shown in Fig. 10(b). In the second case all left inputs of the gates are connected to the same input v. An n-bit $\circ$-tree has inputs $a[n-1:0]$ and a single output b satisfying

$$b = \circ_{i=1}^{n} a_i \, .$$

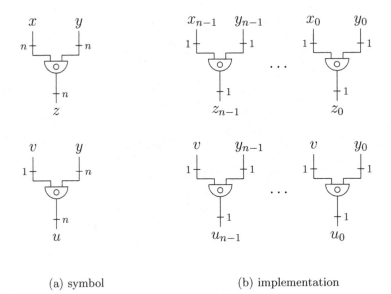

(a) symbol   (b) implementation

Fig. 10. Gates for n-bit wide inputs

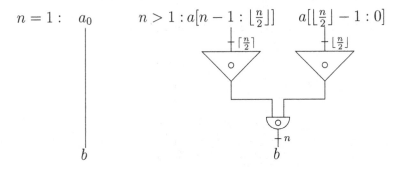

Fig. 11. Implementation of an n-bit $\circ$-tree for $\circ \in \{\wedge, \vee, \oplus\}$

Recursive construction is shown in Fig. 11.

The inputs $a[n - 1 : 0]$ and outputs $zero$ and $nzero$ of an n-zero tester shown in Fig. 12 satisfy

$$zero \equiv a = 0^n$$
$$nzero \equiv a \neq 0^n \ .$$

The implementation uses

$$nzero(a[n - 1 : 0]) = \bigvee_{i=0}^{n-1} a_i \quad , \quad zero = \overline{nzero} \ .$$

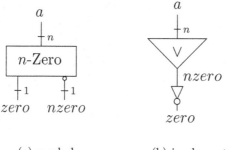

(a) symbol   (b) implementation

Fig. 12. n-bit zero tester

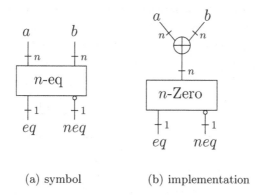

(a) symbol   (b) implementation

Fig. 13. n-bit equality tester

The inputs $a[n-1:0]$, $b[n-1:0]$ and outputs eq, neq of an n-bit *equality tester* in Fig. 13 satisfy

$$eq \equiv a = b \quad , \quad neq \equiv a \neq b .$$

The implementation uses

$$neq(a[n-1:0]) = nzero(a[n-1:0] \oplus b[n-1:0]) \quad , \quad eq = \overline{neq} .$$

An n-*decoder* is a circuit with inputs $x[n-1:0]$ and outputs $y[2^n-1:0]$ satisfying

$$\forall i : y_i = 1 \leftrightarrow \langle x \rangle = i .$$

A recursive construction with $k = \lceil \frac{n}{2} \rceil$ is shown in Fig. 14. For the correctness, one argues in the induction step

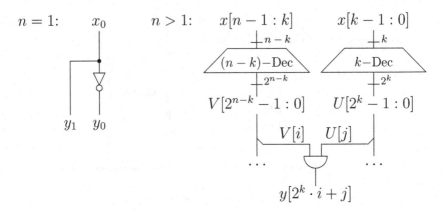

Fig. 14. Implementation of an n-bit decoder

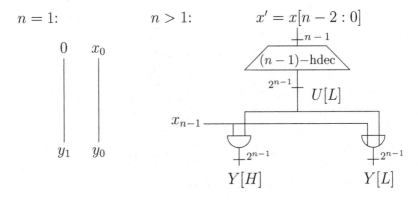

Fig. 15. Recursive construction of n-bit half decoder

$$y[i \cdot 2^k + j] = 1 \leftrightarrow V[i] = 1 \wedge U[j] = 1 \quad \text{(construction)}$$
$$\leftrightarrow \langle x[n-1:k] \rangle = i \wedge \langle x[k-1:0] \rangle = j \quad \text{(ind. hypothesis)}$$
$$\leftrightarrow \langle x[n-1:k]x[k-1:0] \rangle = i \cdot 2^k + j . \quad \text{(Lemma 2.9)}$$

An n-*half decoder* has inputs $x[n-1:0]$ and outputs $y[2^n - 1:0]$ satisfying

$$y = 0^{2^n - \langle x \rangle} 1^{\langle x \rangle} ,$$

i.e., input x is interpreted as a binary number and decoded into a unary number. The remaining output bits are filled with zeros. A recursive construction of n-half decoders is shown in Fig. 15. For the construction of n-half decoders from $(n-1)$-half decoder, we divide the index range into upper and lower half:

$$L = [2^{n-1} - 1:0] \quad , \quad H = [2^n - 1:2^{n-1}] .$$

Also we divide $x[n-1:0]$ into the leading bit x_{n-1} and the low order bits

$$x' = x[n-2:0] \, .$$

In the induction step we then conclude

$$Y[H] \circ Y[L] = x_{n-1} \wedge U[L] \circ (x_{n-1} \vee U(L))$$

$$= \begin{cases} 0^{2^{n-1}} \circ 0^{2^{n-1}-\langle x' \rangle} 1^{\langle x' \rangle} & : \quad x_{n-1} = 0 \\ 0^{2^{n-1}-\langle x' \rangle} 1^{\langle x' \rangle} \circ 1^{2^{n-1}} & : \quad x_{n-1} = 1 \end{cases}$$

$$= \begin{cases} 0^{2^n - \langle x' \rangle} 1^{\langle x' \rangle} & : \quad x_{n-1} = 0 \\ 0^{2^n-(2^{n-1}+\langle x' \rangle)} 1^{2^{n-1}+\langle x' \rangle} & : \quad x_{n-1} = 1 \end{cases}$$

$$= 0^{2^n - \langle x_{n-1} x' \rangle} 1^{\langle x_{n-1} x' \rangle}$$

$$= 0^{2^n - \langle x \rangle} 1^{\langle x \rangle} \, .$$

An n-*parallel prefix* circuit $PP_\circ(n)$ for an associative function $\circ : \mathbb{B} \times \mathbb{B} \to \mathbb{B}$ is a circuit with inputs $x[n-1:0]$ and outputs $y[n-1:0]$ satisfying

$$y_0 = x_0 \quad , \quad y_{i+1} = x_{i+1} \circ y_i \, . \tag{6}$$

For even n a recursive construction of an n-parallel prefix circuit based on $\circ$-gates is shown in Fig. 16. For odd n one can realize an $(n-1)$-bit parallel prefix from Fig. 16 and compute output y_{n-1} as

$$y_{n-1} = x_{n-1} \circ y_{n-2}$$

using one extra $\circ$-gate.

For the correctness of the construction, we first observe that

$$x'_i = x_{2i+1} \circ x_{2i}$$
$$y_{2i} = x_{2i} \circ y'_{i-1}$$
$$y_{2i+1} = y'_i \, .$$

We first show that odd outputs of the circuit satisfy (6). For $i = 0$ we have

$$y_1 = y'_0 \quad \text{(construction)}$$
$$= x'_0 \quad \text{(ind. hypothesis } PP_\circ(n/2))$$
$$= x_1 \circ x_0 \, . \quad \text{(construction)}$$

For $i > 0$ we conclude

$$y_{2i+1} = y'_i \quad \text{(construction)}$$
$$= x'_i \circ y'_{i-1} \quad \text{(ind. hypothesis } PP_\circ(n/2))$$
$$= (x_{2i+1} \circ x_{2i}) \circ y'_{i-1} \quad \text{(construction)}$$
$$= x_{2i+1} \circ (x_{2i} \circ y'_{i-1}) \quad \text{(associativity)}$$
$$= x_{2i+1} \circ y_{2i} \, . \quad \text{(construction)}$$

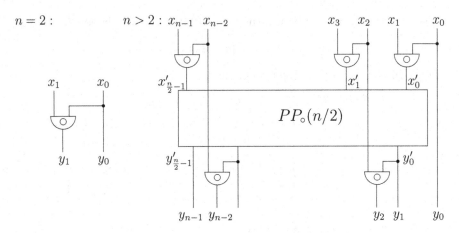

Fig. 16. Recursive construction of an n-bit parallel prefix circuit of the function $\circ$ for an even n

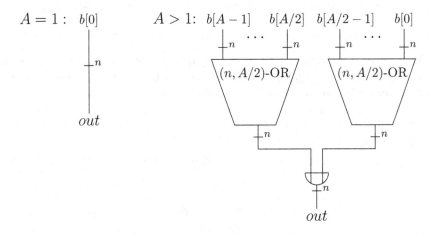

Fig. 17. Recursive construction of an (n, A)-OR tree

For even outputs of the circuit, we easily conclude

$$y_0 = x_0 \quad \text{(construction)}$$
$$i > 0 \rightarrow y_{2i} = x_{2i} \circ y'_{i-1} \quad \text{(construction)}$$
$$= x_{2i} \circ y_{2i-1} . \quad \text{(construction)}$$

An (n, A)-OR tree has A many input vectors $b[i] \in \mathbb{B}^n$ with $i \in [0 : A - 1]$, where $b[i][j]$ with $j \in [0 : n - 1]$ is the j-th bit of input vector $b[i]$. The outputs of the circuit $out[n - 1 : 0]$ satisfy

$$out[j] = \bigvee_{i=0}^{A-1} b[i][j] \, .$$

The implementation of (n, A)-OR trees, for the special case where A is a power of two, is shown in Fig. 17.

3.3 Clocked Circuits

We introduce *two* computational models in which processors are constructed and their correctness is proven. We begin with the usual digital hardware model, where time is counted in hardware *cycles* and signals are binary-valued. Afterwards, we present a more general, detailed hardware model that is motivated by the data sheets of hardware manufacturers. There, time is real-valued and signals may assume the digital values in $\mathbb{B}$ as well as a third value Ω. The detailed hardware model allows arguing about

- hardware with multiple clock domains[4], e.g., in the real time systems that control cars or airplanes [10, 14], and
- the presence and absence of glitches. Glitches are an issue in the construction of memory systems: accesses to dynamic RAM tend to take several hardware cycles and inputs have to be constant in the digital sense *and* free of glitches during this time. The latter requirement cannot be expressed in the usual digital model, and thus the lemmas establishing their absence in our construction would be isolated from the remainder of the theory without the detailed model.

We explain how timing analysis is performed in the detailed model and then show that, with proper timing analysis, the digital model is an abstraction of the detailed model. Thus, in the end, all constructions are correct in the detailed model. Where glitches do not matter – i.e., everywhere except the access to dynamic RAM – we can simply work in the usual and much more comfortable digital model (without having to resort to the detailed hardware model to prove the absence of glitches).

3.3.1 Digital Clocked Circuits

A *digital clocked circuit*, as illustrated in Fig. 18, has four components:

- a special *reset* input,
- special inputs 0 and 1,
- a sequence $x[n-1:0]$ of 1-bit registers, and
- a circuit with inputs $x[n-1:0]$, *reset*, 0, and 1 and outputs $x[n-1:0]in$ and $x[n-1:0]ce$.

---

[4] In this book we do not present such hardware.

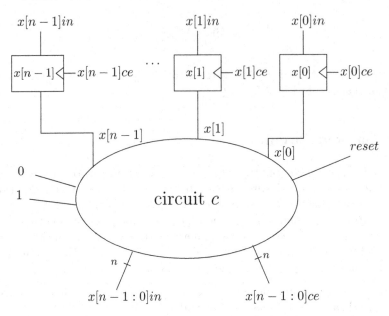

Fig. 18. A digital clocked circuit. Every output signal $x[i]in$ of circuit c is the data input of the corresponding register $x[i]$ and every output $x[i]ce$ produced by circuit c is the clock enable input of the corresponding register

Each register $x[i]$ has

- a data input $x[i]in$,
- a clock enable input $x[i]ce$, and
- a register value $x[i]$ which is also the output signal of the register.

In the digital model we assume that register values as well as all other signals always are in $\mathbb{B}$.

A *hardware configuration* h of a clocked circuit is a snapshot of the current values of the registers:

$$h = x[n-1:0] \in \mathbb{B}^n .$$

A *hardware computation* is a sequence of hardware configurations where the next configuration h' is computed from the current configuration h and the current value of the *reset* signal by a *next hardware configuration* function δ_H:

$$h' = \delta_H(h, reset) .$$

In a hardware computation, we count *cycles* (steps of the digital model) using natural numbers $t \in \mathbb{N} \cup \{-1\}$. The hardware configuration in cycle t of a hardware computation is denoted by $h^t = x^t[n-1:0]$ and the value of signal y during cycle t is denoted by y^t.

The values of the *reset* signal are fixed. Reset is on in cycle -1 and off ever after:

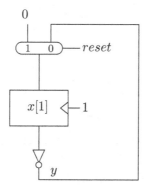

Fig. 19. Simple clocked circuit with a single register

$$reset^t = \begin{cases} 1 & t = -1 \\ 0 & t \geq 0 \,. \end{cases}$$

At power up, register values are binary but unknown. We denote this sequence of unknown binary values at startup by $a[n-1:0]$:

$$x^{-1}[n-1:0] = a[n-1:0] \in \mathbb{B}^n \,.$$

The current value of a circuit signal y in cycle t is defined according to the previously introduced circuit semantics:

$$y^t = \begin{cases} \overline{in1(y)^t} & y \text{ is an inverter} \\ in1(y)^t \circ in2(y)^t & y \text{ is a } \circ\text{-gate}\,. \end{cases}$$

Let $x[n-1:0]in^t$ and $x[n-1:0]ce^t$ be the register input and clock enable signals computed from the current configuration $x^t[n-1:0]$ and the current value of the reset signal $reset^t$. Then the register value $x^{t+1}[i]$ of the next hardware configuration $x^{t+1}[n-1:0] = \delta_H(x^t[n-1:0], reset^t)$ is defined as

$$x^{t+1}[i] = \begin{cases} x[i]in^t & x[i]ce^t = 1 \\ x^t[i] & x[i]ce^t = 0\,, \end{cases}$$

i.e., when the clock enable signal of register $x[i]$ is active in cycle t, the register value of $x[i]$ in cycle $t+1$ is the value of the data input signal in cycle t; otherwise, the register value does not change.

As an example, consider the digital clocked circuit from Fig. 19. There is only one register, thus we abbreviate $x = x[0]$. For cycle -1 we have

$$x^{-1} = a[0]$$
$$reset^{-1} = 1$$
$$xce^{-1} = 1$$
$$xin^{-1} = 0\,.$$

Hence, $x^0 = 0$. For cycles $t \geq 0$ we have

$$reset^t = 0$$
$$xce^t = 1$$
$$xin^t = y^t = \overline{x^t} \ .$$

Hence, we get $x^{t+1} = \overline{x^t}$. An easy induction on t shows that

$$\forall t \geq 0 : x^t = (t \bmod 2) \ .$$

3.3.2 The Detailed Hardware Model

In the detailed hardware model, time is real-valued. Circuit signals y (which include register outputs) are functions

$$y : \mathbb{R} \to \{0, 1, \Omega\}$$

where Ω stands for an either undefined or metastable value.

A circuit in the detailed hardware model is clocked by a clock signal ck which alternates between 0 and 1 in a regular fashion. When the clock signal switches from 0 to 1, we call this a *clock edge*. In order to arrive at the abstraction of the digital hardware model later, we count clock edges – clock edge i marks the start of cycle i in the detailed model. The circuit clock has two parameters:

- the time γ where clock edge 0 occurs,
- the cycle time τ between consecutive clock edges.

For $c \in \mathbb{N} \cup \{-1\}$ this defines the position $e(c)$ of clock edge c as

$$e(c) = \gamma + c \cdot \tau \ .$$

Inspired by data sheets from hardware manufacturers, registers and gates have six timing parameters:

- ρ: the minimal propagation delay of register outputs after clock edges,
- σ: the maximal propagation delay of register outputs after clock edges (we require $0 \leq \rho < \sigma$),
- ts: setup time of register input and clock enable before clock edges,
- th: hold time of register input and clock enable after clock edges,
- α: minimal propagation delay of gates, and
- β: maximal propagation delay of gates[5] (we require $0 < \alpha < \beta$).

---

[5] Defining such delays from voltage levels of electrical signals is nontrivial and can go wrong in subtle ways. For the deduction of a *negative* propagation delay from the data of a very serious hardware catalogue, see [5].

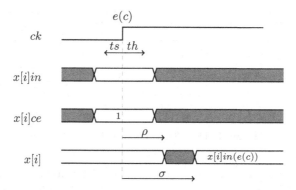

Fig. 20. Detailed timing of a register $x[i]$ with stable inputs and $ce = 1$

This is a simplification. Setup and hold times can be different for register inputs and clock enable signals. Also, the propagation delays of different types of gates are, in general, different. Generalizing our model to this situation is easy but requires more notation.

Let y be any signal. The requirement that this signal satisfies the setup and hold times of registers at clock edge c is defined by

$$stable(y, c) \leftrightarrow \exists a \in \mathbb{B} : \forall t \in [e(c) - ts, e(c) + th] : y(t) = a .$$

The behavior of a register $x[i]$ with stable input and clock enable at edge t is illustrated in Fig. 20.

For $c \in \mathbb{N} \cup \{-1\}$ and $t \in (e(c) + \rho, e(c + 1) + \rho]$, we define the register value $x[i](t)$ and output at time t by a case split:

- Clocking the register at edges $c \geq 0$. The clock enable signal is 1 at edge $e(c)$ and the setup and hold times for the input and clock enable signals are met:
  $$x[i]ce(e(c)) \land stable(x[i]in, c) \land stable(x[i]ce, c) .$$

  Then the data input at edge $e(c)$ becomes the new value of the register, and it becomes visible (at the latest) at time σ after clock edge $e(c)$.
- Not clocking the register at edges $c \geq 0$. The clock enable signal is 0 at edge $e(c)$ and the setup and hold times for it are met:
  $$\overline{x[i]ce(e(c))} \land stable(x[i]ce, c) .$$

  The output stays unchanged for the entire period.
- Register initialization. This is happening when the reset signal ($reset(t)$) is high. In this situation we assume that the register $x[i]$ outputs some value $a[i] \in \mathbb{B}$, which is unknown but is not Ω.
- Any other situation, where the voltage cannot be guaranteed to be recognized as a *known* logical 0 or 1. This includes i) the transition period from

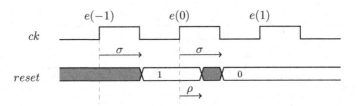

Fig. 21. Detailed timing of the reset signal

ρ to σ after regular clocking, and ii) the entire time interval if there was a violation of the stability conditions of any kind. Usually, a physical register will settle in this situation quickly into an unknown logical value, but in rare occasions the register can "hang" at a voltage level not recognized as 0 or 1 for a long time. This is called *ringing* or *metastability*.

Formally, we define the register semantics of the detailed hardware model in the following way:

$$x[i](t) = \begin{cases} a[i] & reset(t) \\ x[i]in(e(c)) & t \in [e(c) + \sigma, e(c+1) + \rho] \land stable(x[i]in, c) \\ & \land\ stable(x[i]ce, c) \land x[i]ce(e(c)) \land \neg reset(t) \\ x[i](e(c)) & t \in (e(c) + \rho, e(c+1) + \rho] \land stable(x[i]ce, c) \\ & \land\ \neg x[i]ce(e(c)) \land \neg reset(t) \\ \Omega & \text{otherwise .} \end{cases}$$

Notice that during regular clocking in, the output is unknown between $e(c)+\rho$ and $e(c)+\sigma$. This is the case *even if $x[i]in(e(c)) = x[i](e(c))$*, i.e., when writing the same value the register currently contains. In this case a *glitch* on the register output can occur. A glitch (or a spike) is a situation when a signal has the same digital value $x \in \mathbb{B}$ in cycle t and $t+1$ but in the physical model it temporarily has a value not recognized as x. The only way to *guarantee* constant register outputs during the time period is not to clock the register during that time.

We require the reset signal to behave like an output of a register which is clocked at cycles -1 and 0 and is not clocked afterwards (Fig. 21):

$$reset(t) = \begin{cases} 1 & t \in [e(-1) + \sigma, e(0) + \rho] \\ \Omega & t \in (e(0) + \rho, e(0) + \sigma) \\ 0 & \text{otherwise .} \end{cases}$$

Special signals 1 and 0 are always said to be 1 or 0 respectively:

$$1(t) = 1$$
$$0(t) = 0 \ .$$

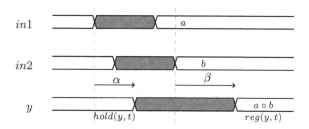

Fig. 22. Detailed timing of a gate y with two inputs

We show a simple lemma, which guarantees that the output from a register does not have any glitches if this register is not clocked.

Lemma 3.3 (glitch-free output of non-clocked register). Assume stable data is clocked into register $x[i]$ at edge $e(c)$:

$$stable(x[i]in, c) \wedge stable(x[i]ce, c) \wedge x[i]ce(e(c)) \ .$$

Assume further that the register is not clocked for the following $K - 1$ clock edges:

$$\forall k \in [1 : K - 1] : stable(x[i]ce(c + k)) \wedge \neg x[i]ce(e(c + k)) \ .$$

Then the value $x[i]in(e(c))$ is visible at the output of register $x[i]$ from time $e(c) + \sigma$ to $e(c + K) + \rho$:

$$\forall t \in [e(c) + \sigma, e(c + K) + \rho] : x[i](t) = x[i]in(e(c)) \ .$$

Proof. One shows by an easy induction on k

$$\forall t \in [e(c) + \sigma, e(c + 1) + \rho] : x[i](t) = x[i]in(e(c))$$

and

$$\forall k \in [1 : K - 1] : \forall t \in (e(c + k) + \rho, e(c + k + 1) + \rho] : x[i](t) = x[i]in(e(c)) \ .$$

$\square$

For the definition of the value $y(t)$ of gates g at time t in the detailed model, we distinguish three cases (see Fig. 22):

- Regular signal propagation. Here, all input signals are binary and stable for the maximal propagation delay β before t. For inverters y this is captured by the following predicate:

$$reg(y, t) \leftrightarrow \exists a \in \mathbb{B} : \forall t' \in [t - \beta, t] : in1(y)(t') = a \ .$$

Gate y in this case outputs $\bar{a}$ at time t. For $\circ$-gates y we define

$$reg(y, t) \leftrightarrow \exists a, b \in \mathbb{B} : \forall t' \in [t - \beta, t] : in1(y)(t') = a \wedge in2(y)(t') = b \ .$$

Then gate y outputs $a \circ b$ at time t.

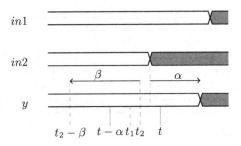

Fig. 23. Illustrating the proof of Lemma 3.4

- Signal holding. Here, signal propagation is not regular anymore but it was regular at some time during the minimal propagation delay α before t:

$$hold(y,t) \leftrightarrow \neg reg(y,t) \wedge \exists t' \in [t-\alpha, t] : reg(y,t') .$$

The gate y in this case still holds the old value $y(t')$ at time t. We will show that the value $y(t')$ is well defined for all t'.
- All other cases where we cannot give any guarantees about $y(t)$.

Lemma 3.4 (well-defined signal holding value). Assume $hold(y,t)$ and $t_1, t_2 \in [t-\alpha, t] \wedge reg(y,t_1) \wedge reg(y,t_2)$. Then we have

$$y(t_1) = y(t_2) .$$

Proof. The proof is illustrated in Fig. 23. Without loss of generality, we have $t_1 < t_2$. Let $z \in \{in1(y), in2(y)\}$ be any input of y. From $reg(y,t_1)$ we infer

$$\exists a \in \mathbb{B} : \forall t' \in [t_1 - \beta, t_1] : z(t') = z(t_1) = a .$$

From

$$0 < t_2 - t_1 < \alpha < \beta$$

we infer

$$t_2 - \beta < t_1 < t_2 .$$

Thus,

$$t_1 \in (t_2 - \beta, t_2).$$

From $reg(y,t_2)$ we get

$$\forall t' \in [t_2 - \beta, t_2] : z(t') = z(t_2)$$

and hence,

$$z(t_2) = z(t_1) = a .$$

For o-gates y we have

$$y(t_1) = in1(t_1) \circ in2(t_1)$$
$$= in1(t_2) \circ in2(t_2)$$
$$= y(t_2) \; .$$

For inverters the argument is equally simple. □

For values t satisfying $hold(y, t)$, we define $lreg(y, t)$ as the last value t' before t when signal propagation was regular:

$$lreg(y, t) = \max\{t' \mid t' < t \wedge reg(y, t')\} \; .$$

Now we can complete the definition of the value of gate y at time t:

$$y(t) = \begin{cases} \overline{in1(y)(t)} & reg(y, t) \wedge y \text{ is an inverter} \\ in1(y)(t) \circ in2(y)(t) & reg(y, t) \wedge y \text{ is a } \circ\text{-gate} \\ y(lreg(y, t)) & hold(y, t) \\ \Omega & \text{otherwise} \; . \end{cases}$$

3.3.3 Timing Analysis

Timing analysis is performed in the detailed model in order to ensure that all register inputs $x[i]in$ and clock enables $x[i]ce$ are stable at clock edges. We capture the conditions for *correct timing* by

$$\forall i, c : stable(x[i]in, c) \wedge stable(x[i]ce, c) \; .$$

After a reminder that $d(y)$ and $sp(y)$ are the lengths of longest and shortest paths from the inputs to y, we define the minimal and the maximal propagation delays of arbitrary signals y relative to the clock edges:

$$tmin(y) = \rho + sp(y) \cdot \alpha,$$
$$tmax(y) = \sigma + d(y) \cdot \beta \; .$$

Note that, in the definitions of $tmin(y)$ and $tmax(y)$, we overestimate propagation delays of signals which are calculated from the special input signals 0 and 1.[6]

In what follows, we define a sufficient condition for correct timing and show that with this condition detailed and digital circuits simulate each other in the sense that for all signals y the value y^c in the digital model during cycle

---

[6] The input signals 0 and 1 of a circuit do in fact have no propagation delay. However, giving a precise definition that takes this into account would make things unnecessarily complicated here since we would need to define and argue about the longest and shortest path without the 0/1 signals. Instead, we prefer to overestimate and keep things simple by using already existing definitions.

c equals the value $y(e(c+1))$ at the *end* of the cycle. In other words, with correct timing the digital model is an abstraction of the detailed model:

$$y^c = y(e(c+1)) \ .$$

Lemma 3.5 (timing and simulation). If for all signals y we have

$$\forall y : tmax(y) + ts \leq \tau$$

and if for all inputs $x[i]in$ and clock enable signals $x[i]ce$ of registers we have

$$\forall i : th \leq tmin(x[i]in) \wedge th \leq tmin(x[i]ce),$$

then

1. $\forall y, c : \forall t \in [e(c) + tmax(y), e(c+1) + tmin(y)] : y(t) = y^c,$
2. $\forall i, c : c \geq 0 \rightarrow stable(x[i]in, c) \wedge stable(x[i]ce, c).$

Proof. By induction on c. For each c, we show statement 1 with the help of the following auxiliary lemma.

Lemma 3.6 (timing and simulation, 1 cycle). Let statement 1 of Lemma 3.5 hold in cycle c for all signals with depth 0:

$$\forall t \in [e(c) + \sigma, e(c+1) + \rho] : x[i](t) = x[i]^c \ ,$$

then the same statement holds for all signals y in cycle c:

$$\forall y : \forall t \in [e(c) + tmax(y), e(c+1) + tmin(y)] : y(t) = y^c \ .$$

Proof. By induction on the depth $d(y)$ of signals. Let the statement hold for signals of depth $d-1$ and let y be a $\circ$-gate of depth d. We show that it holds for y.

Consider Fig. 24. There are inputs z_1, z_2 of y such that

$$d(y) = d(z_1) + 1 \wedge sp(z) = sp(z_2) + 1 \ .$$

Hence,

$$tmax(y) = tmax(z_1) + \beta$$
$$tmin(y) = tmin(z_2) + \alpha \ .$$

By induction we have for all inputs z of y

$$\forall t \in [e(c) + tmax(z), e(c+1) + tmin(z)] : z(t) = z^c \ .$$

Since we have

$$tmin(z_2) \leq tmin(z) \wedge tmax(z) \leq tmax(z_1)$$

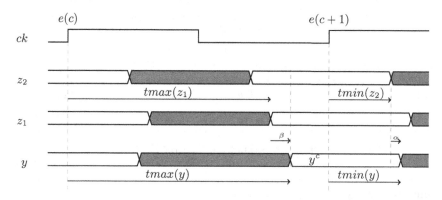

Fig. 24. Computing $tmin(y)$ and $tmax(y)$

for all inputs z of y, we get

$$[e(c) + tmax(y) - \beta, e(c+1) + tmin(y) - \alpha]$$
$$= [e(c) + tmax(z_1), e(c+1) + tmin(z_2)]$$
$$\subseteq [e(c) + tmax(z), e(c+1) + tmin(z)]$$

and thus,

$$\forall t \in [e(c) + tmax(y) - \beta, e(c+1) + tmin(y) - \alpha] : z(t) = z^c .$$

We conclude

$$\forall t \in [e(c) + tmax(y), e(c+1) + tmin(y) - \alpha] : reg(y, t)$$

and

$$y(t) = in1(y)(t) \circ in2(y)(t)$$
$$= in1(y)^c \circ in2(y)^c \quad \text{(ind. hypothesis)}$$
$$= y^c .$$

Now we have to show that

$$\forall t \in (e(c+1) + tmin(y) - \alpha, e(c+1) + tmin(y)] : z(t) = z^c .$$

We choose an arbitrary t in this interval and do a case split on whether the signal is regular or not. In case $reg(y, t)$ holds (actually, it never does, but we don't bother showing that), we have for all inputs z of y

$$\forall t' \in [t - \beta, t] : z(t) = z(t') .$$

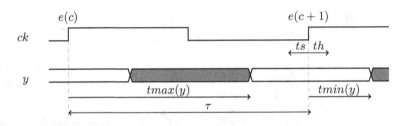

Fig. 25. Stability of register input y

Since $\alpha < \beta$, we have

$$e(c+1) + tmin(y) - \alpha \in [t - \beta, t]$$

and conclude for all inputs z of y

$$z(t) = z(e(c+1) + tmin(y) - \alpha) = z^c ,$$

which implies

$$y(t) = in1(y)^c \circ in2(y)^c$$
$$= y^c .$$

In case $reg(y, t)$ doesn't hold, we get $hold(y, t)$. We have to show that

$$y(lreg(y, t)) = y^c .$$

If $lreg(y, t) \in (e(c+1) + tmin(y) - \alpha, t)$, then we observe that $reg(y, lreg(y, t))$ holds and proceed in the same way as in the first case. Otherwise, we have $lreg(y, t) = e(c+1) + tmin(y) - \alpha$, which also implies

$$y(lreg(y, t)) = y^c .$$

□

We now continue with the proof of Lemma 3.5. For the induction base $c = -1$ and the signals coming from the registers $x[i]$ with $d(x[i]) = 0$, we have

$$tmin(x[i]) = \rho \wedge tmax(x[i]) = \sigma .$$

From the initialization rules in the digital and detailed models we get

$$\forall t \in [e(-1) + \sigma, e(0) + \rho] : x[i](t) = x[i]^{-1} = a[i] \in \mathbb{B}$$

and conclude the proof of part 1 by Lemma 3.6. For part 2 there is nothing to show.

For the induction step we go from c to $c + 1$ and first show part 2 of the lemma. Consider Fig. 25. For register inputs $y = x[i]in$ and clock enable signals $y = x[i]ce$ we have from the induction hypothesis:

$$\forall t \in [e(c) + tmax(y), e(c+1) + tmin(y)] : y(t) = y^c .$$

From the lemma's assumptions we get for all $y = x[i]in, y = x[i]ce$

$$\forall y : th \leq tmin(y) \wedge tmax(y) + ts \leq \tau ,$$

which implies

$$e(c) + tmax(y) \leq e(c) + \tau - ts$$
$$= e(c+1) - ts,$$
$$e(c+1) + tmin(y) \geq e(c+1) + th .$$

Thus,

$$[e(c+1) - ts, e(c+1) + th] \subseteq [e(c) + tmax(y), e(c+1) + tmin(y)]$$

and

$$\forall t \in [e(c+1) - ts, e(c+1) + th] : y(t) = y^c .$$

We conclude $stable(y, c+1)$, which shows part 2 for $c + 1$.

Since all input and clock enable signals for register $x[i]$ are stable at clock edge $c + 1$, we get from the register semantics of the detailed model for all $t \in [e(c+1) + \sigma, e(c+2) + \rho]$:

$$x[i](t) = \begin{cases} x[i]in(e(c+1)) & x[i]ce(e(c+1)) = 1 \\ x[i](e(c+1)) & x[i]ce(e(c+1)) = 0. \end{cases}$$

Observing that for all y we have

$$e(c+1) \in [e(c) + tmax(y), e(c+1) + tmin(y)] ,$$

we conclude with part 1 of the induction hypothesis:

$$x[i](e(c+1)) = x[i]^c$$
$$x[i]in(e(c+1)) = x[i]in^c$$
$$x[i]ce(e(c+1)) = x[i]ce^c .$$

Finally, from the register semantics of the digital model we conclude for $t \in [e(c+1) + \sigma, e(c+2) + \rho]$:

$$x[i](t) = \begin{cases} x[i]in^c & x[i]ce^c = 1 \\ x[i]^c & x[i]ce^c = 0 \end{cases}$$
$$= x[i]^{c+1} .$$

This shows part 1 of the lemma for all signals y with $d(y) = 0$. Applying Lemma 3.6, we get part 1 for all other circuit signals and conclude the proof.

$\square$

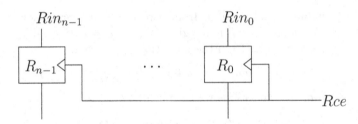

Fig. 26. An n-bit register

3.4 Registers

So far we have shown that there is one basic hardware model, namely the detailed one, but with correct timing it can be abstracted to the digital model (Lemma 3.5). From now on we assume correct timing and stick to the usual digital model unless we need to prove properties not expressible in this model – like the absence of glitches.

Although all memory components can be built from 1-bit registers, it is inconvenient to refer to all memory bits in a computer by numbering them with an index i of a clocked circuit input $x[i]$. It is more convenient to deal with hardware configurations h and to gather groups of such bits into certain memory components $h.M$. For M we introduce n-bit registers $h.R$. In Chap. 4 we add to this no less than 9 (nine) random access memory (RAM) designs. As before, in a hardware computation with memory components, we have

$$h^{t+1} = \delta_H(h^t, reset^t) \ .$$

An n-bit register R consists simply of n many 1-bit registers $R[i]$ with a common clock enable signal Rce as shown in Fig. 26.

Register configurations are n-tuples:

$$h.R \in \mathbb{B}^n \ .$$

Given input signals $Rin(h^t)$ and $Rce(h^t)$, we obtain from the semantics of the basic clocked circuit model:

$$h^{t+1}.R = \begin{cases} Rin(h^t) & Rce(h^t) = 1 \\ h^t.R & Rce(h^t) = 0 \ . \end{cases}$$

Recall that, from the initialization rules for 1-bit registers, after power up register content is binary but unknown (metastability is extremely rare):

$$h^0.R \in \mathbb{B}^n \ .$$

3.5 Drivers and Main Memory

In order to deal with main memory and its connection to caches and processor cores, we introduce several new hardware components: tristate drivers, open

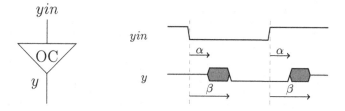

Fig. 27. Open collector driver and its timing diagram

collector drivers, and main memory. For hardware consisting only of gates, inverters, and registers, we have shown in Lemma 3.5 that a design that works in the digital model also works in the detailed hardware model. For tristate drivers and main memory this will not be the case.

3.5.1 Open Collector Drivers and Active Low Signal

A single open collector driver y and its detailed timing is shown in Fig. 27. If the input yin is 0, then the open collector driver also outputs 0. If the input is 1, then the driver is disabled. In detailed timing diagrams, an undefined value due to disabled outputs is usually drawn as a horizontal line in the middle between 0 and 1. In the jargon of hardware designers this is called the *high impedance* state or *high Z* or simply Z. In order to specify behavior and operating conditions of open collector and tristate drivers, we have to permit Z as a signal value for drivers y. Thus, we have

$$y : \mathbb{R} \to \{0, 1, \Omega, Z\} .$$

For the propagation delay of open collector drivers, we use the same parameters α and β as for gates. Regular signal propagation is defined the same way as for inverters:

$$reg(y, t) \leftrightarrow \exists a \in \mathbb{B} : \forall t \in [t - \beta, t] : yin(t) = a .$$

The signal y generated by a single open collector driver is defined as

$$y(t) = \begin{cases} 0 & reg(y, t) \wedge yin(t) = 0 \\ Z & reg(y, t) \wedge yin(t) = 1 \\ y(lreg(y, t)) & hold(y, t) \\ \Omega & \text{otherwise} . \end{cases}$$

In contrast to other gates, it is allowed to connect the outputs of drivers by wires which are often called *buses*. Fig. 28 shows k open collector drivers y_i with inputs $y_i in$ driving a bus b. If all the drivers connected to the open collector bus are disabled, then in the physical design a *pull-up resistor* drives 1 on the bus. The bus value $b(t)$ is then determined as

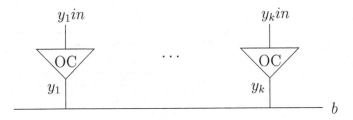

Fig. 28. Open collector drivers y_i connected by a bus b

$$b(t) = \begin{cases} 0 & \exists i : y_i(t) = 0 \\ 1 & \forall i : y_i(t) = Z \\ \Omega & \text{otherwise} . \end{cases}$$

In the digital model, we simply get

$$b^t = \bigwedge_i y_i in^t ,$$

but this abstracts away an important detail: glitches on a driver input can propagate to the bus, for instance when other drivers are disabled. This will not be an issue for the open collector buses constructed here. It is, however, an issue in the control of real time buses [10].

By de Morgan's law, one can use open collector buses together with some inverters to compute the logical OR of signals u_i:

$$b = \bigwedge_i \overline{u_i} = \neg(\bigvee_i u_i) . \tag{7}$$

In control logic, it is often equally easy to generate or use an "active high" signal u or its inverted "active low" version $\overline{u}$. By (7), open collector buses compute an active low OR $\overline{b}$ of control signals u_i without extra cost, if the active low versions $\overline{u_i}$ are available.

n-bit open collector drivers are simply n open collector drivers in parallel. Symbol and construction are shown in Fig. 29.

3.5.2 Tristate Drivers and Bus Contention

Tristate drivers y are controlled by output enable signals yoe[7]. Symbol and timing are shown in Fig. 30. Only when the output enable signal is active, a tristate driver propagates the data input yin to the output y. Like ordinary switching, enabling and disabling tristate drivers involves propagation delays.

---

[7] Like clock enable signals, we model them as active high, but in data sheets for real hardware components they are usually active low.

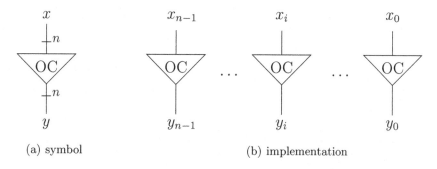

(a) symbol   (b) implementation

Fig. 29. Symbol and construction of an n-bit open collector driver.

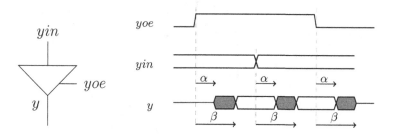

Fig. 30. Tristate driver and its timing diagram

Ignoring propagation delays, a tristate driver computes the following function:

$$tr(in, oe) = \begin{cases} in & oe = 1 \\ Z & oe = 0 \,. \end{cases}$$

For simplicity, we use the same timing parameters as for gates. Regular signal propagation is defined as for gates:

$$reg(y, t) \leftrightarrow \exists a, b \in \mathbb{B} : \forall t \in [t - \beta, t] : yin(t) = a \wedge yoe(t) = b \,.$$

The signal y generated by a single tristate driver is then defined as

$$y(t) = \begin{cases} tr(yin(t), yoe(t)) & reg(y, t) \\ y(lreg(y, t)) & hold(y, t) \\ \Omega & \text{otherwise}\,. \end{cases}$$

Observe that a glitch on an output enable signal can produce a glitch in signal y. In contrast to glitches on open collector buses this will be an issue in our designs involving main memory.

Like open collector drivers, the outputs of tristate drivers can be connected via so called *tristate buses*. The clean way to operate a tristate bus b with

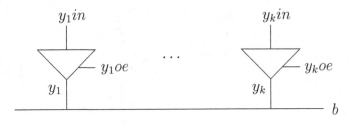

Fig. 31. Tristate drivers y_i connected by a bus b

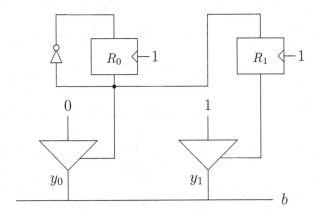

Fig. 32. Switching enable signals of drivers at the same clock edge

drivers y_i as shown in Fig. 31 is to allow at any time t at most one driver to produce a signal different from Z:

$$y_i(t) \neq Z \wedge y_j(t) \neq Z \rightarrow i = j \,. \tag{8}$$

If this invariant is maintained, the following definition of the bus value $b(t)$ at time t is well defined:

$$b(t) = \begin{cases} y_i(t) & \exists i : y_i(t) \neq Z \\ Z & \text{otherwise} \,. \end{cases}$$

The invariant excludes a design like in Fig. 32, where drivers y_0 and y_1 are switched on and off at the same clock edge[8]. In order to understand the possible problem with such a design consider a rising clock edge when $R_0 = y_0 oe$ is turned on and $R_1 = y_1 oe$ is turned off. This can lead to a situation as shown in Fig. 33.

There, we assume that the propagation delay of R_0 is $\rho = 1$ and the propagation delay of R_1 is $\sigma = 2$. Similarly, assume that the enable time of y_0

---

[8] This is not unheard of in practice.

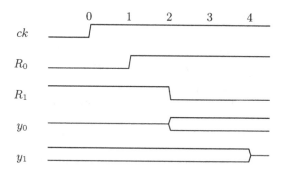

Fig. 33. Possible timing when enable signals are switched at the same clock edge

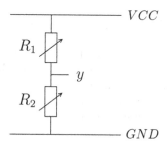

Fig. 34. Output stage of a tristate driver as a pair of variable resistors

Table 5. Output y of a driver regulated by adjustment of two resistors R_1 and R_2.

R_1	R_2	y
low	high	1
high	low	0
high	high	Z
low	low	short circuit

is $\alpha = 1$ and the disable time of y_1 is $\beta = 2$. The resulting signals at a rising edge of clock ck are shown in the detailed timing diagram in Fig. 33. Note that for $2 \leq t \leq 4$ we have $y_0(t) = 0$ and $y_1(t) = 1$. This happens to produce more problems than just a temporarily undefined bus value.

The output circuitry of a driver or a gate can be envisioned as a pair of adjustable resistors as shown in Fig. 34. Resistor R_1 is between the supply voltage VCC and the drivers output y. The other resistor R_2 is between the output and ground GND. Logical values 0 and 1 as high impedance state Z can now be implemented by adjusting the values of the resistors as shown in Table 5.

Of course the circuitry of a well designed single driver will never produce a short circuit by adjusting both resistors to "low". However, as shown in

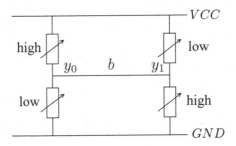

Fig. 35. Short circuit via the bus b when two drivers are enabled at the same time

Fig. 35 the short circuit is still possible via the low resistance path

$$GND \to y_0 \to b \to y_1 \to VCC .$$

This occurs when two drivers are simultaneously enabled and one of the drivers drives 0 while the other driver drives 1. Exactly this situation occurs temporarily in the real-valued time interval $[r + 2, r + 3]$ after each rising clock edge r. In the jargon of hardware designers this is called – temporary – *bus contention*, which clearly sounds much better than "temporary short circuit". But even with the nicer name it remains of course a short circuit. In the best case, it increases power consumption and shortens the life time of the driver. The spikes in power consumption can have the side effect that power supply voltage falls under specified levels; maybe not always, but sporadically when power consumption in other parts of the hardware is high. Insufficient supply voltage then will tend to produce sporadic non reproducible failures in other parts of the hardware.

3.5.3 The Incomplete Digital Model for Drivers

Observe that there is a deceptively natural looking digital model of tristate drivers which has a good and a bad part. The good part is

$$y = \begin{cases} yin(y) & yoe = 1 \\ Z & \text{otherwise} . \end{cases} \tag{9}$$

The bad part – as we will demonstrate later – is the very natural looking condition:

$$y_i^t \neq Z \wedge y_j^t \neq Z \to i = j . \tag{10}$$

The good part, i.e., (9), correctly models the behavior of drivers for times after clock edges where all propagation delays have occurred and when registers are updated. Indeed, if we consider a bus b driven by drivers y_i as a gate with depth

$$d(b) = \max\{d(y_i) \mid i \in [1 : k]\}$$
$$sp(b) = \min\{sp(y_i) \mid i \in [1 : k]\}$$

we can immediately extend Lemma 3.5 to circuits with buses and drivers of both kinds.

Lemma 3.7 (timing and simulation with drivers and buses). Assume that (8) holds for all tristate buses and assume the correct timing

$$\forall y : tmax(y) + ts \leq \tau$$

and

$$\forall i : th \leq tmin(x[i]in) \wedge th \leq tmin(x[i]ce) .$$

Then,

1. $\forall y, c : \forall t \in [e(c) + tmax(y), e(c + 1) + tmin(y)] : y(t) = y^c$,
2. $\forall i, c : c \geq 0 \rightarrow stable(x[i]in, c) \wedge stable(x[i]ce, c)$.

This justifies the use of the digital model as far as register update is concerned. The lemma has, however, a hypothesis coming from the detailed model. Replacing it simply by what we call the bad part of the digital model, i.e., by (10), is the highway to big trouble. First of all, observe that our design in Fig. 33, which switched enable signals at the same clock edge, satisfies it. But in the detailed model (and the real world) we can do worse. We can construct hardware that destroys itself by the short circuits caused by bus contention but which is contention free according to the (bad part of) the digital model.

3.5.4 Self Destructing Hardware

In what follows we will do some arithmetic on time intervals $[a, b]$ where signals change. In our computations of these time bounds we use the following rules:

$$c + [a, b] = [c + a, c + b]$$
$$c \cdot [a, b] = [c \cdot a, c \cdot b]$$
$$[a, b] + [c, d] = [a + c, b + d]$$
$$c + (a, b) = (c + a, c + b)$$
$$c \cdot (a, b) = (c \cdot a, c \cdot b) .$$

Lemma 3.8 (self destructing hardware). For any $\epsilon > 0$ there is a design satisfying (10) which produces continuous bus contention for at least a fraction $\alpha/\beta - \epsilon$ of the total time.

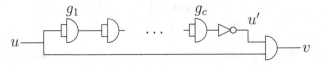

Fig. 36. Generating a pulse of arbitrary width by a sufficiently long delay line

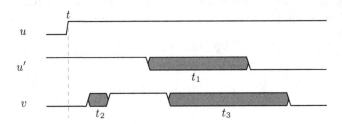

Fig. 37. Timing diagram for a pulse generator

Proof. The key to the construction is the parametrized design of Fig. 36. The timing diagram in Fig. 37 shows that the entire design produces a pulse of length growing with c; hence, we call it a c-pulse generator.

Signal u goes up at time t. The chain of c AND gates just serves as a delay line. The result is finally inverted. Thus, signal u' falls in time interval with

$$t_1 = t + (c+1) \cdot [\alpha, \beta] .$$

The final AND gate produces a pulse v with a rise time in interval t_2 and a fall time in interval t_3 satisfying

$$t_2 = t + [\alpha, \beta]$$
$$t_3 = t + (c+2) \cdot [\alpha, \beta] .$$

Note that, in the digital model, we have for all cycles t

$$v^t = (u^t \wedge \neg u^t) = 0 ,$$

which is indeed correct after propagation delays are over – and that is all the digital model captures. Now consider the design in Fig. 38. In the digital model, v_1 and v_2 are always zero. The only driver ever enabled in the digital model is y_3. Thus, the design satisfies (10) for the digital model.

Now consider the timing diagram in Fig. 39. At each clock edge T, one of registers R_i has a rising edge in time interval

$$t_1 = T + [\rho, \sigma] ,$$

which generates a pulse with rising edge in time interval t_2 and falling edge in time interval t_3 satisfying

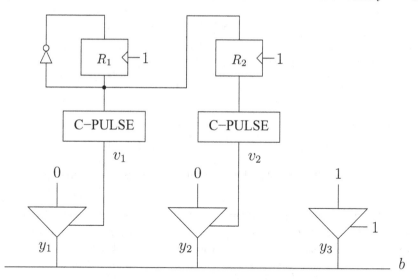

Fig. 38. Generating contention with two pulse generators

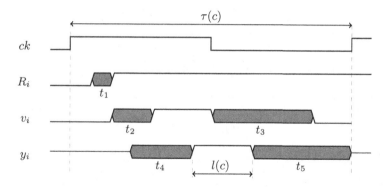

Fig. 39. Timing analysis for the period of bus contention from t_4 to t_5

$$t_2 = T + [\rho, \sigma] + [\alpha, \beta]$$
$$t_3 = T + [\rho, \sigma] + (c + 2) \cdot [\alpha, \beta] \ .$$

Driver y_i then enables in time interval t_4 and disables in time interval t_5, satisfying

$$t_4 = T + [\rho, \sigma] + 2 \cdot [\alpha, \beta]$$
$$t_5 = T + [\rho, \sigma] + (c + 3) \cdot [\alpha, \beta] \ .$$

We choose a cycle time

$$\tau(c) = \sigma + (c + 3) \cdot \beta \ ,$$

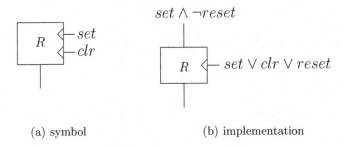

(a) symbol   (b) implementation

Fig. 40. Symbol and implementation of a set-clear flip-flop

such that the timing diagram fits exactly into one clock cycle. In the next cycle, we then have the same situation for the other register and driver. We have contention on bus b at least during time interval

$$C = T + [\sigma + 2 \cdot \beta, \rho + (c + 3) \cdot \alpha]$$

of length

$$\ell(c) = \rho + (c + 3) \cdot \alpha - (\sigma + 2 \cdot \beta) \, .$$

Asymptotically we have

$$\lim_{c \to \infty} \ell(c)/\tau(c) = \alpha/\beta \, .$$

Thus, we choose c such that

$$\ell(c)/\tau(c) \geq \alpha/\beta - \epsilon$$

and the lemma follows.   □

For common technologies, the fraction α/β is around $1/3$. Thus, we are talking about a short circuit for roughly $1/3$ of the time. We should mention that this will overheat drivers to an extent that the packages of the chips tend to explode.

3.5.5 Clean Operation of Tristate Buses

We now construct control logic for tristate buses. We begin with a digital specification, construct a control logic satisfying this (incomplete) specification and then show in the detailed model i) that the bus is free of contention and ii) that signals are free of glitches while we guarantee their presence on the bus.

As a building block of the control, we use the *set-clear flip-flops* from Fig. 40. This is simply a 1-bit register which is set to 1 by activation of the *set* signal and to 0 by activation of the *clr* signal (without activation of the *set* signal). During reset, i.e., during cycle -1, the flip-flops are forced to zero.

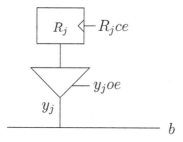

Fig. 41. Registers R_j connected to a bus b by tristate drivers y_j

$$R^0 = 0$$

$$R^{t+1} = \begin{cases} 1 & set^t \\ 0 & \neg set^t \wedge clr^t \\ R^t & \text{otherwise} \end{cases}$$

We consider a situation as shown in Fig. 41 with registers R_j connected to a bus b by tristate drivers y_j for $j \in [1:k]$.

For $i \in \mathbb{N}$ we aim at intervals

$$T_i = [a_i : b_i]$$

of cycles, s.t., $a_i \leq b_i$, and a function

$$send : \mathbb{N} \to [1:k]$$

specifying for each $i \in \mathbb{N}$ the unique index $j = send(i)$ such that register R_j is "sending" on the bus during "time" interval T_i:

$$b^t = \begin{cases} R_j & \exists i : j = send(i) \wedge t \in T_i \\ Z & \text{otherwise} . \end{cases}$$

The sending register R_j is clocked at cycle $a_i - 1$ and is not clocked in the time interval $[a_i : b_i - 1]$:

$$send(i) = j \to R_j ce^{a_i - 1} \wedge \forall t \in [a_i : b_i - 1] : \neg R_j ce^t .$$

At the end of a time interval T_i we consider two possible scenarios:

- Unit $j = send(i)$ continues to operate on the bus in cycle $b_i + 1$. In this case we have
  $$a_{i+1} = b_i + 1 \wedge send(i+1) = send(i) .$$

- Unit j gives up the bus in cycle b_i. In order to guarantee that there is enough time for activating signals in between two time intervals in this case we require
  $$b_i + 1 < a_{i+1} .$$

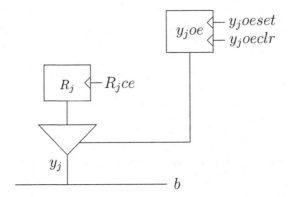

Fig. 42. Generation of output enable signals yoe_j by set-clear flip-flops

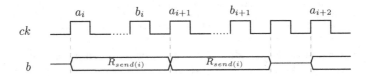

Fig. 43. Idealized timing of clean tristate bus control

For the first time interval, we require

$$0 < a_0 .$$

As shown in Fig. 42, control signals $y_j oe$ are generated as outputs of set-clear flip-flops which in turn are controlled by signals $y_j oeset$ and $y_j oeclr$. The rule for generation of the latter signals is simple: for intervals T_i during which y_j is enabled ($j = send(i)$), the output enable signal is set in cycle $a_i - 1$ (unless unit j was sending in cycle $a_i - 1 = b_{i-1}$) and cleared in cycle b_i (unless unit j will be sending in cycle $b_i + 1 = a_{i+1}$):

$$y_j oeset^t \equiv \exists i : send(i) = j \wedge t = a_i - 1 \wedge t \neq b_{i-1}$$
$$y_j oeclr^t \equiv \exists i : send(i) = j \wedge t = b_i \wedge t \neq a_{i+1} - 1 .$$

An example of idealized timing of the tristate bus control in shown in Fig. 43. Unit $send(i)$ is operating on the bus in two consecutive time intervals T_i and T_{i+1} (the value of the register $R_{send(i)}$ can be updated in the last cycle of the first interval) and then its driver is disabled. Between the end b_{i+1} of interval T_{i+1} and the start a_{i+2} of the next interval T_{i+2}, there is at least one cycle where no driver is enabled in the digital model.

In the digital model, we immediately conclude

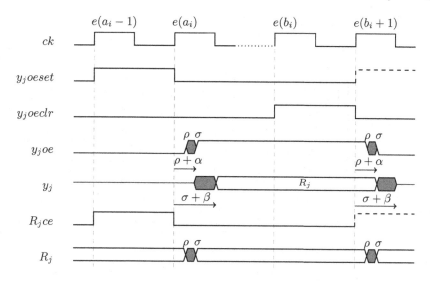

Fig. 44. Timing diagram for clean bus control in case unit j is sending in the interval T_i and is giving up the bus afterwards. Timing of signals $y_j oeset$, $y_j oeclr$, and $R_j ce$ are idealized. Other timings are detailed

$$y_j oe^t \equiv \exists i : send(i) = j \wedge t \in T_i$$

$$b^t = \begin{cases} R_j & \exists i : send(i) = j \wedge t \in T_i \\ Z & \text{otherwise ,} \end{cases}$$

as required in the digital specification. In the detailed model, we can show more. Before we do that, recall that $e(t)$ is the time of the clock edge starting cycle t. Because we are arguing about cycles and time simultaneously we denote cycles with q and times with t.

Lemma 3.9 (tristate bus control). Let a tristate bus be controlled by the logic designed in this section. Then,

- after time $t \geq e(0) + \sigma + \beta$ there is no bus contention:

$$t \geq e(0) + \sigma + \beta \wedge y_i(t) \neq Z \wedge y_j(t) \neq Z \rightarrow i = j ,$$

- if $j = send(i)$, then the content of R_j is glitch free on the bus roughly during T_i:

$$j = send(i) \rightarrow \forall t \in [e(a_i) + \sigma + \beta, e(b_i + 1) + \rho + \alpha] : b(t) = R_j^{a_i} .$$

Proof. Note that the hypotheses of this lemma are all digital. Thus, we can prove them entirely in the digital world.

Consider the timing diagram in Fig. 44. For the outputs of the set-clear flip-flop $y_j oe$, we get after reset

$$e(0) + \sigma \le t \le e(1) + \rho \to y_j oe(t) = 0 \, .$$

For $t > e(1) + \rho$ we get

$$y_j oe(t) = \begin{cases} \Omega & \exists i : send(i) = j \wedge t \in e(a_i) + (\rho, \sigma) \wedge a_i - 1 \ne b_{i-1} \\ 1 & \exists i : send(i) = j \wedge t \in e(a_i) + (\rho, \sigma) \wedge a_i - 1 = b_{i-1} \\ 1 & \exists i : send(i) = j \wedge t \in [e(a_i) + \sigma, e(b_i + 1) + \rho] \\ \Omega & \exists i : send(i) = j \wedge t \in e(b_i + 1) + (\rho, \sigma) \wedge b_i + 1 \ne a_{i+1} \\ 1 & \exists i : send(i) = j \wedge t \in e(b_i + 1) + (\rho, \sigma) \wedge b_i + 1 = a_{i+1} \\ 0 & \text{otherwise} \, . \end{cases}$$

For the outputs y_j of the drivers, it follows that after reset

$$e(0) + \sigma + \beta \le t \le e(1) + \rho + \alpha \to y_j(t) = Z \, .$$

For $t > e(1) + \rho$ we get

$$y_j(t) \ne Z \to \exists i : send(i) = j \wedge t \in [e(a_i) + \rho + \alpha, e(b_i + 1) + \sigma + \beta] \, .$$

Hence,

$$y_j(t) \ne Z \to \exists i : send(i) = j \wedge t \in (e(a_i), e(b_i + 2)) \, .$$

The first statement of the lemma is fulfilled because our requirements on the time intervals where different units are operating on the bus imply

$$e(1) \le e(a_0) \wedge e(b_i + 2) \le e(a_{i+1}).$$

For the second statement of the lemma, we observe that the signal $R_j ce$ is active in cycle $a_i - 1$ and can possibly become active again only in cycle b_i. Using Lemmas 3.3 and 3.5 we conclude that

$$j = send(i) \wedge t \in [e(a_i) + \sigma, e(b_i + 1) + \rho] \to$$
$$R_j(t) = R_j(e(a_i + 1)) = R_j^{a_i} \, .$$

We have shown already about the output enable signals

$$j = send(i) \wedge t \in [e(a_i) + \sigma, e(b_i + 1) + \rho] \to yoe_j(t) = 1 \, .$$

Thus, for the driver values we get

$$j = send(i) \wedge t \in [e(a_i) + \sigma + \beta, e(b_i + 1) + \rho + \alpha] \to y_j(t) = R_j^{a_i} \ne Z \, .$$

From the first part of the lemma we conclude for the value of the bus

$$j = send(i) \wedge t \in [e(a_i) + \sigma + \beta, e(b_i + 1) + \rho + \alpha] \to b(t) = R_j^{a_i} \, .$$

$\square$

Figure 45 shows symbol and implementation of an n-tristate driver. This driver consists simply of n tristate drivers with a common output enable signal.

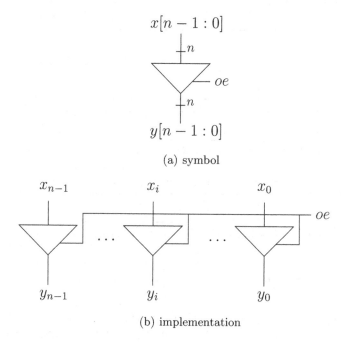

(a) symbol

(b) implementation

Fig. 45. Symbol and construction of an n-tristate driver.

3.5.6 Specification of Main Memory

As a last building block for hardware, we introduce a main memory $h.mm$. It is a line addressable memory

$$h.mm : \mathbb{B}^{29} \rightarrow \mathbb{B}^{64}$$

which is accessed via a tristate bus b with the following components:

- $b.d \in \mathbb{B}^{64}$. In write operations, this is a cache line to be stored in main memory. In the last cycle of read operations, $b.d$ contains the data read from main memory.
- $b.ad \in \mathbb{B}^{29}$. The line address of main memory operations.
- $b.mmreq \in \mathbb{B}$. The request signal for main memory operations.
- $b.mmw \in \mathbb{B}$. The main memory write signal, which denotes that the current main memory request is a write.
- $b.mmack \in \mathbb{B}$. The main memory acknowledgement signal. The main memory activates it in the last cycle of a main memory operation.

An incomplete digital specification of main memory accesses is given by the idealized timing diagram in Fig. 46.

It is often desirable to implement some small portion of the main memory as a read only memory (ROM) and the remaining large part as a random

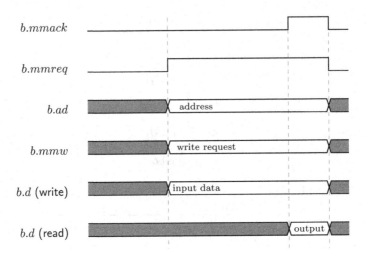

Fig. 46. Timing of main memory operations

access memory (RAM)[9]. The standard use for this is to store boot code in the read only portion of the memory. Since, after power up, the memory content of RAM is unknown, computation will not start in a meaningful way unless at least *some* portion of memory contains code that is known after power up. The reset mechanism of the hardware ensures that processors start by executing the program stored in the ROM. This code usually contains a so called *boot loader* which accesses a large and slow memory device – like a disk – to load further programs, e.g., an operating system to be executed, from the device.

For the purpose of storing a boot loader, we assume the main memory to behave as a ROM for addresses $a = 0^{29-r}b$, where $b \in \mathbb{B}^r$ and $r < 29$.

Operating conditions of the main memory are formulated in the following definitions and requirements:

1. **Stable inputs.** In general, accesses to main memory last several cycles. During such an access, the inputs must be stable:

$$b.mmreq^t \wedge \neg b.mmack^t \wedge X \in mmin(q) \rightarrow b.X^{t+1} = b.X^t \ ,$$

where $mmin(q)$ is the set of inputs of an access active in cycle q:

$$mmin(q) = \{b.ad, b.mmreq, b.mmw\} \cup \begin{cases} b.d & b.mmw^q \\ \emptyset & \text{otherwise} \ . \end{cases}$$

2. **No spurious acknowledgements.** The main memory should never raise a $b.mmack$ signal unless the $b.mmreq$ signal is set:

$$\neg b.mmreq^t \rightarrow \neg b.mmack^t \ .$$

---

[9] Some basic constructions of static RAMs and ROMs are given in Chapter 4.

3. **Memory liveness.** If the inputs are stable, we may assume liveness for the main memory, i.e., every request should be eventually served:

$$b.mmreq^t \rightarrow \exists t' \geq t : b.mmack^{t'} .$$

We denote the cycle in which the main memory acknowledges a request active in cycle t by

$$ack(t) = \min\{x \geq t \mid b.mmack^x = 1\} .$$

4. **Effect of write operations.** If the inputs are stable and the write access is on, then in the next cycle after the acknowledgement, the data from $b.d$ is written to the main memory at the address specified by $b.ad$:

$$mm^{q+1}(x) = \begin{cases} b.d^q & x = b.ad^q \wedge b.mmack^q \wedge b.mmw^q \\ & \wedge\ x[28:r] \neq 0^{29-r} \\ mm^q(x) & \text{otherwise} . \end{cases}$$

The writes only affect the memory content if they are performed to addresses larger than $0^{29-r}1^r$.

5. **Effect of read operations.** If the inputs are stable, then, in the last cycle of the read access, the data from the main memory specified by $b.ad$ is put on $b.d$:

$$b.mmreq^q \wedge \neg b.mmw^q \rightarrow b.d^{ack(q)} = mm^q(b.ad^q) .$$

6. **Tristate driver enable.** The driver $mmbd$ connecting the main memory to bus $b.d$ is never enabled outside of a read access:

$$\neg(\exists q : b.mmreq^q \wedge \neg b.mmw^q \wedge t \in [q, ack(q)]) \rightarrow mmbd^t = Z .$$

Properties 1, 5, and 6 of the digital specification are incomplete with respect to the detailed hardware model; since the absence of glitches is of importance, we complete the specification in the detailed hardware model with the following three conditions:

1. **Timing of inputs.** We require that, during a main memory access, inputs to main memory have to be free of glitches. The detailed specification has a new timing parameter, namely a main memory set up time $mmts$. This setup time has to be large enough to permit a reasonable control automaton (as specified in Sect. 3.6) to compute a next state and a response before the next clock edge.

   Let the memory request be active during time q. We require input components $b.X$ of the bus to have the digital value $b.X^q$ from time $mmts$ before edge $e(q+1)$ until hold time th after edge $e(ack(q)+1)$:

$$t \in [e(q+1) - mmts, e(ack(q)+1) + th] \wedge b.mmreq^q$$
$$\wedge\ X \in mmin(q) \rightarrow b.X(t) = b.X^q . \tag{11}$$

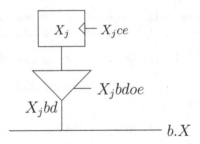

Fig. 47. Registers and their drivers on bus components $b.X$

2. **Timing of outputs.** We also have to specify the timing of responses given by main memory. We require the memory acknowledgement signal $b.mmack(t)$ to have digital value $b.mmack^c$ from time $mmts$ before edge $e(c+1)$ until hold time th after edge $e(c+1)$:

$$t \in [e(c+1) - mmts, e(c+1) + th] \rightarrow b.mmack(t) = b.mmack^c . \quad (12)$$

In case there is an active read request in cycle q, we also require the data output from the memory on bus $b.d$ to have digital value $b.d^{ack(q)}$ from time $mmts$ before edge $e(ack(q) + 1)$ until hold time th after edge $e(ack(q) + 1)$:

$$t \in [e(ack(q) + 1) - mmts, e(ack(q) + 1) + th] \wedge b.mmreq^q$$
$$\wedge \neg b.mmw^q \rightarrow b.d(t) = b.d^{ack(q)} . \quad (13)$$

3. **Absence of bus contention.** Finally, we have to define the absence of bus contention in the detailed model so that clean operation of the tristate bus can be guaranteed. The $mmbd$-driver can only be outside the high Z from start of the cycle starting a read access until the end of the cycle following a read access:

$$\neg(\exists q : b.mmreq^q \wedge \neg b.mmw^q \wedge t \in (e(q), e(ack(q) + 2))) \rightarrow$$
$$mmbd(t) = Z . \quad (14)$$

3.5.7 Operation of Main Memory via a Tristate Bus

We extend the control of the tristate bus from Sect. 3.5.5 to a control of the components of the main memory bus. We consider k units $U(j)$ with $j \in [1 : k]$ capable of accessing main memory. Each unit has output registers $mmreq_j, mmw_j, a_j$, and d_j and an input register Q_j . They are connected to the bus b accessing main memory in the obvious way: bus components $b.X$ with $X \in \{ad, mmreq, mmw\}$ occur only as inputs to the main memory. The situation shown in Fig. 47 for unit $U(j)$ is simply a special case of Fig. 41 with

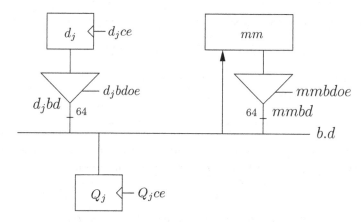

Fig. 48. Registers and main memory with their drivers on bus component $b.d$

$$R_j = X_j$$
$$y_j = X_j bd$$
$$b = b.X .$$

As shown in Fig. 48, bus components $b.d$ can be driven both by the units and by the main memory. If main memory drives the data bus, the data on the bus can be clocked into input register Q_j of unit $U(j)$. If the data bus is driven by a unit, the data on the bus can be stored in main memory. We treat main memory simply as unit $k + 1$. Then we almost have a special case of Fig. 41 with

$$R_j = d_j \quad \text{if } 1 \le j \le k$$
$$y_j = \begin{cases} d_j bd & 1 \le j \le k \\ mmbd & j = k + 1 \end{cases}$$
$$b = b.d .$$

Signal $b.mmack$ is broadcast by main memory. Thus, bus control is not necessary for this signal. We want to extend the proof of Lemma 3.9 to show that all four tristate buses given above are operated in a clean way. We also use the statement of Lemma 3.9 to show that the new control produces memory input without glitches in the sense of the main memory specification. The crucial signals governing the construction of the control are the main memory request signals $mmreq_j$. We compute them in set-clear flip-flops; they are cleared at reset:

$$\forall y : mmreq_y^0 = 0 .$$

For the set and clear signals of the memory request, we use the following discipline:

- a main memory request signal is only set when all request signals are off

$$mmreq_j set^q \to \forall y : mmreq_y^q = 0 \ ,$$

- at most one request signal is turned on at a time (this requires some sort of bus arbitration):

$$mmreq_j set^q \wedge mmreq_{j'} set^q \to j = j' \ ,$$

- a request which starts in cycle q is kept on until the corresponding acknowledgement in cycle $ack(q)$ and is then turned off

$$mmreq_j set^{q-1} \to$$
$$(\forall x \in [q : ack(q) - 1] : \neg mmreq_j clr^x) \wedge mmreq_j clr^{ack(q)} \ .$$

Now we can define access intervals $T_i = [a_i : b_i]$. The start cycle a_i of interval T_i is occurrence number i of the event that any signal $mmreq_j$ turns on. In the end cycle b_i, the corresponding acknowledgement occurs:

$$a_1 = \min\{x \geq 0 : \exists j : mmreq_j set^x\} + 1$$
$$b_i = ack(a_i)$$
$$a_{i+1} = \min\{x > b_i : \exists j : mmreq_j set^x\} + 1 \ .$$

For bus components $b.X$ with $X \in \{ad, mmreq, mmw\}$, we say that a unit $U(j)$ is sending in interval T_i if its request signal is on at the start of the interval:

$$send(i) = j \leftrightarrow mmreq_j^{a_i} = 1 \ .$$

Controlling the bus components $b.X$ with $X \in \{ad, mmreq, mmw\}$ (which occur only as inputs to the main memory) as prescribed in Lemma 3.9[10], we conclude

$$\forall t \in [e(a_i) + \sigma + \beta, e(b_i + 1) + \rho + \alpha] : b.X(t) = X_{send(i)}^{a_i} \ .$$

For the data component $b.d$ of the bus, we define unit j to be sending if its request signal is on in cycle a_i and the request is a write request. We define the main memory to be sending ($send'(i) = k + 1$) if the request in cycle a_i is a read request:

$$send'(i) = \begin{cases} j & mmreq_j^{a_i} = 1 \wedge mmw_j^{a_i} \\ k+1 & \exists j : mmreq_j^{a_i} = 1 \wedge \neg mmw_j^{a_i} \ . \end{cases}$$

Now we control all registers $data_j$ for $j \in [1 : k]$ as prescribed in Lemma 3.9. Absence of bus contention for component $b.d$ follows from the proof of Lemma

---

[10] Note that for signals $X \in \{ad, mmreq\}$ the corresponding time intervals when they are driven on the bus can be larger than the time interval for signal $mmreq$.

3.9 and (14) in the specification of the main memory. For write operations, we conclude by Lemma 3.9:

$$send'(i) \leq k \rightarrow \forall t \in [e(a_i) + \sigma + \beta, e(b_i + 1) + \rho + \alpha] : b.X(t) = X_{send'(i)}^{a_i} .$$

Under reasonable assumptions for timing parameters and cycle time τ, this completes the proof of (11) of the main memory specification requiring that glitches are absent in main memory input.

Lemma 3.10 (clean opeation of memory). Let $\rho + \alpha \geq th$ and $\sigma + \beta + mmts \leq \tau$. Then,

$$X \in mmin(a_i) \wedge t \in [e(a_i + 1) - mmts, e(ack(a_i) + 1) + th] \rightarrow$$
$$b.X(t) = b.X^{a_i} .$$

Equation (13) is needed for timing analysis. In order to meet set up times for the data of input $Q_j in$ of registers Q_j on bus $b.d$, it obviously suffices if

$$mmts \geq ts .$$

However, a larger lower bound for parameter $mmts$ will follow from the construction of particular control automata in Chap. 8.

3.6 Finite State Transducers

Control automata (also called *finite state transducers*) are finite automata which produce an output in every step. Formally, a finite state transducer M is defined by a 6-tuple $(Z, z_0, I, O, \delta_A, \eta)$, where Z is a finite set of states, $I \subseteq \mathbb{B}^\sigma$ is a finite set of *input symbols*, $z_0 \in Z$ is called the *initial state*, $O \subseteq \mathbb{B}^\gamma$ is a finite set of *output symbols*,

$$\delta_A : Z \times I \rightarrow Z$$

is the *transition function*, and

$$\eta : Z \times I \rightarrow O$$

is the *output function*.

Such an automaton performs steps according to the following rules:

- the automaton is started in state z_0,
- if the automaton is in state z and reads input symbol in, then it outputs symbol $\eta(z, in)$ and goes to state $\delta_A(z, in)$.

If the output function does not depend on the input, i.e., if it can be written as

$$\eta : Z \rightarrow O ,$$

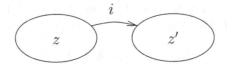

Fig. 49. Graphical representation of a transition $z' = \delta_A(z, i)$

the automaton is called a *Moore automaton*. Otherwise, it is called a *Mealy automaton*.

Automata are often visualized in graphical form. We will do this too in Sect. 8.4.3 when we construct several automata for the control of a cache coherence protocol. State z is drawn as an ellipse with z written inside. A state transition

$$z' = \delta_A(z, i)$$

is visualized by an arrow from state z to state z' with label i as shown in Fig. 49. Initial states are sometimes drawn as a double circle.

In what follows, we show how to implement control automata. We start with the simpler Moore automata and then generalize the construction to Mealy automata.

3.6.1 Realization of Moore Automata

Let $k = \#Z$ be the number of states of the automaton. Then states can be numbered from 0 to $k - 1$, and we can rename the states with numbers from 0 to $k - 1$, taking 0 as the initial state:

$$Z = [0 : k - 1] \quad , \quad z_0 = 0 \ .$$

We code the current state z in a register $S \in \mathbb{B}^k$ by simple unary coding:

$$S = code(z) \leftrightarrow \forall i : S[i] = \begin{cases} 1 & z = i \\ 0 & \text{otherwise} \ . \end{cases}$$

A completely straightforward and naive implementation is shown in Fig. 50. By the construction of the reset logic, we get

$$h^0.S = code(0) \ .$$

Circuits *out* (like output) and *nexts* are constructed such that the automaton is simulated in the following sense: if $h.S = z$, i.e., state z is encoded by the hardware, then

1. $out(h) = \eta(z)$, i.e., automaton and hardware produce the same output,
2. $nexts(h) = code(\delta_A(z, in(h)))$, i.e., in the next cycle the hardware $h'.S$ encodes the next state $\delta_A(z, in(h))$.

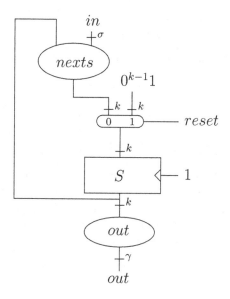

Fig. 50. Naive implementation of a Moore automaton

The following lemma states correctness of the construction shown in Fig. 50.

Lemma 3.11 (Moore automaton). Let

$$h.S = code(z) \wedge \delta_A(z, in(h)) = z' .$$

Then,

$$out(h) = \eta(z) \wedge h'.S = code(z') .$$

For all $i \in [0 : \gamma - 1]$, we construct the i'th output simply by OR-ing together all bits $S[x]$ where $\eta(x)[i] = 1$, i.e., such that the i-th output is on in state x of the automaton:

$$out(h)[i] = \bigvee_{\eta(x)[i]=1} h.S[x] .$$

A straightforward argument shows the first claim of the lemma. Assume $h.S = z$. Then,

$$h.S[x] = 1 \leftrightarrow x = z .$$

Hence,

$$out(h)[i] = 1$$
$$\leftrightarrow \bigvee_{\eta(x)[i]=1} h.S[x] = 1$$
$$\leftrightarrow \exists x : \eta(x)[i] = 1 \wedge h.S[x] = 1$$
$$\leftrightarrow \eta(z)[i] = 1 .$$

Lemma 2.16 gives

$$out(h)[i] = \eta(z)[i] .$$

For states i, j we define auxiliary switching functions

$$\delta_{i,j} : \mathbb{B}^\sigma \to \mathbb{B}$$

from the transition function δ_A of the automaton by

$$\delta_{i,j}(in) = 1 \leftrightarrow \delta_A(i, in) = j ,$$

i.e., function $\delta_{i,j}(in)$ is on if input in takes the automaton from state i to state j. Boolean formulas for functions $\delta_{i,j}$ can be constructed by Lemma 2.20. For each state j, component $nexts[j]$, which models the next state function, is turned on in states x, which transition under input in to state j according to the automaton's transition function:

$$nexts(h)[j] = \bigvee_x h.S[x] \wedge \delta_{x,j}(in(h)) .$$

For the second claim of the lemma, let

$$h.S = code(z)$$
$$\delta_A(z, in(h)) = z' .$$

For any next state j, we then have

$$nexts(h)[j] = 1$$
$$\leftrightarrow \bigvee_x h.S[x] \wedge \delta_{x,j}(in(h)) = 1$$
$$\leftrightarrow \delta_{z,j}(in(h)) = j$$
$$\leftrightarrow \delta_A(z, in(h)) = j .$$

Hence,

$$nexts(h)[j] = \begin{cases} 1 & j = z' \\ 0 & \text{otherwise} . \end{cases}$$

Thus,

$$code(z') = nexts(h)$$
$$= h'.S .$$

3.6.2 Precomputing Outputs of Moore Automata

The previous construction has the disadvantage that the propagation delay of circuit out tends to contribute to the cycle time of the circuitry controlled by

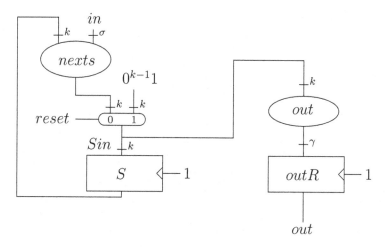

Fig. 51. Implementation of a Moore automaton with precomputed outputs

the automaton. This can by avoided by precomputing the output signals of a Moore automaton as a function of the next state signals as shown in Fig. 51.

As above, one shows

$$Sin(h) = code(z) \rightarrow out(h) = \eta(z) .$$

For $h = h^{-1}$ the reset signal is active and we have

$$Sin(h^{-1}) = 0^{k-1}1 = code(0)$$
$$out(h^{-1}) = \eta(0) .$$

Thus,

$$h^0.S = code(0) \quad \text{and} \quad h^0.outR = \eta(0) .$$

The following lemma states correctness of the construction shown in Fig. 51.

Lemma 3.12 (Moore automaton with precomputed outputs). For $h = h^t$ and $t \geq 0$, let

$$h.S = code(z) \wedge \delta_A(z, in(h)) = z' .$$

Then,

$$h'.S = code(z') \wedge h'.outR = \eta(z') .$$

We have $reset(h) = 0$, and hence, $Sin(h) = nexts(h)$. From above we have

$$h'.S = nexts(h) = code(z')$$

and

$$h'.outR = out(h) = \eta(z') .$$

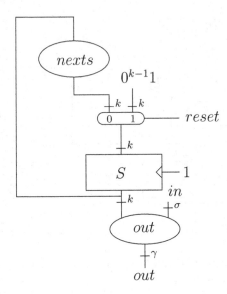

Fig. 52. Simple implementation of a Mealy automaton

3.6.3 Realization of Mealy Automata

Figure 52 shows a simple implementation of a Mealy automaton. Compared to the construction for Moore automata, only the generation of output signals changes; the next state computation stays the same. Output $\eta(z, in)$ now depends both on the current state z and the current input in. For states z and indices i of outputs, we derive from function η the set of switching functions $f_{z,i}$, where

$$f_{z,i}(in) = 1 \leftrightarrow \eta(z, in)[i] = 1 .$$

Output is generated by

$$out(h)[i] = \bigvee_x h.S[x] \wedge f_{x,i}(in(h)) .$$

This generates the outputs of the automaton in the following way.

Lemma 3.13 (Mealy automaton).

$$h.S = code(z) \rightarrow out(h) = \eta(z, in(h))$$

Again, the proof is straightforward:

$$out(h)[i] = 1$$
$$\leftrightarrow \bigvee_x h.S[x] \wedge f_{x,i}(in(h)) = 1$$
$$\leftrightarrow f_{z,i}(in(h)) = 1$$
$$\leftrightarrow \eta(z, in(h))[i] = 1 .$$

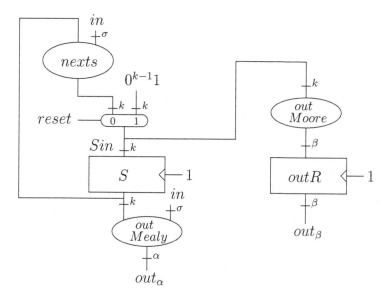

Fig. 53. Separate realization of Moore and Mealy components

3.6.4 Partial Precomputation of Outputs of Mealy Automata

We describe two optimizations that can reduce the delay of outputs of Mealy automata. The first one is trivial. We divide the output components $out[j]$ into two classes: i) Mealy components $\eta[k](z, in)$, which have a true dependency on the input variables, and ii) Moore components that can be written as $\eta[k](z)$, i.e., that only depend on the current state. Suppose we have α Mealy components and β Moore components with $\gamma = \alpha + \beta$. Obviously, one can precompute the Moore components as in a Moore automaton and realize the Mealy components as in the previous construction of Mealy automata. The resulting construction is shown without further correctness proof in Fig. 53.

However, quite often, more optimization is possible since Mealy components usually depend only on very few input bits of the automaton. As an example, consider a Mealy output depending only on two input bits:

$$\eta(z, in)[j] = f(z, in[1:0]) .$$

For $x, y \in \mathbb{B}$, we derive Moore outputs $f_{x,y}(z)$ that precompute $\eta(z, in)[j]$ if $in[1:0] = xy$:

$$f_{x,y}(z) = f(z, xy) .$$

Output $\eta(z, in)[j]$ in this case is computed as

$$\eta(z, in)[j] = f(z, in[1:0])$$
$$= \bigvee_{x,y\in\mathbb{B}} (in[1:0] = xy) \wedge f_{x,y}(z) .$$

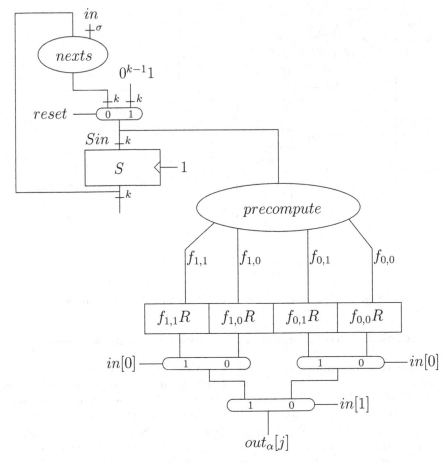

Fig. 54. Partial precomputation of a Mealy output depending on two input bits

Now, we precompute automata outputs $f_{x,y}(Sin(h))$ and store them in registers $f_{x,y}R$ as shown in Fig. 54.

As for precomputed Moore signals, one shows

$$h.S = code(z) \rightarrow h.f_{x,y}R = f_{x,y}(z) \ .$$

For the output $out_\alpha[j]$ of the multiplexer tree, we conclude

$$
\begin{aligned}
out_\alpha[j](h) &= h.f_{in[1:0]}R \\
&= f_{in[1:0]}(z) \\
&= \eta(z, in[1:0])[j] \ .
\end{aligned}
$$

This construction has the advantage that only the multiplexers contribute to the delay of the control signals generated by the automaton. In general, for Mealy signals which depend on k input bits, we have k levels of multiplexers.

4

Nine Shades of RAM[1]

The processors of multi-core machines communicate via a shared memory in a highly nontrivial way. Thus, not surprisingly, memory components play an important role in the construction of such machines. We start in Sect. 4.1 with a basic construction of (static) random access memory (RAM). Next, we derive in Sect. 4.2 five specialized designs: read only memory (ROM), multi-bank RAM, cache state RAM, and special purpose register RAM (SPR RAM). In Sect. 4.3 we then generalize the construction to multi-port RAM; this is RAM with more than one address and data port. We need multi-port RAMs in 4 flavours: 3-port RAM for the construction of general purpose register files, general 2-port RAM, 2-port combined multi-bank RAM-ROM, and 2-port cache state RAM.

For the correctness proof of a RAM construction, we consider a hardware configuration h which has the abstract state of the RAM $h.S$ as well as the hardware components implementing this RAM. The abstract state of the RAM is coupled with the state of its implementation by means of an *abstraction relation*. Given that both the abstract RAM specification and RAM implementation have the same inputs, we show that their outputs are also always the same.

The material in this section builds clearly on [12]. The new variations of RAMs (like general 2-port RAM or 2-port cache state RAM), that we have introduced, are needed in later chapters. Correctness proofs for the various flavours of RAM are quite similar. Thus, if one lectures about this material, it suffices to present only a few of them in the classroom.

4.1 Basic Random Access Memory

As illustrated in Fig. 55, an (n, a)-static RAM S or SRAM is a portion of a clocked circuit with the following inputs and outputs:

---

[1] The title of this chapter is inspired by the song "Forty Shades of Green" written in 1959 by Johnny Cash and not by a recent novel.

M. Kovalev et al.: A Pipelined Multi-core MIPS Machine, LNCS 9000, pp. 83–98, 2014.
© Springer International Publishing Switzerland 2014

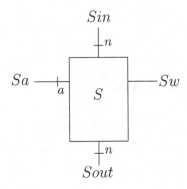

Fig. 55. Symbol for an (n, a)-SRAM

- an n-bit data input Sin,
- an a-bit address input Sa,
- a write signal Sw, and
- an n-bit data output $Sout$.

Internally, the static RAM contains 2^a many n-bit registers $S(x) \in \mathbb{B}^n$. Thus, it is modeled as a function

$$h.S : \mathbb{B}^a \to \mathbb{B}^n .$$

The initial content of the RAM after reset is unknown:

$$\forall x : h^0.S(x) \in \mathbb{B}^n .$$

The output of the RAM is the register content selected by the address input:

$$Sout(h) = h.S(Sa(h)) .$$

For addresses $x \in \mathbb{B}^a$ we define the next state transition function for SRAM as

$$h'.S(x) = \begin{cases} Sin(h) & Sa(h) = x \wedge Sw(h) = 1 \\ h.S(x) & \text{otherwise} . \end{cases}$$

The implementation of an SRAM is shown in Fig. 56. We use 2^a many n-bit registers $R^{(i)}$ with $i \in [0 : 2^a - 1]$ and an a-decoder with outputs $X[2^a - 1 : 0]$ satisfying

$$X(i) = 1 \leftrightarrow i = \langle Sa(h) \rangle .$$

The inputs of register $R^{(i)}$ are defined as

$$h.R^{(i)}in = Sin(h)$$
$$h.R^{(i)}ce = Sw(h) \wedge X[i] .$$

For the next state computation we get

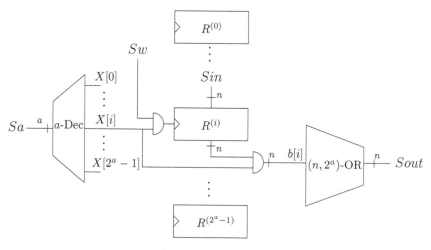

Fig. 56. Construction of an (n, a)-SRAM

$$h'.R^{(i)} = \begin{cases} Sin(h) & i = \langle Sa(h) \rangle \wedge Sw(h) \\ h.R^{(i)} & \text{otherwise .} \end{cases}$$

The i-th input vector $b[i]$ to the OR-tree is constructed as

$$b[i] = X[i] \wedge h.R^{(i)}$$
$$= \begin{cases} h.R^{(i)} & i = \langle Sa(h) \rangle \\ 0^n & \text{otherwise .} \end{cases}$$

Thus,

$$Sout(h) = \bigvee_{i=0}^{2^a - 1} b[i]$$
$$= h.R^{(\langle Sa(h) \rangle)} .$$

As a result, when we choose

$$h.S(x) = h.R^{(\langle x \rangle)}$$

as the defining equation of our abstraction relation, the presented construction implements an SRAM.

4.2 Single-Port RAM Designs

4.2.1 Read Only Memory (ROM)

An (n, a)-ROM is a memory with a drawback and an advantage. The drawback: it can only be read. The advantage: its content is known after power

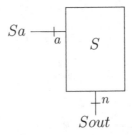

Fig. 57. Symbol of an (n, a)-ROM

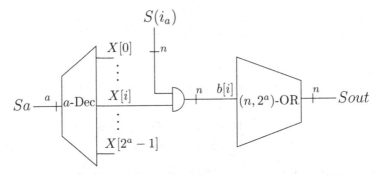

Fig. 58. Construction of an (n, a)-ROM

up. It is modeled by a mapping $S : \mathbb{B}^a \to \mathbb{B}^n$, which does not depend on the hardware configuration h. The construction is obtained by a trivial variation of the basic RAM design from Fig. 56: replace each register $R^{(i)}$ by the constant input $S(bin_a(i)) \in \mathbb{B}^n$. Since the ROM cannot be written, there are no data in, write, or clock enable signals; the hardware constructed in this way is a circuit. Symbol and construction are given in Figs. 57 and 58.

4.2.2 Multi-bank RAM

Let $n = 8k$ be a multiple of 8. An (n, a)-multi-bank RAM $S : \mathbb{B}^a \to \mathbb{B}^{8k}$ is basically an (n, a)-RAM with separate bank write signals $bw(i)$ for each byte $i \in [0 : k - 1]$ (see Fig. 59). It has

- a data input $Sin \in \mathbb{B}^{8k}$,
- a data output $Sout \in \mathbb{B}^{8k}$,
- an address input $Sa \in \mathbb{B}^a$, and
- bank write signals $Sbw[i] \in \mathbb{B}$ for $i \in [0 : k - 1]$.

Data output is defined exactly as for the ordinary RAM:

$$Sout(h) = h.S(Sa(h)) .$$

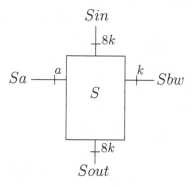

Fig. 59. Symbol of an (n, a)-multi-bank RAM

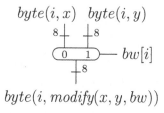

Fig. 60. Computation of output byte i of a modify circuit

For the definition of the next state, we first introduce auxiliary function

$$modify : \mathbb{B}^{8k} \times \mathbb{B}^{8k} \times \mathbb{B}^{k} \to \mathbb{B}^{8k} \ .$$

This function selects bytes from two provided strings according to the provided byte write signals. Let $y, x \in \mathbb{B}^{8k}$ and $bw \in \mathbb{B}^{k}$. Then, for all $i \in [0 : k - 1]$,

$$byte(i, modify(x, y, bw)) = \begin{cases} byte(i, y) & bw[i] = 1 \\ byte(i, x) & bw[i] = 0 \ , \end{cases}$$

i.e., for all i with active $bw[i]$ one replaces byte i of x by byte i of y. The next state of multi-bank RAM is then defined as

$$h'.S(x) = \begin{cases} modify(h.S(x), Sin(h), Sbw(h)) & x = \langle Sa(h) \rangle \\ h.S(x) & \text{otherwise} \ . \end{cases}$$

As shown in Fig. 60, each byte of the output of a modify circuit is simply computed by an 8-bit wide multiplexer.

The straightforward construction of a multi-bank RAM uses k separate so called *banks*. These are $(8, a)$-RAMs $S^{(i)}$ for $i \in [0 : k - 1]$. For each i, bank $S^{(i)}$ is wired as shown in Fig. 61:

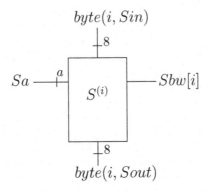

Fig. 61. Bank i of an (n, a)-multi-bank RAM

$$S^{(i)}a = Sa(h)$$
$$S^{(i)}in = byte(i, Sin(h))$$
$$S^{(i)}out = byte(i, Sout(h))$$
$$S^{(i)}w = Sbw(h)[i] \ .$$

We abstract the state $h.S$ for this construction as

$$byte(i, h.S(x)) = h.S^{(i)}(x) \ .$$

Correctness now follows in a lengthy – but completely straightforward – way from the specification of ordinary RAM. For the outputs we have

$$
\begin{aligned}
byte(i, Sout(h)) &= S^{(i)}out(h) \quad \text{(construction)}\\
&= h.S^{(i)}(S^{(i)}a(h)) \quad \text{(construction)}\\
&= h.S^{(i)}(Sa(h)) \quad \text{(construction)}\\
&= byte(i, h.S(Sa(h))) \ . \quad \text{(state abstraction)}
\end{aligned}
$$

For the new state of the multi-bank RAM and address $x \neq Sa(h)$, we have

$$
\begin{aligned}
byte(i, h'.S(x)) &= h'.S^{(i)}(x) \quad \text{(state abstraction)}\\
&= h.S^{(i)}(x) \quad \text{(construction)}\\
&= byte(i, h.S(x)) \ . \quad \text{(state abstraction)}
\end{aligned}
$$

For the new state and address $x = Sa(h)$:

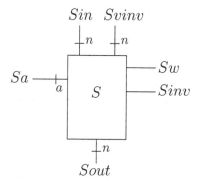

Fig. 62. Symbol of an (n, a)-CS RAM

$$byte(i, h'.S(x)) = h'.S^{(i)}(x) \quad \text{(state abstraction)}$$

$$= \begin{cases} S^{(i)}in(h) & S^{(i)}w(h) = 1 \\ h.S^{(i)}(x) & S^{(i)}w(h) = 0 \end{cases} \quad \text{(construction)}$$

$$= \begin{cases} byte(i, Sin(h)) & Sbw(h)[i] = 1 \\ h.S^{(i)}(x) & Sbw(h)[i] = 0 \end{cases} \quad \text{(construction)}$$

$$= \begin{cases} byte(i, Sin(h)) & Sbw(h)[i] = 1 \\ byte(i, h.S(x)) & Sbw(h)[i] = 0 \, . \end{cases} \quad \text{(state abstraction)}$$

As a result, we have

$$h'.S(x) = modify(h.S(x), Sin(h), Sbw(h)) \, .$$

4.2.3 Cache State RAM

The symbol of an (n, a)-cache state RAM or CS RAM is shown in Fig. 62. This type of RAM is used later for holding the status bits of caches. It has two extra inputs:

- a control signal $Sinv$ – on activation, a special value is forced into all registers of the RAM. Later, we will use this to set a value that indicates that all cache lines are invalid[2] and
- an n-bit input $Svinv$ providing this special value. This input is usually wired to a constant value in $\mathbb{B}^n$.

Activation of $Sinv$ takes precedence over ordinary write operations:

---

[2] I.e., not a copy of meaningful data in our programming model. We explain this in much more detail later.

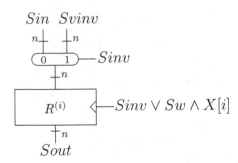

Fig. 63. Construction block of an (n, a)-cache state RAM

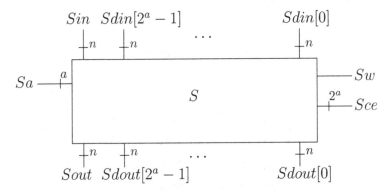

Fig. 64. Symbol of an (n, a)-SPR RAM

$$h'.S(x) = \begin{cases} Svinv(h) & Sinv(h) = 1 \\ Sin(h) & x = Sa(h) \wedge Sw(h) = 1 \wedge Sinv(h) = 0 \\ h.S(x) & \text{otherwise .} \end{cases}$$

The changes in the implementation for each register $R^{(i)}$ are shown in Fig. 63. The clock enable is also activated by $Sinv$ and the data input comes from a multiplexer:

$$R^{(i)}ce = Sinv(h) \vee X[i] \wedge Sw(h)$$

$$R^i in = \begin{cases} Svinv(h) & Sinv(h) = 1 \\ Sin(h) & \text{otherwise .} \end{cases}$$

4.2.4 SPR RAM

An (n, a)-SPR RAM as shown in Fig. 64 is used for the realization of special purpose register files and in the construction of fully associative caches. It behaves both as an (n, a)-RAM and as a set of 2^a many n-bit registers. It has the following inputs and outputs:

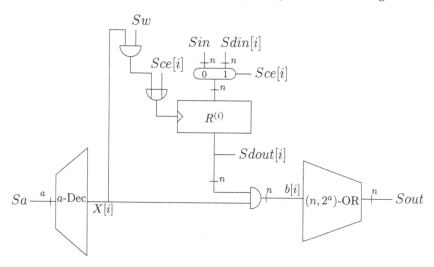

Fig. 65. Construction of an (n, a)-SPR RAM

- an n-bit data input Sin,
- an a-bit address input Sa,
- an n-bit data output $Sout$,
- a write signal Sw,
- for each $i \in [0 : 2^a - 1]$ an individual n-bit data input $Sdin[i]$ for register $R^{(i)}$,
- for each $i \in [0 : 2^a - 1]$ an individual n-bit data output $Sdout[i]$ for register $R^{(i)}$, and
- for each $i \in [0 : 2^a - 1]$ an individual clock enable signal $Sce[i]$ for register $R^{(i)}$.

Ordinary data output is generated as usual, and the individual data outputs are simply the outputs of the internal registers:

$$Sout(h) = h.S(Sad(h))$$
$$Sdout(h)[i] = h.S(bin_a(i)) \, .$$

Register updates to $R^{(i)}$ can be performed either by Sin for regular writes or by $Sdin[i]$ if the special clock enables are activated. Special writes take precedence over ordinary writes:

$$h'.S(x) = \begin{cases} Sdin(h)[\langle x \rangle] & Sce(h)[\langle x \rangle] = 1 \\ Sin(h) & Sce(h)[\langle x \rangle] = 0 \wedge Sw(h) = 1 \\ h.S(x) & \text{otherwise} \, . \end{cases}$$

A single address decoder with outputs $X[i]$ and a single OR-tree suffices. Figure 65 shows the construction satisfying

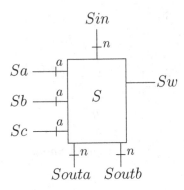

Fig. 66. Symbol of an (n, a)-GPR RAM

$$R^{(i)}ce = Sce(h)[i] \vee X[i] \wedge Sw(h)$$
$$R^{(i)}in = \begin{cases} Sdin(h)[i] & Sce(h)[i] = 1 \\ Sin(h) & \text{otherwise} . \end{cases}$$

4.3 Multi-port RAM Designs

4.3.1 3-port RAM for General Purpose Registers

An (n, a)-GPR RAM is a three-port RAM that we use later for general purpose registers. As shown in Fig. 66, it has the following inputs and outputs:

- an n-bit data input Sin,
- three a-bit address inputs Sa, Sb, Sc,
- a write signal Sw, and
- two n-bit data outputs $Souta, Soutb$.

As for ordinary SRAM, the state of the 3-port RAM is a mapping

$$h.S : \mathbb{B}^a \to \mathbb{B}^n .$$

Reads are controlled by address inputs $Sa(h)$ and $Sb(h)$:

$$Souta(h) = h.S(Sa(h))$$
$$Soutb(h) = h.S(Sb(h)) .$$

Writing is performed under control of address input $Sc(h)$:

$$h'.S(x) = \begin{cases} Sin(h) & Sc(h) = x \wedge Sw(h) = 1 \\ h.S(x) & \text{otherwise} . \end{cases}$$

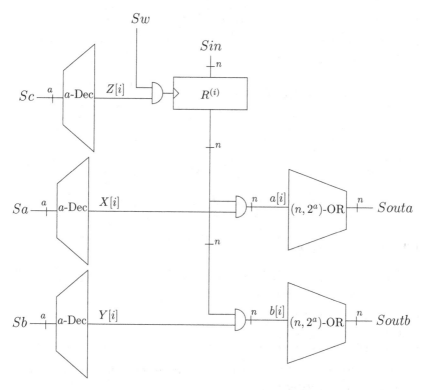

Fig. 67. Construction of an (n, a)-GPR RAM

The implementation shown in Fig. 67 is a straightforward variation of the
design for ordinary SRAM. One uses three different a-decoders with outputs
$X[0 : 2^a - 1], Y[0 : 2^a - 1], Z[0 : 2^a - 1]$ satisfying

$$X[i] = 1 \leftrightarrow i = \langle Sa(h) \rangle$$
$$Y[i] = 1 \leftrightarrow i = \langle Sb(h) \rangle$$
$$Z[i] = 1 \leftrightarrow i = \langle Sc(h) \rangle .$$

Clock enable signals are derived from the decoded Sc address:

$$R^{(i)}ce = Z[i] \wedge Sw(h) .$$

Outputs $Souta, Soutb$ are generated by two $(n, 2^a)$-bit OR-trees with inputs
$a[i]$, $b[i]$ satisfying

$$a[i] = X[i] \wedge h.R^{(i)}$$
$$Souta(h) = \bigvee a[i]$$
$$b[i] = Y[i] \wedge h.R^{(i)}$$
$$Soutb(h) = \bigvee b[i] .$$

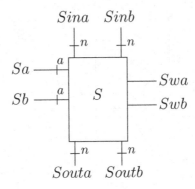

Fig. 68. Symbol of an (n, a)-2-port RAM

4.3.2 General 2-port RAM

A general (n, a)-2-port RAM is shown in Fig. 68. This is a RAM with the following inputs and outputs:

- two data inputs $Sina, Sinb$,
- two addresses Sa, Sb,
- two write signals Swa, Swb.

The data outputs are determined by the addresses as in the 3-port RAM for general purpose registers:

$$Souta(h) = h.S(Sa(h))$$
$$Soutb(h) = h.S(Sb(h)) \ .$$

The 2-port RAM allows simultaneous writes to two addresses. In case both write signals are active and both addresses point to the same port we have to resolve the conflict: the write via the a port will take precedence:

$$h'.S(x) = \begin{cases} Sina(h) & x = Sa(h) \wedge Swa(h) = 1 \\ Sinb(h) & x = Sb(h) \wedge Swb(h) = 1 \wedge \overline{x = Sa(h) \wedge Swa(h) = 1} \\ h.S(x) & \text{otherwise} \ . \end{cases}$$

Only two address decoders with outputs $X[0 : 2^a - 1]$, $Y[0 : 2^a - 1]$ are necessary. They satisfy

$$X[i] = 1 \ \leftrightarrow i = \langle Sa(h) \rangle$$
$$Y[i] = 1 \ \leftrightarrow i = \langle Sb(h) \rangle \ .$$

Figure 69 shows the changes to each register $R^{(i)}$. Clock enable is activated in case a write via the a address or via the b address occurs. The input is chosen from the corresponding data input by a multiplexer:

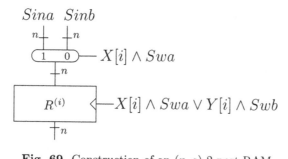

$$X[i] \wedge Swa$$

$$X[i] \wedge Swa \vee Y[i] \wedge Swb$$

Fig. 69. Construction of an (n, a)-2-port RAM

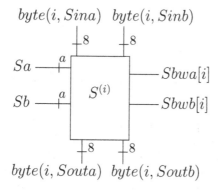

Fig. 70. Bank i of an (n, a)-2-port multi-bank RAM

$$R^{(i)}ce = Swa(h) \wedge X[i] \vee Swb(h) \wedge Y[i]$$

$$R^{(i)}in = \begin{cases} Sina(h) & Swa(h) \wedge X[i] \\ Sinb(h) & \text{otherwise .} \end{cases}$$

As required in this implementation, writes via port a take precedence over writes via port b to the same address.

Output is generated as for GPR RAMs.

4.3.3 2-port Multi-bank RAM-ROM

In Sect. 3.5.6, we have already explained why it is often desirable to implement some small portion of the main memory as a ROM and the remaining large part as a RAM. In the implementation of the sequential MIPS processor that we construct in Chap. 6, every instruction is executed in a single cycle. Hence, we need a memory construction, which allows us to fetch an instruction and to access data in a single cycle. For this purpose we construct a 2-port multi-bank RAM-ROM out of a 2-port multi-bank RAM and a 2-port ROM.

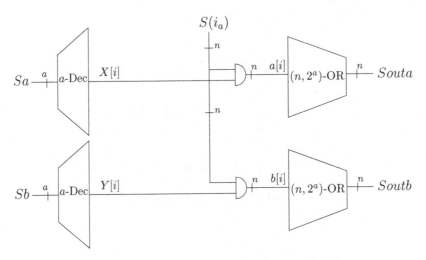

Fig. 71. Construction of an (n, a)-2-port ROM

A straightforward implementation of an $(8k, a)$-2-port multi-bank RAM uses k many $(8, a)$-2-port RAMs. Wiring for bank i is shown in Fig. 70. Figure 71 shows the implementation of an (n, a)-2-port ROM.

For $r < a$ we define a combined (n, r, a)-2-port multi-bank RAM-ROM, where $n = 8k$, as a device that behaves for small addresses $a = 0^{a-r}b$ with $b \in \mathbb{B}^r$ like ROM and on the other addresses like RAM. Just like an ordinary 2-port RAM, we model the state of the (n, r, a)-2-port multi-bank RAM-ROM as

$$h.S : \mathbb{B}^a \to \mathbb{B}^n$$

and define its output as

$$Souta(h) = h.S(Sa(h))$$
$$Soutb(h) = h.S(Sb(h)) \,.$$

Write operations, however, only affect addresses larger than $0^{a-r}1^r$. Moreover, we only need the writes to be performed through port b of the memory (port a will only be used for instruction fetches):

$$h'.S(x) = \begin{cases} modify(h.S(x), Sin(h), Sbw(h)) & x[a-1:r] \neq 0^{a-r} \\ & \wedge\, x = \langle Sb(h) \rangle \\ h.S(x) & \text{otherwise} \,. \end{cases}$$

The symbol for an (n, r, a)-2-port multi-bank RAM-ROM and a straightforward implementation involving an (n, a)-2-port multi-bank RAM, an (n, r)-2-port ROM, and two zero testers is shown in Figs. 72 and 73.

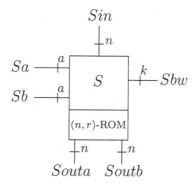

Fig. 72. Symbol of an (n, r, a)-2-port multi-bank RAM-ROM

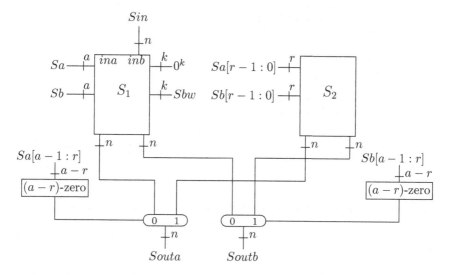

Fig. 73. Construction of an (n, r, a)-2-port multi-bank RAM-ROM

4.3.4 2-port Cache State RAM

Exactly as the name indicates, an (n, a)-2-port CS RAM is a RAM with all features of a 2-port RAM and a CS RAM . Its symbol is shown in Fig. 74. Inputs and outputs are:

- two data inputs $Sina, Sinb$,
- two addresses Sa, Sb,
- two write signals Swa, Swb,
- a control signal $Sinv$, and
- an n-bit input $Svinv$ providing a special data value.

Address decoding, data output generation, and execution of writes is as for 2-port RAMs. In write operations, activation of signal $Sinv$ takes precedence

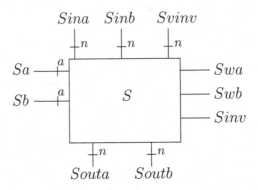

Fig. 74. Symbol of an (n, a)-2-port CS RAM

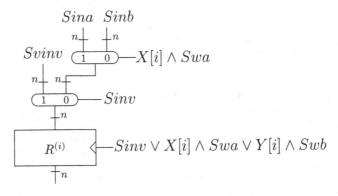

Fig. 75. Construction block of an (n, a)-2-port CS RAM

over everything else:

$$h'.S(x) = \begin{cases} Svinv(h) & Sinv(h) = 1 \\ Sina(h) & Sinv(h) = 0 \wedge x = Sa(h) \wedge Swa(h) = 1 \\ Sinb(h) & Sinv(h) = 0 \wedge x = Sb(h) \wedge Swb(h) = 1 \\ & \wedge \overline{x = Sa(h) \wedge Swa(h) = 1} \\ h.S(x) & \text{otherwise} . \end{cases}$$

The changes in the implementation for each register $R^{(i)}$ are shown in Fig. 75. The signals generated are:

$$R^{(i)}ce = Sinv(h) \vee X[i] \wedge Swa(h) \vee Y[i] \wedge Swb(h)$$

$$R^{(i)}in = \begin{cases} Svinv(h) & Sinv(h) = 1 \\ Sina(h) & Sinv(h) = 0 \wedge X[i] \wedge Swa(h) \\ Sinb(h) & \text{otherwise} . \end{cases}$$

5

Arithmetic Circuits

For later use in processors with the MIPS instruction set architecture (ISA), we construct several circuits: as the focus in this book is on correctness and not so much on efficiency of the constructed machine, only the most basic adders and incrementers are constructed in Sect. 5.1. For more advanced constructions see, e.g., [12]. An arithmetic unit (AU) for binary and two's complement numbers is studied in Sect. 5.2. In our view, understanding the correctness proofs of this section is a must for anyone wishing to understand fixed point arithmetic.

With the help of the AU we construct in Sect. 5.3 an arithmetic logic unit (ALU) for the MIPS ISA in a straightforward way. Differences to [12] are simply due to differences in the encoding of ALU operations between the MIPS ISA considered here and the DLX ISA considered in [12].

Also the shift unit considered in Sect. 5.4 is basically from [12]. Shift units are not completely trivial. We recommend to cover this material in the classroom.

As branch instructions in the DLX and the MIPS instruction set architectures are treated in quite different ways, the new Sect. 5.5 with a branch condition evaluation unit had to be included here.

5.1 Adder and Incrementer

An *n-adder* is a circuit with inputs $a[n-1:0] \in \mathbb{B}^n$, $b[n-1:0] \in \mathbb{B}^n$, $c_0 \in \mathbb{B}$ and outputs $c_n \in \mathbb{B}$ and $s[n-1:0] \in \mathbb{B}^n$ satisfying the specification

$$\langle c_n, s[n-1:0]\rangle = \langle a[n-1:0]\rangle + \langle b[n-1:0]\rangle + c_0 \, .$$

We use the symbol from Fig. 76 for n-adders.

A full adder is obviously a 1-adder. A recursive construction of a very simple n-adder, called *carry chain adder*, is shown in Fig. 77. The correctness follows directly from the correctness of the basic addition algorithm for binary numbers (Lemma 2.11).

M. Kovalev et al.: A Pipelined Multi-core MIPS Machine, LNCS 9000, pp. 99–115, 2014.
© Springer International Publishing Switzerland 2014

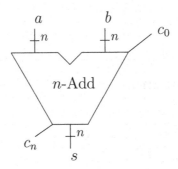

Fig. 76. Symbol of an n-adder

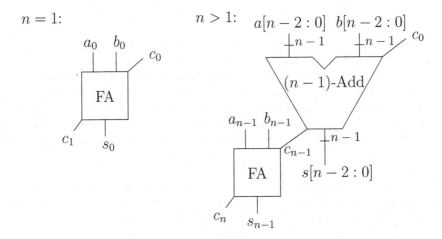

Fig. 77. Recursive construction of a carry chain adder

It is often convenient to ignore the carry out bit c_n of the n-adder and to talk only about the sum bits $s[n-1:0]$. With the help of Lemma 2.10, we can then rewrite the specification of the n-adder as

$$\langle s \rangle = ((\langle a \rangle + \langle b \rangle + c_0) \bmod 2^n).$$

An n-*incrementer* is a circuit with inputs $a[n-1:0] \in \mathbb{B}^n, c_0 \in \mathbb{B}$ and outputs $c_n \in \mathbb{B}$ and $s[n-1:0] \in \mathbb{B}^n$ satisfying

$$\langle c_n, s[n-1:0] \rangle = \langle a[n-1:0] \rangle + c_0 .$$

Throwing away the carry bit c_n and using Lemma 2.10, we can rewrite this as

$$\langle s \rangle = ((\langle a \rangle + c_0) \bmod 2^n).$$

We use the symbol from Fig. 78 for n-incrementers. Obviously, incrementers can be constructed from n-adders by tying the b input to 0^n. As shown in

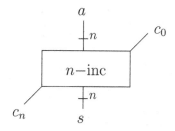

Fig. 78. Symbol of an n-incrementer

$n = 1$: $n > 1$:

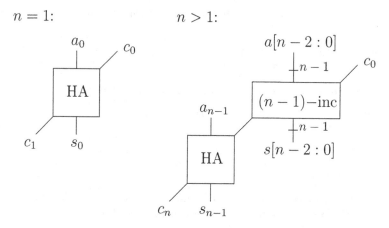

Fig. 79. Recursive construction of a carry chain incrementer

Sect. 3.2 a full adders whose b input is tied to zero can be replaced with a half adder. This yields the construction of carry chain incrementers shown in Fig. 79.

5.2 Arithmetic Unit

The symbol of an n-arithmetic unit or short n-AU is shown in Fig. 80. It is a circuit with the following inputs:

- operand inputs $a = a[n-1:0], b = b[n-1:0]$ with $a, b \in \mathbb{B}^n$,
- control input $u \in \mathbb{B}$ distinguishing between unsigned (binary) and signed (two's complement) numbers,
- control input $sub \in \mathbb{B}$ indicating whether input b should be subtracted from or added to input a,

and the following outputs:

- result $s[n-1:0] \in \mathbb{B}^n$,

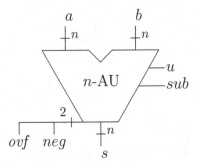

Fig. 80. Symbol of an n-arithmetic unit

- overflow bit $ovf \in \mathbb{B}$, and
- negative bit $neg \in \mathbb{B}$.

We define the exact result $S \in \mathbb{Z}$ of an arithmetic unit as

$$S = \begin{cases} [a] + [b] & (u, sub) = 00 \\ [a] - [b] & (u, sub) = 01 \\ \langle a \rangle + \langle b \rangle & (u, sub) = 10 \\ \langle a \rangle - \langle b \rangle & (u, sub) = 11 \,. \end{cases}$$

For the result of the ALU, we pick the representative of the exact result in B_n resp. T_n and represent it in the corresponding format

$$s = \begin{cases} twoc_n(S \text{ tmod } 2^n) & u = 0 \\ bin_n(S \bmod 2^n) & u = 1 \,, \end{cases}$$

i.e., we have

$$[s] = (S \text{ tmod } 2^n) \quad \text{if} \quad u = 0$$
$$\langle s \rangle = (S \bmod 2^n) \quad \text{if} \quad u = 1 \,.$$

Overflow and negation signals are defined with respect to the exact result. The overflow bit is computed only for the case of two's complement numbers; for binary numbers it is always 0 since the architecture we introduce later does not consider unsigned overflows:

$$ovf = \begin{cases} S \notin T_n & u = 0 \\ 0 & u = 1 \end{cases}$$
$$neg = S < 0 \,.$$

Data Paths

We introduce special symbols $+_n$ and $-_n$ to denote addition and subtraction of n-bit binary numbers mod 2^n:

$$a +_n b = bin_n(\langle a \rangle + \langle b \rangle \bmod 2^n)$$
$$a -_n b = bin_n(\langle a \rangle - \langle b \rangle \bmod 2^n) \,.$$

The following lemma asserts that, for signed and unsigned numbers, the sum bits s can be computed in exactly the same way.

Lemma 5.1 (computing sum bits). Compute the sum bits as

$$s = \begin{cases} a +_n b & sub = 0 \\ a -_n b & sub = 1 \,, \end{cases}$$

then

$$[s] = (S \text{ tmod } 2^n) \quad \text{if} \quad u = 0$$
$$\langle s \rangle = (S \bmod 2^n) \quad \text{if} \quad u = 1 \,.$$

Proof. For $u = 1$ this follows directly from the definitions. For $u = 0$ we have from Lemma 2.14 and Lemma 2.2:

$$[s] \equiv \langle s \rangle \bmod 2^n$$
$$\equiv \left(\begin{cases} \langle a \rangle + \langle b \rangle & sub = 0 \\ \langle a \rangle - \langle b \rangle & sub = 1 \end{cases} \right) \bmod 2^n$$
$$\equiv \left(\begin{cases} [a] + [b] & sub = 0 \\ [a] - [b] & sub = 1 \end{cases} \right) \bmod 2^n$$
$$\equiv S \bmod 2^n \,.$$

From $[s] \in T_n$ and Lemma 2.5 we conclude

$$[s] = (S \text{ tmod } 2^n) \,.$$

□

The main data paths of an n-AU are shown in Fig. 81. The following lemma asserts that the sum bits are computed correctly.

Lemma 5.2 (correctness of arithmetic unit). The sum bits $s[n-1:0]$ in Fig. 81 satisfy

$$s = \begin{cases} a +_n b & sub = 0 \\ a -_n b & sub = 1 \,. \end{cases}$$

Proof. From the construction of the circuit, we have

$$d = b \oplus sub$$
$$= \begin{cases} b & sub = 0 \\ \bar{b} & sub = 1 \,. \end{cases}$$

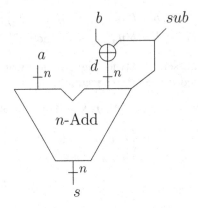

Fig. 81. Data paths of an n-arithmetic unit

From the specification of an n-adder, Lemma 2.10, and the subtraction algorithm for binary numbers (Lemma 2.15), we conclude

$$\langle s \rangle = \left(\left(\begin{cases} \langle a \rangle + \langle b \rangle & sub = 0 \\ \langle a \rangle + \langle \bar{b} \rangle + 1 & sub = 1 \end{cases} \right) \bmod 2^n \right)$$

$$= \left(\left(\begin{cases} \langle a \rangle + \langle b \rangle & sub = 0 \\ \langle a \rangle - \langle b \rangle & sub = 1 \end{cases} \right) \bmod 2^n \right) .$$

Application of $bin_n(\cdot)$ to both sides completes the proof of the lemma.   □

Negative Bit

We start with the case $u = 0$, i.e., with two's complement numbers. We have

$$\begin{aligned} S &= [a] \pm [b] \\ &= [a] + [d] + sub \\ &\le 2^{n-1} - 1 + 2^{n-1} - 1 + 1 \\ &= 2^n - 1, \\ S &\ge -2^{n-1} - 2^{n-1} \\ &= -2^n . \end{aligned}$$

Thus,

$$S \in T_{n+1} .$$

According to Lemma 2.14 we use sign extension to extend operands to $n + 1$ bits:

$$[a] = [a_{n-1}a]$$
$$[d] = [d_{n-1}d] \ .$$

We compute an extra sum bit s_n by the basic addition algorithm:

$$s_n = a_{n-1} \oplus d_{n-1} \oplus c_n \ ,$$

and conclude

$$S = [s[n:0]].$$

Again by Lemma 2.14 this is negative if and only if the sign bit s_n is 1:

$$S < 0 \leftrightarrow s_n = 1 \ .$$

As a result, we have the following lemma.

Lemma 5.3 (two's complement negative bit).

$$u = 0 \rightarrow neg = a_{n-1} \oplus d_{n-1} \oplus c_n$$

For the case $u = 1$, i.e., for binary numbers, a negative result can only occur in the case of subtraction, i.e., if $sub = 1$. In this case we argue along the lines of the correctness proof for the subtraction algorithm:

$$\begin{aligned}
S &= \langle a \rangle - \langle b \rangle \\
&= \langle a \rangle - [0b] \\
&= \langle a \rangle + [1\bar{b}] + 1 \\
&= \langle a \rangle + \langle \bar{b} \rangle - 2^n + 1 \\
&= \langle c_n s[n-1:0] \rangle - 2^n \\
&= 2^n(c_n - 1) + \underbrace{\langle s[n-1:0] \rangle}_{\in B_n} \ .
\end{aligned}$$

If $c_n = 1$ we have $S = \langle s \rangle \geq 0$. If $c_n = 0$ we have

$$\begin{aligned}
S &= -2^n + \langle s[n-1:0] \rangle \\
&\leq -2^n + 2^n - 1 \\
&= -1 \ .
\end{aligned}$$

Thus,

$$u = 1 \rightarrow neg = sub \wedge \overline{c_n} \ ,$$

and together with Lemma 5.3 we can define the negative bit computation.

Lemma 5.4 (negative bit).

$$\begin{aligned}
neg = {}& \overline{u} \wedge (a_{n-1} \oplus d_{n-1} \oplus c_n) \vee \\
& u \wedge sub \wedge \overline{c_n}
\end{aligned}$$

Overflow Bit

We compute the overflow bit only for the case of two's complement numbers, i.e., when $u = 0$. We have

$$
\begin{aligned}
S &= [a] + [d] + sub \\
&= -2^{n-1}(a_{n-1} + d_{n-1}) + \langle a[n-2:0] \rangle + \langle d[n-2:0] \rangle + sub \\
&= -2^{n-1}(a_{n-1} + d_{n-1}) + \langle c_{n-1} s[n-2:0] \rangle - c_{n-1} 2^{n-1} + c_{n-1} 2^{n-1} \\
&= -2^{n-1}(a_{n-1} + d_{n-1} + c_{n-1}) + 2^{n-1}(c_{n-1} + c_{n-1}) + \langle s[n-2:0] \rangle \\
&= -2^{n-1} \langle c_n s_{n-1} \rangle + 2^n c_{n-1} + \langle s[n-2:0] \rangle \\
&= -2^n c_n - 2^{n-1} s_{n-1} + 2^n c_{n-1} + \langle s[n-2:0] \rangle \\
&= 2^n(c_{n-1} - c_n) + [s[n-1:0]] \,.
\end{aligned}
$$

We claim

$$
S \in T_n \leftrightarrow c_{n-1} = c_n \,.
$$

If $c_n = c_{n-1}$ we obviously have $S = [s]$, thus $S \in T_n$. If $c_n = 1$ and $c_{n-1} = 0$ we have

$$
-2^n + [s] \le -2^n + 2^{n-1} - 1 = -2^{n-1} - 1 < -2^{n-1}
$$

and if $c_n = 0$ and $c_{n-1} = 1$, we have

$$
2^n + [s] \ge 2^n - 2^{n-1} > 2^{n-1} - 1 \,.
$$

Thus, in the two latter cases, we have $S \notin T_n$. Because

$$
c_n \ne c_{n-1} \leftrightarrow c_n \oplus c_{n-1} = 1 \,,
$$

we get the following lemma for the overflow bit computation.

Lemma 5.5 (overflow bit).

$$
ovf = \overline{u} \wedge c_n \oplus c_{n-1}
$$

5.3 Arithmetic Logic Unit (ALU)

Figure 82 shows a symbol for the n-ALU constructed here. Width n should be even. The circuit has the following inputs:

- operand inputs $a = a[n-1:0]$, $b = b[n-1:0]$ with $a, b \in \mathbb{B}^n$,
- control inputs $af[3:0] \in \mathbb{B}^4$ and $i \in \mathbb{B}$ specifying the operation that the ALU performs with the operands,

and the following outputs:

- result $alures[n-1:0] \in \mathbb{B}^n$,
- overflow bit $ovfalu \in \mathbb{B}$.

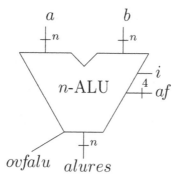

Fig. 82. Symbol of an n-arithmetic logic unit

Table 6. Specification of ALU operations

$af[3:0]$	i	$alures[31:0]$	$ovfalu$
0000	*	$a +_n b$	$[a] + [b] \notin T_n$
0001	*	$a +_n b$	0
0010	*	$a -_n b$	$[a] - [b] \notin T_n$
0011	*	$a -_n b$	0
0100	*	$a \wedge b$	0
0101	*	$a \vee b$	0
0110	*	$a \oplus b$	0
0111	0	$\overline{a \vee b}$	0
0111	1	$b[n/2 - 1 : 0]0^{n/2}$	0
1010	*	$0^{n-1}([a] < [b] \ ? \ 1 : 0)$	0
1011	*	$0^{n-1}(\langle a \rangle < \langle b \rangle \ ? \ 1 : 0)$	0

The results that must be generated are specified in Table 6. There are three groups of operations:

- Arithmetic operations.
- Logical operations. At first sight, the result $b[n/2 : 0]0^{n/2}$ might appear odd. This ALU function is later used to load the upper half of an n-bit constant using the immediate fields of an instruction.
- Test and set instructions. They compute an n-bit result $0^{n-1}z$ where only the last bit is of interest. The result of these instructions can be computed by performing a subtraction in the AU and then testing the negative bit.

Figure 83 shows the fairly obvious data paths of an n-ALU. The missing signals are easily constructed. We subtract if $af[1] = 1$. For test and set operations with $af[3] = 1$, output z is simply the negative bit neg. The overflow bit can only differ from zero if we are doing an arithmetic operation. Thus, we have

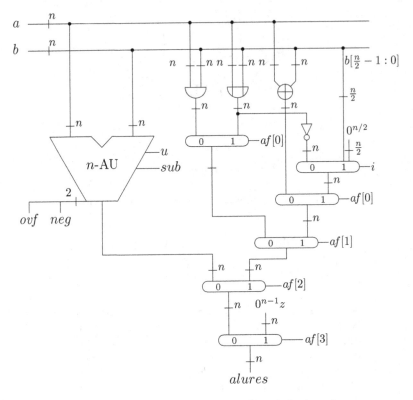

Fig. 83. Data paths of an n-arithmetic logic unit

$$sub = af[1]$$
$$z = neg$$
$$u = af[0]$$
$$ovfalu = ovf \wedge \overline{af[3]} \wedge \overline{af[2]}.$$

5.4 Shift Unit

n-shift operations have two operands:

- a bit vector $a[n - 1 : 0] \in \mathbb{B}^n$ that is to be shifted and
- a shift distance $i \in [0 : n - 1]$.

Shifts come in five flavors: cyclical left shift slc, cyclical right shift src, logical left shift sll, logical right shift srl, and arithmetic right shift sra. The result of such an n-shift has n bits and is defined as

$$slc(a, i)[j] = a[j - i \bmod n]$$
$$src(a, i)[j] = a[j + i \bmod n]$$
$$sll(a, i)[j] = \begin{cases} a[j - i] & j \geq i \\ 0 & \text{otherwise} \end{cases}$$
$$srl(a, i)[j] = \begin{cases} a[j + i] & j \leq n - 1 - i \\ 0 & \text{otherwise} \end{cases}$$
$$sra(a, i)[j] = \begin{cases} a[j + i] & j \leq n - 1 - i \\ a_{n-1} & \text{otherwise} \end{cases}$$

or, equivalently, as

$$slc(a, i) = a[n - i - 1 : 0]a[n - 1 : n - i]$$
$$src(a, i) = a[i - 1 : 0]a[n - 1 : i]$$
$$sll(a, i) = a[n - i - 1 : 0]0^i$$
$$srl(a, i) = 0^i a[n - 1 : i]$$
$$sra(a, i) = a_{n-1}^i a[n - 1 : i] \,.$$

From the definition we immediately conclude how to compute right shifts using left shifts.

Lemma 5.6 (left right shift).

$$src(a, i) = slc(a, n - i \bmod n)$$

Proof.

$$j + i = j - (-i)$$
$$\equiv j - (n - i) \bmod n$$

$\square$

Here, we only build shifters for numbers n which are a power of two:

$$n = 2^k, \quad k \in \mathbb{N} \,.$$

Basic building blocks for all following shifter constructions are (n, b)-cyclic left shifters or short (n, b)-SLCs for $b \in [1 : n - 1]$. They have

- input $a[n - 1 : 0] \in \mathbb{B}^n$ for the data to be shifted,
- input $s \in \mathbb{B}$ indicating whether to shift or not,
- data outputs $a'[n - 1 : 0] \in \mathbb{B}^n$ satisfying

$$a' = \begin{cases} slc(a, b) & s = 1 \\ a & \text{otherwise} \end{cases}$$

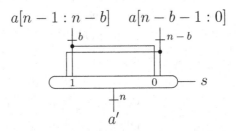

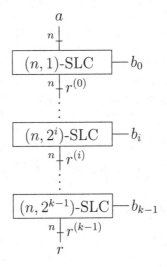

Fig. 84. Implementation of an (n, b)-SLC $((n, b)$-cyclic left shifter)

Fig. 85. Implementation of a n-SLC (cyclic n-left shifter)

Figure 84 shows a construction of an (n, b)-SLC.

A cyclic n-left shifter or short n-SLC is a circuit with

- data inputs $a[n - 1 : 0] \in \mathbb{B}^n$,
- control inputs $b[k - 1 : 0] \in \mathbb{B}^k$, which provide the binary representation of the shift distance,
- data outputs $r[n - 1 : 0] \in \mathbb{B}^n$ satisfying

$$r = slc(a, \langle b \rangle) .$$

Figure 85 shows a construction of a cyclic n-SLC as a stack of $(n, 2^i)$-SLCs. An easy induction on $i \in [0 : k - 1]$ shows

$$r^{(i)} = slc(a, \langle b[i : 0] \rangle) .$$

A cyclic n-right-left shifter n-SRLC is a circuit with

- data inputs $a[n - 1 : 0] \in \mathbb{B}^n$,

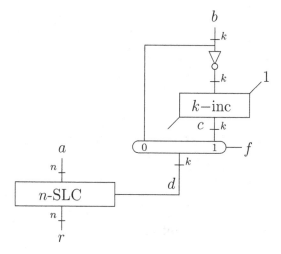

Fig. 86. Implementation of an n-SRLC (cyclic n-right-left shifter)

- control inputs $b[k-1:0] \in \mathbb{B}^k$, which provide the binary representation of the shift distance,
- a control input $f \in \mathbb{B}$ indicating the shift direction, and
- data outputs $r[n-1:0] \in \mathbb{B}^n$ satisfying

$$r = \begin{cases} slc(a, \langle b \rangle) & f = 0 \\ src(a, \langle b \rangle) & f = 1 . \end{cases}$$

Figure 86 shows a construction of n-SRLCs. The output $c[k-1:0]$ of the k-incrementer satisfies

$$\langle c \rangle = (\langle \bar{b} \rangle + 1 \bmod n)$$
$$= (n - \langle b \rangle \bmod n) ,$$

which follows from the subtraction algorithm for binary numbers (Lemma 2.15).

The output d of the multiplexer then satisfies

$$\langle d \rangle = \begin{cases} \langle b \rangle & f = 0 \\ n - \langle b \rangle \bmod n & f = 1 . \end{cases}$$

The correctness of the construction now follows from Lemma 5.6.

An n-shift unit n-SU (see Fig. 87) has

- inputs $a[n-1:0]$ providing the data to be shifted,
- inputs $b[k-1:0]$ determining the shift distance,
- inputs $sf[1:0]$ determining the kind of shift to be executed, and

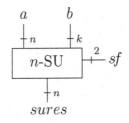

Fig. 87. Symbol of an n-shift unit

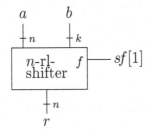

Fig. 88. Right-left shifter of an n-shift unit

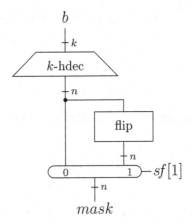

Fig. 89. Mask computation of an n-shift unit

- outputs $sures[n-1:0]$ satisfying

$$sures = \begin{cases} sll(a, \langle b \rangle) & sf = 00 \\ srl(a, \langle b \rangle) & sf = 10 \\ sra(a, \langle b \rangle) & sf = 11 \,. \end{cases}$$

A construction of an n-SU is shown in Figs. 88, 89, 90.

Let $i = \langle b \rangle$. Then the cyclic right-left shifter in Fig. 88 produces output

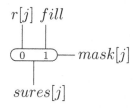

Fig. 90. Result computation of an n-shift unit

Table 7. Specification of branch condition evaluation

$bf[3:0]$	$bcres$
0010	$[a] < 0$
0011	$[a] \geq 0$
100*	$a = b$
101*	$a \neq b$
110*	$[a] \leq 0$
111*	$[a] > 0$

$$r = \begin{cases} a[n-i-1:0]a[n-1:n-i] & sf[1] = 0 \\ a[i-1:0]a[n-i:i] & sf[1] = 1 . \end{cases}$$

The output of the circuit in Fig. 89 produces a mask

$$mask = \begin{cases} 0^{n-i}1^i & sf[1] = 0 \\ 1^i 0^{n-i} & sf[1] = 1 . \end{cases}$$

For each index $j \in [0:n-1]$, the multiplexer in Fig. 90 replaces the shifter output $r[j]$ by the $fill$ bit if this is indicated by the mask bit $mask[j]$. As a result we get

$$sures = \begin{cases} a[n-i-1:0]fill^i & sf[1] = 0 \\ fill^i a[n-i:i] & sf[1] = 1 . \end{cases}$$

By setting

$$fill = sf[0] \wedge a_{n-1} ,$$

we conclude

$$sures = \begin{cases} sll(a,i) & sf = 00 \\ srl(a,i) & sf = 10 \\ sra(a,i) & sf = 11 . \end{cases}$$

5.5 Branch Condition Evaluation Unit

An n-BCE (see Fig. 91) has

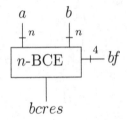

Fig. 91. Symbol of an n-branch condition evaluation unit

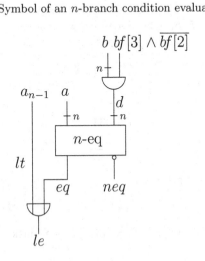

Fig. 92. Computation of auxiliary signals in an n-branch condition evaluation unit

- inputs $a[n-1:0], b[n-1:0] \in \mathbb{B}^n$,
- inputs $bf[3:0] \in \mathbb{B}^4$ selecting the condition to be tested,
- output $bcres \in \mathbb{B}$ specified by Table 7.

The auxiliary circuit in Fig. 92 computes obvious auxiliary signals satisfying

$$d = b \wedge (bf[3] \wedge \overline{bf[2]})$$
$$= \begin{cases} b & bf[3:2] = 10 \\ 0_n & \text{otherwise} \end{cases}$$
$$eq \equiv a = d$$
$$\equiv \begin{cases} a = b & bf[3:2] = 10 \\ [a] = 0 & \text{otherwise} \end{cases}$$
$$neq = \overline{eq}$$
$$lt = [a] < 0$$

$$le \equiv [a] < 0 \vee \begin{cases} a = b & bf[3:2] = 10 \\ [a] = 0 & \text{otherwise} \end{cases}.$$

The result $bcres$ can then be computed as

$$\begin{aligned} bcres \equiv \; & bf[3:1] = 001 \wedge (\overline{bf[0]} \wedge lt \vee bf[0] \wedge \overline{lt}) \\ & \vee \; bf[3:2] = 10 \wedge (\overline{bf[1]} \wedge eq \vee bf[1] \wedge \overline{eq}) \\ & \vee \; bf[3:2] = 11 \wedge (\overline{bf[1]} \wedge le \vee bf[1] \wedge \overline{le}) \\ \equiv \; & \overline{bf[3]} \wedge \overline{bf[2]} \wedge bf[1] \wedge (bf[0] \oplus lt) \\ & \vee \; bf[3] \wedge \overline{bf[2]} \wedge (bf[1] \oplus eq) \\ & \vee \; bf[3] \wedge bf[2] \wedge (bf[1] \oplus le). \end{aligned}$$

6

A Basic Sequential MIPS Machine

We define the basic MIPS instruction set architecture (ISA) without delayed branch, interrupt mechanism and devices. The first Sect. 6.1 of this chapter is very short. It contains a very compact summary of the instruction set architecture (and the assembly language) in the form of tables, which define the ISA **if** one knows how to interpret them. In Sect. 6.2 we provide a succinct and completely precise interpretation of the tables, leaving out only the co-processor instructions and the system call instruction. From this we derive in Sect. 6.3 the hardware of a sequential, i.e., not pipelined, MIPS processor and provide a proof that this processor construction is correct.

This chapter differs from its counter part in [12] in several ways:

- The ISA is MIPS instead of DLX. Most of the resulting modifications are already handled in the control logic of the ALU and the shift unit[1].
- The machine implements each instruction in one very long hardware cycle and uses only precomputed control. It is not meant to be an efficient sequential implementation and serves later only as a reference machine. This turns *most* portions of the correctness proof into straightforward bookkeeping exercises, which would be terribly boring if presented in the classroom. We included this bookkeeping only as a help for readers, who want to use this book as a blueprint for formal proofs.
- Because the byte addressable memory of the ISA is embedded in the implementation into a 64-bit wide hardware memory, shifters have to be used both for the load and store operations of words, half words, and bytes. In [12] the memory is 32 bits wide, the shifters for loads and stores are present; they must be used for accesses of half words or bytes. However, [12] provides no proof that with the help of these shifters loads and stores of half words or bytes work correctly. Subsequent formal correctness proofs for hardware from [12] as presented in [1,3,6] restricted loads and stores to word accesses, and thus, did not provide these proofs either. We present

---

[1] In contrast to [9] we do not tie register 0 to 0. We also do not consider interrupts and address translation in this book.

M. Kovalev et al.: A Pipelined Multi-core MIPS Machine, LNCS 9000, pp. 117–160, 2014.

these proofs here; they hinge on the software condition that accesses are aligned and turn out to be not completely trivial.

6.1 Tables

In the "Effect" row of the tables we use the following shorthands: $m = m_d(ea(c))$ where $ea(c) = rs(c) +_{32} sxtimm(c)$, $rx = gpr(rx(c))$ for $x \in \{t, s, d\}$ (except for the coprocessor instructions, where $rd = rd(c)$ and $rt = rt(c)$), and $iindex$ stands for $iindex(c)^2$. In the table for J-type instructions, R31 stands for $gpr(31_5)$. Arithmetic operations $+$ and $-$ are modulo 2^{32}. Sign extension is denoted by sxt and zero extension by zxt.

6.1.1 I-type

opcode	Instruction	Syntax	d	Effect
Data Transfer				
100 000	lb	lb rt rs imm	1	rt = sxt(m)
100 001	lh	lh rt rs imm	2	rt = sxt(m)
100 011	lw	lw rt rs imm	4	rt = m
100 100	lbu	lbu rt rs imm	1	rt = 0^{24}m
100 101	lhu	lhu rt rs imm	2	rt = 0^{16}m
101 000	sb	sb rt rs imm	1	m = rt[7:0]
101 001	sh	sh rt rs imm	2	m = rt[15:0]
101 011	sw	sw rt rs imm	4	m = rt
Arithmetic, Logical Operation, Test-and-Set				
001 000	addi	addi rt rs imm		rt = rs + sxt(imm)
001 001	addiu	addiu rt rs imm		rt = rs + sxt(imm)
001 010	slti	slti rt rs imm		rt = ([rs] < [sxt(imm)] ? 1_{32} : 0_{32})
001 011	sltiu	sltiu rt rs imm		rt = ($\langle$rs$\rangle$ < $\langle$sxt(imm)$\rangle$? 1_{32} : 0_{32})
001 100	andi	andi rt rs imm		rt = rs $\wedge$ zxt(imm)
001 101	ori	ori rt rs imm		rt = rs $\vee$ zxt(imm)
001 110	xori	xori rt rs imm		rt = rs $\oplus$ zxt(imm)
001 111	lui	lui rt imm		rt = imm0^{16}

opcode	rt	Instr.	Syntax	Effect
Branch				
000 001	00000	bltz	bltz rs imm	pc = pc + ([rs] < 0 ? sxt(imm00) : 4_{32})
000 001	00001	bgez	bgez rs imm	pc = pc + ([rs] $\geq$ 0 ? sxt(imm00) : 4_{32})
000 100		beq	beq rs rt imm	pc = pc + (rs = rt ? sxt(imm00) : 4_{32})
000 101		bne	bne rs rt imm	pc = pc + (rs $\neq$ rt ? sxt(imm00) : 4_{32})
000 110	00000	blez	blez rs imm	pc = pc + ([rs] $\leq$ 0 ? sxt(imm00) : 4_{32})
000 111	00000	bgtz	bgtz rs imm	pc = pc + ([rs] > 0 ? sxt(imm00) : 4_{32})

---

[2] Formal definitions for predicates and functions used here are given in Sect. 6.2.

6.1.2 R-type

opcode	fun	Instruction	Syntax	Effect
Shift Operation				
000000	000 000	sll	sll *rd rt sa*	rd = sll(rt,$\langle$sa$\rangle$)
000000	000 010	srl	srl *rd rt sa*	rd = srl(rt,$\langle$sa$\rangle$)
000000	000 011	sra	sra *rd rt sa*	rd = sra(rt,$\langle$sa$\rangle$)
000000	000 100	sllv	sllv *rd rt rs*	rd = sll(rt,$\langle$rs$\rangle$)
000000	000 110	srlv	srlv *rd rt rs*	rd = srl(rt,$\langle$rs$\rangle$)
000000	000 111	srav	srav *rd rt rs*	rd = sra(rt,$\langle$rs$\rangle$)
Arithmetic, Logical Operation				
000000	100 000	add	add *rd rs rt*	rd = rs + rt
000000	100 001	addu	addu *rd rs rt*	rd = rs + rt
000000	100 010	sub	sub *rd rs rt*	rd = rs − rt
000000	100 011	subu	subu *rd rs rt*	rd = rs − rt
000000	100 100	and	and *rd rs rt*	rd = rs $\wedge$ rt
000000	100 101	or	or *rd rs rt*	rd = rs $\vee$ rt
000000	100 110	xor	xor *rd rs rt*	rd = rs $\oplus$ rt
000000	100 111	nor	nor *rd rs rt*	rd = $\neg$(rs $\vee$ rt)
Test Set Operation				
000000	101 010	slt	slt *rd rs rt*	rd = ([rs] < [rt] ? 1_{32} : 0_{32})
000000	101 011	sltu	sltu *rd rs rt*	rd = ($\langle$rs$\rangle$ < $\langle$rt$\rangle$? 1_{32} : 0_{32})
Jumps, System Call				
000000	001 000	jr	jr *rs*	pc = rs
000000	001 001	jalr	jalr *rd rs*	rd = pc + 4_{32} pc = rs
000000	001 100	sysc	sysc	System Call

Coprocessor Instructions

opcode	fun	rs	Instruction	Syntax	Effect
010000	011 000	10000	eret	eret	Exception Return
010000		00100	movg2s	movg2s *rd rt*	spr[rd] := gpr[rt]
010000		00000	movs2g	movs2g *rd rt*	gpr[rt] := spr[rd]

6.1.3 J-type

opcode	Instr.	Syntax	Effect
Jumps			
000 010	j	j *iindex*	pc = (pc+4_{32})[31:28]iindex00
000 011	jal	jal *iindex*	pc = (pc+4_{32})[31:28]iindex00 R31 = pc + 4_{32}

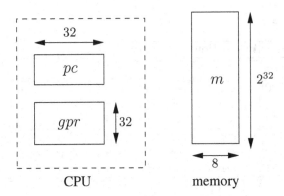

Fig. 93. Visible data structures of MIPS ISA

6.2 MIPS ISA

In this section we give the precise formal interpretation of the basic MIPS ISA without the coprocessor instructions and the system call instruction.

6.2.1 Configuration and Instruction Fields

A basic *MIPS configuration* c has only three user visible data structures (Fig. 93):

- $c.pc \in \mathbb{B}^{32}$ – the program counter (PC).
- $c.gpr : \mathbb{B}^5 \to \mathbb{B}^{32}$ – the general purpose register (GPR) file consisting of 32 registers, each 32 bits wide. For register addresses $x \in \mathbb{B}^5$, the content of general purpose register x in configuration c is denoted by $c.gpr(x) \in \mathbb{B}^{32}$.
- $c.m : \mathbb{B}^{32} \to \mathbb{B}^8$ – the processor memory. It is byte addressable; addresses have 32 bits. Thus, for memory addresses $a \in \mathbb{B}^{32}$, the content of memory location a in configuration c is denoted by $c.m(a) \in \mathbb{B}^8$.

Program counter and general purpose registers belong to the central processing unit (CPU).

Let K be the set of all basic MIPS configurations. A mathematical definition of the ISA will be given by a function

$$\delta : K \to K \,,$$

where

$$c' = \delta(c)$$

is the configuration reached from configuration c, if the next instruction is executed. An ISA computation is a sequence (c^i) of ISA configurations with $i \in \mathbb{N}$ satisfying

$$c^0.pc = 0^{32}$$
$$c^{i+1} = \delta(c^i) \, ,$$

i.e., initially the program counter points to address 0^{32} and in each step one instruction is executed. In the remainder of this section we specify the ISA simply by specifying function δ, i.e., by specifying $c' = \delta(c)$ for all configurations c.

Recall that for numbers $y \in \mathbb{B}^n$ we abbreviate the binary representation of y with n bits as

$$y_n = bin_n(y) \, ,$$

e.g., $1_8 = 00000001$ and $3_8 = 00000011$. For memories $m : \mathbb{B}^{32} \to \mathbb{B}^8$, addresses $a \in \mathbb{B}^{32}$, and numbers d of bytes, we define the content of d consecutive memory bytes starting at address a informally by

$$m_d(a) = m(a +_{32} (d-1)_{32}) \circ \ldots \circ m(a).$$

Formally, we define it in the inductive form as

$$m_1(a) = m(a)$$
$$m_{d+1}(a) = m(a +_{32} d_{32}) \circ m_d(a) \, .$$

The current instruction $I(c)$ to be executed in configuration c is defined by the 4 bytes in memory addressed by the current program counter:

$$I(c) = c.m_4(c.pc) \, .$$

Because all instructions are 4 bytes long, one requires that instructions are *aligned* on 4 byte boundaries [3] or, equivalently, that

$$c.pc[1:0] = 00 \, .$$

The six high order bits of the current instruction are called the op-code:

$$opc(c) = I(c)[31:26] \, .$$

There are three instruction types: R-, J-, and I-type. The current instruction type is determined by the following predicates:

$$rtype(c) \equiv opc(c) = 0*0^4$$
$$jtype(c) \equiv opc(c) = 0^41*$$
$$itype(c) = \overline{rtype(c) \vee jtype(c)} \, .$$

---

[3] In case this condition is violated a so called misalignment interrupt is raised. Since we do not treat interrupts in our construction, we require all ISA computations to have only aligned instructions.

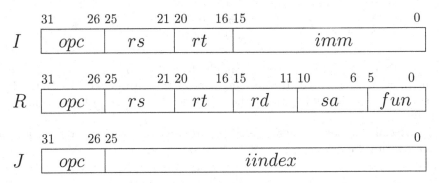

Fig. 94. Types and fields of MIPS instructions

Depending on the instruction type, the bits of the current instruction are subdivided as shown in Fig. 94. Register addresses are specified in the following fields of the current instruction:

$$rs(c) = I(c)[25 : 21]$$
$$rt(c) = I(c)[20 : 16]$$
$$rd(c) = I(c)[15 : 11] .$$

For R-type instructions, ALU-functions to be applied to the register operands can be specified in the function field:

$$fun(c) = I(c)[5 : 0] .$$

Three kinds of immediate constants are specified: the shift amount sa in R-type instructions, the immediate constant imm in I-type instructions, and an instruction index $iindex$ in J-type (like jump) operations:

$$sa(c) = I(c)[10 : 6]$$
$$imm(c) = I(c)[15 : 0]$$
$$iindex(c) = I(c)[25 : 0] .$$

Immediate constant imm has 16 bits. In order to apply ALU functions to it, the constant can be extended with 16 high order bits in two ways: zero extension and sign extension:

$$zxtimm(c) = 0^{16}imm(c)$$
$$sxtimm(c) = imm(c)[15]^{16}imm(c)$$
$$= I(c)[15]^{16}imm(c) .$$

In case of sign extension, Lemma 2.14 guarantees that the value of the constant interpreted as a two's complement number does not change:

$$[sxtimm(c)] = [imm(c)] .$$

6.2.2 Instruction Decoding

For every mnemonic mn of a MIPS instruction from the tables above, we define a predicate $mn(c)$ which is true, if instruction mn is to be executed in configuration c. For instance,

$$lw(c) \equiv opc(c) = 100011$$
$$bltz(c) \equiv opc(c) = 0^5 1 \wedge rt(c) = 0^5$$
$$add(c) \equiv rtype(c) \wedge fun(c) = 10^5 \ .$$

The remaining predicates directly associated to the mnemonics of the assembly language are derived in the same way from the tables. We group the basic instruction set into 5 groups and define for each group a predicate that holds, if an instruction from that group is to be executed:

- ALU-operations of I-type are recognized by the leading three bits of the opcode, resp. $I(c)[31:29]$; ALU-operations of R-type - by the two leading bits of the function code, resp. $I(c)[5:4]$:

$$alur(c) \equiv rtype(c) \wedge fun(c)[5:4] = 10$$
$$\equiv rtype(c) \wedge I(c)[5:4] = 10$$
$$alui(c) \equiv itype(c) \wedge opc(c)[5:3] = 001$$
$$\equiv itype(c) \wedge I(c)[31:29] = 001$$
$$alu(c) = alur(c) \vee alui(c) \ .$$

- Shift unit operations are of R-type and are recognized by the three leading bits of the function code. If bit $fun(c)[2]$ of the function code is on, the shift distance is taken from register specified by $rs(c)$[4]:

$$su(c) \equiv rtype(c) \wedge fun(c)[5:3] = 000$$
$$\equiv rtype(c) \wedge I(c)[5:3] = 000$$
$$suv(c) = su(c) \wedge fun(c)[2]$$
$$= su(c) \wedge I(c)[2] \ .$$

- Loads and stores are of I-type and are recognized by the three leading bits of the opcode:

$$l(c) \equiv opc(c)[5:3] = 100$$
$$\equiv I(c)[31:29] = 100$$
$$s(c) \equiv opc(c)[5:3] = 101$$
$$\equiv I(c)[31:29] = 101$$
$$ls(c) = l(c) \vee s(c)$$
$$\equiv opc(c)[5:4] = 10$$
$$\equiv I(c)[31:30] = 10 \ .$$

---

[4] Mnemonics with suffix v as "variable"; one would expect instead for the other shifts a suffix i as "immediate".

- Branches are of I-Type and are recognized by the three leading bits of the opcode:

$$b(c) \equiv itype(c) \wedge opc(c)[5:3] = 000$$
$$\equiv itype(c) \wedge I(c)[31:29] = 000 \;.$$

- Jumps are defined in a brute force way:

$$jump(c) = jr(c) \vee jalr(c) \vee j(c) \vee jal(c)$$
$$jb(c) = jump(c) \vee b(c) \;.$$

6.2.3 ALU-Operations

We can now go through the ALU-operations in the tables one by one and give them precise interpretations. We do this for two examples.

add(c)

The table specifies the effect as $rd = rs + rt$. This is to be interpreted as an operation on the corresponding register contents: on the right hand side of the equation – for configuration c, i.e., before execution of the instruction; on the left hand side – for configuration c':

$$c'.gpr(rd(c)) = c.gpr(rs(c)) +_{32} c.gpr(rt(c)) \;.$$

Other register contents and the memory content do not change:

$$c'.gpr(x) = c.gpr(x) \quad \text{for} \quad x \neq rd(c)$$
$$c'.m = c.m \;.$$

The program counter is advanced by four bytes to the next instruction:

$$c'.pc = c.pc +_{32} 4_{32} \;.$$

addi(c)

The second operand is now the sign extended immediate constant:

$$c'.gpr(x) = \begin{cases} c.gpr(rs(c)) +_{32} sxtimm(c) & x = rt(c) \\ c.gpr(x) & \text{otherwise} \end{cases}$$
$$c'.m = c.m$$
$$c'.pc = c.pc +_{32} 4_{32} \;.$$

It is clear how to derive precise specifications for the remaining ALU-operations, but we take a shortcut exploiting the fact that we have already constructed an ALU that was specified in Table 6.

This table defines functions $alures(a, b, af, i)$ and $ovf(a, b, af, i)$. As we do not treat interrupts in this book, we use only the first of these functions here. We observe that in all ALU operations a function of the ALU is performed. The left operand is always

$$lop(c) = c.gpr(rs(c)) \ .$$

For R-type operations the right operand is the register specified by the rt field of R-type instructions. For I-type instructions it is the sign extended immediate operand if $opc(c)[2] = I(c)[28] = 0$ or zero extended immediate operand if $opc(c)[2] = 1$. Thus, we define immediate fill bit $ifill(c)$, extended immediate constant $xtimm(c)$, and right operand $rop(c)$ in the following way:

$$ifill(c) = \begin{cases} imm(c)[15] & opc(c)[2] = 0 \\ 0 & opc(c)[2] = 1 \end{cases}$$
$$= imm(c)[15] \wedge \overline{opc(c)[2]}$$
$$= imm(c)[15] \wedge \overline{I(c)[28]}$$
$$xtimm(c) = \begin{cases} sxtimm(c) & opc(c)[2] = 0 \\ zxtimm(c) & opc(c)[2] = 1 \end{cases}$$
$$= ifill(c)^{16} imm(c)$$
$$rop(c) = \begin{cases} c.gpr(rt(c)) & rtype(c) \\ xtimm(c) & \text{otherwise} \ . \end{cases}$$

Comparing Table 6 with the tables for I-type and R-type instructions we see that bits $af[2:0]$ of the ALU control can be taken from the low order fields of the opcode for I-type instructions and from the low order bits of the function field for R-type instructions:

$$af(c)[2:0] = \begin{cases} fun(c)[2:0] & rtype(c) \\ opc(c)[2:0] & \text{otherwise} \end{cases}$$
$$= \begin{cases} I(c)[2:0] & rtype(c) \\ I(c)[28:26] & \text{otherwise} \ . \end{cases}$$

For bit $af[3]$ things are more complicated. For R-type instructions it can be taken from the function code. For I-type instructions it must only be forced to 1 for the two test and set operations, which can be recognized by $opc(c)[2:1] = 01$:

$$af(c)[3] = \begin{cases} fun(c)[3] & rtype(c) \\ \overline{opc(c)[2]} \wedge opc(c)[1] & \text{otherwise} \end{cases}$$
$$= \begin{cases} I(c)[3] & rtype(c) \\ \overline{I(c)[28]} \wedge I(c)[27] & \text{otherwise} \ . \end{cases}$$

The i-input of the ALU distinguishes for $af[3:0] = 0111$ between the *lui*-instruction of I-type for $i = 0$ and the *nor*-instruction of R-type for $i = 1$. Thus, we set it to $itype(c)$. The result of the ALU computed with these inputs is denoted by

$$ares(c) = alures(lop(c), rop(c), af(c), itype(c)) \ .$$

Depending on the instruction type, the destination register $rdes$ is specified by the rd field or the rt field:

$$rdes(c) = \begin{cases} rd(c) & rtype(c) \\ rt(c) & \text{otherwise} \ . \end{cases}$$

A summary of *all* ALU operations is then

$$alu(c) \rightarrow$$

$$c'.gpr(x) = \begin{cases} ares(c) & x = rdes(c) \\ c.gpr(x) & \text{otherwise} \end{cases}$$

$$c'.m = c.m$$
$$c'.pc = c.pc +_{32} 4_{32} \ .$$

6.2.4 Shift Unit Operations

Shift operations come in two flavors: i) for $fun(c)[2] = 0$ the shift distance $sdist(c)$ is an immediate operand specified by the sa field of the instruction. For $fun(c)[2] = 1$ the shift distance is specified by the last bits of the register specified by the rs field:

$$sdist(c) = \begin{cases} sa(c) & fun(c)[2] = 0 \\ c.gpr(rs(c))[4:0] & fun(c)[2] = 1 \ . \end{cases}$$

The left operand that is shifted is always the register specified by the rt-field:

$$slop(c) = c.gpr(rt(c)) \ .$$

and the control bits $sf[1:0]$ are taken from the low order bits of the function field:

$$sf(c) = fun(c)[1:0] \ .$$

The result of the shift unit computed with these inputs is denoted by

$$sres(c) = sures(slop(c), sdist(c), sf(c)) \ .$$

For shift operations the destination register is always specified by the rd field. Thus, the shift unit operations can be summarized as

$$su(c) \rightarrow$$

$$c'.gpr(x) = \begin{cases} sres(c) & x = rd(c) \\ c.gpr(x) & \text{otherwise} \end{cases}$$

$$c'.m = c.m$$

$$c'.pc = c.pc +_{32} 4_{32} .$$

6.2.5 Branch and Jump

A branch condition evaluation unit was specified in Table 7. It computes the function $bcres(a, b, bf)$. We use this function with the following parameters:

$$blop(c) = c.gpr(rs(c))$$
$$brop(c) = c.gpr(rt(c))$$
$$bf(c) = opc(c)[2:0] \circ rt(c)[0]$$
$$= I(c)[28:26]I[16] .$$

and define the result of a branch condition evaluation as

$$bres(c) = bcres(blop(c), brop(c), bf(c)) .$$

The next program counter $c'.pc$ is usually computed as $c.pc +_{32} 4_{32}$. This order is only changed in jump instructions or in branch instructions, where the branch is taken, i.e., the branch condition evaluates to 1. We define

$$jbtaken(c) = jump(c) \vee b(c) \wedge bres(c) .$$

In case of a jump or a branch taken, there are three possible jump targets

Branch Instructions $b(c)$

Branch instructions involve a *relative* branch. The PC is incremented by a branch distance:

$$b(c) \wedge bres(c) \rightarrow$$
$$bdist(c) = imm(c)[15]^{14}imm(c)00$$
$$btarget(c) = c.pc +_{32} bdist(c) .$$

Note that the branch distance is a kind of a sign extended immediate constant, but due to the alignment requirement the low order bits of the jump distance must be 00. Thus, one uses the 16 bits of the immediate constant for bits $[17:2]$ of the jump distance. Sign extension is used for the remaining bits. Note also that address arithmetic is modulo 2^{32}. We have

$$\langle c.pc \rangle + \langle bdist(c) \rangle \equiv [c.pc] + [imm(c)00] \bmod 2^{32} .$$

Thus, backward jumps are realized with negative $[imm(c)]$.

R-type Jumps $jr(c)$ and $jalr(c)$

The branch target is specified by the rs field of the instruction:

$$jr(c) \lor jalr(c) \rightarrow btarget(c) = c.gpr(rs(c)) \; .$$

J-type Jumps $j(c)$ and $jal(c)$

The branch target is computed in a rather peculiar way: i) the PC is incremented by 4, ii) *then* bits $[27 : 0]$ are replaced by the *iindex* field of the instruction:

$$j(c) \lor jal(c) \rightarrow btarget(c) = (c.pc +_{32} 4_{32})[31 : 28]iindex(c)00 \; .$$

Now we can define the next PC computation for *all* instructions as

$$btarget(c) = \begin{cases} c.pc +_{32} bdist(c) & b(c) \land bres(c) \\ c.gpr(rs(c)) & jr(c) \lor jalr(c) \\ (c.pc +_{32} 4_{32})[31 : 28]iindex(c)00 & \text{otherwise} \end{cases}$$

$$c'.pc = \begin{cases} btarget(c) & jbtaken(c) \\ c.pc +_{32} 4_{32} & \text{otherwise} \; . \end{cases}$$

Jump and Link $jal(c)$ and $jalr(c)$

Jump and link instructions are used to implement calls of procedures. Besides setting the PC to the branch target, they prepare the so called *link address*

$$linkad(c) = c.pc +_{32} 4_{32}$$

and save it in a register. For the R-type instruction $jalr$, this register is specified by the rd field. J-type instruction jal does not have an rs field, and the link address is stored in register 31 ($= \langle 1^5 \rangle$). Branch and jump instructions do not change the memory.

Therefore, for the update of registers in branch and jump instructions, we have:

$$jb(c) \rightarrow$$

$$c'.gpr(x) = \begin{cases} linkad(c) & jalr(c) \land x = rd(c) \lor jal(c) \land x = 1^5 \\ c.gpr(x) & \text{otherwise} \end{cases}$$

$$c'.m = c.m \; .$$

6.2.6 Sequences of Consecutive Memory Bytes

Recall that for $i \in [0 : k - 1]$ we define byte i of string $a \in \mathbb{B}^{8 \cdot k}$ as

$$byte(i, a) = a[8 \cdot (i + 1) - 1 : 8 \cdot i] .$$

A trivial observation is stated in the following lemma.

Lemma 6.1 (bytes of concatenation). Let $a \in \mathbb{B}^8$, let $b \in \mathbb{B}^{8 \cdot d}$ and let $c = a \circ b$. Then,

$$\forall i \in [d : 0] : byte(i, c) = \begin{cases} a & i = d \\ byte(i, b) & i < d \end{cases}$$

Proof.

$$byte(i, c) = a \circ b[8 \cdot (i + 1) - 1 : 8 \cdot i]$$
$$= \begin{cases} a & i = d \\ b[8 \cdot (i + 1) - 1 : 8 \cdot i] & i < d \end{cases}$$
$$= \begin{cases} a & i = d \\ byte(i, b) & i < d . \end{cases}$$

$\square$

The state of byte addressable memory with 32-bit addresses is modeled as a mapping

$$m : \mathbb{B}^{32} \rightarrow \mathbb{B}^8 ,$$

where for each address $x \in \mathbb{B}^{32}$ one interprets $m(x) \in \mathbb{B}^8$ as the current value of memory location x. Recall that we defined the content $m_d(x)$ of d consecutive locations starting at address x by

$$m_1(x) = m(x)$$
$$m_{d+1}(x) = m(x +_{32} d_{32}) \circ m_d(x) .$$

The following simple lemma is used to localize bytes in sequences of consecutive memory locations.

Lemma 6.2 (bytes in sequences).

$$\forall i < d : byte(i, m_d(x)) = m(x +_{32} i_{32})$$

Proof. By induction on d. For $d = 1$ we have $i = 0$. Thus, $i_{32} = 0^{32}$ and

$$byte(0, m_1(x)) = m(x) = m(x +_{32} 0^{32}) = m(x +_{32} i_{32}) .$$

For the induction step from d to $d + 1$, we have by Lemma 6.1, definition $m_{d+1}(x)$, and the induction hypothesis:

$$\forall i < d+1 : byte(i, m_{d+1}(x)) = \begin{cases} m(x +_{32} d_{32}) & i = d \\ byte(i, m_d(x)) & i < d \end{cases}$$

$$= \begin{cases} m(x +_{32} i_{32}) & i = d \\ m(x +_{32} i_{32}) & i < d \end{cases}$$

$$= m(x +_{32} i_{32}) .$$

$\square$

6.2.7 Loads and Stores

Load and store operations access a certain number $d(c) \in \{1, 2, 4\}$ of bytes of memory starting at a so called *effective address* $ea(c)$. Letters b, h, and w in the mnemonics define the width: b stands for $d = 1$ resp. a byte access; h stands for $d = 2$ resp. a half word access, and w stands for $d = 4$ resp. a word access. Inspection of the instruction tables gives

$$d(c) = \begin{cases} 1 & opc(c)[0] = 0 \\ 2 & opc(c)[1:0] = 01 \\ 4 & opc(c)[1:0] = 11 . \end{cases}$$

$$= \begin{cases} 1 & I(c)[26] = 0 \\ 2 & I(c)[27:26] = 01 \\ 4 & I(c)[27:26] = 11 . \end{cases}$$

Addressing is always relative to a register specified by the rs field. The offset is specified by the immediate field:

$$ea(c) = c.gpr(rs(c)) +_{32} sxtimm(c) .$$

Note that the immediate constant is sign extended. Thus, negative offsets can be realized in the same way as negative branch distances. Effective addresses are required to be *aligned*. If we interpret them as binary numbers they have to be divisible by the width $d(c)$:

$$d(c) \mid \langle ea(c) \rangle$$

or equivalently

$$ls(c) \wedge d(c) = 2 \rightarrow ea(c)[0] = 0 \quad , \quad ls(c) \wedge d(c) = 4 \rightarrow ea(c)[1:0] = 00 .$$

Stores

A store instruction takes the low order $d(c)$ bytes of the register specified by the rt field and stores them as $m_{d(c)}(ea(c))$. The PC is incremented by 4 (but we have already defined that on page 128). Other memory bytes and register values are not changed:

$$s(c) \rightarrow$$

$$c'.m(x) = \begin{cases} byte(i, c.gpr(rt(c))) & x = ea(c) +_{32} i_{32} \wedge i < d(c) \\ c.m(x) & \text{otherwise} \end{cases}$$

$$c'.gpr = c.gpr$$

A word of caution in case you plan to enter this into a CAV system: the first case of the "definition" of $c'.m(x)$ is very well understandable for humans, but actually it is a shorthand for the following: if

$$\exists i : x = ea(c) +_{32} i_{32}$$

then update $c.m(x)$ with the hopefully unique i satisfying this condition. In this case we can compute this i by solving the equation

$$x = ea(c) +_{32} i_{32}$$

resp.

$$\langle x \rangle = (\langle ea(c) \rangle + i \bmod 2^{32}) .$$

From alignment we conclude

$$\langle ea(c) \rangle + i \leq 2^{32} - 1 .$$

Hence,

$$(\langle ea(c) \rangle + i \bmod 2^{32}) = \langle ea(c) \rangle + i .$$

And we have to solve

$$\langle x \rangle = \langle ea(c) \rangle + i$$

as

$$i = \langle x \rangle - \langle ea(c) \rangle .$$

This turns the above definition into

$$c'.m(x) = \begin{cases} byte(\langle x \rangle - \langle ea(c) \rangle, c.gpr(rt(c))) & \langle x \rangle - \langle ea(c) \rangle \in [0 : d(c) - 1] \\ c.m(x) & \text{otherwise} , \end{cases}$$

which is not so readable for humans.

Loads

Loads, like stores, access $d(c)$ bytes of memory starting at address $ea(c)$. The result is stored in the low order $d(c)$ bytes of the destination register, which is specified by the rt field of the instruction. This leaves $32 - 8 \cdot d(c)$ bits of the destination register to be filled by some bit $fill(c)$. For unsigned loads (with a suffix "u" in the mnemonics) the fill bit is zero; otherwise it is sign extended by the leading bit of $c.m_{d(c)}(ea(c))$. In this way a load result $lres(c) \in \mathbb{B}^{32}$ is computed and the general purpose register specified by the rt field is updated. Other registers and the memory are left unchanged:

$$u(c) = opc(c)[2]$$

$$fill(c) = \begin{cases} 0 & u(c) \\ c.m(ea(c) +_{32} (d(c) - 1)_{32})[7] & \text{otherwise} \end{cases}$$

$$lres(c) = fill(c)^{32-8 \cdot d(c)} c.m_{d(c)}(ea(c))$$

$$l(c) \rightarrow$$

$$c'.gpr(x) = \begin{cases} lres(c) & x = rt(c) \\ c.gpr(x) & \text{otherwise} \end{cases}$$

$$c'.m = c.m .$$

6.2.8 ISA Summary

We collect all previous definitions of destination registers for the general purpose register file into

$$Cad(c) = \begin{cases} 1^5 & jal(c) \\ rd(c) & rtype(c) \\ rt(c) & \text{otherwise} . \end{cases}$$

Also we collect the data $gprin$ to be written into the general purpose register file. For technical reasons, we define on the way an intermediate result C that collects the possible GPR input from arithmetic, shift, and jump instructions:

$$C(c) = \begin{cases} sres(c) & su(c) \\ linkad(c) & jal(c) \vee jalr(c) \\ ares(c) & \text{otherwise} \end{cases}$$

$$gprin(c) = \begin{cases} lres(c) & l(c) \\ C(c) & \text{otherwise} . \end{cases}$$

Finally, we collect in a general purpose register write signal all situations when some general purpose register is updated:

$$gprw(c) = alu(c) \vee su(c) \vee l(c) \vee jal(c) \vee jalr(c) .$$

Now we can summarize the MIPS ISA in three rules concerning the updates of PC, general purpose registers, and memory:

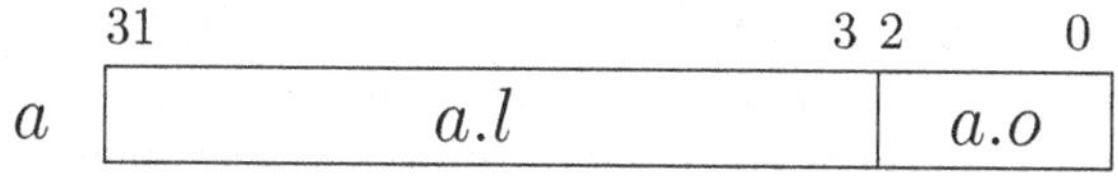

Fig. 95. Line address $a.l$ and offset $a.o$ of a byte address a

$$c'.pc = \begin{cases} btarget(c) & jbtaken(c) \\ c.pc +_{32} 4_{32} & \text{otherwise} \end{cases}$$

$$c'.gpr(x) = \begin{cases} gprin(c) & x = Cad(c) \wedge gprw(c) \\ c.gpr(x) & \text{otherwise} \end{cases}$$

$$c'.m(x) = \begin{cases} byte(i, c.gpr(rt(c))) & x = ea(c) +_{32} i_{32} \wedge i < d(c) \wedge s(c) \\ c.m(x) & \text{otherwise} \, . \end{cases}$$

6.3 A Sequential Processor Design

From the ISA specification, we derive a hardware implementation of the basic MIPS processor. It will execute every MIPS instruction in a single hardware cycle, and it will be so close to the ISA specification that the correctness proof is reduced to a very simple bookkeeping exercise. This basic implementation, however, is far from naive. In the following chapter we turn this implementation into a provably correct pipelined processor design with almost ridiculously little effort.

6.3.1 Software Conditions

As was required in the ISA specification, the hardware implementation only needs to work if all memory accesses of the ISA computation (c^i) are *aligned*, i.e.,

$$\forall i > 0 : c^i.pc[1:0] = 00 \wedge$$
$$ls(c^i) \rightarrow (d(c^i) = 2 \rightarrow ea(c^i)[0] = 0 \wedge$$
$$d(c^i) = 4 \rightarrow ea(c^i)[1:0] = 00) \, .$$

As illustrated in Fig. 95, we divide addresses $a \in \mathbb{B}^{32}$ into *line address* $a.l \in \mathbb{B}^{29}$ and *offset* $a.o \in \mathbb{B}^3$ as

$$a.l = a[31:3]$$
$$a.o = a[2:0] \, .$$

When we later introduce caches, $a.l$ will be the address of a cache line in the cache and $a.o$ will denote the offset of a byte in the cache line.

For the time being we will assume that there is a *code region* $CR \subset \mathbb{B}^{29}$ such that all instructions are fetched from addresses with a line address in CR. We also assume that there is a data region $DR \subset \mathbb{B}^{29}$ such that all addresses of loads and stores have a line address in DR:

$$\forall i : c^i.pc.l \in CR$$

$$\forall i : ls(c^i) \rightarrow ea(c^i).l \in DR .$$

For the time being we will also assume that these regions are disjoint:

$$DR \cap CR = \emptyset .$$

Moreover, in the next section we require the code region CR to always include the addresses which belong to the ROM portion of the hardware memory.

6.3.2 Hardware Configurations and Computations

The hardware configuration h of the implementation has four components:

- a program counter $h.pc \in \mathbb{B}^{32}$,
- a general purpose register file $h.gpr : \mathbb{B}^5 \rightarrow \mathbb{B}^{32}$,
- a *double word addressable* hardware memory $h.m : \mathbb{B}^{29} \rightarrow \mathbb{B}^{64}$. In later constructions it is replaced by separate data and instruction caches. Here it is a single $(64, r, 29)$-2-port multi-bank RAM-ROM. We use port a of this memory for instruction fetch from the code region and port b for performing loads and stores to the data region. Hence, we refer to port a as the *instruction port* and to port b as the *data port* of the hardware memory $h.m$. We assume that the ROM portion of the memory is always included into the code region:

$$CR \supseteq \{0^{29-r}b \mid b \in \mathbb{B}^r\}.$$

Wider memory speeds up aligned loads and stores of half words and words and will later speed up communication between caches and main memory. For the hardware, this comes at the price of shifters for loading or storing words, half words, or bytes. We also need to develop some machinery for tracking the byte addressed data in line addressable hardware memory.

A hardware computation is a sequence (h^t) with $t \in \mathbb{N} \cup \{-1\}$, where configuration h^t denotes the state of the hardware at cycle t. The hardware construction given in the remainder of this chapter defines a hardware transition function

$$h^{t+1} = \delta_H(h^t, reset^t) .$$

We assume the reset signal to be high in cycle -1 and to be low afterwards[5]:

$$reset^t = \begin{cases} 1 & t = -1 \\ 0 & \text{otherwise} . \end{cases}$$

---

[5] That is the reason why we count hardware states starting from -1 and ISA states starting from 0.

6.3.3 Memory Embedding

Let $m : \mathbb{B}^{32} \to \mathbb{B}^8$ be a byte addressable memory like $c.m$ in the ISA specification, and let $cm : \mathbb{B}^{29} \to \mathbb{B}^{64}$ be a line addressable memory like $h.m$ in the intended hardware implementation. Let $A \subseteq \mathbb{B}^{29}$ be a set of line addresses like CR and DR. We define in a straightforward way a relation $cm \sim_A m$ stating that with respect to the addresses in A memory m is embedded in memory cm by

$$\forall a \in A : cm(a) = m_8(a0^3) \ .$$

Thus, illustrating with dots, each line of memory cm contains 8 consecutive bytes of memory m, namely

$$cm(a) = m(a +_{32} 7_{32}) \circ \ldots \circ m(a) \ .$$

We are interested to localize the single bytes of sequences $m_d(x)$ in the line addressable memory cm. We are only interested in access widths, which are powers of two and at most 8 bytes[6]:

$$d \in \{2^k \mid k \in [0 : 3]\} \ .$$

Also we are only interested in so called *accesses* (x, d) which are aligned in the following sense: if $d = 2^k$ with $k \geq 1$ (i.e., to more than a single byte), then the last k bits of address x must all be zero:

$$d = 2^k \wedge k \geq 1 \to x[k - 1 : 0] = 0^k \ .$$

For accesses of this nature and $i < d$, the expressions $x.o +_{32} i_{32}$ that are used in Lemma 6.2 to localize bytes of $m_d(x)$ in byte addressable memory have three very desirable properties: i) their numerical value is at most 7, hence, ii) computing their representative mod 8 in B_3 gives the right result, and iii) all bytes are embedded in the same cache line. This is shown in the following technical lemma.

Lemma 6.3 (properties of aligned addresses). Let (x, d) be aligned and $i < d$. Then,

1. $\langle x.o \rangle + i \leq 7$,
2. $\langle x.o +_3 i_3 \rangle = \langle x.o \rangle + i$,
3. $x +_{32} i_{32} = x.l \circ (x.o +_3 i_3)$.

Proof. We prove three statements of the lemma one by one.

1. By alignment and because $i < d = 2^k$ we have

---

[6] Double precision floating point numbers are 8 bytes long.

$$\langle x.o \rangle + i = \begin{cases} \langle x[2:k] \circ x[k-1:0] \rangle + i & k \leq 2 \\ \langle x[k-1:0] \rangle + i & k = 3 \end{cases}$$

$$= \begin{cases} \langle x[2:k] \circ 0^k \rangle + i & k \leq 2 \\ \langle 0^3 \rangle + i & k = 3 \end{cases}$$

$$\leq \begin{cases} 7 - (2^k - 1) + d - 1 & k \leq 2 \\ 7 & k = 3 \end{cases}$$

$$= 7 .$$

2. By the definition of $+_3$ and part 1 of the lemma we have

$$\langle x.o \rangle + i = \langle x.o \rangle + \langle i_3 \rangle$$
$$= (\langle x.o \rangle + \langle i_3 \rangle \bmod 8)$$
$$= \langle x.o +_3 i_3 \rangle .$$

3. We write

$$x = x.l \circ x.o$$
$$i_{32} = 0^{29} \circ i_3 .$$

Adding the offset and the line components separately, we get by part 2 of the lemma

$$\langle x.o \rangle + \langle i_3 \rangle = \langle 0 \circ (x.o +_3 i_3) \rangle$$
$$\langle x.l \rangle + \langle 0^{29} \rangle = \langle x.l \rangle .$$

Because the carry of the addition of the offsets to position 4 is 0, we get from Lemma 2.12:

$$\langle x \rangle + \langle i_{32} \rangle = \langle x.l \circ (x.o +_3 i_3) \rangle < 2^{32} .$$

Hence,

$$(\langle x \rangle + \langle i_{32} \rangle \bmod 2^{32}) = \langle x.l \circ (x.o +_3 i_3) \rangle .$$

Applying $bin_{32}(\ )$ to this equation proves part 3 of the lemma.

□

In Lemma 6.2 we showed for all accesses (aligned or not)

$$\forall i < d : byte(i, m_d(x)) = m(x +_{32} i_{32}) .$$

Using Lemma 6.3 we specialize this for aligned accesses.

Lemma 6.4 (bytes in sequences for aligned accesses). Let (x, d) be aligned and $i < d$. Then,

$$byte(i, m_d(x)) = m(x.l \circ (x.o +_3 i_3)) .$$

This allows a reformulation of the embedding relation $\sim_A$:

Lemma 6.5 (embedding for bytes). Relation $cm \sim_A m$ holds iff for all byte addresses $x \in \mathbb{B}^{32}$ with $x.l \in A$

$$byte(\langle x.o \rangle, cm(x.l)) = m(x) \ .$$

Proof. Assume for line addresses $a \in \mathbb{B}^{29}$ we have

$$\forall a \in A : cm(a) = m_8(a0^3) \ .$$

Then access $(a0^3, 8)$ is aligned and Lemma 6.4 can be reformulated for single bytes:

$$\forall i < 8 : byte(i, cm(a)) = byte(i, m_8(a0^3))$$
$$= m(a \circ i_3) \ .$$

Now we rewrite byte address $a \circ i_3$ as

$$a \circ i_3 = x = x.l \circ x.o$$

and get

$$byte(\langle x.o \rangle, cm(x.l)) = m(x) \ .$$

For the opposite direction of the proof we assume

$$\forall x \in \mathbb{B}^{32} : x.l \in A \rightarrow byte(\langle x.o \rangle, cm(x.l)) = m(x) \ .$$

We instantiate

$$x = x.l \circ x.o = a \circ i_3 \ ,$$

and get for all $i < 8$ and $a \in A$

$$byte(\langle i_3 \rangle, cm(a)) = m(a \circ i_3) \ .$$

We further derive

$$\forall i < 8 : byte(i, cm(a)) = byte(\langle i_3 \rangle, cm(a))$$
$$= m(a \circ i_3)$$
$$= m(a \circ (0^3 +_3 i_3))$$
$$= byte(i, m_8(a0^3)) \quad \text{(Lemma 6.4)},$$

which implies

$$cm(a) = m_8(a0^3) \ .$$

$\square$

Finally, we can formulate for aligned accesses (x, d), how the single bytes of consecutive sequences $m_d(x)$ are embedded in memory cm.

Lemma 6.6 (embedding for aligned accesses). Let relation $cm \sim_A m$ hold, (x, d) be aligned, $x.l \in A$, and $i < d$. Then,

$$byte(i, m_d(x)) = byte(\langle x.o \rangle + i, cm(x.l)) .$$

Proof.

$$
\begin{aligned}
byte(i, m_d(x)) &= m(x.l \circ (x.o +_3 i_3)) && \text{(Lemma 6.4)} \\
&= byte(\langle x.o +_3 i_3 \rangle, cm(x.l)) && \text{(Lemma 6.5)} \\
&= byte(\langle x.o \rangle + i, cm(x.l)) && \text{(Lemma 6.3)}
\end{aligned}
$$

$\square$

For aligned word accesses $(d = 4)$ and indices $i < 3$, we get an important special case:

$$
\begin{aligned}
byte(i, m_4(x)) &= byte(\langle x[2]00 \rangle + i, cm(x.l)) \\
&= byte(4 \cdot x[2] + i, cm(x.l)) \\
&= \begin{cases} byte(i, cm(x.l)) & x[2] = 0 \\ byte(4 + i, cm(x.l) & x[2] = 1 . \end{cases}
\end{aligned}
$$

Concatenating bytes we can rewrite the embedding relation for aligned word accesses.

Lemma 6.7 (embedding for word accesses). Let relation $cm \sim_A m$ hold, $x \in \mathbb{B}^{32}$, $x.l \in A$, and $x[1:0] = 00$. Then,

$$
m_4(x) = \begin{cases} cm(x.l)[31:0] & x[2] = 0 \\ cm(x.l)[63:32] & x[2] = 1 . \end{cases}
$$

6.3.4 Defining Correctness for the Processor Design

We define in a straightforward way a *simulation relation* $sim(c, h)$ stating that hardware configuration h encodes ISA configuration c by

$$sim(c, h) \equiv$$

1. $h.pc = c.pc \land$
2. $h.gpr = c.gpr \land$
3. $h.m \sim_{CR} c.m \land$
4. $h.m \sim_{DR} c.m,$

i.e., every hardware memory location $h.m(a)$ for $a \in CR \cup DR$ contains the contents of eight ISA memory locations:

$$c.m(a111) \circ \ldots \circ c.m(a000) = h.m(a) .$$

By Lemma 6.5 this is equivalent to

$$\forall x \in \mathbb{B}^{32} : x.l \in CR \cup DR \rightarrow c.m(x) = byte(\langle x[2:0]\rangle, h.m(x[31:3])) .$$

We will construct the hardware such that one ISA instruction is emulated in every hardware cycle and that we can show the following lemma.

Lemma 6.8 (MIPS one step). Let alignment and disjointness of code and data regions hold for configuration c^i. Then

$$\forall i \geq 0 : sim(c^i, h^i) \rightarrow sim(c^{i+1}, h^{i+1}).$$

This is obviously the induction step in the correctness proof of the MIPS construction.

Lemma 6.9 (MIPS correctness). There exists an initial ISA configuration c^0 such that

$$\forall i \geq 0 : sim(c^i, h^i) .$$

At first glance it seems that the lemmas are utterly useless, because after power up hardware registers come up with unknown binary content. With unknown content of the code region, one does not know the program that is executed, and thus, one cannot prove alignment and the disjointness of code and data regions. That is of course a very real problem whenever one tries to boot any real machine. We have already seen the solution: for the purpose of booting, the code region occupies the bottom part of the address range:

$$CR = \{0^{29-r}b \mid b \in \mathbb{B}^r\}$$

for some small $r < 29$. The hardware memory is, therefore, realized as a combined $(64, r, 29)$-2-port multi-bank RAM-ROM. The content of the ROM-portion is known after power up and contains the boot loader. Thus, Lemma 6.9 works at least literally for programs in ROM. After the boot loader has loaded more *known* programs, one can define new code and data regions CR' and DR' and discharge (with extra arguments) the hypotheses of Lemma 6.8 for the new regions[7] .

As already mentioned earlier, our hardware construction will closely follow the ISA specification, and there will be many signals X occurring both in the ISA specification and in the hardware implementation. We will distinguish them by their argument. $X(c)$ is the ISA signal whereas $X(h)$ is the corresponding hardware signal.

---

[7] In a pipelined processor, in between a switch to a new code and data region one has to make sure that the pipe is drained. This is achieved, for instance, with instruction *eret* (return from exception). Since in this book instruction *eret* and other instructions which drain the pipe as a side effect are not specified, we assume the code and data regions to be fixed initially and unchanged afterwards. As a result, a slight adaptation of the proofs would be necessary if one wants to argue formally about self-modifying code. For details refer to [12].

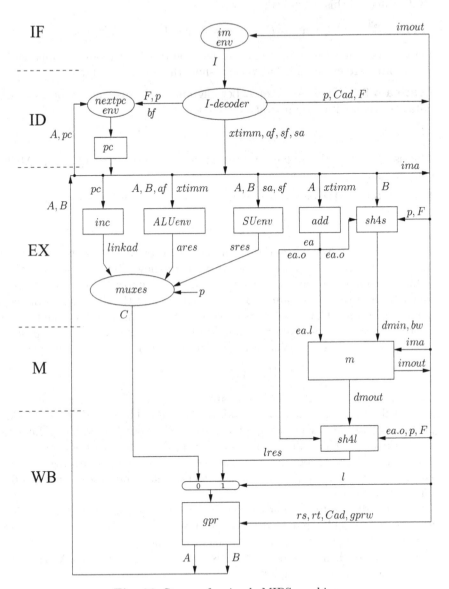

Fig. 96. Stages of a simple MIPS machine

6.3.5 Stages of Instruction Execution

Aiming at pipelined implementations later on, we construct the basic implementation of a MIPS processor in a very structured way. We split instruction execution into 5 stages, that we describe first in a preliminary and somewhat informal way (see Fig. 96):

- *IF* – instruction fetch. The program counter pc is used to access the instruction port of memory m in order to fetch the current instruction I.
- *ID* – instruction decode:
  - In an instruction decoder predicates p and functions f depending only on the current instruction are computed. The predicates p correspond to the predicates in the ISA specification. Functions f include the function bits af and sf controlling ALU and shift unit as well as the extended immediate constant $xtimm$. Some trivial functions f simply select some fields F of the instruction I, like rs or rt.
  - The general purpose register file is accessed with addresses rs and rt. For the time being we call the result $A = gpr(rs)$ and $B = gpr(rt)$.
  - Result A is used to compute the next program counter in the next PC environment.
- *EX* – execute. Using only results from the *ID* stage the following results are computed by the following circuits:
  - the link address $linkad$ for the link-instructions by an incrementer,
  - the result $ares$ of the ALU by an ALU-environment,
  - the result $sures$ of the shift unit by a shift unit environment,
  - the preliminary input C for the general purpose register file from $linkad$, $ares$, and $sres$ by a small multiplexer tree,
  - effective address ea for loads and stores by an adder,
  - the shifted operand $dmin$ and the byte write signals $bw[i]$ for store instructions in an sh4s-environment[8].
- *M* – memory. Store instructions update the hardware memory m through the data port (port b). For store instructions, line $ea.l$ of the hardware memory is accessed. The output of the data port of the hardware memory m is called $dmout$.
- *WB* – write back. For load instructions the output of the data port $dmout$ is shifted in an sh4l-environment and if necessary modified by a fill bit. The result $lres$ is combined with C to the data input $gprin$ of the general purpose register file. The gpr is updated.

6.3.6 Initialization

PC initialization and the instruction port environment $imenv$ is shown in Fig. 97. We have

$$h^0.pc = 0^{32} = c^0.pc \ .$$

Thus, condition 1 of relation sim holds for $i = 0$. We take no precautions to prevent writes to $h.gpr$ or $h.m$ during cycle -1 and define

---

[8] sh4s is a shorthand for "shift for store" and sh4l is a shorthand for "shift for load".

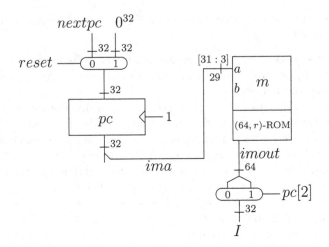

Fig. 97. PC initialization and the instruction port environment

$$c^0.gpr = h^0.gpr$$
$$c^0.m_8(a000) = h^0.m(a) .$$

Hence, we can conclude

$$sim(c^0, h^0) .$$

We assume that the software conditions stated in Sec. 6.3.1 hold for all ISA computations that start from c^0.

From now on let $i > 0$ and $c = c^i$, $h = h^i$ and assume $sim(c, h)$. In the remainder of the chapter we consider every stage of instruction execution in detail and show that Lemma 6.8 holds for our construction, i.e., that simulation relation

$$sim(c', h')$$

holds, where $c' = c^{i+1}$ and $h' = h^{i+1}$. When in the proofs we invoke part k of the simulation relation for $k \in [1 : 4]$, we abbreviate this as $(sim.k)$. When we argue about hardware construction and semantics of hardware components, like memories, we abbreviate by (H).

6.3.7 Instruction Fetch

The treatment of the instruction fetch stage is short. The instruction port of the hardware memory $h.m$ is addressed with bits

$$ima(h) = h.pc[31 : 3] = h.pc.l .$$

It satisfies

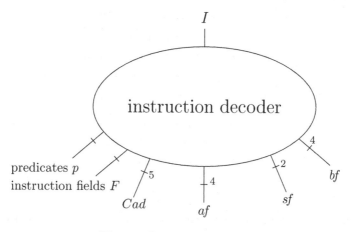

Fig. 98. Instruction decoder

$$h.pc[31:3] = c.pc[31:3] \quad (sim.1)$$
$$\in CR .$$

Using Lemma 6.7 we conclude that the hardware instruction $I(h)$ fetched by the circuitry in Fig. 97 is

$$I(h) = \begin{cases} h.m(h.pc[31:3])[63:32] & h.pc[2] = 1 \\ h.m(h.pc[31:3])[31:0] & h.pc[2] = 0 \end{cases}$$
$$= c.m_4(c.pc[31:2]00) \quad (\text{Lemma 6.7, } sim.3)$$
$$= c.m_4(c.pc) \quad (\text{alignment})$$
$$= I(c) .$$

Thus, instruction fetch is correct.

Lemma 6.10 (instruction fetch).

$$I(h) = I(c)$$

6.3.8 Instruction Decoder

The instruction decoder belongs to the instruction decode stage. As shown in Fig. 98 it computes the hardware version of functions $f(c)$ that only depend on the current instruction $I(c)$, i.e., which can be written as

$$f(c) = f'(I(c)) .$$

For example,

$$rtype(c) \equiv opc(c) = 0{*}0^4$$
$$\equiv I(c)[31:26] = 0{*}0^4$$
$$rtype'(I[31:0]) \equiv I[31:26] = 0{*}0^4$$
$$rtype(c) = rtype'(I(c))$$

or

$$rd(c) = I(c)[15:11]$$
$$rd'(I[31:0]) = I[15:11]$$
$$rd(c) = rd'(I(c)) \ .$$

Predicates

This trivial transformation, however, gives a straightforward way to construct circuits for all predicates $p(c)$ from the ISA specification that depend only on the current instruction:

- Construct a boolean formula for p'. This is always possible by Lemma 2.20. In the above example

$$rtype'(I) = \overline{I[31]} \wedge \overline{I[29]} \wedge \overline{I[28]} \wedge \overline{I[27]} \wedge \overline{I[26]} \ .$$

- Translate the formula into a circuit and connect the inputs of the circuit to the hardware instruction register. The output $p(h)$ of the circuit satisfies

$$p(h) = p'(I(h))$$
$$= p'(I(c)) \quad \text{(Lemma 6.10)}$$
$$= p(c) \ .$$

Thus, the instruction decoder produces correct instruction predicates.

Lemma 6.11 (instruction predicates). For all predicates p depending only on the current instruction:
$$p(h) = p(c) \ .$$

Instruction Fields

All instruction fields F have the form

$$F(c) = I(c)[m:n] \ .$$

Compute the hardware version as

$$F(h) = I(h)[m:n]$$
$$= I(c)[m:n] \quad \text{(Lemma 6.10)}$$
$$= F(c) \ .$$

Lemma 6.12 (instruction fields). For all instruction fields F:
$$F(h) = F(c) \ .$$

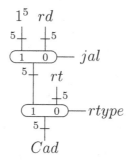

Fig. 99. C address computation

C Address

The output $Cad(h)$ in Fig. 99 computes the address of the destination register for the general purpose register file. By Lemmas 6.11 and 6.12 it satisfies

$$Cad(h) = \begin{cases} 1^5 & jal(h) \\ rd(h) & rtype(h) \\ rt(h) & \text{otherwise} \end{cases}$$

$$= \begin{cases} 1^5 & jal(c) \\ rd(c) & rtype(c) \\ rt(c) & \text{otherwise} \end{cases}$$

$$= Cad(c) .$$

Extended Immediate Constant

The fill bit $ifill(c)$ is a predicate and $imm(c)$ is a field of the instruction. Thus, we can compute the extended immediate constant in hardware as

$$\begin{aligned} xtimm(h) &= ifill(h)^{16}imm(h) \\ &= ifill(c)^{16}imm(c) \quad \text{(Lemmas 6.11 and 6.12)} \\ &= xtimm(c) . \end{aligned}$$

Lemma 6.13 (immediate constant).

$$xtimm(h) = xtimm(c) .$$

Function Fields for ALU, SU, and BCE

Figure 100 shows the computation of the function fields af, i, sf, and bf for the ALU, the shift unit, and the branch condition evaluation unit.

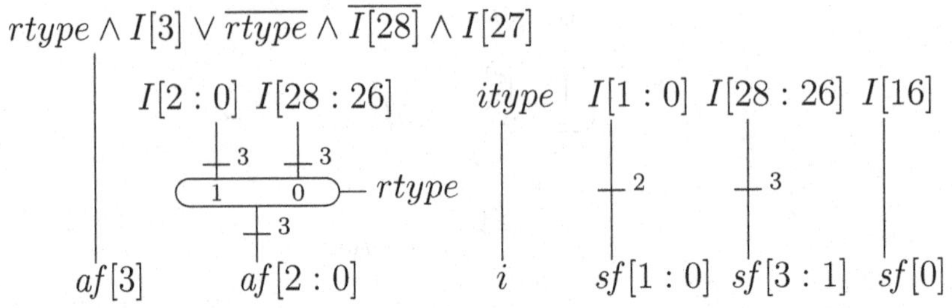

$$rtype \wedge I[3] \vee \overline{rtype} \wedge \overline{I[28]} \wedge I[27]$$

Fig. 100. Computation of function fields for ALU, SU, and BCE

Outputs $af(h)[2:0]$ satisfy by Lemmas 6.11 and 6.12

$$af(h)[2:0] = \begin{cases} I(h)[2:0] & rtype(h) \\ I(h)[28:26] & \text{otherwise} \end{cases}$$

$$= \begin{cases} I(c)[2:0] & rtype(c) \\ I(c)[28:26] & \text{otherwise} \end{cases}$$

$$= af(c) .$$

One shows

$$i(h) = i(c)$$
$$sf(h) = sf(c)$$
$$bf(h) = bf(c)$$

in the same way. Bit $af[3](c)$ is a predicate. Thus, $af(h)$ is computed in the function decoder as a predicate and we get by Lemma 6.11

$$af[3](h) = af[3](c) .$$

We summarize in the following lemma.

Lemma 6.14 (C address and function fields).

$$Cad(h) = Cad(c)$$
$$af(h) = af(c)$$
$$i(h) = i(c)$$
$$sf(h) = sf(c)$$
$$bf(h) = bf(c)$$

That finishes – fortunately – the bookkeeping of what the instruction decoder does.

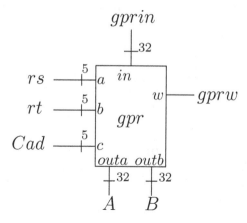

Fig. 101. General purpose register file

6.3.9 Reading from General Purpose Registers

The general purpose register file $h.gpr$ of the hardware as shown in Fig. 101 is a 3-port GPR RAM with two read ports and one write port. The a and b addresses of the file are connected to $rs(h)$ and $rt(h)$. For the data outputs $gprouta$ and $gproutb$, we introduce the shorthands A and B

$$
\begin{aligned}
A(h) &= gprouta(h) \\
&= h.gpr(rs(h)) \quad (H) \\
&= c.gpr(rs(h)) \quad (sim.2) \\
&= c.gpr(rs(c)) \quad (\text{Lemma } 6.12) \\
B(h) &= c.gpr(rt(c)) . \quad (\text{similarly})
\end{aligned}
$$

Thus, the outputs of the GPR RAM are correct.

Lemma 6.15 (GPR outputs).

$$
\begin{aligned}
A(h) &= c.gpr(rs(c)) \\
B(h) &= c.gpr(rt(c))
\end{aligned}
$$

6.3.10 Next PC Environment

Branch Condition Evaluation Unit

The BCE-unit is wired as shown in Fig. 102. By Lemmas 6.15 and 6.14 as well as the correctness of the BCE implementation from Sect. 5.5 we have

$$
\begin{aligned}
bres(h) &= bcres(A(h), B(h), bf(h)) \\
&= bcres(c.gpr(rs(c)), c.gpr(rt(c)), bf(c)) \\
&= bres(c) .
\end{aligned}
$$

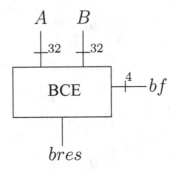

Fig. 102. The branch condition evaluation unit and its operands

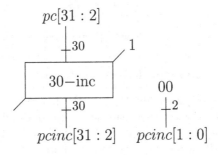

Fig. 103. Incrementing an aligned PC with a 30-incrementer

Thus, the branch condition evaluation unit produces the correct result.

Lemma 6.16 (BCE result).

$$bres(h) = bres(c)$$

Incremented PC

The computation of an incremented PC as needed for the next PC environment as well as for the link instructions is shown in Fig. 103. Because the PC can be assumed to be aligned[9] the use of a 30-incrementer suffices. Using the correctness of the incrementer from Sect. 5.1 we get

$$
\begin{aligned}
pcinc(h) &= (h.pc[31:2] +_{30} 1_{30})00 \\
&= (c.pc[31:2] +_{30} 1_{30})00 \quad (sim.1) \\
&= c.pc[31:2]00 +_{32} 1_{30}00 \quad (\text{Lemma 2.12}) \\
&= c.pc +_{32} 4_{32} . \quad (\text{alignment})
\end{aligned}
$$

Thus, the incremented PC is correct.

---
[9] Otherwise a misalignment interrupt would be signalled.

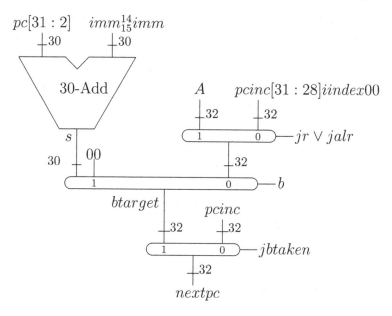

Fig. 104. Next PC computation

Lemma 6.17 (incremented PC).

$$pcinc(h) = c.pc +_{32} 4_{32}$$

Next PC Computation

The circuit computing the next PC input, which was left open in Fig. 97 when we treated the instruction fetch, is shown in Fig. 104.

Predicates $p \in \{jr, jalr, jump, b\}$ are computed in the instruction decoder. Thus, we have

$$p(c) = p(h)$$

by Lemma 6.11.

We compute $jbtaken$ in the obvious way and conclude by Lemma 6.16

$$jbtaken(h) = jump(h) \vee b(h) \wedge bres(h)$$
$$= jump(c) \vee b(c) \wedge bres(c)$$
$$= jbtaken(c) \, .$$

We have by Lemmas 6.15, 6.17, and 6.12

$$A(h) = c.gpr(rs(c))$$
$$pcinc(h) = c.pc +_{32} 4_{42}$$
$$imm(h)[15]^{14}imm(h)00 = imm(c)[15]^{14}imm(c)00$$
$$= bdist(c) \, .$$

For the computation of the 30-bit adder, we argue as in Lemma 6.17:

$$
\begin{aligned}
s(h)00 &= (h.pc[31:2] +_{30} imm(h)[15]^{14}imm(h))00 \\
&= (c.pc[31:2] +_{30} imm(c)[15]^{14}imm(c))00 \quad (sim.1, \text{ Lemma } 6.12) \\
&= c.pc[31:2]00 +_{32} imm(c)[15]^{14}imm(c)00 \quad (\text{Lemma } 2.12) \\
&= c.pc +_{32} bdist(c) . \quad (\text{alignment})
\end{aligned}
$$

We conclude

$$
\begin{aligned}
btarget(h) &= \begin{cases} c.pc +_{32} bdist(c) & b(c) \\ c.gpr(rs(c)) & jr(c) \vee jalr(c) \\ (c.pc +_{32} 4_{32})[31:28]iindex(c)00 & j(c) \vee jal(c) \end{cases} \\
&= btarget(c) .
\end{aligned}
$$

Exploiting

$$
reset(h) = 0
$$

and the semantics of register updates we conclude

$$
\begin{aligned}
h'.pc &= nextpc(h) \\
&= \begin{cases} btarget(c) & jbtaken(c) \\ c.pc +_{32} 4_{32} & \text{otherwise} \end{cases} \\
&= c'.pc .
\end{aligned}
$$

Thus, we have shown the following lemma.

Lemma 6.18 (next PC).

$$
h'.pc = c'.pc
$$

This is $sim.1$ for the next configuration.

6.3.11 ALU Environment

We begin with the treatment of the execute stage. The ALU environment is shown in Fig. 105. For the ALU's left operand, we have

$$
\begin{aligned}
lop(h) &= A(h) \\
&= c.gpr(rs(c)) \quad (\text{Lemma } 6.15) \\
&= lop(c) .
\end{aligned}
$$

For the right operand, it follows by Lemmas 6.15 and 6.13

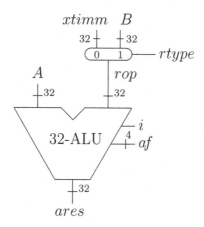

Fig. 105. ALU environment

$$rop(h) = \begin{cases} B(h) & rtype(h) \\ xtimm(h) & \text{otherwise} \end{cases}$$

$$= \begin{cases} c.gpr(rt(c)) & rtype(c) \\ xtimm(c) & \text{otherwise} \end{cases}$$

$$= rop(c) .$$

For the result $ares$ of the ALU, we get

$$\begin{aligned} ares(h) &= alures(lop(h), rop(h), itype(h), af(h)) \quad \text{(Sect. 5.3)} \\ &= alures(lop(c), rop(c), itype(c), af(c)) \quad \text{(Lemma 6.11)} \\ &= ares(c) . \end{aligned}$$

We summarize in the following lemma.

Lemma 6.19 (ALU result).

$$ares(h) = ares(c)$$

Note that in contrast to previous lemmas the proof of this lemma is not just bookkeeping; it involves the not so trivial correctness of the ALU implementation from Sect. 5.3.

6.3.12 Shift Unit Environment

The computation of the operands of the shift unit is shown in Fig. 106. The left operand of the shifter is tied to B. Thus,

$$\begin{aligned} slop(h) &= B(h) \\ &= c.gpr(rt(c)) \quad \text{(Lemma 6.15)} \\ &= slop(c) . \end{aligned}$$

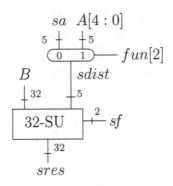

Fig. 106. Shift unit environment

For the shift distance we have by Lemmas 6.12 and 6.15

$$sdist(h) = \begin{cases} sa(h) & fun(h)[2] = 0 \\ A(h)[4:0] & fun(h)[2] = 1 \end{cases}$$

$$= \begin{cases} sa(c) & fun(c)[2] = 0 \\ c.gpr(rs(c))[4:0] & fun(c)[2] = 1 \end{cases}$$

$$= sdist(c) .$$

Using the non trivial correctness of the shift unit implementation from Sect. 5.4 we get

$$sres(h) = sures(slop(h), sdist(h)), sf(h)) \quad \text{(Sect. 5.4)}$$
$$= sures(slop(c), sdist(c), sf(c)) \quad \text{(Lemma 6.14)}$$
$$= sres(c) .$$

Thus, the result produced by the shift unit is correct.

Lemma 6.20 (shift unit result).

$$sres(h) = sres(c)$$

6.3.13 Jump and Link

The value *linkad* that is saved in jump and link instructions is identical with the incremented PC *pcinc* from the next PC environment (Lemma 6.17):

$$linkad(h) = pcinc(h) = c.pc +_{32} 4_{32} = linkad(c) . \tag{15}$$

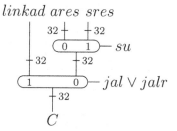

Fig. 107. Collecting results into signal C

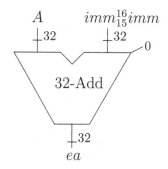

Fig. 108. Effective address computation

6.3.14 Collecting Results

Figure 107 shows a small multiplexer-tree collecting results $linkad$, $ares$, and $sres$ into an intermediate result C. Using Lemmas 6.19, 6.20, and 6.11 as well as (15) we conclude

$$C(h) = \begin{cases} sres(h) & su(h) \\ linkad(h) & jal(h) \vee jalr(h) \\ ares(h) & \text{otherwise} \end{cases}$$
$$= C(c) \,.$$

Thus, the intermediate result $C(h)$ is correct.

Lemma 6.21 (C result).
$$C(h) = C(c)$$

6.3.15 Effective Address

The effective address computation is shown in Fig. 108. We have

$$ea(h) = A(h) +_{32} imm(h)[15]^{16}imm(h) \quad \text{(Sect. 5.1)}$$
$$= c.gpr(rs(c)) +_{32} sxtimm(c) \quad \text{(Lemmas 6.15 and 6.12)}$$
$$= ea(c) \,.$$

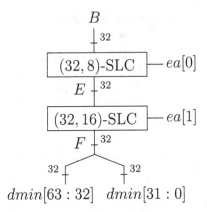

Fig. 109. Shifter for store operations in the sh4s-environment

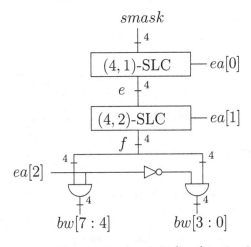

Fig. 110. Computation of byte write signals $bw[7:0]$ in the sh4s-environment

Thus, the effective address computation is correct.

Lemma 6.22 (effective address).

$$ea(h) = ea(c)$$

6.3.16 Shift for Store Environment

Figure 109 shows a shifter construction and the data inputs for the data port of the hardware memory $h.m$. The shifter construction serves to align the B operand with the 64-bit wide memory. A second small shifter construction generating the byte write signals is shown in Fig. 110.

The initial mask signals are generated as

$$smask(h)[3:0] = s(h) \wedge (I(h)[27]^2 I(h)[26]1) \ .$$

One easily verifies that

$$smask(h) = \begin{cases} 0000 & \neg s(c) \\ 0001 & s(c) \wedge d(c) = 1 \\ 0011 & s(c) \wedge d(c) = 2 \\ 1111 & s(c) \wedge d(c) = 4 \end{cases}$$

resp.

$$smask(h)[i] = 1 \leftrightarrow s(c) \wedge i < d(c) \ .$$

In case $s(c) = 0$, we immediately get

$$bw(h) = 0^8 \ .$$

By alignment we have

$$(d(c) = 2 \rightarrow ea(c)[0] = 0) \wedge (d(c) = 4 \rightarrow ea(c)[1:0] = 00) \ .$$

Using $ea(c) = ea(h)$ from Lemma 6.22 and correctness of SLC-shifters we conclude for $s(c) = 1$:

$$\begin{aligned} e(h)[j] = 1 &\leftrightarrow \exists i < d(c) : j = \langle ea(c)[0] \rangle + i \\ f(h)[j] = 1 &\leftrightarrow \exists i < d(c) : j = \langle ea(c)[1:0] \rangle + i \\ bw(h)[j] = 1 &\leftrightarrow \exists i < d(c) : j = \langle ea(c)[2:0] \rangle + i \ . \end{aligned}$$

Similarly we have for the large shifter from Fig. 109 and for $i < d(c)$

$$\begin{aligned} byte(i, B(h)) &= byte(i + \langle ea(c)[0] \rangle, E(h)) \\ &= byte(i + \langle ea(c)[1:0] \rangle, F(h)) \\ &= byte(i + \langle 0ea(c)[1:0] \rangle, dmin(h)) \\ &= byte(i + \langle 1ea(c)[1:0] \rangle, dmin(h)) \\ &= byte(i + \langle ea(c)[2:0] \rangle, dmin(h)) \ . \end{aligned}$$

Using $B(h) = c.gpr(rt(c))$ from Lemma 6.15, we summarize this for the shifters supporting the store operations.

Lemma 6.23 (shift for store). If $s(c) = 1$, i.e., if a store operation is performed in ISA configuration c, then

$$bw(h)[j] = 1 \leftrightarrow \exists i < d(c) : j = \langle ea(c).o \rangle + i$$
$$\forall i < d(c) : byte(i, c.gpr(rt(c))) = byte(i + \langle ea(c).o \rangle, dmin(h)) \ .$$

This concludes the treatment of the execute stage.

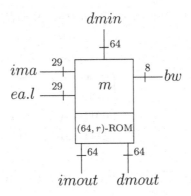

Fig. 111. Wiring of the hardware memory

6.3.17 Memory Stage

In the memory stage we access port b of hardware memory $h.m$ with the line address $ea.l$ and the signals $bw(h)[7:0]$ and $dmin(h)$ constructed above. Figure 111 shows wiring of the hardware memory. We proceed to prove the induction step for $h.m$.

Lemma 6.24 (hardware memory).

$$\forall a \in CR \cup DR : h'.m(a) = c.m_8(a000).$$

Proof. By Lemma 6.5 this is equivalent to

$$\forall x \in \mathbb{B}^{32} : x.l \in CR \cup DR : c'.m(x) = byte(\langle x[2:0]\rangle, h'.m(x[31:3])).$$

and we will prove the lemma for the data region in this form.

By induction hypotheses, $sim.3$, and $sim.4$ we have

$$\forall a \in CR \cup DR : h.m(a) = c.m_8(a000).$$

For $s(c) = 0$ no store is executed and in the ISA computation we have $c'.m = c.m$. In the hardware computation we have $bmask(h) = 0^4$ and $bw(h)[7:0] = 0^8$; hence, $h'.m = h.m$. With the induction hypothesis we conclude trivially for all $a \in CR \cup DR$:

$$
\begin{aligned}
h'.m(a) &= h.m(a) \\
&= c.m_8(a000) \quad (sim.3, \ sim.4) \\
&= c'.m_8(a000) \ .
\end{aligned}
$$

For $s(c) = 1$ we get from the ISA specification:

$$
c'.m(x) = \begin{cases} byte(i, c.gpr(rt(c))) & x = ea(c) +_{32} i_{32} \wedge i < d(c) \\ c.m(x) & \text{otherwise} \ . \end{cases}
$$

For $x \in \mathbb{B}^{32}$ and $i < d(c)$ we derive:

$$x = ea(c) +_{32} i_{32} \leftrightarrow x = ea(c).l \circ (ea(c).o +_3 i_3) \qquad \text{(Lemma 6.3)}$$
$$\leftrightarrow x.o = ea(c).o +_3 i_3 \land x.l = ea(c).l$$
$$\leftrightarrow \langle x.o \rangle = \langle ea(c).o +_3 i_3 \rangle \land x.l = ea(c).l \qquad \text{(Lemma 2.7)}$$
$$\leftrightarrow \langle x.o \rangle = \langle ea(c).o \rangle + i \land x.l = ea(c).l . \qquad \text{(Lemma 6.3)}$$

Hence,

$$c'.m(x) = \begin{cases} byte(i, c.gpr(rt(c))) & \langle x.o \rangle = \langle ea(c).o \rangle + i \land i < d(c) \\ & \land x.l = ea(c).l \\ c.m(x) & \text{otherwise} . \end{cases}$$

In Lemma 6.22 we have already concluded that

$$ea(h) = ea(c).$$

Moreover, we know from the software conditions that $ea(c).l \in DR$. Thus, for any $a \in CR$ we have

$$h'.m(a) = h.m(a)$$
$$= c.m_8(a000) \quad (sim.3)$$
$$= c'.m_8(a000) .$$

For the hardware memory the specification of the 2-port multi-bank RAM-ROM gives for all $a \in DR$:

$$h'.m(a) = \begin{cases} modify(h.m(a), dmin(h), bw(h)) & a = ea(c).l \\ h.m(a) & \text{otherwise} . \end{cases} \qquad (16)$$

With $x \in \mathbb{B}^{32}$, $a = x.l \in DR$, $j = \langle x.o \rangle \in \mathbb{B}_3$, and the definition of function $modify$, we rewrite (16) as

$$byte(\langle x.o \rangle, h'.m(x.l))$$
$$= byte(j, h'.m(a))$$
$$= \begin{cases} byte(j, dmin(h)) & bw(h)[j] \land a = ea(c).l \\ byte(j, h.m(a)) & \text{otherwise} \end{cases}$$
$$= \begin{cases} byte(i, c.gpr(rt(c))) & j = \langle ea(c).o \rangle + i \land i < d(c) \\ & \land a = ea(c).l \qquad \text{(Lemma 6.23)} \\ byte(j, h.m(a)) & \text{otherwise} \end{cases}$$
$$= \begin{cases} byte(i, c.gpr(rt(c))) & j = \langle ea(c).o \rangle + i \land i < d(c) \\ c.m(x) & \text{otherwise} \qquad (sim.4, \text{Lemma 6.5}) \end{cases}$$
$$= c'.m(x) .$$

$\square$

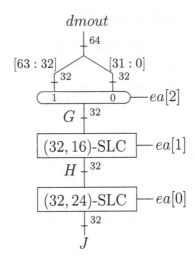

Fig. 112. Shifter for load operations in the sh4l-environment

6.3.18 Shifter for Load

The only remaining stage is the write back stage. A shifter construction supporting load operations is shown in Fig. 112. Assume $l(c)$ holds, i.e., a load instruction is executed. Because $c.m \sim_{DR} h.m$ holds by induction hypothesis, we can use Lemma 6.6 to locate for $i < d(c)$ the bytes to be loaded in $h.m$ and subsequently – using memory semantics – in $dmout(h)$. Then we simply track the effect of the two shifters taking into account that a 24-bit left shift is the same as an 8-bit right shift:

$$
\begin{aligned}
&byte(i, c.m_d(ea(c)) \\
&= byte(\langle ea(c).o \rangle + i, h.m(ea(c).l)) \quad \text{(Lemma 6.6)} \\
&= byte(\langle ea(h).o \rangle + i, h.m(ea(h).l)) \quad \text{(Lemma 6.22)} \\
&= byte(\langle ea(h).o \rangle + i, dmout(h)) \quad \text{(H)} \\
&= byte(\langle ea(h)[1:0] \rangle + i, G(h)) \quad \text{(H)} \\
&= byte(\langle ea(h)[0] \rangle + i, H(h)) \quad \text{(H)} \\
&= byte(i, J(h)) \, . \quad \text{(H)}
\end{aligned}
$$

Hence, we can conclude the following lemma.

Lemma 6.25 (shift for load).

$$
J(h)[8d(c) - 1 : 0] = c.m_{d(c)}(ea(c))
$$

By setting

$$
fill(h) = J(h)[7] \wedge lb(h) \vee J(h)[15] \wedge lh(h)
$$

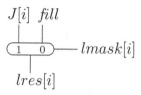

Fig. 113. Fill bit computation for loads

we conclude

$$s(c) \wedge d(c) \neq 4 \rightarrow fill(h) = fill(c) .$$

Similar to the mask $smask$ for store operations we generate a load mask

$$lmask(h) = I(h)[27]^{16}I(h)[26]^{8}1^{8} .$$

In case of load operations ($l(c)$ holds) it satisfies

$$lmask(h) = \begin{cases} 0^{24}1^{8} & d(c) = 1 \\ 0^{16}1^{16} & d(c) = 2 \\ 1^{32} & d(c) = 4 \end{cases}$$
$$= 0^{32-8 \cdot d(c)}1^{8 \cdot d(c)} .$$

As shown in Fig. 113 we insert the fill bit at positions i where the corresponding mask bit $lmask[i]$ is zero:

$$lres(h)[i] = \begin{cases} fill(h) & lmask(h)[i] = 0 \\ J(h)[i] & lmask(h)[i] = 1 . \end{cases}$$

By Lemma 6.25 we show that the load result is correct.

Lemma 6.26 (load result).

$$lres(h) = fill(c)^{32-8 \cdot d(c)}c.m_{d(c)}$$
$$= lres(c)$$

6.3.19 Writing to the General Purpose Register File

Figure 114 shows the last multiplexer connecting the data input of the general purpose register file with intermediate result C and the result $lres$ coming from the sh4l-environment. The write signal $gprw$ of the general purpose register file and the predicates su, jal, $jalr$, l controlling the muxes are predicates p computed in the instruction decoder. By Lemma 6.11 we have for them

$$p(c) = p(h) .$$

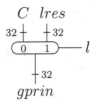

Fig. 114. Computing the data input of the general purpose register file

Using Lemmas 6.21 and 6.26 we conclude

$$gprin(h) = \begin{cases} lres(h) & l(h) \\ C(h) & \text{otherwise} \end{cases}$$

$$= \begin{cases} lres(c) & l(c) \\ C(c) & \text{otherwise} \end{cases}$$

$$= gprin(c) \, .$$

Using RAM semantics, induction hypothesis $sim.2$, and Lemma 6.14 we complete the induction step for the general purpose register file:

$$h'.gpr(x) = \begin{cases} gprin(h) & gprw(h) \wedge x = Cad(h) \\ h.gpr(x) & \text{otherwise} \end{cases}$$

$$= \begin{cases} gprin(c) & gprw(c) \wedge x = Cad(c) \\ c.gpr(x) & \text{otherwise} \end{cases}$$

$$= c'.gpr(x) \, .$$

This concludes the proof of Lemma 6.8 as well as the correctness proof of the entire (simple) processor.

7

Pipelining

In this chapter we deviate from [12] and present somewhat simpler proofs in the spirit of [6]. Pipelining without speculative instruction fetch introduces delay slots after branch and jump instruction. The corresponding simple changes to ISA and reference implementation are presented in Sect. 7.1.

In Sect. 7.2 we use what we call *invisible registers* to partition the reference implementation into pipeline stages. Replacing the invisible registers by pipeline registers and controlling the updates of the pipeline stages by a very simple stall engine we produce a basic pipelined implementation of the MIPS ISA. As in [12] and [6] we use scheduling functions which, for all pipeline stages k and hardware cycles t, keep track of the number of the sequential instruction $I(k,t)$ which is processed in cycle t in stage k of the pipelined hardware. The correctness proof intuitively then hinges on two observations:

1. The circuits of stage k in the sequential hardware σ and the pipelined hardware π are almost identical; the one difference (for the instruction address ima) is handled by an interesting special case in the proof.
2. If X_π is a signal of circuit stage k of the pipelined machine and X_σ is its counter part in the sequential reference machine, then the value of X_π in cycle t equals the value of X_σ before execution of instruction $I(k,t)$. In algebra $X_\pi^t = X_\sigma^{I(k,t)}$.

Although we are claiming to follow the simpler proof pattern from [6] the correctness proof presented here comes out considerably longer than its counter parts in [12] and [6]. The reason is a slight gap in the proof as presented in [12]: the second observation above is almost but not quite true. In every cycle it only holds for the signals which are *used* in the processing of the instruction $I(k,t)$ currently processed in stage k. Proofs with slight gaps are wrong[1] and should be fixed. Fixing the gap discussed here is not hard: one formalizes the concept of signals used for the processing of an instruction and then does the

---

[1] Just as husbands which are almost never cheating are not true husbands.

M. Kovalev et al.: A Pipelined Multi-core MIPS Machine, LNCS 9000, pp. 161–206, 2014.
© Springer International Publishing Switzerland 2014

bookkeeping, which is lengthy and should not be presented fully in the classroom. In [6], where the correctness of the pipelined hardware was formally proven, the author clearly had to fix this problem, but he dealt with it in different way: he introduced extra hardware in the reference implementation, which forced signals, which are not used to zero. This makes observation 2 above strictly true.

Forwarding circuits and their correctness are studied in Sect. 7.3. The material is basically from [12] but we work out the details of the pipe fill phase more carefully.

The elegant general stall engine in Sect. 7.4 is from [6]. Like in [6], where the liveness of pipelined processors is formally proven, the theory of scheduling functions with general stall engines is presented here in much greater detail than in [12]. The reason for this effort becomes only evident at the very end of this book: due to possible interference between bus scheduler of the memory system and stall engines of the processors, liveness of pipelined multi-core machines is a delicate and nontrivial matter.

7.1 MIPS ISA and Basic Implementation Revisited

7.1.1 Delayed PC

What we have presented so far – both in the definition of the ISA and in the implementation of the processor – was a sequential version of MIPS. For pipelined machines we introduce one change to the ISA.

So far in an ISA computation (c^i) new program counters $c^{i+1}.pc$ were computed by instruction $I(c^i)$ and the next instruction

$$I(c^{i+1}) = c^{i+1}.m_4(c^{i+1}.pc)$$

was fetched with this PC. In the new ISA the instruction fetch after a new PC computation is delayed by 1 instruction. This is achieved by leaving the next PC computation unchanged but i) introducing a $delayed\ PC$ (DPC) $c.dpc$ which simply stores the PC of the previous instruction and ii) fetching instructions with this delayed PC. At the start of computations the two program counters are initialized such that the first two instructions are fetched from addresses 0_{32} and 4_{32}. Later we always obtain the delayed PC from the value of the regular PC in the previous cycle:

$$c^0.dpc = 0_{32}$$
$$c^0.pc = 4_{32}$$
$$c^{i+1}.dpc = c^i.pc$$
$$I(c^i) = c^i.m_4(c^i.dpc) \ .$$

The reason for this change is technical and stems from the fact that, in basic 5-stage pipelines, instruction fetch and next PC computation are distributed over two pipeline stages. The introduction of the delayed PC permits to model the effect of this in the *sequential ISA*. In a nutshell, PC and DPC are a tiny bit of visible pipeline in an otherwise completely sequentially programming model.

The 4 bytes after a jump or branch instruction are called a *delay slot*, because the instruction in the delay slot is always executed before the branch or jump takes effect.

The semantics of jump and branch instructions stays unchanged. This means that for computation of the link address and of the jump target we still use the regular PC and not the delayed PC. For instance, for the link address we have

$$linkad(c) = c.pc +_{32} 4_{32} .$$

In case there are no jumps or branches in delay slots[2] and the current instruction $I(c^i) = c^i.m_4(c^i.dpc)$ is a jump or branch instruction, we have for $i > 0$:

$$c^i.dpc = c^{i-1}.pc$$
$$c^i.pc = c^{i-1}.pc +_{32} 4_{32}$$
$$= c^i.dpc +_{32} 4_{32} ,$$

which for the link address gives us

$$linkad(c^i) = c^i.pc +_{32} 4_{32}$$
$$= c^i.dpc +_{32} 8_{32} .$$

So in case of $jal(c^i)$ or $jalr(c^i)$ we save the return address, which points to the first instruction after a delay slot. Relative jumps are also computed with respect to the instruction in the delay slot in contrast to the ISA from the previous chapter, where they were computed with respect to the branch or jump instruction itself.

7.1.2 Implementing the Delayed PC

The changes in the simple non pipelined implementation for the new ISA are completely obvious and are shown in Fig. 115.

The resulting new design σ is a sequential implementation of the MIPS ISA for pipelined machines. We denote hardware configurations of this machine by h_σ. The simulation relation $sim(c, h_\sigma)$ from Sect. 6.3.4 is extended with the obvious coupling for the DPC:

$$sim(c, h_\sigma) \equiv$$

---

[2] A software condition which one has to maintain for the ISA to be meaningful.

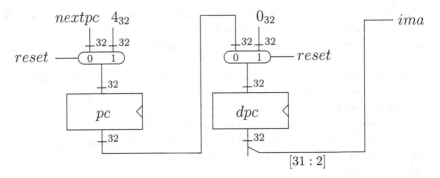

Fig. 115. Implementation of the delayed PC

1. $h_\sigma.pc = c.pc \wedge$
2. $h_\sigma.dpc = c.dpc \wedge$
3. $h_\sigma.gpr = c.gpr \wedge$
4. $h_\sigma.m \sim_{CR} c.m \wedge$
5. $h_\sigma.m \sim_{DR} c.m.$

For ISA computations (c^t) of the new pipelined instruction set one shows in the style of the previous chapter under the same software conditions the correctness of the modified implementation for the new (and real) instruction set.

Lemma 7.1 (MIPS with delayed PC). There is an initial ISA configuration c^0 such that

$$\forall t \geq 0 : sim(c^t, h_\sigma^t) .$$

Note that absence of jump or branch instructions in the delay slot is necessary for the ISA to behave in the expected way, but is not needed for the correctness proof of the sequential MIPS implementation.

7.1.3 Pipeline Stages and Visible Registers

When designing processor hardware one tries to solve a fairly well defined optimization problem that is formulated and studied at considerable length in [12]. In this text we focus on correctness proofs and only remark that one tries i) to spend (on average) as few as possible hardware cycles per executed ISA instruction and ii) to keep the cycle time (as, e.g., introduced in the detailed hardware model) as small as possible. In the first respect the present design is excellent. With a single processor one cycle per instruction is hard to beat. As far as cycle time is concerned, it is a perfect disaster: the circuits of every single stage contribute to the cycle time.

In a basic 5 stage pipeline one partitions the circuits of the sequential design into 5 circuit stages $cir(i)$ with $i \in [0 : 4]$, such that

- the circuit stages have roughly the same delay which then is roughly 1/5 of the original cycle time and
- connections between circuit stages are as simple as possible.

We have already introduced the stages in Fig. 96 of Chap. 6. That the cycle times in each stage are roughly equal cannot be shown here, because we have not introduced a detailed and realistic enough delay model. The interested reader is referred to [12].

Simplicity of inter stage connections is desirable, because in pipelined implementations most of theses connections are realized as register stages. And registers cost money without computing anything new. For a study of how much relative cost is increased by such registers we refer the reader again to [12].

We conclude this section by a bookkeeping exercise about the interconnections between the circuit stages. We stress that we do almost nothing at all here. We simply add the delayed PC and redraw Fig. 96 according to some very simple rules:

1. Whenever a signal crosses downwards from one stage to the next we draw a dotted box around it and rename it (before or after it crosses the boundary). Exception to those are signal ima used for instruction fetch and signals rs and rt used to address the GPR file during instruction decode. For those signals we don't draw a box, since we do not pipeline them later.
2. We collapse the circuits between stages into circles labelled $cir(i)$.

The result is shown in Fig. 116. We observe two kinds of pipeline stages: i) circuit stages $cir(i)$ and ii) *register stages* $reg(k)$ consisting either of registers or memories of the sequential design or of dotted boxes for renamed signals. Most of the figure should be self explaining, we add a few remarks:

- Circuit stage $cir(1)$ and register stage $reg(1)$ are the *IF* stage. $cir(1)$ consists only of the instruction port environment, which is presently read only and hence behaves like a circuit. Signal I contains the instruction that was fetched.
- Circuit stage $cir(2)$ and register stage $reg(2)$ are the *ID* stage. The circuit stage consists of the instruction decoder and the next PC environment. Signals A and B have been renamed *before* they enter circuit stage $cir(2)$. Signal Bin is only continued under the synonym B, but signal Ain is both used in the next PC environment and continued under the synonym A. The signals going from the instruction decoder to the next PC environment are denoted by $i2nextpc$:

$$i2nextpc = (bf, jump, jr, jalr, b, imm, iindex) \,.$$

Register stage 2 contains program counters pc and dpc, the operands A and B fetched from the GPRs, the incremented PC renamed to link address $linkad$, and the signals $i2ex$ going from the instruction decoder to the *EX* stage:

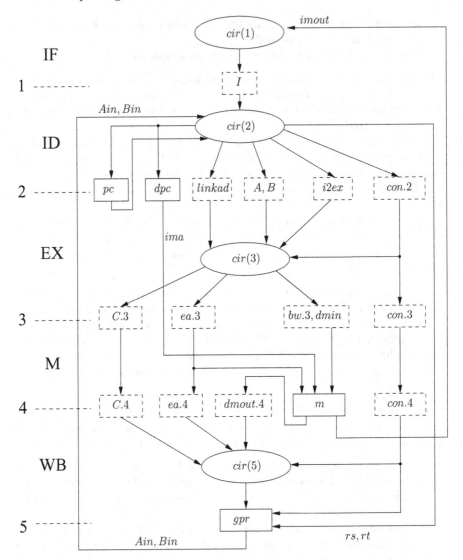

Fig. 116. Arranging the sequential MIPS design into pipeline stages

$$i2ex = (xtimm, af, sf, i, sa, smask) .$$

For some signals x there exist versions in various register stages k. In such situations we denote the version in register stage $reg(k)$ by $x.k$. In this sense we find in all register stages $k \geq 2$ versions $con.k$ of control signals that were precomputed in the instruction decoder. This group of signals comprises predicates $p.k$, instruction fields $F.k$ and the C-address $Cad.k$:

$$con.k = (\ldots, p.k, \ldots, F.k, \ldots, Cad.k) .$$

- Circuit stage $cir(3)$ and register stage $reg(3)$ are the execute stage. The circuit stage comprises the ALU-environment, the shift unit environment, an incrementer for the computation of $linkad$, multiplexers for the collection of $ares$, $sures$, and $linkad$ into intermediate result C, an adder for the computation of the effective address, and the sh4s-environment.
  Register stage 3 contains a version $C.3$ of intermediate result C, the effective address $ea.3$, the byte write signals $bw.3$, the data input $dmin$ for the hardware memory, and the copy $con.3$ of the control signals.
- Circuit stage $cir(4)$ and register stage $reg(4)$ are the M stage. The circuit stage consists only of wires; so we have not drawn it here. Register stage 4 contains a version $C.4$ of C, the output of the data port $dmout.4$ as well as versions $con.4$ and $ea.4$ of the control signals and the effective address. Note that we also have included the hardware memory m itself in this register stage.
- Circuit stage $cir(5)$ and register stage $reg(5)$ are the WB stage. The circuit stage contains the sh4l-environment (controlled by $ea.4.o$) and a multiplexer collecting $C.4$ and result $lres$ of the sh4l-environment into the data input $gprin$ of the general purpose register file. Register stage 5 consists of the general purpose register file.

For the purpose of constructing a first pipelined implementation of a MIPS processor we can simplify this picture even further:

- We distinguish in register stages k only between $visible$ (in ISA) registers pc, dpc and memories m, gpr on one side and other signals $x.k$ on the other side.
- Straight connections by wires, which in Fig. 116 are drawn as straight lines, are now included into the circuits $cir(i)$[3].
- For $k \in [1:5]$ circuit stage $cir(k)$ is input for register stage $k+1$ and for $k \in [1:4]$ register stage k is input to circuit stage $cir(k+1)$. We only hint these connections with small arrows and concentrate on the other connections.

We obtain Fig. 117. In the next section we will transform this simple figure with very little effort into a pipelined implementation of a MIPS processor.

7.2 Basic Pipelined Processor Design

7.2.1 Transforming the Sequential Design into a Pipelined Design

We transform the sequential processor design σ of the last section into a pipelined design π whose hardware configurations we will denote by h_π. We also introduce some shorthands for registers or memories R and circuit signals X in either design:

---

[3] This does not change circuits $cir(1)$ and $cir(2)$.

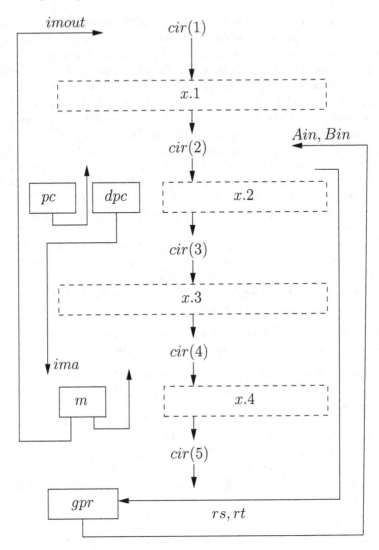

Fig. 117. Simplified view of register and circuit stages

$$R_\sigma^t = h_\sigma^t.R$$
$$R_\pi^t = h_\pi^t.R$$
$$X_\sigma^t = X(h_\sigma^t)$$
$$X_\pi^t = X(h_\pi^t) \, .$$

For signals or registers only occurring in the pipelined design, we drop the sub-script π. If an equation holds for all cycles (like equations describing hardware construction) we drop the index t.

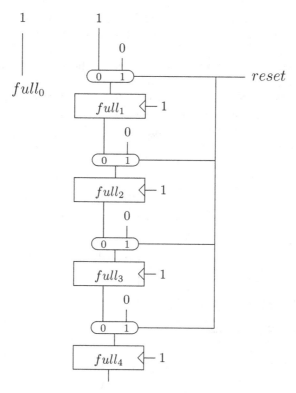

Fig. 118. Tracking full register stages with a basic stall engine

Table 8. Full bits track the filling of the register stages

t	0	1	2	3	≥ 4
$full_0^t$	1	1	1	1	1
$full_1^t$	0	1	1	1	1
$full_2^t$	0	0	1	1	1
$full_3^t$	0	0	0	1	1
$full_4^t$	0	0	0	0	1

The changes to design σ are explained very quickly:

- We turn all dotted boxes of all register stages into pipeline *registers* with the same name. Because their names do not occur in the ISA, they are only visible in the hardware design but not to the ISA programmer. Therefore they are called *non visible* or *implementation* registers. We denote visibility of a register or memory R by predicate $vis(R)$:

$$vis(R) = R \in \{pc, dpc, m, gpr\} .$$

- For indices k of register stages, we collect in $reg(k)$ all registers and memories of register stage k. We use a common clock enable ue_k for all registers of $reg(k)$.
- Initially after reset all register stages except the program counters contain no meaningful data. In the next 5 cycles they are filled one after another (Table 8). We introduce the hardware from Fig. 118 to keep track of this. There are 5 full bits $full[0 : 4]$, where the bit $full_k^t$ means that circuit stage $cir(k + 1)$ contains meaningful data in cycle t.
Formally we define

$$full_0 = 1$$
$$\forall k \geq 1 : full_k^0 = 0$$
$$\forall k \geq 1 : full_k^{t+1} = full_{k-1}^t .$$

We show

$$full[0 : 4]^t = \begin{cases} 1^{t+1}0^{4-t} & t \leq 3 \\ 1^5 & t \geq 4 \end{cases} \tag{17}$$

by the following simple lemma.

Lemma 7.2 (full bits).

$$\forall k, t \geq 0 : full_k^t = \begin{cases} 0 & t < k \\ 1 & t \geq k \end{cases}$$

Proof. For $k = 0$ we have for all $t \geq 0$:

$$t \geq 1 > 0 = k \quad , \quad full_0^t = 1 .$$

Thus, the lemma holds for $k = 0$. For $k \geq 1$ the lemma is shown by induction on t. For $t = 0$ we have

$$t < k \quad , \quad full_k^0 = 0 .$$

Thus, the lemma holds after reset. Assume the lemma holds for cycle t. Then

$$full_k^{t+1} = full_{k-1}^t$$
$$= \begin{cases} 0 & t < k - 1 \\ 1 & t \geq k - 1 \end{cases}$$
$$= \begin{cases} 0 & t + 1 < k \\ 1 & t + 1 \geq k . \end{cases}$$

$\square$

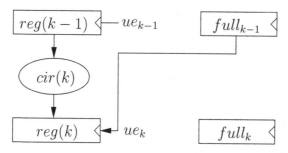

Fig. 119. Updating register stage k under control of the full bit $full_{k-1}$

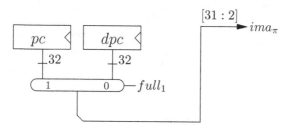

Fig. 120. Computation of the instruction address in the pipelined machine

Full bits being set to 0 prevent the update of register stages. This is also called stalling a register stage; we call the hardware therefore a basic *stall engine*. Other stall engines are introduced later.

- For any register stage k we update registers and memories in $reg(k)$ only if their input contains meaningful data, which is the case when the previous stage is full. As illustrated in Fig. 119 we set the update enable signal as

$$ue_k = full_{k-1} \ .$$

For registers in stage 1 we have a special case, where the signal $full_0$ is not coming from a register, but is always tied to 1.

- For memories m and gpr we take the precomputed signals $bw.3$ and $gprw.4$ from the precomputed control and AND them, respectively, with the corresponding update enable signals to get the new write signals:

$$bw_\pi = bw.3_\pi \wedge ue_4$$
$$gprw_\pi = gprw.4_\pi \wedge ue_5 \ .$$

- The address of the instruction is now computed as shown in Fig. 120 as

$$ima_\pi = \begin{cases} dpc_\pi.l & full_1 = 0 \\ pc_\pi.l & full_1 = 1 \ . \end{cases}$$

This has the remarkable effect that we fetch from the PC in all cycles except the very first one. Thus, the important role of the delayed PC is not in the hardware implementation but in the ISA, where it exposes the effect of the fact that instruction fetch and next PC computation are distributed over two stages. If we would join the two stages into a single one (by omitting the I-register), we would gain back the original instruction set, but we would ruin the efficiency of the design by roughly doubling the cycle time.

These are all changes we make to the sequential design σ.

7.2.2 Scheduling Functions

In the sequential design, there was a trivial correspondence between the hardware cycle t and the instruction $I(c^t)$ executed in that cycle. In the pipelined design π the situation is more complicated, because in 5 stages there are up to 5 different instructions which are in various stages of completion. For instructions $I(c^i)$ of the sequential computation we use the shorthand

$$I_i = I(c^i) .$$

We introduce scheduling functions

$$I : [1 : 5] \times \mathbb{N} \to \mathbb{N} ,$$

which keep track of the instructions being processed every cycle in every circuit stage. Intuitively, if

$$I(k, t) = i ,$$

then the registers of register stage k in cycle t are in the state *before* executing instruction I_i. In case register stage $k-1$ is full, this is equivalent to saying that instruction I_i during cycle t is being processed in circuit stage k. If register stage $k-1$ is not full, then circuit stage k does not have any meaningful input during cycle t, but I_i will be the next instruction which will eventually be processed by circuit stage k when register stage $k - 1$ becomes full. For both cases if $I(k, t) = i$ we say that instruction I_i is in circuit stage k during cycle t. Note that if some stages of the pipeline are not full, then one instruction is said to be present in several circuit stages simultaneously.

Formally the functions are defined with the help of the update enable functions ue_k in the following way:

$$\forall k : I(k, 0) = 0$$

$$I(1, t + 1) = \begin{cases} I(1, t) + 1 & ue_1^t = 1 \\ I(1, t) & \text{otherwise} \end{cases}$$

$$\forall k \geq 2 : I(k, t + 1) = \begin{cases} I(k - 1, t) & ue_k^t = 1 \\ I(k, t) & \text{otherwise} , \end{cases}$$

i.e., after reset every stage is in the state before executing instruction I_0. In circuit stage 1 we fetch a new instruction and increase the scheduling function

Table 9. Scheduling functions for the first 6 cycles

t	0	1	2	3	4	5
I(1,t)	0	1	2	3	4	5
I(2,t)	0	0	1	2	3	4
I(3,t)	0	0	0	1	2	3
I(4,t)	0	0	0	0	1	2
I(5,t)	0	0	0	0	0	1

every cycle (in the basic stall engine introduced thus far, stage 1 is always updated). A register stage k which has a predecessor stage $k - 1$ is updated or not in cycle t as indicated by the ue_t signal. If it is updated then the data of instruction $I(k, t)$ is written into the registers of stage k, and the circuit stage k in cycle $t + 1$ gets the instruction from the previous stage. Later we prove an easy lemma showing that this instruction is equal to the instruction in stage k in cycle t increased by one. If register stage k is not updated in cycle t then the scheduling function for this stage stays the same. Table 9 shows the development of the scheduling function in our basic pipeline for the first 6 cycles.

The definition of the scheduling functions can be viewed in the following way: imagine we extend each register stage $reg(k)$ by a so called *ghost* register $I(k, \quad)$ that can store arbitrary natural numbers. In real machines that is of course impossible because registers are finite, but for the purpose of mathematical argument we can add the ghost registers to the construction and update them like all other registers of their stage by ue_k. If we initialize the ghost register $I(1, \quad)$ of stage 1 with 0 and increase it by 1 every cycle, then the pipeline of ghost registers simply clocks the index of the current instruction through the pipeline together with the real data.

Augmenting real configurations for the purpose of mathematical argument by ghost components is a useful proof technique. No harm is done to the real construction as long as no information flows from the ghost components to the real components.

With the help of Lemma 7.2 we show the following property of the scheduling functions.

Lemma 7.3 (scheduling functions). For all $k \geq 1$ and for all t

$$I(k, t) = \begin{cases} 0 & t < k \\ t - k + 1 & t \geq k . \end{cases}$$

Proof. By induction on t. For $t = 0$ we have for all k

$$t < k \quad , \quad I(k, t) = 0 .$$

This shows the base case of the induction. Assume the lemma holds for t. In the induction step we consider two cases:

- $k = 1$: the claim of the lemma simplifies to

$$I(1, t+1) = (t+1) - 1 + 1$$
$$= t + 1$$

and we have by the definition of $I(1, \ )$ and by induction hypothesis for t:

$$I(1, t+1) = I(1, t) + 1$$
$$= t + 1 .$$

- $k \geq 2$: we have by Lemma 7.2

$$ue_k^t = full_{k-1}^t = (t \geq k - 1) .$$

Thus, by the definition of $I(1, \ )$ and by induction hypothesis for t we have

$$I(k, t+1) = \begin{cases} I(k, t) & \neg ue_k^t \\ I(k-1, t) & ue_k^t \end{cases}$$

$$= \begin{cases} I(k, t) & t < k - 1 \\ I(k-1, t) & t \geq k - 1 \end{cases}$$

$$= \begin{cases} 0 & t < k - 1 \\ t - (k-1) + 1 & t \geq k - 1 \end{cases}$$

$$= \begin{cases} 0 & t + 1 < k \\ t + 1 - k + 1 & t + 1 \geq k . \end{cases}$$

□

The following lemma relates the indices $I(k, t)$ and $I(k-1, t)$ in adjacent pipeline stages. They differ by 1 iff stage $k - 1$ is full.

Lemma 7.4 (scheduling function difference). Let $k > 1$, then

$$I(k-1, t) = \begin{cases} I(k, t) & full_{k-1}^t = 0 \\ I(k, t) + 1 & full_{k-1}^t = 1 . \end{cases}$$

Proof. By Lemmas 7.3 and 7.2 we have

$$I(k-1, t) - I(k, t)$$

$$= \begin{cases} 0 & t < k - 1 \\ t - (k-1) + 1 & t \geq k - 1 \end{cases} - \begin{cases} 0 & t < k \\ t - k + 1 & t \geq k \end{cases}$$

$$= \begin{cases} 0 - 0 & t < k - 1 \\ 1 - 0 & t = k - 1 \\ t - k + 2 - (t - k + 1) & t > k - 1 \end{cases}$$

$$= \begin{cases} 0 & t < k - 1 \\ 1 & t \geq k - 1 \end{cases}$$

$$= full_{k-1}^t .$$

□

From Lemma 7.4 we immediately conclude for $k > 1$

$$I(k,t) = I(k-1,t) - full^t_{k-1}$$

and for any $k' < k$ we have

$$I(k',t) = I(k,t) + \sum_{j=k'}^{k-1} full^t_j \ .$$

7.2.3 Use of Invisible Registers

Not all registers or memories R are used in all instructions $I(c^i)$. In the correctness theorem we need to show correct simulation of invisible registers only in situations when they are used. Therefore, we define for each invisible register X a predicate $used(X, I)$ which must *at least* be true for all instructions I, which require register X to be used for the computation. Some invisible registers will always be correctly simulated, though not all of them are always used. We define

$$\forall X \in \{I, i2ex, linkad, con.2, con.3, con.4, bw.3\} : used(X, I) = 1 \ .$$

Invisible register A is used when the GPR memory is addressed with rs, and B is used when it is accessed with rt.

We first define auxiliary predicates $A\text{-}used(I)$ and $B\text{-}used(I)$ that we will need later. Recall that in Sect. 6.3.8 we have written the functions $f(c)$ and the predicates $p(c)$ that only depend on the current instruction $I(c)$ as

$$f(c) = f'(I(c)) \qquad \text{and} \qquad p(c) = p'(I(c)) \ .$$

We will use the same notation here. Inspection of the tables summarizing the MIPS ISA gives

$$A\text{-}used(I) = alur'(I) \vee (su'(I) \wedge fun'(I)[2]) \vee jr'(I) \vee jalr'(I)$$
$$\vee \ (itype'(I) \wedge \neg lui'(I))$$
$$B\text{-}used(I) = s'(I) \vee beq'(I) \vee bne'(I) \vee su'(I) \vee alur'(I) \ .$$

Now we simply define[4]

$$used(A, I) = A\text{-}used(I)$$
$$used(B, I) = B\text{-}used(I) \ .$$

Registers $C.3$ and $C.4$ are used when the GPR memory is written but no load is performed:

---

[4] The notation is obviously redundant here, but later we also use *A-used* and *B-used* as hardware signals.

$$\forall X \in \{C.3, C.4\} : used(X, I) = gprw'(I) \wedge \neg l'(I) \ .$$

Registers $ea.3$ and $ea.4$ are used in load and store operations:

$$\forall X \in \{ea.3, ea.4\} : used(X, I) = l'(I) \vee s'(I) \ .$$

Register $dmin$ is used only in stores:

$$used(dmin, I) = s'(I) \ .$$

Finally, $dmout.4$ is used in loads:

$$used(dmout.4, I) = l'(I) \ .$$

7.2.4 Software Condition SC-1

We keep the software conditions of the sequential construction: alignment and no self modification due to disjoint code and data regions.

The new condition comes from the connection from circuit stage 2 to register stage 5 by the rs and rt signals. The scheduling functions for stages 2 and 5 are

$$I(2, t) = \begin{cases} 0 & t < 2 \\ t - 1 & t \geq 2 \end{cases}$$

$$I(5, t) = \begin{cases} 0 & t < 5 \\ t - 4 & t \geq 5 \ . \end{cases}$$

Thus, the indices of the instructions in stages ID and WB differ by

$$I(2, t) - I(5, t) = \begin{cases} 0 - 0 & t < 2 \\ t - 1 - 0 & 2 \leq t \leq 4 \\ t - 1 - (t - 4) & t \geq 5 \end{cases}$$

$$= \begin{cases} 0 & t < 2 \\ t - 1 & 2 \leq t \leq 4 \\ 3 & t \geq 5 \ . \end{cases}$$

Hence,

$$I(2, t) - I(5, t) \leq 3 \ . \tag{18}$$

Assume in cycle t instruction $I(2, t) = i$ is in circuit stage 2, i.e., the ID stage. Then signals rs and rt of this instruction overtake up to 3 instructions in circuit stages 2,3, and 4. If any of these overtaken instructions write to some general purpose register x and instruction i tries to read it - as in our basic design directly from the general purpose register file, then the data read will be stale; more recent data from an overtaken instruction is on the way to the

GPR but has not reached it yet. For the time being we will simply formulate a software condition SC-1 saying that this situation does not occur; we only prove that the basic pipelined design π works for ISA computations (c^i) which obey this condition. In later sections we will improve the design and get rid of the condition.

Therefore we formalize for $x \in \mathbb{B}^5$ and ISA configurations c two predicates:

- $writesgpr(x, i)$ - meaning ISA configuration c^i writes $gpr(x)$:

$$writesgpr(x, i) \equiv gprw(c^i) \wedge Cad(c^i) = x .$$

- $readsgpr(x, i)$ - meaning ISA configuration c^i reads $gpr(x)$. Reading $gpr(x)$ can occur via rs or the rt address, i.e., if A or B are used with address x:

$$readsgpr(x, i) \equiv used(A, I(c^i)) \wedge rs(c^i) = x \vee used(B, I(c^i)) \wedge rt(c^i) = x .$$

Now we can define the new software condition SC-1: for all i and x, if I_i writes $gpr(x)$, then instructions I_{i+1}, I_{i+2}, I_{i+3} don't read $gpr(x)$:

$$writesgpr(x, i) \rightarrow \forall j \in [i + 1 : i + 3] : \neg readsgpr(x, j) .$$

7.2.5 Correctness Statement

Now that we can express what instruction $I(k, t)$ is in stage k in cycle t and whether an invisible register is used in that instruction, we can formulate the invariant coupling states h_π^t of the pipelined machine with the set of states h_σ^i of the sequential machine that are processed in cycle t of the pipelined machine, i.e., the set

$$\{h_\sigma^{I(k,t)} \mid k \in [1 : 5]\} .$$

We intend to prove by induction on t the following simulation.

Lemma 7.5 (basic pipeline). Assume software condition SC-1, alignment, and no self modification. For $k \in [1 : 5]$ let $R \in reg(k)$ be a register or memory of register stage k. Then,

$$R_\pi^t = \begin{cases} R_\sigma^{I(k,t)} & vis(R) \\ R_\sigma^{I(k,t)-1} & full_k^t \wedge \neg vis(R) \wedge used(R, I_\sigma^{I(k,t)-1}) . \end{cases}$$

By Lemma 7.1 we already know $sim(c^t, h_\sigma^t)$. In particular we have for predicates p only depending on the current instruction I:

$$p(c^i) = p(h_\sigma^i) .$$

Thus, Lemma 7.5 also establishes a simulation between the pipelined computation (h_π^t) and the ISA computation (c^i).

Except for the subtraction of 1 from $I(k, t)$ for non visible registers, the induction hypothesis is quite intuitive: pipelined data $h_\pi^t.R$ in stage k in cycle

t is identical to the corresponding sequential data $h_\sigma^i.R$ resp. $c^i.R$ or $X(h_\sigma^{i-1})$ resp. $X(c^{i-1})$, where $i = I(k,t)$ is the index of the sequential instruction that is executed in cycle t in stage k of the pipelined machine.

The subtraction of 1 can be motivated by the fact that in the pipelined machine instructions i pass the pipeline from stage 1 to 5 unloading their results into the visible registers of stage k, when they are clocked into $reg(k)$. Now assume register stage $reg(k)$ contains a visible register R and a non visible register Q and let $I(k,t) = i$. Then by the intuitive portion of the induction hypothesis $R_\pi^t = R_\sigma^i$. Thus, the previous instruction $i-1$ is completed for the visible register R_π in stage k and the content of R_π is the content of register R_σ after execution of instruction $i-1$ resp. *before* execution of instruction i. The invisible register also contains the data produced by instruction $i-1$ (!), but since this register corresponds to a *signal* in ISA, then this signal has to be defined as a function of c^{i-1}. Indeed, if we did define it as a function of c^i (as we do with the visible registers), then this would correspond to the data produced by instruction i. Of course this is just motivation and is not to be confused with a proof.

7.2.6 Correctness Proof of the Basic Pipelined Design

We denote by $inv(k,t)$ the statement of Lemma 7.5 for stage k and cycle t.

Initialization of Register Stages

For $t = 0$ we have
$$full_k^0 = 1 \leftrightarrow k = 0 .$$
Thus, there is nothing to show for invisible registers. Initially we also have
$$\forall k : I(k,0) = 0 .$$
For visible registers one gets
$$pc_\pi^0 = 4 = pc_\sigma^0 = pc_\sigma^{I(2,0)}$$
$$dpc_\pi^0 = 0 = dpc_\sigma^0 = dpc_\sigma^{I(2,0)} .$$

The initial content of general purpose registers and hardware memory of the sequential machine is defined by the content of the pipelined machine after reset:
$$m_\pi^0 = m_\sigma^0 = m_\sigma^{I(4,0)}$$
$$gpr_\pi^0 = gpr_\sigma^0 = gpr_\sigma^{I(5,0)} .$$

Thus, we have
$$\forall k : inv(k,0) .$$

No Updates

Assume the lemma holds for t. We show for each stage k separately that the lemma holds for stage k and $t + 1$. For all stages we always proceed in the same way. There are two cases. The easy case is

$$ue_k^t = 0 \,,$$

i.e., register stage k is not updated in cycle t. By the definition of full bits we know

$$full_k^{t+1} = full_{k-1}^t = ue_k^t = 0 \,.$$

Thus, for invisible registers $R \in reg(k)$ there is nothing to show either. For the scheduling functions $ue_k^t = 0$ implies

$$I(k, t + 1) = I(k, t) \,.$$

Recall, that the byte write signals for the hardware memory and the write signal for the GPR memory are defined as

$$bw_\pi = bw.3_\pi \wedge ue_4$$
$$gprw_\pi = gprw.4_\pi \wedge ue_5 \,.$$

Hence, for visible registers or memories R of $reg(k)$ we get by induction hypothesis $inv(k, t)$:

$$
\begin{aligned}
R_\pi^{t+1} &= R_\pi^t \\
&= R_\sigma^{I(k,t)} \\
&= R_\sigma^{I(k,t+1)} \,.
\end{aligned}
$$

This shows $inv(k, t + 1)$ for stages k that are not updated in cycle t.

Scheduling Functions for Updated Stages

Lemma 7.6 (scheduling functions for updated stages).

$$ue_k^t \to I(k, t + 1) = I(k, t) + 1$$

Proof. We have $ue_k^t = full_{k-1}^t = 1$. For $k = 1$ we have by definition of the scheduling functions:

$$I(1, t + 1) = I(1, t) + 1 \,.$$

For $k \geq 2$, we have by Lemma 7.4 and the definition of the scheduling functions:

$$
\begin{aligned}
I(k, t + 1) &= I(k - 1, t) \\
&= I(k, t) + 1 \,.
\end{aligned}
$$

$\square$

Proof Obligations for the Induction Step

The case $ue_k^t = full_{k-1}^t = 1$ is handled for each stage separately. There are, however, for stages $k \in [1:5]$ and cycles t, general proof obligations $P(k,t)$ we have to show for visible registers, invisible registers, and memories in each register stage $reg(k)$, which will allow us to prove the induction step.

Let cycles t and instruction indices i correspond via

$$I(k,t) = i .$$

Then we define proof obligations $P(k,t)$ in the following way:

- For $k = 2$, visible registers of register stage $reg(2)$ in machines σ and π have identical inputs:

$$R \in \{pc, dpc\} \rightarrow Rin_\pi^t = Rin_\sigma^i .$$

- For $k = 4$, data memories in stage $reg(4)$ always have identical byte write signals bw and have the same effective address input ea and data input $dmin$ in case of a store operation:

$$bw_\pi^t = bw_\sigma^i$$
$$s_\sigma^i \rightarrow ea_\pi^t = ea_\sigma^i \wedge dmin_\pi^t = dmin_\sigma^i .$$

- For $k = 5$, GPRs in stage $reg(5)$ always have identical GPR write signal $gprw$, and have the same write address Cad and the same data input $gprin$ in case if instruction i is writing to GPRs:

$$gprw_\pi^t = gprw_\sigma^i$$
$$gprw_\sigma^i \rightarrow Cad_\pi^t = Cad_\sigma^i \wedge gprin_\pi^t = gprin_\sigma^i .$$

- For any k, invisible registers of register stage $reg(k)$ in machines σ and π that are used have identical inputs:

$$R \in reg(k) \wedge \neg vis(R) \wedge used(R, I_\sigma^i) \rightarrow Rin_\pi^t = Rin_\sigma^i .$$

Note that, in the sequential machine, an input to an invisible register in cycle i is the same as the "value" of the invisible register in cycle i. This is due to the fact that invisible "registers" are actually signals in a sequential machine.

Very simple arguments show that $P(k,t)$ and $inv(k,t)$ implies $inv(k,t+1)$, i.e., proving $P(k,t)$ suffices to complete the induction step for stage k.

Lemma 7.7 (basic pipeline induction step).

$$ue_k^t \wedge P(k,t) \wedge inv(k,t) \rightarrow inv(k,t+1)$$

Proof. Let $R \in reg(k)$. The proof hinges on Lemma 7.6 and splits cases in the obvious way:

- $R \in \{pc, dpc\}$ is a visible register. Because the register has in both machines the same input, it gets updated in both machines in the same way:

$$R_\pi^{t+1} = Rin_\pi^t$$
$$= Rin_\sigma^i$$
$$= R_\sigma^{i+1}$$
$$= R_\sigma^{I(k,t+1)} .$$

- R is invisible and used in c^i, where $i = I(k,t) = I(k, t+1) - 1$. Then R_π is updated, but in the sequential machine Rin and R are just synonyms:

$$R_\pi^{t+1} = Rin_\pi^t$$
$$= Rin_\sigma^i$$
$$= R_\sigma^i$$
$$= R_\sigma^{I(k,t)}$$
$$= R_\sigma^{I(k,t+1)-1} .$$

- $R = m$ is a hardware memory. From Sec. 6.3.16 we have

$$\neg s_\sigma^i \rightarrow bw_\sigma^i = 0^8.$$

Moreover, from the software conditions we know that $ea_\sigma^i.l \in DR$ and that the data region DR is disjoint from the ROM portion of the hardware memory. Then for all $a \in \mathbb{B}^{29}$ we get

$$m_\pi^{t+1}(a) = \begin{cases} modify(m_\pi^t(a), dmin_\pi^t, bw_\pi^t) & a = ea_\pi^t.l \\ m_\pi^t(a) & \text{otherwise} \end{cases}$$
$$= \begin{cases} modify(m_\sigma^i(a), dmin_\sigma^i, bw_\sigma^i) & a = ea_\sigma^i.l \\ m_\sigma^i(a) & \text{otherwise} . \end{cases}$$
$$= m_\sigma^{i+1}(a)$$
$$= m_\sigma^{I(k,t+1)}(a) .$$

- $R = gpr$ is a GPR memory. Then we conclude:

$$gpr_\pi^{t+1}(x) = \begin{cases} gprin_\pi^t & gprw_\pi^t \wedge x = Cad_\pi^t \\ gpr_\pi^t(x) & \text{otherwise} \end{cases}$$
$$= \begin{cases} gprin_\sigma^i & gprw_\sigma^i \wedge x = Cad_\sigma^i \\ gpr_\sigma^i(x) & \text{otherwise} \end{cases}$$
$$= gpr_\sigma^{i+1}(x)$$
$$= gpr_\sigma^{I(k,t+1)}(x) .$$

$\square$

It remains to prove hypothesis $P(k, t)$ of Lemma 7.7 for each stage k separately under the assumption that the simulation relation holds for all stages in cycle t and update enable for stage k is on.

Lemma 7.8 (proof obligations basic pipeline).

$$(\forall k' : inv(k', t)) \wedge ue_k^t \to P(k, t) \ .$$

Proof. We prove the statement of the lemma by a case split on stage k. For each *circuit stage* $cir(k)$ we identify a set of input signals $in(k)$ of the stage which are identical in cycle t of π and in the configuration i of σ:

$$in(k)_\pi^t = in(k)_\sigma^i \ .$$

We then show that these inputs determine the relevant outputs Rin, $dmin$, etc. of the circuit stage. Because the circuit stages are identical in both machines, this suffices for showing that the outputs which are used have identical values. Unfortunately, the proofs require simple but tedious bookkeeping about the invisible registers used. The only real action is in the proofs for signals Ain, Bin, and ima.

Stage *IF* ($k=1$)

We first consider the address input ima of the instruction port. We consider the multiplexer in Fig. 120, which selects between visible registers $pc, dpc \in reg(2)$, and distinguish two cases:

- $t = 0$. Then $full_1^t = 0$ and $I(1, 0) = I(2, 0) = 0$. We conclude with $inv(2, 0)$:

$$\begin{aligned}
ima_\pi^0 &= dpc_\pi^0.l \\
&= dpc_\sigma^{I(2,0)}.l \\
&= dpc_\sigma^0.l \\
&= ima_\sigma^0 \\
&= ima_\sigma^{I(1,0)} \ .
\end{aligned}$$

- $t \geq 1$. Then $full_1^t = 1$. By Lemma 7.4 we have

$$i = I(1, t) = I(2, t) + full_1^t = I(2, t) + 1 \ .$$

Using $inv(2, t)$ and the definition of the delayed PC we conclude:

$$\begin{aligned}
ima_\pi^t &= pc_\pi^t.l \\
&= pc_\sigma^{I(2,t)}.l \\
&= dpc_\sigma^{I(2,t)+1}.l \\
&= dpc_\sigma^i.l \\
&= ima_\sigma^i \ .
\end{aligned}$$

From the software condition we know that $ima_\sigma^i \in CR$ and that the content of the code region does not change during the execution. Using $inv(4, t)$ we get

$$
\begin{aligned}
imout_\pi^t &= m_\pi^t(ima_\pi^t) \\
&= m_\sigma^{I(4,t)}(ima_\sigma^i) \\
&= m_\sigma^0(ima_\sigma^i) \\
&= m_\sigma^i(ima_\sigma^i) \\
&= imout_\sigma^i .
\end{aligned}
$$

Thus, the instruction port environment has in both machines the same input; therefore it produces the same output:

$$
Iin_\pi^t = Iin_\sigma^i ,
$$

i.e., we have shown $P(1, t)$ and thus by Lemma 7.7 $inv(1, t + 1)$.

Stage ID ($k = 2$)

From $ue_2^t = full_1^t$ we know that $t > 0$. Hence, by Lemma 7.4 we have:

$$
I(1, t) = I(2, t) + 1 .
$$

Let

$$
i = I(2, t) = I(1, t) - 1 .
$$

There are three kinds of input signals for the circuits $cir(2)$ of this stage:

- Signal from invisible register $I \in reg(1)$. It is always used. With $inv(1, t)$ we get:
$$
I_\pi^t = I_\sigma^{I(1,t)-1} = I_\sigma^i .
$$
This already determines the inputs of invisible registers $con.2$ and $i2ex$:
$$
R \in \{con.2, i2ex\} \rightarrow Rin_\pi^t = Rin_\sigma^i .
$$
It also determines the signals $i2nextpc$ from the instruction decoder to the next PC environment so that we have for these signals:
$$
i2nextpc_\pi^t = i2nextpc_\sigma^i .
$$

- Signals from visible registers $pc, dpc \in reg(2)$ which are inputs to the next PC environment. From $inv(2, t)$ we get immediately:
$$
R \in \{pc, dpc\} \rightarrow R_\pi^t = R_\sigma^i .
$$

- For inputs Ain and Bin of circuit stage $cir(2)$ we have to make use of software condition SC-1, which is stated on the MIPS ISA level. Hence, we assume here that the sequential MIPS implementation is correct (Lemma 7.1), i.e., that we always have

$$\forall j \geq 0 : sim(c^j, h^j_\sigma).$$

Let register A be used in instruction i to access $gpr \in reg(5)$ via rs:

$$used(A, I^i_\sigma).$$

Let

$$x = rs^t_\pi = rs^i_\sigma = rs(c^i) ,$$

i.e., instruction $I(2,t)$ reads $gpr(x)$:

$$readsgpr(x, I(2,t)) .$$

By (18) we have

$$I(5,t) \leq I(2,t) + 3 = i + 3 .$$

If any of instructions $I(3,t)$, $I(4,t)$, $I(5,t)$ would write $gpr(x)$, this would violate software condition SC-1. Thus,

$$\forall k \in [3:5] : \neg writesgpr(x, I(k,t)) .$$

Hence,

$$gpr_\sigma^{I(2,t)}(x) = gpr_\sigma^{I(5,t)}(x) .$$

Using $inv(5,t)$ we conclude:

$$
\begin{aligned}
Ain^t_\pi &= gpr^t_\pi(x) \\
&= gpr_\sigma^{I(5,t)}(x) \\
&= gpr_\sigma^{I(2,t)}(x) \\
&= Ain^i_\sigma .
\end{aligned}
$$

Arguing about signal $Bin = B'$ in the same way we conclude

$$used(B, I^i_\sigma) \rightarrow Bin^t_\pi = Bin^i_\sigma .$$

For the input to invisible register $linkad$ we have from $inv(2,t)$ and because $t \geq 1$:

$$
\begin{aligned}
linkadin^t_\pi &= pcinc^t_\pi \\
&= pc^t_\pi +_{32} 4_{32} \\
&= pc^i_\sigma +_{32} 4_{32} \\
&= linkadin^i_\sigma .
\end{aligned}
$$

It remains to argue about the inputs of visible registers pc and dpc, i.e., about signals $nextpc$ and register pc which is the input of dpc. For the input pc of dpc we have from $inv(2, t)$ and because $t \geq 1$:

$$dpcin_\pi^t = pc_\pi^t = pc_\sigma^i = dpcin_\sigma^i .$$

For the computation of the $nextpc$ signal there are four cases:

- $be_\sigma^i \vee bne_\sigma^i$. This is the easiest case, because it implies $used(A, I_\sigma^i) \wedge used(B, I_\sigma^i)$ and we have

$$in_\pi^t = in_\sigma^i$$

  for all inputs $in \in \{A, B, i2nextpc\}$ of the next PC environment. Because the environment is identical in both machines we conclude

$$pcin_\pi^t = nextpc_\pi^t = nextpc_\sigma^i = pcin_\sigma^i$$

  and are done.
- $b_\sigma^i \wedge \neg(be_\sigma^i \vee bne_\sigma^i)$. Then we have $used(A, I_\sigma^i)$ and for signal d in the branch evaluation unit we have

$$d_\pi^t = 0^{32} = d_\sigma^i .$$

  And hence,

$$jbtaken_\pi^t = jbtaken_\sigma^i$$
$$btarget_\pi^t = btarget_\sigma^i$$
$$nextpc_\pi^t = nextpc_\sigma^i .$$

- $jr_\sigma^i \vee jalr_\sigma^i$. Then $used(A, I_\sigma^i)$ and

$$nextpc_\pi^t = Ain_\pi^t = Ain_\sigma^i = nextpc_\sigma^i .$$

- $j_\sigma^i \vee jal_\sigma^i$. Then with $inv(2, t)$ we have:

$$nextpc_\pi^t = (pc_\pi^t +_{32} 4_{32})iindex_\pi^t 00$$
$$= (pc_\sigma^i +_{32} 4_{32})iindex_\sigma^i 00$$
$$= nextpc_\sigma^i .$$

- In all other cases we have:

$$nextpc_\pi^t = pc_\pi^t +_{32} 4_{32} = pc_\sigma^i +_{32} 4_{32} = nextpc_\sigma^i .$$

This concludes the proof of $P(2, t)$.

Stage EX ($k = 3$)

From $ue_3^t = full_2^t$ we know that $t > 1$. Hence, by Lemma 7.4 we have:

$$I(2, t) = I(3, t) + 1 .$$

Let

$$i = I(3, t) = I(2, t) - 1 .$$

We have to consider three kinds of input signals for the circuits $cir(3)$ of this stage:

- Invisible registers $i2ex$, $con.2$, and $linkad$. They are always used. Using $inv(2, t)$ we get:

$$X \in \{i2ex, con.2, linkad\} \rightarrow X_\pi^t = X_\sigma^{I(2,t)-1} = X_\sigma^i .$$

  Because $con.2 = con.3in$ this shows $P(3, t)$ for the pipelined control register $con.3$,
- Invisible registers A and B. From $inv(2, t)$ we have:

$$X \in \{A, B\} \wedge used(X, I_\sigma^i) \rightarrow X_\pi^t = X_\sigma^i .$$

We proceed to show $P(3, t)$ for registers $dmin$, $bw.3$, register ea, and register $C.3$ separately:

- For ea we have

$$used(ea, I_\sigma^i) = l_\sigma^i \vee s_\sigma^i$$
$$l_\sigma^i \vee s_\sigma^i \rightarrow used(A, I_\sigma^i) .$$

  Register $i2ex$ is always used. Because ea depends only on A and $i2ex$ we conclude from $inv(2, t)$:

$$eain_\pi^t = eain_\sigma^i .$$

- For $bw.3$, the signal $smask_\pi^t$ is also taken from $i2ex$, which is always used. Hence, we have

$$smask_\pi^t = smask_\sigma^i .$$

We do a case split on whether a store is performed or not:
  - $\neg s_\sigma^i$. In this case we have

$$smask_\pi^t = smask_\sigma^i$$
$$= 0000 .$$

  Thus, we get

$$bw.3in_\pi^t = 0^8$$
$$= bw_\sigma^i$$
$$= bw.3in_\sigma^i .$$

- s_σ^i. For this case we have already shown that

$$eain_\pi^t = eain_\sigma^i .$$

Since computation of byte-write signals depends only on $smask$ and $eain$, we obviously get

$$bw.3in_\pi^t = bw_\sigma^i = bw.3in_\sigma^i .$$

- For $dmin$ we have

$$used(dmin, I_\sigma^i) = s_\sigma^i$$
$$s_\sigma^i \rightarrow itype_\sigma^i \wedge \neg lui_\sigma^i$$

and hence,

$$used(dmin, I_\sigma^i) \rightarrow used(A, I_\sigma^i) \wedge used(B, I_\sigma^i) .$$

With $inv(2,t)$ we conclude

$$X_\pi^t = X_\sigma^i$$

for all inputs X of $cir(3)$ and conclude trivially

$$dminin_\pi^t = dminin_\sigma^i .$$

- For $C.3$ we need a larger case split. We have

$$used(C.3, I_\sigma^i) = alu_\sigma^i \vee su_\sigma^i \vee jal_\sigma^i \vee jalr_\sigma^i .$$

This results in 4 subcases:
- $alur_\sigma^i \vee su_\sigma^i \wedge fun_\sigma^i[3]$. Then

$$used(A, I_\sigma^i) \wedge used(B, I_\sigma^i) .$$

With $inv(2,t)$ we trivially conclude as above

$$C.3in_\pi^t = C.3in_\sigma^i .$$

- $alui_\sigma^i$. Then $used(A, I_\sigma^i)$ and

$$rop_\pi^t = xtimm_\pi^t = xtimm_\sigma^i = rop_\sigma^i .$$

Hence, $alures$ is independent of B and we conclude

$$C.3in_\pi^t = alures_\pi^t = alures_\sigma^i = C.3in_\sigma^i .$$

- $su_\sigma^i \wedge \neg fun_\sigma^i[3]$. Then $used(A, I_\sigma^i)$ and

$$sdist_\pi^t = sa_\pi^t = sa_\sigma^i = sdist_\sigma^i .$$

Hence $sures$ is independent of B and we conclude

$$C.3in_\pi^t = sures_\pi^t = sures_\sigma^i = C.3in_\sigma^i .$$

- $jal_\sigma^i \vee jalr_\sigma^i$. Then

$$C.3in_\pi^t = linkad_\pi^t = linkad_\sigma^i = C.3in_\sigma^i .$$

This concludes the proof of $P(3,t)$.

Stage M $(k = 4)$

From $ue_4^t = full_3^t$ we know that $t > 2$. Hence, by Lemma 7.4 we have:

$$I(3, t) = I(4, t) + 1 .$$

Let

$$i = I(4, t) = I(3, t) - 1 .$$

We have to argue about 3 kinds of signals:

- $X \in \{dmin, con.3, ea.3, C.3\}$. From $inv(3, t)$ we have:

$$used(X, I_\sigma^i) \rightarrow X_\pi^t = X_\sigma^{I(3,t)-1} = X_\sigma^i .$$

  This shows $P(4, t)$ for the data inputs of registers $con.4$, $ea.4$, and $C.4$.
- $dmout.4$. We have

$$used(dmout.4, I_\sigma^i) \rightarrow l_\sigma^i \wedge used(ea, I_\sigma^i) .$$

Using $inv(3, t)$ for ea and $dmin$ as well as $inv(4, t)$ for m we get:

$$\begin{aligned}
dmout_\pi^t &= m_\pi^t(ea.l_\pi^t) \\
&= m_\sigma^i(ea.l_\sigma^{I(3,t)-1}) \\
&= dmout_\sigma^i .
\end{aligned}$$

This shows $P(4, t)$ for the input $dmout$ of register $dmout.4$.
- memory inputs. The register $bw.3$ is always used. Thus, we have from $inv(3, t)$:

$$\begin{aligned}
bw.3_\pi^t &= bw_\sigma^{I(3,t)-1} \\
&= bw_\sigma^i \\
bw_\pi^t &= bw.3_\pi^t \wedge ue_4^t \\
&= bw_\sigma^i ,
\end{aligned}$$

For the effective address and the data input to the hardware memory we have

$$s_\sigma^i \rightarrow used(ea.3, I_\sigma^i) \wedge used(dmin, I_\sigma^i) .$$

As shown above, this implies in case of s_σ^i:

$$\begin{aligned}
dmin_\pi^t &= dmin_\sigma^i \\
ea_\pi^t &= ea.3_\pi^t \\
&= ea_\sigma^i .
\end{aligned}$$

Stage WB ($k = 5$)

From $ue_5^t = full_4^t$ we know that $t > 3$. Hence, by Lemma 7.4 we have

$$I(4, t) = I(5, t) + 1 .$$

Let

$$i = I(5, t) = I(4, t) - 1 .$$

We only have to consider the input registers of the stage and to show $P(4, t)$ for the general purpose register file:

- All input registers are invisible thus let $X \in \{C.4, dmout.4, ea.4, con.4\}$. From $inv(4, t)$ we have:

$$used(X, I_\sigma^i) \rightarrow X_\pi^t = X_\sigma^i .$$

- Signal $gprw.4$ is a component of $con.4$. Thus, we have:

$$gprw.4_\pi^t = gprw_\sigma^i$$
$$gprw_\pi^t = gprw.4_\pi^t \wedge ue_5^t$$
$$= gprw_\sigma^i .$$

Signal $Cad.4$ is a component of $con.4$. Thus

$$Cad.4_\pi^t = Cad_\sigma^i .$$

Assume $gprw_\sigma^i$, i.e., the general purpose register file, is written. We have to consider two subcases:

– A load is performed. Then $dmout.4$ and $ea.4$ are both used, load result $lres$ is identical for both computations and the data input $gprin$ for the general purpose register file comes for both computations from $lres$:

$$l_\sigma^i \rightarrow used(dmout.4, I_\sigma^i) \wedge used(ea.4, I_\sigma^i)$$
$$dmin_\pi^t = lres_\pi^t$$
$$= lres_\sigma^i$$
$$= dmin_\sigma^i .$$

– No load is performed. Then $C.4$ is used and it is put to the data input $gprin$:

$$\neg s_\sigma^i \rightarrow used(C.4, I_\sigma^i)$$
$$dmin_\pi^t = C.4_\pi^t$$
$$= C_\sigma^i$$
$$= dmin_\sigma^i .$$

This completes the proof of $P(5, t)$, the proof of Lemma 7.8, and the correctness proof of the basic pipeline design.

$\square$

7.3 Forwarding

Software condition SC-1 forbids to read a general purpose register $gpr(x)$ that is written by instruction i in the following three instructions $i + 1$, $i + 2$, and $i + 3$. We needed this condition because with the basic pipelined machine constructed so far we had to wait until the written data had reached the general purpose register file, simply because that's where we accessed them. This situation is greatly improved by the forwarding circuits studied in this section.

7.3.1 Hits

The improvement is based on two very simple observations. Let cycle t be the cycle when we want to read in circuit stage $cir(2)$ register content $gpr(x)$ into register A or B. First, it is easy to recognize instructions in the deeper register stages $reg(k)$, with $k \in [2 : 4]$, that write into $gpr(x)$:

- The stage must be full:
$$full_k^t .$$

  Otherwise it contains no meaningful data.
- The C-address must coincide with the rs address or the rt address (note that these addresses are signals of circuit stage $cir(2)$):
$$Cad.k^t = rs^t \quad \text{or} \quad Cad.k^t = rt^t .$$

- The instruction in stage k must write to the general purpose register file:
$$gprw.k^t .$$

We introduce for registers A and B separate predicates characterizing this situation:
$$hit_A[k] \equiv full_k \wedge Cad.k = rs \wedge gprw.k.$$
$$hit_B[k] \equiv full_k \wedge Cad.k = rt \wedge gprw.k .$$

Second, in case we have a hit in stage $reg(2)$ or $reg(3)$ and the instruction is not a load instruction, then the data we want to fetch into A or B can be found as the input of the C register of the following circuit stage, i.e., as $C.3in$ or $C.4in$. In case of a hit in stage $reg(4)$ we can find the required data at the data input $grpin$ of the general purpose register file, even for loads.

7.3.2 Forwarding Circuits

All we have to do now is to construct circuits recognizing hits and forwarding the required data – where possible – to circuit stage $cir(2)$. In case of simultaneous hits in several stages we are interested in the data of the most

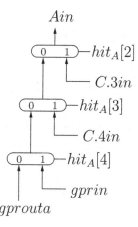

Fig. 121. Forwarding circuit For_A

recent instruction producing a hit. This is the "top" instruction in the pipe (i.e., with the smallest k) producing a hit:

$$top_A[k] = hit_A[k] \wedge \bigwedge_{j<k} \overline{hit_A[j]}.$$

$$top_B[k] = hit_B[k] \wedge \bigwedge_{j<k} \overline{hit_B[j]} .$$

Obviously, top hits are unique, i.e., for $X \in \{A, B\}$ we have

$$top_X[i] \wedge top_X[j] \to i = j .$$

Figure 121 shows the forwarding circuit For_A. If we find nothing to forward we access the general purpose register file as in the basic design. We have:

$$Ain = \begin{cases} C.3in & top_A[2] \\ C.4in & top_A[3] \\ gprin & top_A[4] \\ gprouta & \text{otherwise} . \end{cases}$$

Construction of the forwarding circuit For_B is completely analogous.

7.3.3 Software Condition SC-2

Forwarding will only fail if instruction i is a load with destination $gpr(x)$ and the register x is read by one of the next two instructions $i + 1$ or $i + 2$. Hence, we formulate a weaker software condition SC-2 which takes care of such situations:

$$l(c^i) \wedge Cad(c^i) = x \wedge j \in [i+1 : i+2] \rightarrow \neg readsgpr(x, j) .$$

The correctness statement formulated in Lemma 7.5 stays the same as before. Only software condition SC-1 is replaced by conditions SC-2.

7.3.4 Scheduling Functions Revisited

For the correctness proof we need a very technical lemma which states in a nutshell that in the pipeline instructions are not lost.

Lemma 7.9 (no instructions lost). Let $s(t)$ be the number of full stages in between stages 2 and 5:

$$s(t) = \sum_{j=2}^{4} full_j^t .$$

Further, let

$$i = I(2,t) = I(5,t) + s(t) ,$$

let $s(t) > 0$ and $0 \le j < s(t)$. Then

$$I(2+j,t) = i - j \qquad \text{and} \qquad full_{2+j}^t ,$$

i.e., any instruction $i - j$ between i and $i - s(t)$ is found in the full register stage $2 + j$ between stages 2 and 5.

Proof. From Lemma 7.3 we get

$$I(2,t) = \begin{cases} 0 & t < 2 \\ t-1 & t \ge 2 \end{cases}$$

$$= I(5,t) + s(t)$$

$$\ge 1 .$$

Hence, $t \ge 2$ and

$$I(2,t) = t - 1 \ge s(t) .$$

Thus,

$$t \ge s(t) + 1 > 1 + j ,$$

which implies

$$t \ge 2 + j .$$

Applying again Lemma 7.3 we get

$$I(2+j,t) = \begin{cases} 0 & t < 2+j \\ t-(2+j)+1 & t \ge 2+j \end{cases}$$

$$= t - 1 - j$$

$$= i - j .$$

From Lemma 7.2 we get

$$full_{2+j}^t = t \ge j + 2 = 1 .$$

$\square$

7.3.5 Correctness Proof

The only case in the proof affected by the addition of the two forwarding circuits For_A and For_B is the proof of $P(2, t)$ in Lemma 7.8 for signals Ain and Bin. Also the order in which proof obligations $P(k, t)$ are shown becomes important: one proves $P(2, t)$ after $P(3, t)$, $P(4, t)$, and $P(5, t)$.

We present the modified proof for Ain. The proof for Bin is completely analogous. Assume

$$ue_2^t = full_1^t = 1 ,$$

and let

$$i = I(2, t) .$$

Our goal is to show that the forwarding circuit outputs the same content of the GPR register file, as we get in the sequential configuration i:

$$Ain_\pi^t = gpr_\sigma^i(rs_\sigma^i)$$
$$= Ain_\sigma^i .$$

As before, in order to make use of the software condition which is stated on the MIPS ISA level, we assume that the sequential MIPS implementation is correct (Lemma 7.1), i.e., that we always have

$$\forall j \geq 0 : sim(c^j, h_\sigma^j).$$

Let us consider some full stage $k \in [2 : 4]$:

$$k \in [2 : 4] \wedge full_k^t .$$

Then by Lemma 7.2 stage k and all preceding stages must be full in cycle t

$$\forall j \leq k : full_j^t ,$$

and we can use induction hypothesis $inv(j, t)$ for the invisible registers. Let

$$k = 2 + \alpha \quad \text{with} \quad \alpha \in [0 : 2] .$$

For the scheduling function for stages k and $k + 1$ we get by Lemma 7.4

$$I(2 + \alpha, t) = I(k, t)$$
$$= \begin{cases} I(2, t) & k = 2 \\ I(2, t) - \sum_{j=2}^{k-1} full_j^t & k > 2 \end{cases}$$
$$= i - (k - 2)$$
$$= i - \alpha$$
$$I(3 + \alpha, t) = I(k + 1, t)$$
$$= I(k, t) - full_k^t$$
$$= i - \alpha - 1 .$$

Lemma 7.10 (hit signal). Let $i = I(2, t)$ and

$$x = rs_\sigma^i \wedge k = 2 + \alpha \wedge full_k^t .$$

Then,

$$hit_A^t[k] = writesgpr(x, i - \alpha - 1) .$$

Proof. For the hit signal under consideration we can conclude with $inv(k, t)$ for the invisible registers $Cad.k$ and $gprw.k$ and with $inv(1, t)$ for the signal rs:

$$
\begin{aligned}
hit_A[k]^t &\equiv full_k^t \wedge Cad.k_\pi^t = rs_\pi^t \wedge gprw.k_\pi^t \\
&\equiv Cad_\sigma^{I(k,t)-1} = rs_\sigma^i \wedge gprw_\sigma^{I(k,t)-1} \\
&\equiv Cad_\sigma^{i-\alpha-1} = x \wedge gprw_\sigma^{i-\alpha-1} \\
&\equiv writesgpr(x, i - \alpha - 1) .
\end{aligned}
$$

$\square$

Now assume

$$hit_A[k]^t \wedge k = 2 + \alpha \wedge x = rs_\sigma^i .$$

Then by Lemma 7.10 we have $writesgpr(x, i - \alpha - 1)$. For $\alpha \in [0 : 1]$ and exploiting the fact that instruction i reads GPR x we can also conclude from software condition SC-2 that instruction $i - \alpha - 1$ is not a load instruction:

$$\alpha \in [0 : 1] \wedge hit_A[2 + \alpha]^t \rightarrow \neg l(c^{i-\alpha-1}) .$$

This in turn implies that registers $C.3$ and $C.4$ are used by instruction $i-\alpha-1$, i.e.,

$$used(C.(3 + \alpha), I(c^{i-\alpha-1})) ,$$

and that the content of these registers is written into register x by this instruction. Thus, we can apply $P(3, t)$ and $P(4, t)$ to conclude

$$
\begin{aligned}
C.(3 + \alpha)in_\pi^t &= C.(3 + \alpha)_\sigma^{I(3+\alpha,t)} \\
&= C.(3 + \alpha)_\sigma^{i-\alpha-1} \\
&= gprin_\sigma^{i-\alpha-1} \\
&= gpr_\sigma^{i-\alpha}(x) .
\end{aligned}
$$

If we have $hit_A[2 + \alpha]^t$ for $\alpha = 2$ we conclude from $gprw_\sigma^{i-\alpha-1}$ and the proof of $P(5, t)$

$$
\begin{aligned}
gprin_\pi^t &= gprin_\sigma^{I(5,t)} \\
&= gprin_\sigma^{I(3+\alpha,t)} \\
&= gprin_\sigma^{i-\alpha-1} \\
&= gpr_\sigma^{i-\alpha}(x) .
\end{aligned}
$$

The proof of $P(2, t)$ for Ain can now be completed. There are two major cases:

- There exists a hit: $\exists \alpha \in [0:2] : hit_A[2+\alpha]^t$. In this case we take the smallest such α and have

$$top_A[2+\alpha]^t .$$

For the output Ain of forwarding circuit For_A we conclude

$$Ain_\pi^t = \begin{cases} C.(3+\alpha)in^t & \alpha \le 1 \\ gprin_\pi^t & \alpha = 2 \end{cases}$$

$$= gpr_\sigma^{i-\alpha}(x) .$$

If $\alpha = 0$ we have

$$gpr_\sigma^{i-\alpha}(x) = gpr_\sigma^i(x)$$

and we are done. Otherwise we have

$$I(2+\alpha, t) = I(2, t) - \alpha \qquad \text{and} \qquad \alpha \ge 1 .$$

Since all the stages up to stage $2+\alpha$ are full, we can apply Lemma 7.9 to conclude

$$j \in [0:\alpha-1] \rightarrow full_{2+j}^t \wedge I(2+j, t) = i - j .$$

From $\neg hit_A[2+j]^t$ we conclude by Lemma 7.10 for all such j

$$\neg writesgpr(x, i - j - 1) .$$

This implies again

$$gpr_\sigma^{i-\alpha}(x) = gpr_\sigma^i(x)$$

and we are done.

- No hit exists: $\forall \alpha \in [0:2] : \neg hit_A[2+\alpha]^t$. For the output Ain of the forwarding circuit we have

$$Ain_\pi^t = gpr_\pi^t(x)$$
$$= gpr_\sigma^{I(5,t)}(x) .$$

If $I(5, t) = i$ we are done. Otherwise let $s(t)$ denote the number of full stages between 2 and 4 and we have

$$I(5, t) = i - s(t) .$$

Applying again Lemma 7.9 we conclude for the instructions $i - j$ between i and $i - s(t)$

$$j \in [0:s(t)-1] \rightarrow full_{2+j}^t \wedge I(2+j, t) = i - j .$$

From $\neg hit_A[2+j]^t$ we conclude by Lemma 7.10 for all such j

$$\neg writesgpr(x, i - j - 1) .$$

This implies

$$gpr_\sigma^{I(5,t)}(x) = gpr_\sigma^{i-s(t)}(x)$$
$$= gpr_\sigma^i(x)$$

and we are done.

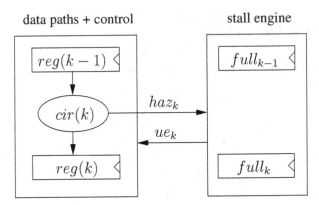

data paths + control   stall engine

Fig. 122. Signals between data paths and control and the stall engine

7.4 Stalling

In this last section of the pipelining chapter we use a non trivial stall engine, which permits to improve the pipelined machine π such that we can drop software condition SC-2. As shown in Fig. 122 the new stall engine receives from every circuit stage $cir(k)$ an input signal haz_k indicating that register stage $reg(k)$ should not be clocked, because correct input signals are not available.

In case a hazard signal haz_k is active the improved stall engine will stall the corresponding circuit stage $cir(k)$, but it will keep clocking the other stages if this is possible without overwriting instructions. Care has to be taken that the resulting design is live, i.e., that stages generating hazard signals are not blocking each other.

7.4.1 Stall Engine

The stall engine we use here was first presented in [6]. It is quickly described but is far from trivial. The signals involved for stages k are:

- full signals $full_k$ for $k \in [0 : 4]$,
- update enable signals ue_k for $k \in [1 : 5]$,
- stall signals $stall_k$ indicating that stage k should presently not be clocked for $k \in [1 : 6]$; the stall signal for stage 6 is only introduced to make definitions more uniform,
- hazard signal haz_k generated by circuit stage k for $k \in [1 : 5]$.

As before, circuit stage 1 is always full (i.e., $full_0 = 1$) and circuit stages 2 to 5 are initially empty. Register stage $reg(6)$ does not exist, and thus it is never stalled:

$$full_0 = 1$$
$$full[1:4]^0 = 0^4$$
$$stall_6 = 0 .$$

We specify the new stall engine with 3 equations. Only full circuit stages k with full input registers (registers $reg(k-1)$) are stalled. This happens in two situations: if a hazard signal is generated in circuit stage k or if the subsequent stage $k+1$ is stalled and clocking registers in stage k would overwrite data needed in the next stage:

$$stall_k = full_{k-1} \wedge (haz_k \vee stall_{k+1}) .$$

Stage k is updated, when the preceding stage $k-1$ is full and stage k itself is not stalled:

$$
\begin{aligned}
ue_k &= full_{k-1} \wedge \overline{stall_k} \\
&= full_{k-1} \wedge \overline{(full_{k-1} \wedge (haz_k \vee stall_{k+1}))} \\
&= full_{k-1} \wedge (\overline{full_{k-1}} \vee \overline{(haz_k \vee stall_{k+1})}) \\
&= full_{k-1} \wedge \overline{full_{k-1}} \vee full_{k-1} \wedge \overline{(haz_k \vee stall_{k+1})}) \\
&= full_{k-1} \wedge \overline{(haz_k \vee stall_{k+1})} .
\end{aligned}
$$

A stage is full in cycle $t+1$ in two situations: i) if new data were clocked in during the preceding cycle or ii) if it was full before and the old data had to stay where they are because the next stage was stalled:

$$full_k^{t+1} = ue_k^t \vee full_k^t \wedge stall_{k+1}^t .$$

Because

$$(stall_{k+1} \wedge full_k) = stall_{k+1} ,$$

this can be simplified to

$$full_k^{t+1} = ue_k^t \vee stall_{k+1}^t .$$

The corresponding hardware is shown in Fig. 123.

7.4.2 Hazard Signals

In the new design only stage 2 generates a hazard signal, namely A resp. B is used and forwarding is desirable but not possible due to a hit in stage 2 or 3 which corresponds to a load:

$$haz_2 = haz_A \vee haz_B$$
$$haz_A = A\text{-}used \wedge (top_A[2] \wedge con.2.l \vee top_A[3] \wedge con.3.l)$$
$$haz_B = B\text{-}used \wedge (top_B[2] \wedge con.2.l \vee top_B[3] \wedge con.3.l) .$$

For the time being, we set all other hazard signals to zero:

$$k \neq 2 \rightarrow haz_k = 0 .$$

This completes the construction of the new design.

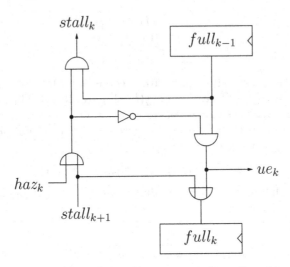

Fig. 123. Hardware of one stage of the stall engine

7.4.3 Correctness Statement

The correctness statement formulated in Lemma 7.5 stays the same as before. Software conditions *SC*-1 resp. *SC*-2 are dropped. Only alignment of memory accesses and the disjointness of the code and data regions are assumed.

7.4.4 Scheduling Functions

The correctness proof follows the pattern of previous proofs, but due to the non trivial stall engine the arguments about scheduling functions now become considerably more complex. Before we can adapt the overall proof we have to show the counter parts of Lemmas 7.4 and 7.9 for the new stall engine. We begin with three auxiliary technical results.

Lemma 7.11 (stall lemma 1). Let $k \geq 2$. Then,

$$full_{k-1} \wedge ue_{k-1} \rightarrow ue_k ,$$

i.e., if a full stage $k - 1$ is clocked then the previous data are clocked into the next stage.

Proof. By contradiction. Assume

$$
\begin{aligned}
0 = ue_k \\
= full_{k-1} \wedge \neg stall_k \\
= \neg stall_k .
\end{aligned}
$$

Thus,

$$\begin{aligned}
stall_k &= 1 \\
stall_{k-1} &= full_{k-2} \wedge (haz_{k-1} \vee stall_k) \\
&= full_{k-2} \\
ue_{k-1} &= full_{k-2} \wedge \neg stall_{k-1} \\
&= stall_{k-1} \wedge \neg stall_{k-1} \\
&= 0 .
\end{aligned}$$

$\square$

Lemma 7.12 (stall lemma 2).

$$\neg full_k^t \wedge \neg ue_k^t \rightarrow \neg full_k^{t+1} ,$$

i.e., an empty stage k that is not clocked, stays empty.

Proof.

$$\begin{aligned}
full_k^{t+1} &= ue_k^t \vee stall_{k+1}^t \\
&= stall_{k+1}^t \\
&= full_k^t \wedge (haz_{k+1} \vee stall_{k+2}) \\
&= 0 .
\end{aligned}$$

$\square$

Lemma 7.13 (stall lemma 3).

$$\neg full_{k-1}^t \vee \neg ue_k^t \rightarrow I(k, t+1) = I(k, t) ,$$

i.e., the scheduling function of stage k that does not have a full input stage $k - 1$ or that is not clocked, stays the same.

Proof. By the definitions of the scheduling functions we have

$$\neg ue_k^t \rightarrow I(k, t+1) = I(k, t) .$$

By the definition of the update enable signals we have

$$\neg full_{k-1}^t \rightarrow \neg ue_k^t .$$

$\square$

We can now state the crucial counterpart of Lemma 7.4.

Lemma 7.14 (scheduling function difference with stalling). Let $k \geq 2$. Then,

$$I(k - 1, t) = I(k, t) + full_{k-1}^t .$$

Table 10. Case split according to bits $full_{k-1}^t$, ue_{k-1}^t, and ue_k^t in the proof of Lemma 7.15

$full_{k-1}^t$	ue_{k-1}^t	ue_k^t	$I(k-1,t)$	$I(k-1,t+1)$	$I(k,t+1)$	$full_{k-1}^{t+1}$
0	0	0	i	i	i	0
0	1	0	i	$i+1$	i	1
1	0	0	$i+1$	$i+1$	i	1
1	0	1	$i+1$	$i+1$	$i+1$	0
1	1	1	$i+1$	$i+2$	$i+1$	1

Proof. By induction on t. For $t = 0$ the lemma is obviously true because initially we have $full_{k-1}^0 = 0$ and $I(k-1,0) = I(k,0) = 0$ for all $k \geq 2$.

For the induction step from t to $t+1$ we assume that the lemma holds for t and prove an auxiliary lemma.

Lemma 7.15 (stall lemma 4).

$$ue_k^t \rightarrow I(k,t+1) = I(k,t) + 1 \wedge full_k^{t+1} ,$$

i.e., after stage k is clocked, it is full and its scheduling function is increased by one.

Proof. In the proof we distinguish two cases. If $k = 1$ then ue_1^t implies

$$I(1,t+1) = I(1,t) + 1$$

by the definition of the scheduling functions. Now let $k \geq 2$. By the definitions of ue and $full$, we have

$$ue_k^t \rightarrow full_{k-1}^t \wedge full_k^{t+1} .$$

Thus we have by the definition of the scheduling functions and the induction hypothesis of Lemma 7.14

$$\begin{aligned} I(k,t+1) &= I(k-1,t) \\ &= I(k,t) + full_{k-1}^t \\ &= I(k,t) + 1 . \end{aligned}$$

$\square$

Lemma 7.14 for $t+1$ is now proven by a case split. Let

$$I(k,t) = i .$$

The major case split is according to bit $full_{k-1}^t$ as shown in Table 10:

- $full_{k-1}^t = 0$. By Lemma 7.13 and the induction hypothesis we have

$$I(k,t+1) = I(k,t) = I(k-1,t) = i .$$

We consider subcases according to bit ue_{k-1}:

- $ue^t_{k-1} = 0$. By Lemma 7.12 and the definitions of the scheduling functions we conclude

$$\neg full^{t+1}_{k-1} \wedge I(k-1, t+1) = I(k-1, t) = i \ .$$

- $ue^t_{k-1} = 1$. By Lemma 7.15 and the induction hypothesis we get

$$full^{t+1}_{k-1} \wedge I(k-1, t+1) = I(k-1, t) + 1 = i + 1 \ .$$

In both subcases we have

$$I(k-1, t+1) = I(k, t+1) + full^{t+1}_{k-1} \ .$$

- $full^t_{k-1} = 1$. By induction hypothesis we have

$$I(k-1, t) = I(k, t) + 1 = i + 1 \ .$$

By the definition of scheduling functions and Lemma 7.15 we get

$$(I(k-1, t+1), I(k, t+1)) = \begin{cases} (i+1, i) & \neg ue^t_{k-1} \wedge \neg ue^t_k \\ (i+1, i+1) & \neg ue^t_{k-1} \wedge ue^t_k \\ (i+2, i+1) & ue^t_{k-1} \wedge ue^t_k \ . \end{cases}$$

We consider subcases according to bits $ue[k-1:k]^t \in \mathbb{B}^2$, where

$$ue^t_{k-1} \rightarrow ue^t_k$$

by Lemma 7.11:
- $ue^t_{k-1} = 1$. Then,

$$full^{t+1}_{k-1} = ue^t_{k-1} \vee stall^t_k$$
$$= 1 \ .$$

- $ue^t_{k-1} = 0$. Then,

$$full^{t+1}_{k-1} = stall^t_k$$
$$ue^t_k = full^t_{k-1} \wedge \neg stall^t_k$$
$$= \neg stall^t_k$$
$$= \neg full^{t+1}_{k-1} \ .$$

In both subcases we have

$$I(k-1, t+1) = I(k, t+1) + full^{t+1}_{k-1} \ .$$

$\square$

From Lemma 7.14 we conclude the same formula as for the machine without stalling for any $k' < k$:

$$I(k',t) = I(k,t) + \sum_{j=k'}^{k-1} full_j^t .$$

The counterpart of Lemma 7.9 can now easily be shown.

Lemma 7.16 (no instructions lost with stalling). Let $s(t)$ be the number of full stages in between stages 2 and 5:

$$s(t) = \sum_{j=2}^{4} full_j^t .$$

Let

$$i = I(2,t) = I(5,t) + s(t).$$

For $j \in [-1 : s(t) - 1]$ we define numbers $a(j,t)$ by[5]

$$a(-1,t) = 1$$
$$a(j,t) = \min\{x \mid x > a(j-1,t) \wedge full_x^t\} .$$

Then,

$$\forall j \in [0 : s(t) - 1] : full_{a(j,t)}^t \wedge I(a(j,t),t) = i - j .$$

Proof. The lemma follows by an easy induction on j. For $j = -1$ there is nothing to show. Assume the lemma holds for j. By the minimality of $a(j+1,t)$ we have

$$\forall x : a(j,t) < x < a(j+1,t) \rightarrow \neg full_x^t .$$

By Lemma 7.14 we get

$$I(a(j+1,t),t) = I(a(j,t),t) - \sum_{x=a(j,t)}^{a(j+1,t)-1} full_x^t$$
$$= I(a(j,t),t) - 1$$
$$= I(2,t) - j - 1$$
$$= I(2,t) - (j+1) .$$

$\square$

We are now also able to state the version of Lemma 7.10 for the machine with stalling.

---

[5] For $j \in [0 : s(t) - 1]$, the function $a(j,t)$ returns the index of the $(j+1)$-th full stage, starting to count from stage 2 .

Lemma 7.17 (hit signal with stalling). Let $i = I(2,t)$ and the numbers $s(t)$ and $a(j,t)$ be defined as in the previous lemma. Further, let $\alpha \in [0 : s(t) - 1]$ and let

$$x = rs_\sigma^i \wedge k = a(\alpha, t) \wedge full_k^t .$$

Then,

$$hit_A^t[k] = writesgpr(x, i - \alpha - 1) .$$

Proof. For the hit signal under consideration we can conclude with $inv(k,t)$, $inv(2,t)$ and Lemma 7.16:

$$
\begin{aligned}
hit_A[k]^t &\equiv full_k^t \wedge Cad.k_\pi^t = rs_\pi^t \wedge gprw.k_\pi^t \\
&\equiv Cad_\sigma^{I(k,t)-1} = rs_\sigma^i \wedge gprw_\sigma^{I(k,t)-1} \\
&\equiv Cad_\sigma^{i-\alpha-1} = x \wedge gprw_\sigma^{i-\alpha-1} \\
&\equiv writesgpr(x, i - \alpha - 1) .
\end{aligned}
$$

$\square$

7.4.5 Correctness Proof

The correctness proof for the pipelined processor with forwarding and stalling follows the lines of previous proofs. The reduction of the induction step to the proof obligations $P(k,t)$ and the subsequent proofs of $P(3,t)$, $P(4,t)$, and $P(5,t)$ relied only on Lemma 7.4 which is now simply replaced by Lemma 7.14.

The proof of $P(1,t)$ is simpler. Let

$$i = I(1,t) .$$

We have by Lemma 7.14:

$$
\begin{aligned}
ima_\pi^t &= \begin{cases} pc_\pi^t.l & full_1^t \\ dpc_\pi^t.l & \neg full_1^t \end{cases} \\
&= \begin{cases} pc_\sigma^{I(2,t)}.l & full_1^t \\ dpc_\sigma^{I(2,t)}.l & \neg full_1^t \end{cases} \\
&= \begin{cases} pc_\sigma^{i-1}.l & full_1^t \\ dpc_\sigma^i.l & \neg full_1^t \end{cases} \\
&= dpc_\sigma^i.l \\
&= ima_\sigma^i.l .
\end{aligned}
$$

In the proof of $P(2,t)$ for Ain recall that proof obligations $P(k,t)$ only have to be shown for cycles with active enable signals ue_k^t. For $k = 2$ we have

$$ue_2^t \rightarrow \neg haz_2^t .$$

Let $i = I(2,t)$ and $x = rs_\sigma^i$. Further, let the numbers $s(t)$ and $a(j,t)$ be defined as in Lemma 7.16. We now consider two cases:

- There is an instruction in the pipeline in circuit stages 2, 3, or 4 which is writing to register x and this is the most recent instruction writing to this register:

$$\exists k \in [2:4] : hit_A^t[k] \wedge top_A^t[k] .$$

This implies that there exists α such that $k = a(\alpha, t)$. Applying Lemma 7.17 we get

$$writesgpr(x, i - \alpha - 1) .$$

For all $\alpha' \in [0 : \alpha - 1]$ we know by definition of $a(j, t)$ that

$$a(\alpha', t) < a(\alpha, t) \wedge full_{a(\alpha', t)}^t .$$

Since we have chosen the most recent instruction writing to x we have

$$\neg hit_A^t[a(\alpha', t)]$$

and get by Lemma 7.17

$$\neg writesgpr(x, i - \alpha' - 1) .$$

Hence, we have

$$\forall j \in [i - \alpha, i - 1] : \neg writesgpr(x, j) .$$

Using the hardware construction, Lemma 7.16, and $inv(k, t)$ we derive

$$Ain_\pi^t = \begin{cases} C.3in_\pi^t & k = 2 \\ C.4in_\pi^t & k = 3 \\ gprin_\pi^t & k = 4 \end{cases}$$

$$= \begin{cases} C.3in_\sigma^{i-\alpha-1} & k = 2 \\ C.4in_\sigma^{i-\alpha-1} & k = 3 \\ gprin_\sigma^{i-\alpha-1} & k = 4 . \end{cases}$$

Since we don't have an active hazard signal in stage 2, we can conclude that instruction $i - \alpha - 1$ is not a load instruction:

$$0 = con.k.l_\pi^t = con.k.l_\sigma^{I(k,t)-1} = con.k.l_\sigma^{i-\alpha-1} .$$

Hence, we get

$$Ain_\pi^t = gprin_\sigma^{i-\alpha-1}$$
$$= gpr_\sigma^{i-\alpha}(x)$$
$$= gpr_\sigma^i(x) .$$

- No hit in stages 2 to 4 exists:

$$\forall k \in [2:4] : \neg hit_A^t[k].$$

Applying Lemma 7.17 we get

$$\forall j \in [i - s(t), i - 1] : \neg writesgpr(x, j) .$$

and further derive

$$
\begin{aligned}
Ain_\pi^t &= gprouta_\pi^t \\
&= gpr_\sigma^{I(5,t)}(x) \\
&= gpr_\sigma^{i-s(t)}(x) \\
&= gpr_\sigma^i(x) .
\end{aligned}
$$

7.4.6 Liveness

We have to show that all active hazard signals are eventually turned off, so that no stage is stalled forever. By the definition of the stall signals we have

$$\neg stall_{k+1}^t \wedge \neg haz_k^t \rightarrow \neg stall_k^t ,$$

i.e., a stage whose successor stage is not stalled and whose hazard signal is off is not stalled either. From

$$stall_6 = haz_5 = haz_4 = haz_3 = 0$$

we conclude

$$k \geq 3 \rightarrow \neg stall_k ,$$

i.e., stages $k \geq 3$ are never stalled. Stages k with empty input stage $k - 1$ are never stalled. Thus it suffices to show the following lemma.

Lemma 7.18 (pipelined MIPS liveness).

$$full_1^t \wedge haz_2^t \wedge haz_2^{t+1} \rightarrow \neg haz_2^{t+2} ,$$

i.e., with a full input stage, stage 2 is not stalled for more than 2 successive cycles.

Proof. From the definitions of the signals in the stall engine we conclude successively:

$$
\begin{aligned}
stall_2^t &= stall_2^{t+1} = 1 \\
full_1^{t+1} &= 1 \\
ue_2^t &= ue_2^{t+1} = 0 .
\end{aligned}
$$

Using

$$stall_3 = stall_4 = 0$$

we conclude successively

$$full_2^{t+1} = full_2^{t+2} = 0$$
$$ue_3^{t+1} = 0$$
$$full_3^{t+2} = 0 \ .$$

Thus in cycle $t + 2$ stages 2 and 3 are both empty, hence the hit signals of these stages are off:

$$X \in \{A, B\} \rightarrow hit_X[2]^{t+2} = hit_X[3]^{t+2} = 0 \ ,$$

which implies

$$haz_2^{t+2} = 0 \ .$$

$\square$

8

Caches and Shared Memory

In this chapter we implement a cache based shared memory system and prove that it is sequentially consistent. Sequential consistency means: i) answers of read accesses to the memory system behave as if all accesses to the memory system were performed in some sequential order and ii) this order is consistent with the local order of accesses [7]. Cache coherence is maintained by the classical MOESI protocol as introduced in [16]. That a sequentially consistent shared memory system can be built at the gate level is in a sense *the* fundamental result of multi-core computing. Evidence that it holds is overwhelming: such systems are since decades part of commercial multi-core processors. Much to our surprise, when preparing the lectures for this chapter, we found in the open literature only one (undocumented) published gate level design of a cache based shared memory system [17]. Closely related to our subject, there is of course also an abundance of literature in the model checking community showing for a great variety of cache protocols, that desirable invariants - including cache coherence - are maintained, if accesses to the memory system are performed *atomically* at arbitrary caches in an arbitrary *sequential* order. In what follows we will call this variety of protocols *atomic protocols*. For a survey on the verification techniques for cache coherence protocols see [13], and for the model checking of the MOESI protocol we refer the reader to [4]. Atomic protocols and shared memory hardware differ in several important aspects:

- Accesses to shared memory hardware are as often as possible performed in parallel. After all, the purpose of multi-core computing is gaining speed by parallelism. If memory accesses were sequential as in the atomic protocols, memory would be a sequential bottleneck.
- Accesses to cache based hardware memory systems take one, two, or many more hardware cycles. Thus, they are certainly *not* performed in an atomic fashion.

Fortunately, we will be able to use the model checked invariants *literally* as lemmas in the hardware correctness proof presented here, but very consider-

M. Kovalev et al.: A Pipelined Multi-core MIPS Machine, LNCS 9000, pp. 207–310, 2014.
© Springer International Publishing Switzerland 2014

able extra proof effort will be required to establish a simulation between the hardware computation and the atomic protocol. After it is established one can easily conclude sequential consistency of the hardware system, because the atomic computation is sequential to begin with.

In Sect. 8.1 we introduce what we call *abstract caches* and show that the common basic types of single caches (direct mapped, k-way set associative, fully associative) can be modelled as abstract caches. This will later permit to simplify notation considerably. It also permits to unify *most* of the theory of shared memory constructions for all basic cache types. However, presently our definition of abstract caches does not yet include eviction addresses. The construction we present involves direct mapped caches, and we have to deal with eviction addresses below the abstract cache level. Modifying this small part of the construction and the corresponding arguments to other types of basic caches should not be hard. Modification of the definition of abstract caches such that they can be used completely as a black box is still future work. In the classroom it suffices to show that direct mapped caches can be modeled as abstract caches.

In Sect. 8.2 we develop formalism permitting to deal with i) atomic protocols, ii) hardware shared memory systems, and iii) simulations between them. It is the best formalism we can presently come up with. Suggestions for improvement are welcome. If one aims at correctness proofs there is no way to avoid this section (or an improved version of it) in the classroom.

Section 8.3 formulates in the framework of Sect. 8.2 the classical theory of the atomic MOESI protocol together with some auxiliary technical results that are needed later. Also we have enriched the standard MOESI protocol by a treatment of compare-and-swap (CAS) operations. We did this for two reasons: i) compare-and-swap operations are essential for the implementation of locks. Thus, multi-core machines without such operations are of limited use to put it mildly, ii) compare-and-swap is *not* a read followed by a conditional write; it is an *atomic* read followed by a conditional write, and this makes a large difference for the implementation.

A hardware-level implementation of the protocol for the direct mapped caches is presented in Sect. 8.4. It has the obvious three parts: i) data paths, ii) control automata, and iii) bus arbiter. The construction of data paths and control automata is not exactly straightforward. Caches in the data part generally consist of general 2-port RAMs, because they have to be able to serve their processor and to participate in the snooping bus protocol at the same time. We have provided each processor with two control automata: a master automaton processing requests of the processor and a slave automaton organizing the cache response to the requests of other masters on the bus. The arbiter does round robin scheduling of bus requests. One should sleep an extra hour at night before presenting this material in the classroom.

The correctness proof for the shared memory system is presented in Sect. 8.5. An outline of the proof is given at the start of the section. Roughly speaking, the proof contains the following kinds of arguments: i) showing that

bus arbitration guarantees at any time that at most one master automaton
is not idle, ii) showing the absence of bus contention (except on open collector buses[1]), among other things by showing that during global transactions
(involving more than one cache) master and participating slave automata
stay "in sync", iii) concluding that control signals and data "somehow corresponding to the atomic protocol" are exchanged via the buses, iv) abstracting
memory accesses in the sense of Sect. 8.2 from the hardware computation and
ordering them sequentially by their end cycle; it turns out that for accesses
with identical end cycles it does not matter how we order them among each
other, and v) showing (by induction on the end cycles of accesses) that the
data exchanged via the buses are *exactly* the data exchanged by the atomic
protocol, if it were run in the memory system configuration at the end cycle of the access. This establishes simulation and allows us to conclude that
cache invariants are maintained in the hardware computation (because hardware simulates the atomic protocol, and there it was model-checked that the
invariants are maintained).

Many of the arguments of parts i) to iv) are tedious bookkeeping; in the
classroom it suffices to just state the corresponding lemmas and to present only
a few typical proofs. However, even in this preliminary/bookkeeping phase of
the proof the order of arguments is of great importance: the absence of bus
contention often hinges on the cache invariants. Part v) is not only hard; it
turns out that it is also highly dependent on properties of the particular cache
protocol we are using. Thus, reinspection of the corresponding portions of the
proof is necessary, if one wants to establish shared memory correctness for a
different protocol.

8.1 Concrete and Abstract Caches

Caches are small and fast memories between the fast processor and the large
but slow main memory. Transporting data between main memory and cache
costs extra time, but this time is usually gained back because once data are in
the cache they are usually accessed several times (this is called locality) and
each of these accesses is much faster than an access to main memory. Also
caches are extra hardware units which increase cost. Because here we do not
consider hardware cost and cycle time, we cannot give quantitative arguments
why adding caches is cost effective. We refer the interested reader to [12]. Here
we are interested in explanations why the caches work.

There are three standard cache constructions: i) direct mapped, ii) k-way
associative, and iii) fully associative. In this section we review these three
constructions and then show that – as far as their memory content is concerned
– they all can be abstracted to what we call *abstract caches*. The correctness

---

[1] We do not use open collector buses to communicate with the main memory. Hence,
we do not worry about absence of bus contention on them.

Table 11. Synonyms and names of cache states s

s	synonym	name
10000	M	modified
01000	O	owned
00100	E	exclusive
00010	S	shared
00001	I	invalid

proof of the shared memory construction of the subsequent sections will then to a very large extent be based on abstract caches.

8.1.1 Abstract Caches and Cache Coherence

We use very specific parameters: an address length of 32 bits, line addresses of 29 bits, a line size of 8 bytes[2]. When it comes to states of cache lines, we exclusively consider the 5 states of the MOESI protocol [16]. We code the 5 states of the MOESI protocol in unary in the state set

$$S = \{00001, 00010, 00100, 01000, 10000\}\,.$$

For the states, we use the synonyms and names from Table 11.

In the digital model, main memory is simply a line addressable memory with configuration

$$mm : \mathbb{B}^{29} \to \mathbb{B}^{64}\,.$$

An abstract cache configuration aca has the following components:

- data memory $aca.data : \mathbb{B}^{29} \to \mathbb{B}^{64}$ - simply a line addressable memory,
- state memory $aca.s : \mathbb{B}^{29} \to S$ mapping each line address a to its current state $aca.s(a)$.

We denote the set of all possible abstract cache configurations by K_{aca}.

If a cache line a with $a \in \mathbb{B}^{29}$ has state I, i.e., $aca.s(a) = I$, then the data $aca.data(a)$ of this cache line is considered *invalid* or meaningless, otherwise it is considered *valid*. When cache line a has valid data, we also say that we have an abstract *cache hit* in cache line a:

$$ahit(aca, a) \equiv aca.s(a) \neq I\,.$$

In case of a hit, we require the data output $acadout(aca, a)$ of an abstract cache to be $aca.data(a)$ and the state output $acasout(aca, a)$ to be $aca.s(a)$:

$$ahit(aca, a) \to acadout(aca, a) = aca.data(a) \land acasout(aca, a) = aca.s(a)\,.$$

---

[2] If line size was larger than the width of the memory bus, one would have to use sectored caches. This would mildly complicate the control automata.

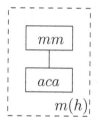

Fig. 124. An abstract cache *aca* and a main memory *mm* are abstracted to a single memory $m(h)$

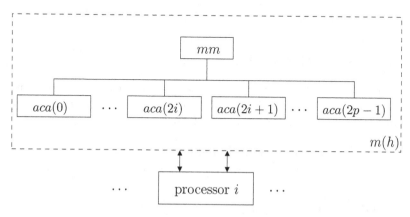

Fig. 125. Many caches $ca(i)$ and a main memory *mm* are abstracted to a shared memory $m(h)$

From a single abstract cache *aca* and a main memory *mm* as sketched in Fig. 124 one can define an *implemented* memory $m : \mathbb{B}^{29} \to \mathbb{B}^{64}$ by

$$m(a) = \begin{cases} aca.data(a) & ahit(aca, a) \\ mm(a) & \text{otherwise} . \end{cases}$$

In this definition, valid data in the cache hide the data in main memory.

A much more practical and interesting situation arises if P many abstract caches $aca(i)$ are coupled with a main memory *mm* as shown in Fig. 125 to get the abstraction of a *shared memory*. We intend to connect such a shared memory system with p processors. The number of caches will be $P = 2p$. For $i \in [0 : p-1]$ we will connect processor i with cache $aca(2i)$, which will replace the instruction port of the data memory, and with cache $aca(2i + 1)$, which will replace the data port of the data memory.

Again, we want to get a memory abstraction by hiding the data in main memory by the data in caches. But this only works if we have an invariant stating *coherence* resp. *consistency* of caches, namely that valid data in different caches are identical:

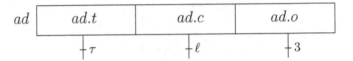

Fig. 126. Decomposition of a byte address ad

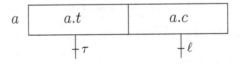

Fig. 127. Decomposition of a line address a

$$aca(i).s(a) \neq I \wedge aca(j).s(a) \neq I \rightarrow aca(i).data(a) = aca(j).data(a).$$

The purpose of cache coherence protocols like the one considered in this chapter is to maintain this invariant. With this invariant the following definition of an implemented memory m is well defined

$$m(a) = \begin{cases} aca(i).data(a) & ahit(aca(i), a) \\ mm(a) & \text{otherwise} . \end{cases}$$

8.1.2 Direct Mapped Caches

All cache constructions considered here use the decomposition of byte addresses $ad \in \mathbb{B}^{32}$ into three components as shown in Fig. 126:

- a line offset $ad.o \in \mathbb{B}^3$ within lines,
- a cache line address $ad.c \in \mathbb{B}^\ell$. This is the (short) address used to address the (small) RAMs constituting the cache,
- a tag $ad.t \in \mathbb{B}^\tau$ with
$$\tau + \ell + 3 = 32 ,$$

which completes cache line addresses to line addresses:

$$ad.l = ad.t \circ ad.c .$$

For line addresses $a \in \mathbb{B}^{29}$ this gives a decomposition into two components as shown in Fig. 127.

We structure the hardware configurations h of our constructions by introducing cache components $h.ca$. Direct mapped caches have the following cache line addressable components:

- data memory $h.ca.data : \mathbb{B}^\ell \rightarrow \mathbb{B}^{64}$ implemented as a multi-bank RAM,
- tag memory $h.ca.tag : \mathbb{B}^\ell \rightarrow \mathbb{B}^\tau$ implemented as an ordinary static RAM, and
- state memory $h.ca.s : \mathbb{B}^\ell \rightarrow \mathbb{B}^5$ implemented as a cache state RAM.

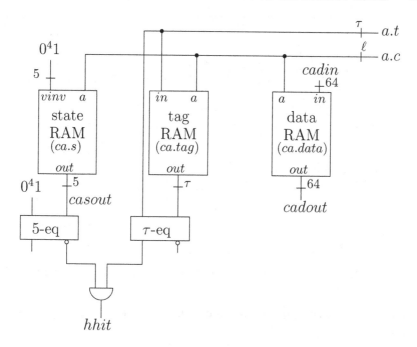

Fig. 128. Data paths of a direct mapped cache $h.ca$

The standard construction of the data paths of a direct mapped cache is shown in Fig. 128. Note that cache states are stored in a cache state RAM. This permits to make all cache lines invalid by activation of the inv signal. Any data with line address a are stored at cache line address $a.c$. At any time this is only possible for a single address a[3]. The tag $a.t$ completing the cache line address $a.c$ to a line address $a.l$ is stored in $ca.tag(a.c)$.

The hardware hit signal is computed as

$$hhit(h.ca, a) \equiv h.ca.s(a.c) \neq I \wedge h.ca.tag(a.c) = a.t \ .$$

We define the abstract cache $aca(h)$ for a direct mapped cache by

$$aca(h).s(a) = \begin{cases} h.ca.s(a.c) & hhit(h.ca, a) \\ I & \text{otherwise} \end{cases}$$

$$aca(h).data(a) = \begin{cases} h.ca.data(a.c) & hhit(h.ca, a) \\ * & \text{otherwise ,} \end{cases}$$

where $*$ simply indicates a "don't care" entry for invalid data.

---

[3] That caches are smaller than main memory is achieved by mapping many line addresses to the same cache line address.

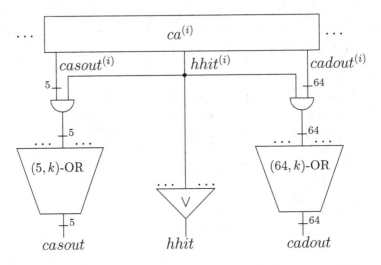

Fig. 129. Connection of way i to the data paths of a k-way associative cache

Lemma 8.1 (direct mapped cache abstraction). $aca(h)$ is an abstract cache.

Proof. The hardware hit signal $hhit(h, a)$ is active for the addresses where the abstract hit signal is on:

$$hhit(h.ca, a) \equiv h.sa.s(a.c) \neq I \wedge h.ca.tag(a.c) = a.t$$
$$\equiv aca(h).s(a) \neq I$$
$$\equiv ahit(aca(h), a) \,.$$

In case of an abstract hit $ahit(aca(h), a)$ we also have a concrete hit $hhit(h.ca, a)$. For the data and state outputs of the direct mapped cache in this case, we conclude

$$cadout(h.ca, a) = h.ca.data(a.c)$$
$$= aca(h).data(a)$$
$$= acadout(aca(h), a)$$
$$casout(h.ca, a) = h.ca.s(a.c)$$
$$= aca(h).s(a)$$
$$= acasout(aca(h), a) \,.$$

$\square$

8.1.3 k-way Associative Caches

As shown in Fig. 129, k-way associative caches (also called set associative caches) consist of k copies $h.ca^{(i)}$ of direct mapped caches for $i \in [0 : k - 1]$

which are called *ways*. Individual hit signals $hhit^{(i)}$, cache data out signals $cadout^{(i)}$, and cache state out signals $casout^{(i)}$ are computed in each way i as

$$hhit^{(i)}(h.ca, a) = hhit(h.ca^{(i)}, a)$$
$$cadout^{(i)}(h.ca, a) = cadout(h.ca^{(i)}, a)$$
$$casout^{(i)}(h.ca, a) = casout(h.ca^{(i)}, a) \ .$$

A hit in any of the individual caches constitutes a hit in the set associative cache:

$$hhit(h.ca, a) = \bigvee_i hhit^{(i)}(h.ca, a) \ .$$

Joint data output $cadout(h.ca, a)$ and state output $casout(h.ca, a)$ are obtained by multiplexing the individual data and state outputs under control of the individual hit signals:

$$cadout(h.ca, a) = \bigvee_i cadout^{(i)}(h.ca, a) \wedge hhit^{(i)}(h.ca, a)$$
$$casout(h.ca, a) = \bigvee_i casout^{(i)}(h.ca, a) \wedge hhit^{(i)}(h.ca, a) \ .$$

Initialization and update of the cache must maintain the invariant that valid tags in different ways belonging to the same cache line address are distinct:

$$i \neq j \wedge h.ca^{(i)}.s(a.c) \neq I \wedge h.ca^{(j)}.s(a.c) \neq I \rightarrow$$
$$h.ca^{(i)}.tag(a.c) \neq h.ca^{(j)}.tag(a.c) \ .$$

This implies that for every line address a, a hit can occur in at most one way.

Lemma 8.2 (hit unique).

$$hhit^{(i)}(h.ca, a) \wedge hhit^{(j)}(h.ca, a) \rightarrow i = j$$

Proof. Assume

$$hhit^{(i)}(h.ca, a) \wedge hhit^{(j)}(h.ca, a) \wedge i \neq j \ .$$

Then,

$$h.ca^{(i)}.s(a.c) \neq I \wedge h.ca^{(j)}.s(a.c) \neq I$$

and

$$h.ca^{(j)}.tag(a.c) = a.t$$
$$= h.ca^{(i)}.tag(a.c) \ .$$

This contradicts the invariant. $\square$

We can now define $aca'(h)$ by

$$aca'(h).s(a) = \begin{cases} h.ca^{(i)}.s(a.c) & hhit^{(i)}(h.ca, a) \\ I & \text{otherwise} \end{cases}$$

$$aca'(h).data(a) = \begin{cases} h.ca^{(i)}.data(a.c) & hhit^{(i)}(h.ca, a) \\ * & \text{otherwise} . \end{cases}$$

This is well defined by Lemma 8.2.

Lemma 8.3 (k-way associative cache abstraction). $aca'(h)$ is an abstract cache.

Proof. We have

$$\begin{aligned} hhit(h.ca, a) &= \exists i : hhit(h.ca^{(i)}, a) \\ &\equiv aca'(h).s(a) \neq I \\ &\equiv ahit(aca'(h), a) . \end{aligned}$$

In case of an abstract hit $ahit(aca'(h), a)$ we also have by Lemma 8.2 a unique concrete hit $hhit(h.ca^{(i)}, a)$. For the data and state outputs of the k-way associative cache, we conclude

$$\begin{aligned} cadout(h.ca, a) &= h.ca^{(i)}.data(a.c) \\ &= aca'(h).data(a) \\ &= acadout(aca'(h), a) \\ casout(h.ca, a) &= h.ca^{(i)}.s(a.c) \\ &= aca'(h).s(a) \\ &= acasout(aca'(h), a) . \end{aligned}$$

$\square$

8.1.4 Fully Associative Caches

These RAMs have the same components $h.ca.s$, $h.ca.tag$, and $h.ca.data$ as direct mapped caches, but data for any line address a can be stored at any cache line and is addressed with a cache line address $b \in \mathbb{B}^\alpha$:

- Data memory $h.ca.data : \mathbb{B}^\alpha \to \mathbb{B}^{64}$ is implemented as an SPR RAM.
- Tag memory $h.ca.tag : \mathbb{B}^\alpha \to \mathbb{B}^{29}$ is implemented as an SPR RAM. The tag RAM has width 29 so that it can store entire line addresses.
- State memory $h.ca.s : \mathbb{B}^\alpha \to \mathbb{B}^5$ is implemented as an SPR RAM extended with the invalidation option of a cache state RAM[4].

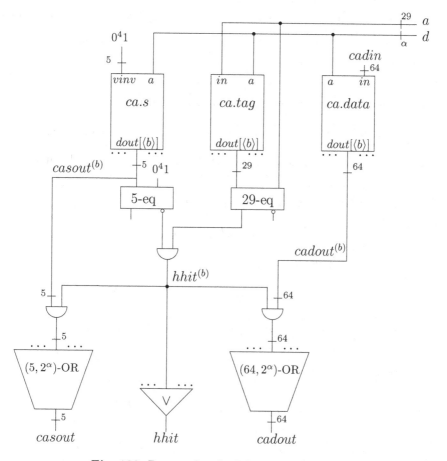

Fig. 130. Data paths of a fully associative cache

A fully associative cache can be viewed as a k-way associative cache with $k = 2^\alpha$ and $l = 0$.

Figure 130 shows the data paths of a fully associative cache. The RAMs are addressed by a cache line address $d \in \mathbb{B}^\alpha$ which is only used for updating the cache. For each of the RAMs X, one needs simultaneous access to all register contents $X[\langle b \rangle]$ for every cache line address $b \in \mathbb{B}^\alpha$. This, together with the 2^α equality testers that we use in the hit signal computation, makes fully associative caches expensive.

A hit for line address a occurs at cache line address b if a can be found in the tag RAM at address b and the state of this cache line is valid:

$$hhit^{(b)}(h.ca, a) \equiv h.ca.tag(b) = a \wedge h.ca.s(b) \neq I \ .$$

---

[4] We leave the construction of such a RAM as an easy exercise for the reader.

A hit for the entire fully associative cache occurs if at least one of the lines contains the valid data for a:

$$hhit(h.ca, a) = \bigvee_b hhit^{(b)}(h.ca, a) \ .$$

One maintains the invariant that valid tags are distinct:

$$b \neq b' \wedge h.ca.s(b) \neq I \wedge h.ca.s(b') \neq I \rightarrow h.ca.tag(b) \neq h.ca.tag(b') \ .$$

Along the lines of the proof of Lemma 8.2 this permits to show the uniqueness of cache lines producing a hit.

Lemma 8.4 (fully associative hit unique).

$$hhit^{(b)}(h.ca, a) \wedge hhit^{(b')}(h.ca, a) \rightarrow b = b'$$

Outputs are constructed as

$$cadout(h.ca, a) = \bigvee_b ca.data(b) \wedge hhit^{(b)}(h.ca, a)$$

$$casout(h.ca, a) = \bigvee_b ca.s(b) \wedge hhit^{(b)}(h.ca, a) \ .$$

We define $aca''(h)$ by

$$aca''(h).s(a) = \begin{cases} h.ca.s(b) & hhit^{(b)}(h.ca, a) \\ I & \text{otherwise} \end{cases}$$

$$aca''(h).data(a) = \begin{cases} h.ca.data(b) & hhit^{(b)}(h.ca, a) \\ * & \text{otherwise} \ . \end{cases}$$

Lemma 8.5 (fully associative cache abstraction). $aca''(h)$ is an abstract cache.

Proof. We have

$$hhit(h.ca, a) = \bigvee_b hhit^{(b)}(h.ca, a)$$

$$\equiv aca''(h).s(a) \neq I$$

$$\equiv ahit(aca''(h), a) \ .$$

In case of an abstract hit $ahit(aca''(h), a)$ we also have by Lemma 8.4 a unique concrete hit $hhit^{(b)}(h.ca, a)$. For the data and state outputs of the direct mapped cache, we conclude

$$cadout(h.ca, a) = h.ca.data(b)$$
$$= aca''(h).data(a)$$
$$= acadout(aca''(h), a)$$
$$casout(h.ca, a) = h.ca.s(b)$$
$$= aca''(h).s(a)$$
$$= acasout(aca''(h), a) .$$

□

So far, we have not yet explained how to update caches. For different types of concrete caches this is done in different ways. In what follows we elaborate details only for direct mapped caches.

8.2 Notation

We summarize a large portion of the notation we are going to use in the remainder of this book.

8.2.1 Parameters

Our construction uses the following parameters:

- p – denotes the number of processors. The set of processor IDs is $[0 : p-1]$.
- $P = 2p$ – denotes the number of caches. There is one instruction cache and one data cache per processor. The set of cache indices is $[0 : P - 1]$.

8.2.2 Memory and Memory Systems

The user visible memory model we aim at is a line addressable multi-bank RAM, i.e., memory configurations are mappings

$$m : \mathbb{B}^{29} \to \mathbb{B}^{64} .$$

The set of all possible memory configurations is denoted by K_m.

A user visible memory will be realized by several flavors of *memory systems*. A memory system configuration has components:

- $ms.mm : \mathbb{B}^{29} \to \mathbb{B}^{64}$. This is simply line addressable memory.
- $ms.aca : [0 : P - 1] \to K_{aca}$. This is simply a sequence of abstract cache configurations.

The set of memory system configurations is denoted by K_{ms}. In memory systems we will always keep data caches consistent, i.e., we maintain the invariant

$$ms.aca(i).s(a) \neq I \wedge ms.aca(j).s(a) \neq I \rightarrow$$
$$ms.aca(i).data(a) = ms.aca(j).data(a) \ .$$

From memory systems ms we abstract memories $m(ms)$ in a way described before:

$$m(ms)(a) = \begin{cases} ms.aca(i).data(a) & ms.aca(i).s(a) \neq I \\ ms.mm(a) & \text{otherwise} \ . \end{cases}$$

For line addresses $a \in \mathbb{B}^{29}$, we project all components $ms.mm(a)$ and $aca(i).X(a)$ with $X \in \{data, s\}$ belonging to address a in the *memory system slice* $\Pi(ms, a)$:

$$\Pi(ms, a) = (ms.aca(0).data(a), ms.aca(0).s(a),$$
$$\dots,$$
$$ms.aca(P-1).data(a), ms.aca(P-1).s(a),$$
$$ms.mm(a)) \ .$$

This definition would be shorter if memory systems were tensors. Then a slice would simply be the submatrix with coordinate a^5.

8.2.3 Accesses and Access Sequences

Memories will be accessed sequentially by accesses. Memory systems will be accessed sequentially or in parallel by accesses.

The set of accesses is defined as K_{acc}. An access $acc \in K_{acc}$ has the following components:

- processor address $acc.a[28 : 0]$ (line address),
- processor data $acc.data[63 : 0]$ – the input data in case of a write or a compare-and-swap (CAS),
- comparison data $acc.cdata[31 : 0]$ – the data for comparison in case of a CAS access,
- the byte write signals $acc.bw[7 : 0]$ for write and CAS accesses,
- write signal $acc.w$,
- read signal $acc.r$,

---

[5] Actually, we could choose notation coming closer to this if we define an abstract cache configuration for cache i and line a as

$$aca(i, a) = (aca(i, a).s, aca(i, a).data) \ .$$

Then the abstract cache component of a memory system slice is defined like a row of a matrix:

$$\Pi(ms, a) = (ms.aca([0 : P-1], a), ms.mm(a)) \ .$$

- CAS signal $acc.cas$, and
- flush request $acc.f$.

At most one of the bits w, r, cas, or f must be on. In case none of these bits is one, we call such an access *void*. A void access does not update memory and does not produce an answer.

For technical reasons, we also require the byte write signals to be off in read accesses and to mask one of the words in case of CAS accesses:

$$acc.r \rightarrow acc.bw = 0^8$$

$$acc.cas \rightarrow acc.bw \in \{0^4 1^4, 1^4 0^4\} \,.$$

For CAS accesses, we define the predicate $test(acc, d)$, which compares $acc.cdata$ with the upper or the lower word of the data $d \in \mathbb{B}^{64}$ depending on the byte write signal $acc.bw[0]$:

$$test(acc, d) \equiv acc.cdata = \begin{cases} d[63 : 32] & \neg acc.bw[0] \\ d[31 : 0] & acc.bw[0] \,. \end{cases}$$

As the name suggests, access sequences are finite or infinite sequences of accesses. As with caches and abstract caches we use the same notation acc both for single accesses and access sequences. Access sequences come in two flavors:

- Sequential access sequences. These are simply mappings $acc : \mathbb{N} \rightarrow K_{acc}$ in the infinite case and $acc : [0 : n - 1] \rightarrow K_{acc}$ for some n in the finite case.
- Multi-port access sequences

$$acc : [0 : P - 1] \times \mathbb{N} \rightarrow K_{acc} \,,$$

where $acc(i, k)$ denotes access number k to cache (port) i.

8.2.4 Sequential Memory Semantics

Semantics of single accesses acc operating on a memory m is specified by a memory update function

$$\delta_M : K_m \times K_{acc} \rightarrow K_m$$

and the answers

$$dataout(m, acc) \in \mathbb{B}^{64}$$

of read and CAS accesses. Let

$$m' = \delta_M(m, acc) \,.$$

Then memory is updated like a multi-bank memory:

$$m'(a) = \begin{cases} modify(m(a), acc.data, acc.bw) & acc.a = a \wedge (acc.w \ \vee \\ & acc.cas \wedge test(acc, m(acc.a))) \\ m(a) & \text{otherwise .} \end{cases}$$

For CAS accesses, if the data comparison $test(acc, m(acc.a))$ succeeds, we call the CAS access *positive*. Otherwise we call it *negative*.

The answers $dataout(m, acc)$ of read or CAS accesses are defined as

$$acc.r \vee acc.cas \rightarrow dataout(m, acc) = m(acc.a) .$$

Void and flush accesses do not have any affect on the memory and do not produce an answer.

The change of memory state by sequential access sequences acc of accesses and the corresponding outputs $dataout[i]$ are defined in the obvious way by

$$\Delta_M^0(m, acc) = m$$
$$\Delta_M^{i+1}(m, acc) = \delta_M(\Delta_M^i(m, acc), acc[i])$$
$$dataout(m, acc)[i] = dataout(\Delta_M^i(m, acc), acc[i]) .$$

An easy induction on y shows that performing $x + y$ accesses is the same as first performing x and then y accesses.

Lemma 8.6 (decomposition of access sequences). Let

$$m' = \Delta_M^x(m, acc[0 : x - 1]) .$$

Then,

$$\Delta_M^{x+y}(m, acc[0 : x + y - 1]) = \Delta_M^y(m', acc[x : x + y - 1]) .$$

8.2.5 Sequentially Consistent Memory Systems

For multi-port access sequences acc, we denote by $msdout(ms, acc, i, k)$ the answer of the system to read or CAS access $acc(i, k)$ if the initial configuration of the memory system is ms.

A sequential ordering of the accesses is simply a bijective mapping

$$seq : [0 : P - 1] \times \mathbb{N} \to \mathbb{N} ,$$

which respects the local order of accesses, i.e., which satisfies

$$k < k' \rightarrow seq(i, k) < seq(i, k') .$$

A memory system ms is called *sequentially consistent* if for any multi-port access sequence acc there exists a sequential ordering seq satisfying the following condition. Let the sequential access sequence acc' be defined as

$$acc'[seq(i,k)] = acc(i,k) \,,$$

then for read accesses the answer $msdout(ms, acc, i, k)$ to access $acc(i, k)$ of the multi-port access sequence acc is the same as the answer to access $seq(i, k)$ of the sequential access sequence acc':

$$acc(i,k).r \vee acc(i,k).cas \rightarrow$$
$$msdout(ms, acc, i, k) = dataout(m(ms), acc')[seq(i, k)] \,.$$

By the definition of function $dataout$ this is equivalent to

$$
\begin{aligned}
msdout(ms, acc, i, k) &= dataout(m(ms), acc')[seq(i, k)] \\
&= dataout(\Delta_M^{seq(i,k)}(m(ms), acc'), acc'[seq(i, k)])) \\
&= \Delta_M^{seq(i,k)}(m(ms), acc')(acc'[seq(i, k)].a) \\
&= \Delta_M^{seq(i,k)}(m(ms), acc')(acc(i, k).a) \,.
\end{aligned}
$$

8.2.6 Memory System Hardware Configurations

We collect the components of a memory system into the following components of hardware configuration h:

- main memory component $h.mm$,
- (direct mapped) cache components $h.ca(i)$; in theses components we collect cache RAMs $h.ca(i).X$ for $X \in \{data, s, tag\}$ which we have already introduced, but later we also add registers $h.ca(i).Y$ of the cache control and the data paths of cache i.

We denote by

$$aca(i) = aca(h.ca(i))$$

the abstract cache abstracted from cache RAMs $h.ca(i).X$ of cache i as explained in Sect. 8.1.2. For hardware cycles t, we abbreviate the states of hardware cache i and abstract cache i in cycle t as

$$
\begin{aligned}
ca(i)^t &= h^t.ca(i) \\
aca(i)^t &= aca(h^t.ca(i)) \,.
\end{aligned}
$$

For components $X \in \{data, s\}$ of abstract caches and components Y of hardware cache $h.ca(i)$, we use the notation

$$
\begin{aligned}
ca(i).Y^t &= h^t.ca(i).Y \\
aca(i).X^t &= aca(h^t.ca(i)) \,.
\end{aligned}
$$

The hardware constitutes a memory system

$$ms(h) = (ms(h).mm, ms(h).aca)$$

with

$$ms(h).mm = h.mm$$
$$ms(h).aca(i) = aca(h.ca(i)) \, ,$$

which in turn permits the definition of a memory abstraction

$$m(h) = m(ms(h)) \, .$$

8.3 Atomic MOESI Protocol

We specify the MOESI protocol in five steps:

1. For any system of abstract caches $ms.aca(i)$ and main memory $ms.mm$ we formulate the *state invariants* for the five states M, O, E, S, I involved in the protocol.
2. We present the protocol in a way that is common in literature, namely by tables prescribing how to run the protocol *one access at a time*. We give this version of the protocol a special name and call it *atomic*, because it performs each access sequentially in an atomic way without interference of any other access.
3. We translate the master and slave tables into switching functions $C1, C2$, and $C3$.
4. Using functions Ci we give an algebraic specification of the atomic MOESI protocol.
5. We specify how the caches and, if applicable, the main memory exchange data after the protocol information of step 2 has been exchanged.

We then review the classical proof that a system of caches $ca(i)$ and main memory mm running the atomic MOESI protocol behaves like memory. Observe that the atomic system is sequentially consistent for completely trivial reasons: it runs sequentially.

The beauty of the protocol as introduced in [16] is that it permits a parallel implementation which nevertheless simulates the atomic protocol. The first such construction in the open literature is the undocumented design of OpenSPARC T1 and T2 processors [17]. Here we present, to the best of our knowledge, the first such construction which is documented and accompanied by a correctness proof. Indeed, the classical result that state invariants are preserved in the atomic protocol is a crucial lemma in our proof. It is, however, only a part of our main induction hypothesis.

8.3.1 Invariants

For the memory system ms under consideration, we abbreviate

$$mm = ms.mm$$
$$aca = ms.aca \ .$$

One calls the data in a cache line *clean* if this data are known to be the same as in the main memory, otherwise it is called *dirty*. A line is *exclusive* if the line is known to be only in one cache, otherwise it is called *shared*. The intended meaning of the states is:

- E – exclusive clean (the data are in one cache and are clean).
- S – shared (the data might be in other caches and might be not clean).
- M – exclusive modified (the data are in one cache and might be not clean).
- O – owned (the data might be in other caches and might be not clean; the cache with this line in owned state is responsible for writing it back to the memory or sending it on demand to other caches).
- I – invalid (the data are meaningless).

This intended meaning is formalized in a crucial set of *state invariants*:

1. States E and M are exclusive; in other caches the line is invalid:

$$aca(i).s(a) \in \{E, M\} \wedge j \neq i \to aca(j).s(a) = I \ ,$$

2. state E is clean:

$$aca(i).s(a) = E \to aca(i).data(a) = mm(a) \ .$$

3. Shared lines, i.e., lines in state S, are clean or they have an owner:

$$aca(i).s(a) = S \to aca(i).data(a) = mm(a) \vee \exists j \neq i : aca(j).s(a) = O \ .$$

4. Data in lines in nonexclusive state are identical:

$$aca(i).s(a) = S \wedge aca(j).s(a) \in \{O, S\} \to$$
$$aca(i).data(a) = aca(j).data(a) \ .$$

5. If a line is non-exclusive, i.e., in state S or O, other copies must be invalid or in a non exclusive state. Moreover the owner is unique:

$$aca(i).s(a) = S \wedge j \neq i \to aca(j).s(a) \in \{I, O, S\}$$
$$aca(i).s(a) = O \wedge j \neq i \to aca(j).s(a) \in \{I, S\} \ .$$

We introduce the notation $sinv(ms)(a)$ to denote that the state invariants hold for cache line address a with a system aca of abstract caches and main memory mm. For cycle numbers t, we denote by $SINV(t)$ the fact that the state invariants hold for the memory system $ms(h)$ abstracted from the hardware for all cycles $t' \in [0 : t]$, i.e., from cycle 0 after reset until t:

$$sinv(ms) \equiv \forall a : sinv(ms)(a)$$
$$SINV(t) \equiv \forall t' \in [0 : t] : sinv(ms(h^{t'})) \ .$$

One easily checks that the state invariants hold if all cache lines are invalid. In the hardware construction, this will be the state of caches after reset.

Lemma 8.7 (invalid state satisfies invariants).

$$(\forall a, i : aca(i).s(a) = I) \rightarrow sinv(ms)$$

8.3.2 Defining the Protocol by Tables

We stress the fact that the atomic protocol is a sequential protocol operating on a multi-port memory system ms. Its semantics is defined by two functions:

- A transition function

$$\delta_1 : K_{ms} \times K_{acc} \times [0 : P - 1] \rightarrow K_{ms} \; ,$$

  where

$$ms' = \delta_1(ms, acc, i)$$

  defines the new memory system if *single* access acc is applied to (cache) port i of memory system ms.
- An output function

$$pdout1 : K_{ms} \times K_{acc} \times [0 : P - 1] \rightarrow \mathbb{B}^{64} \; ,$$

  where

$$d = pdout1(ms, acc, i)$$

  specifies for read and CAS accesses (i.e., accesses with $acc.r$ or $acc.cas$) memory system output d as response to access acc at port i in memory system configuration ms.

We abbreviate

$$mm' = ms'.mm$$
$$aca' = ms'.aca \; .$$

The processing of accesses is summarized in Tables 131(a) and 131(b).

   We first describe somewhat informally how the tables are interpreted. In Sect. 8.3.4 we translate this description into an algebraic specification.

   Every access $acc(i, k)$ is processed by cache $aca(i)$ which is called the *master* of the access. Actions of the master are specified in Table 131(a). The master determines the local state $aca(i).s(acc(i, k).a)$ of cache line $acc.a$ and the *type* of the access, i.e., whether the access is a read, a write, a flush, or a CAS. The state determines the row of the table to be used. The type of the access determines the column. For a hit with a CAS access, we distinguish cases when the data comparison succeeds (CAS+) and when it fails (CAS-). In case of a cache miss on CAS, the master cannot predict whether the test will succeed or fail and runs the protocol just like in case of a write miss.

   There are two kinds of table entries in the master table: i) single states and ii) others. A single state indicates that a cache can handle the access

master	read	write	flush	CAS-	CAS+
M	M	M	I	M	M
O	O	Ca, im, bc ch?O:M	I	O	Ca, im, bc ch?O:M
E	E	M	I	E	M
S	S	Ca, im, bc ch?O:M	I	S	Ca, im, bc ch?O:M
I	Ca ch?S:E	Ca, im M	I	Ca, im M	

(a) Master state transitions

slave	Ca, ¬im, ¬bc read miss	Ca, im, ¬bc write or CAS miss	Ca, im, bc write or CAS hit
M	ch, di O	di I	-
O	ch, di O	di I	ch S
E	ch, di S	di I	-
S	ch S	I	ch S
I	I	I	I

(b) Slave state transitions

Fig. 131. Protocol state transitions

without contacting the other caches; for some flushes it still may have to write back a cache line to main memory. In case i) the table entry specifies the next state of the cache line. The table does not explicitly state how data are to be processed; this is implicitly specified by the fact that we aim at a memory construction and by the state invariants. We will make this explicit in Sect. 8.3.4.

In case there is more than a single state in the master table entry, the protocol is run in four steps. Three steps concern the exchange of signals belonging to the memory protocol and the next state computation. The fourth step involves the processing of the data and is only implicitly specified.

1. Out of three master protocol signals Ca, im, bc the master activates the ones specified in the table entry. These signals are broadcast to the other caches $ca(j)$, $j \neq i$ which are called the *slaves* of the access. The intuitive meaning of the signals is:
   - Ca – intention of the master to cache line $acc.a$ after the access is processed.
   - im – intention of the master to modify (write) the line.

- bc – intention of the master to broadcast the line after the write has been performed. This signal is activated after a write or a positive CAS hit with non exclusive data.

2. The slaves j determine the local state $aca(j).s(acc.a)$ of cache line $acc.a$, which determines the row of Table 131(b) to be used. The column is determined by the values of the master protocol signals Ca, im, and bc. Each slave $aca(j)$ goes to a new state as prescribed in the slave table entry and activates two slave protocol signals $ch(j)$ and $di(j)$ as indicated by the slave table entry used. The intuitive meaning of the signals is:
   - $ch(j)$ – cache hit in slave $aca(j)$.
   - $di(j)$ – data intervention by slave $aca(j)$. Slave $aca(j)$ has the cache line needed by the master and will put it on a bus, from which the master can read it.

   The individual signals are ORed together (in active low form on an open collector bus) and made accessible to the master as

$$ch = \bigvee_{j \neq i} ch(j) \quad , \quad di = \bigvee_{j \neq i} di(j) \ .$$

3. The master determines the new state of the cache line accessed as a function of the slaves' responses as indicated by the table entry used. The notation $ch\ ?\ X : Y$ is an expression borrowed from C and means

$$ch\ ?\ X : Y = \begin{cases} X & ch \\ Y & \neg ch \ . \end{cases}$$

4. The master processes the data. This step is discussed in Sect. 8.3.4.

8.3.3 Translating the Tables into Switching Functions

We extract from the tables three sets of switching functions. They correspond to phases of the protocol, and we specify them in the order, in which they are used in the protocol:

- $C1$ – this function is used by the master. It depends on a state[6] $s \in S$ and the type of the access $acc.type \in \mathbb{B}^4$, where

$$acc.type = (acc.r, acc.w, acc.cas, acc.f) \ .$$

The function $C1$ computes the master protocol signals $C1.Ca$, $C1.im$, and $C1.bc$. Thus,

---

[6] Recall that we encode the cache states in the unary form as

$$S = \{00001, 00010, 00100, 01000, 10000\} \ .$$

$$C1 : S \times \mathbb{B}^4 \to \mathbb{B}^3 \ .$$

The component functions $C1.X$ are defined by translating the master protocol table, i.e., looking up the corresponding cell $(s, type)$ in Table 131(a)
and choosing the necessary protocol bits accordingly:

$$\forall X \in \{Ca, im, bc\} : C1(s, type).X = 1 \leftrightarrow$$
$$\text{master table entry } (s, type) \text{ contains } X.$$

In case of a cache hit on CAS ($acc.cas = 1$ and $s \neq I$), we always choose
the column CAS+, since in case of CAS- the access is performed locally
and the protocol signals are not put on the bus anyway.
Using the construction of Lemma 2.20 for each component $C1.X$, the above
switching function can be turned into a switching circuit that we also call
$C1$. A symbol for this circuit is shown in Fig. 132.

- $C2$ – this function is used by slaves. It depends on a cache state $s \in S$
  and the master protocol signals Ca, im, and bc. It computes slave protocol
  signals $C2.ch$ and $C2.di$, i.e., the slave response, and the next state $C2.ss'$
  for slaves. Thus,

$$C2 : S \times \mathbb{B}^3 \to \mathbb{B}^2 \times S \ .$$

For component $X \in \{ch, di\}$, functions $C2.X$ are defined by translating the
slave protocol table, i.e., looking up the corresponding cell (s, Ca, im, bc)
in Table 131(b) and choosing the necessary protocol bits accordingly:

$$\forall X \in \{ch, di\} : C2(s, Ca, im, bc).X = 1 \leftrightarrow$$
$$\text{slave table entry } (s, Ca, im, bc) \text{ contains } X.$$

$C2$ also computes the next state of the slave:

$$C2(s, Ca, im, bc).ss' = s' \leftrightarrow$$
$$\text{slave table entry } (s, Ca, im, bc) \text{ contains } s'.$$

A symbol for the corresponding circuit is also shown in Fig. 132.

- $C3$ – this function depends on a state $s \in S$, the type of the access $acc.type$
  and the slave response ch. It computes the next state $C3.ps'$ of the master.
  Thus,

$$C3 : S \times \mathbb{B}^4 \times \mathbb{B} \to S \ .$$

The function is defined by translating the master protocol table:

$$C3(s, type, ch).ps' = s' \leftrightarrow$$
$$\text{master table entry } (s, type) \text{ contains } s'$$
$$\vee \, \exists s'' : ch \wedge \text{master table entry } (s, type) \text{ contains } ch \, ? \, s' : s''$$
$$\vee \, \exists s'' : \overline{ch} \wedge \text{master table entry } (s, type) \text{ contains } ch \, ? \, s'' : s'.$$

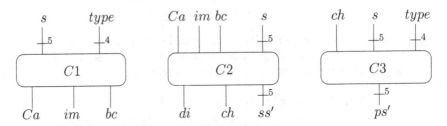

Fig. 132. Symbols for circuits $C1$, $C2$, and $C3$ computing the protocol signals and next state functions of the MOESI protocol

In case of a cache hit on CAS ($acc.cas = 1$ and $s \neq I$), we always choose the column CAS+, since in case of CAS- the state of the master is not changed at all and the output of $C3$ is simply ignored[7].

The corresponding symbol for circuit $C3$ is shown in Fig. 132.

8.3.4 Algebraic Specification

For the following definitions we assume $sinv(ms)$, i.e., that the state invariants hold for the memory system ms before the (sequential and atomic) processing of access acc at port i.

For all components x of an access acc, we abbreviate

$$x = acc.x .$$

Note that a in this section and below, where applicable, denotes the line address $acc.a$. Also, the functions we define depend on arguments $ms.aca$ and $ms.mm$. For brevity of notation we will omit these arguments most of the time – but not always – in the remainder of this section. We now proceed to define the effect of applying accesses acc to port i of the memory system ms by specifying functions $ms' = \delta_1(ms, acc, i)$ and $d = pdout1(ms, acc, i)$.

We only specify the components that do change. We define a hit at atomic abstract cache $aca(i)$ by

$$hit(aca, a, i) \equiv aca(i).s(a) \neq I .$$

We further identify local read and write accesses. A local read access is either a read hit or a CAS hit with the negative test result. A local write is either a write hit to exclusive data or a positive CAS hit to exclusive data:

$$rlocal(aca, acc, i) = hit(aca, a, i) \wedge (r \vee cas \wedge \neg test(acc, aca(i).data(a)))$$
$$wlocal(aca, acc, i) = hit(aca, a, i) \wedge (w \vee cas \wedge test(acc, aca(i).data(a)))$$
$$\wedge aca(i).s(a) \in \{E, M\} .$$

---

[7] In Sect. 8.3.4 we treat cache hits on CAS with the negative test result the same way as read hits and do not update the state of the cache line.

We say that an access to a cache system configuration aca at port i is *local*, if it is a local read or a local write. An access is called *global* if it is not local and not a flush:

$$local(aca, acc, i) = rlocal(aca, acc, i) \lor wlocal(aca, acc, i)$$
$$global(aca, acc, i) = \neg local(aca, acc, i) \land \neg f .$$

Summarizing definitions given above, we have specified four types of accesses: local reads (including negative CAS hits), local writes (including positive CAS hits), global accesses, and flushes.

Now we define the transition function $ms' = \delta_1(ms, acc, i)$ and the output function $d = pdout1(ms, acc, i)$ for every possible type of accesses. We aim at the following:

- to maintain the state invariants, i.e., to have $sinv(ms')$,
- to have the resulting memory abstraction $m(ms')$ behave as if access acc had been applied with ordinary memory semantics to the previous memory abstraction $m(ms)$:

$$m(ms') = \delta_M(m(ms), acc) ,$$

- the response d to read accesses to be equal to the response given by the memory abstraction $m(ms)$:

$$pdout1(ms, acc, i) = dataout(m(ms), acc) = m(ms)(acc.a) .$$

Flush

A flush invalidates abstract cache line a and writes back the cache line in case it is modified or owned:

$$f \rightarrow aca'(i).s(a) = I \land (aca(i).s(a) \in \{M, O\} \rightarrow mm'(a) = aca(i).data(a)) .$$

Note that we allow invalidation of any cache line, even the one which is initially in state E, S, or I. The main memory in that case is not updated.

Local Write Accesses

Local write accesses update the local cache line addressed by a and change the state to M:

$$wlocal(aca, acc, i) \rightarrow$$
$$aca'(i).data(a) = modify(aca(i).data(a), data, bw)$$
$$aca'(i).s(a) = C3(aca(i).s(a), acc.type, *).ps'$$
$$= M .$$

In case of positive CAS hits we also need to specify the output of the memory system. We do this later in this section.

Global Accesses

For global accesses we run the MOESI protocol in an atomic way:

$$global(aca, acc, i) \rightarrow$$
$$mprot = C1(aca(i).s(a), acc.type)$$
$$\forall j : sprot(j) = C2(aca(i).s(a), mprot)$$
$$\forall X \in \{ch, di\} : sprot.X = \bigvee_{j \neq i} sprot(j).X$$
$$\forall j : aca'(j).s(a) = \begin{cases} C3(aca(i).s(a), acc.type, sprot.ch).ps' & i = j \\ C2(aca(i).s(a), mprot).ss' & i \neq j \end{cases}.$$

Next, we specify the data broadcast $bdata$ via the bus during a global transaction. If the broadcast signal $mprot(i).bc$ is active then the master broadcasts the modified result $modify(aca(i).data(a), data, bw)$. If a slave activates the data intervention signal then it is responsible for putting the data on the bus. The intervening slave j is unique by the state invariants $sinv(ms)$. In other cases the data are fetched from the main memory :

$$global(aca, acc, i) \rightarrow$$
$$bdata = \begin{cases} modify(aca(i).data(a), data, bw) & mprot(i).bc \\ aca(j).data(a) & sprot(j).di \\ mm(a) & \text{otherwise} . \end{cases}$$

During a global access the caches signaling a cache hit $sprot(j).ch$ store the broadcast result if the master activates a broadcast signal $mprot(i).bc$:

$$\forall j \neq i : global(aca, acc, i) \wedge mprot(i).bc \wedge sprot(j).ch \rightarrow$$
$$aca'(j).data(a) = bdata .$$

Note that in case of a write hit or a positive CAS hit the master and the affected slaves store the same data for address a.

For global CAS accesses we define the test data as the old value stored in cache i if we have a hit (which means that the broadcast signal is on) or as the data obtained from the bus otherwise:

$$global(aca, acc, i) \wedge cas \rightarrow tdata = \begin{cases} aca(i).data(a) & mprot(i).bc \\ bdata & \text{otherwise} . \end{cases}$$

Negative CAS misses are grouped together with the regular read misses into global reads:

$$rglobal(aca, acc, i) = global(aca, acc, i) \wedge (r \vee cas \wedge \neg test(acc, tdata)) .$$

A global write is a global access which is either a write or which is a CAS with the positive result of the test:

$$wglobal(aca, acc, i) = global(aca, acc, i) \wedge (w \vee cas \wedge test(acc, tdata)) .$$

In case of a global read the master copies the missing cache line from the bus without modifications:

$$rglobal(aca, acc, i) \rightarrow aca'(i).data(a) = bdata .$$

In case of a global write the master either modifies its old data in case if it is a hit (which means that the broadcast signal is on) or modifies the data obtained from the bus:

$$wglobal(aca, acc, i) \rightarrow$$

$$aca'(i).data(a) = \begin{cases} modify(aca(i).data(a), data, bw) & mprot(i).bc \\ modify(bdata, data, bw) & \text{otherwise} . \end{cases}$$

Answers of Reads

For a read request or a CAS request, we return either the data from the local cache or the data fetched from the bus:

$$r \vee cas \rightarrow pdout1(ms, acc, i) = \begin{cases} aca(i).data(a) & hit(aca, a, i) \\ bdata & \text{otherwise} . \end{cases}$$

Iterated Transitions

For memory systems ms, sequential access sequences acc', sequences is of ports, and step numbers n, we define the effect of n steps of the atomic protocol in the obvious way:

$$\Delta_1^0(ms, acc', is) = ms$$
$$\Delta_1^{n+1}(ms, acc', is) = \delta_1(\Delta_1^n(ms, acc', is), acc'[n], is[n]) .$$

The following lemma is proven by an easy induction on y.

Lemma 8.8 (decomposition of 1 step accesses). Let

$$ms' = \Delta_1^x(ms, acc', is) .$$

Then,

$$\Delta_1^{x+y}(ms, acc', is) = \Delta_1^y(ms', acc'[x : x + y - 1], is[x : x + y - 1]) .$$

8.3.5 Properties of the Atomic Protocol

In the atomic execution of the MOESI protocol the state invariants are preserved.

Lemma 8.9 (invariants maintained). Let $ms' = \delta_1(ms, acc, i)$. Then,

$$sinv(ms) \to sinv(ms') \,.$$

Proof. The proof of this lemma is error prone, so it is usually shown by model checking [4, 13].   □

An easy proof shows that we have achieved two more goals that were stated before.

Lemma 8.10 (memory abstraction 1 step). Let $ms' = \delta_1(ms, acc, i)$ and the state invariants $sinv(ms)$ hold. Then,

- the resulting memory abstraction $m(ms')$ behaves as if access acc would have been applied with ordinary memory semantics to the previous memory abstraction $m(ms)$:

$$m(ms') = \delta_M(m(ms), acc) \,,$$

- the response to read accesses is equal to the response given by the memory abstraction $m(ms)$:

$$pdout1(ms, acc, i) = dataout(m(ms), acc) = m(ms)(acc.a) \,.$$

By induction on y we show that the memory abstraction after y steps of the atomic protocol is equal to the y memory steps applied to the initial memory abstraction of the system.

Lemma 8.11 (memory abstraction 1 step iterative). Let the state invariants $sinv(ms)$ hold. Then,

$$m(\Delta_1^y(ms, acc', is')) = \Delta_M^y(m(ms), acc')) \,.$$

The following technical lemma formalizes the fact that the abstract protocol with an access acc only operates on memory system slice $\Pi(ms, acc.a)$. The reader might have observed that this address does not even occur in the tables specifying the protocol, because everybody understands, that line address $aca.a$ (alone) is concerned in each cache. Readers familiar with cache designs will of course observe that read, write, or CAS accesses acc can trigger flushes evicting cache lines with line addresses $a' \neq acc.a$; but these are treated as separate accesses in our arguments.

Lemma 8.12 (properties 1 step). Let $ms' = \delta_1(ms, acc, i)$ and $a = acc.a$. Then,

1. Local read accesses don't change the memory system:

$$rlocal(ms.aca, acc, i) \rightarrow ms' = ms .$$

2. Slices different from slice a of the memory system are not changed

$$b \neq a \rightarrow \Pi(ms', b) = \Pi(ms, b) .$$

3. Possible changes to slice a only depend on slice a:

$$\forall ms_1, ms_2 : \Pi(ms_1, a) = \Pi(ms_2, a) \rightarrow$$
$$\Pi(\delta_1(ms_1, acc, i), a) = \Pi(\delta_1(ms_2, acc, i), a) .$$

4. Answers of reads to address a depend only on slice a:

$$\forall ms_1, ms_2 : \Pi(ms_1, a) = \Pi(ms_2, a) \rightarrow$$
$$pdout1(ms_1, acc, i) = pdout1(ms_2, acc, i) .$$

Proof. The proof for every case is based on the following arguments.

1. For local reads we specified no change of ms.
2. In the definition of function δ_1 we only specified components that change. Slices other than slice a were not among them.
3. This is a simple bookkeeping exercise, where one has to compare all parts of the definition of function δ_1 for the two memory system configurations ms_1 and ms_2[8]
4. Bookkeeping exercise.

$\square$

8.4 Gate Level Design of a Shared Memory System

We present the construction of a gate level design of a shared memory system in the following order.

1. We specify in this section the interface between processors $p(j)$ and caches $ca(i)$ and the interface between caches ca and the main memory bus b. Bus b is extended by components $b.mprot$ and $b.sprot$ for the exchange of protocol signals. These components are implemented as an open collector bus.
2. We specify the data paths of each (direct mapped) cache $ca(i)$. These data paths have three obvious components for the data, tag, and state RAMs of the cache. The data paths for the state RAM include circuits $C1$, $C2$, and $C3$ introduced in Sect. 8.3.3 implementing the tables of the MOESI protocol. Each cache $ca(i)$ may have to serve two purposes simultaneously:

---

[8] This proof can be avoided if one defines function δ_1 directly as a function of slice $\Pi(ms, a)$, but this definition does not match the hardware design so well.

i) serving its processor as a master of accesses and ii) participating as a slave in the protocol. Therefore, all RAMs $ca(i).data$, $ca(i).tag$, and $ca(i).s$ will be implemented as dual ported RAMs.

3. We present control automata. Each cache $ca(i)$ has two such automata: one for accesses where $ca(i)$ is master and one for accesses when $ca(i)$ is slave. Thus, in a system with P caches we have $2P$ control automata. Showing that master and slave automata are in some sense synchronized while they are handling the same access will be a crucial part of the correctness proof.

4. Accesses requiring cooperation of caches via the memory bus b are called *global* accesses. In case several caches want to initiate a global access at the same time (as masters) a *bus arbiter* has to grant the bus to one of them and deny it to the others. Construction of the bus arbiter is presented at the end of this section.

In this and the following chapter for signals and RAMs X of cache i we use equivalent notations $ca(i).X$ and $X(i)$. We will also sometimes omit index (i) if talking about internal computation of signals in a single cache.

8.4.1 Specification of Interfaces

We need to establish interfaces between

1. processors p and their caches; this is done by signals,
2. the caches $ca(i)$ and the bus b; this is done (mostly) via dedicated registers.

$p \rightarrow ca$ Interface

Signals from a processor p to its cache $ca(i)$:

- $ca(i).preq \in \mathbb{B}$ – processor request signal,
- $ca(i).pdin \in \mathbb{B}^{64}$ – processor data coming into the cache,
- $ca(i).pcdin \in \mathbb{B}^{64}$ – compare data for CAS requests,
- $ca(i).pa \in \mathbb{B}^{29}$ – processor line address,
- $ca(i).type \in \mathbb{B}^3 = (ca(i).pr, ca(i).pw, ca(i).pcas)$ – type of an access; exactly one of these bits should be active for every request,
- $ca(i).bw \in \mathbb{B}^8$ - byte write signals. They must be off for read requests and half of them must be off for CAS requests:

$$ca(i).preq \land ca(i).pr \rightarrow ca(i).bw = 0^8$$

$$ca(i).preq \land ca(i).pcas \rightarrow ca(i).bw \in \{0^4 1^4, 1^4 0^4\}.$$

Recall that our main memory (Sect. 3.5.6) behaves as a ROM for addresses $0^{29-r} b^r$, where $b \in \mathbb{B}^r$ for some small r. As a result, any write performed to this memory region has no effect. Yet, in the sequential memory semantics given in Sect. 8.2.4, we consider the whole memory to be writable. To resolve

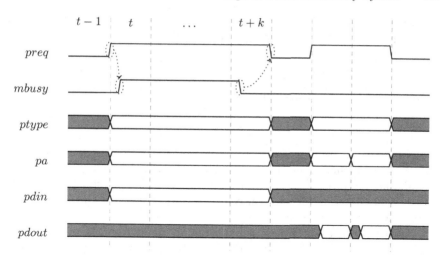

Fig. 133. The timing diagram for a k-cycle write access followed by two consecutive 1-cycle read accesses

that problem we add a software condition, stating that the processors never issue write and CAS requests to addresses smaller than or equal to $0^{29-r}1^r$:

$$ca(i).preq \land ca(i).pa[28:r] = 0^{29-r} \rightarrow ca(i).bw = 0^8.$$

$ca \rightarrow p$ Interface

Signals from cache to processor:

- $ca(i).mbusy \in \mathbb{B}$ – memory system is busy (generated by control automaton of the cache),
- $ca(i).pdout \in \mathbb{B}^{64}$ – data output to processor.

$p \leftrightarrow ca$ Protocol

We need to define a protocol for interaction between a processor and its caches (data and instruction cache). Communication between processor p and its cache ca is done under the following rules:

- p starts a request by activating $preq$,
- ca in the same cycle acknowledges the request by raising (Mealy[9]) signal $mbusy$ (unless a one-cycle access is performed),
- ca finishes with lowering $mbusy$, and
- p disables $preq$ in the next cycle.

---

[9] Recall, that a Mealy output of the control automaton is a function of the input and the current state.

The timing diagram for a $k-$cycle (write) cache access is depicted in Fig. 133.
    Cycle t is the first cycle of an access iff

$$\neg mbusy^{t-1} \wedge preq^t \; .$$

Cycle $t' \geq t$ is the last cycle of an access iff

$$\neg mbusy^{t'} \wedge preq^{t'} \; .$$

Observe that 1-cycle accesses are desirable and indeed possible (in case of local reads, including negative CAS hits). Then signal $mbusy$ is not raised at all and the processor can immediately start a new request in cycle $t+1$. The timing diagram for two consecutive 1$-$cycle read accesses is depicted in Fig. 133.
    Once the processor request signal is raised, inputs from the processor must be stable[10] until the cache takes away the $mbusy$ signal. In order to formalize this condition we identify the cache input signals of cache $ca(i)$ in cycle t as

$$cain(i,t) = \{pa, type, pbw, preq\} \cup \begin{cases} \{pdin\} & ca(i).pw^t \\ \{pdin, pcdin\} & ca(i).pcas^t \\ \emptyset & \text{otherwise} \end{cases}$$

and then require

$$ca(i).preq^t \wedge ca(i).mbusy^t \wedge X \in cain(i,t) \rightarrow ca(i).X^{t+1} = ca(i).X^t \; .$$

Memory Bus

The memory bus b is subdivided into 4 sets of bus lines. The first three sets are already known from the main memory specification in Sect. 3.5 and contain regular tristate lines. The corresponding outputs are connected to these lines via the tristate drivers. The fourth set of lines supports the cache protocol and is an open collector bus:

- $b.d \in \mathbb{B}^{64}$ – for transmitting data contained in a cache line,
- $b.ad \in \mathbb{B}^{29}$ – memory line address,
- $b.mmreq \in \mathbb{B}$, $b.mmw \in \mathbb{B}$, $b.mmack \in \mathbb{B}$ – memory protocol lines,
- $b.prot \in \mathbb{B}^5$ – cache protocol lines.

$ca \leftrightarrow b$ Interface

The following dedicated registers are used between cache $ca(i)$ and bus b:

- $ca(i).bdout \in \mathbb{B}^{64}$ – cache data output to the bus,

---

[10] Stability in the digital sense is enough here; the processors never access main memory directly.

- $ca(i).bdin \in \mathbb{B}^{64}$ – cache data input from the bus,
- $ca(i).badout \in \mathbb{B}^{29}$ – (master) line address output to the bus,
- $ca(i).badin \in \mathbb{B}^{29}$ – (slave) line address input from the bus,
- $ca(i).mmreq \in \mathbb{B}$ – cache request to the main memory (a set-clear flip-flop),
- $ca(i).mmw \in \mathbb{B}$ – cache write signal to the main memory (a set-clear flip-flop),
- $ca(i).mprotout \in \mathbb{B}^3$, $ca(i).sprotout \in \mathbb{B}^2$ – master and slave protocol data output to the bus,
- $ca(i).mprotin \in \mathbb{B}^3$, $ca(i).sprotin \in \mathbb{B}^2$ – slave and master protocol data input from the bus.

For the signal $b.mmack$ we do not introduce a dedicated input register and sample this signal directly from the bus.

For the tristate lines of the memory bus we use the control logic developed in Sect. 3.5. We use set-clear flip-flops for the generation of the output enable signals Xoe with $X \in \{mmreq, mmw, bdout, badout\}$. The ownership of the tristate lines of the memory bus is controlled by a fair master arbiter (Sect. 8.4.5). To run a transaction on the bus, cache i raises a request signal

$$ca(i).req$$

to the arbiter and waits until the arbiter activates signal $grant[i]$. Construction of the arbiter makes sure that at most one grant signal is active at a time. Register $ca(i).req$ is implemented as a set-clear flip-flop. Control signals for all set-clear flip-flops are generated by the control automata of the cache.

As shown in Fig. 134, the cache protocol signals are inverted before they are put on the open collector bus and before they are clocked from the bus into a register. Thus, by de Morgan's law we have for every component $x \in [0:4]$:

$$\neg b.prot[x] = \neg(\bigwedge_j \neg ca(j).bprotout[x])$$

$$= \bigvee_j ca(j).bprotout[x] \ .$$

The following synonyms for the protocol signals are used:

$$b.mprot.Ca = b.mprot[2] = \neg b.prot[4]$$
$$b.mprot.im = b.mprot[1] = \neg b.prot[3]$$
$$b.mprot.bc = b.mprot[0] = \neg b.prot[2]$$
$$b.sprot.ch = b.sprot[1] = \neg b.prot[1]$$
$$b.sprot.di = b.sprot[0] = \neg b.prot[0] \ .$$

When several slaves signal a data intervention, further bus arbitration appears to be necessary, since only one cache should access the bus at a time. However,

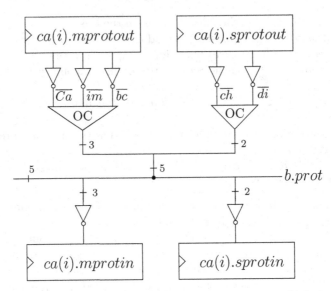

Fig. 134. Using de Morgan's law to compute the OR of active high signals on the open collector bus *b.prot*

arbitration is not necessary as long as only one slave will forward the required cache line. This is guaranteed by the cache coherency protocol, where we do not raise di in case of a miss on data in state S. However, the protocol provides that all caches keep the same data when it is shared, so that we could in principle forward the data if we arbitrate the data intervention. A possible arbitration algorithm for data intervention in a "shared clean miss" case would be to select $ca(i)$ with the smallest i, s.t., di is active. This can be efficiently implemented using a parallel prefix OR circuit.

8.4.2 Data Paths of Caches

The data paths for the data RAM, state RAM, and tag RAM are presented in Figs. 135, 137, 136 respectively.

The control signals for the data paths are generated by the control automata described in the following section. Let us try to get a first understanding of the designs.

In general RAMs are controlled from two sides: i) from the processor side using port a and ii) from the bus side using port b. Auxiliary registers $ca(i).dataouta'$, $ca(i).tagouta'$, $ca(i).souta'$, and $ca(i).soutb'$ latch the outputs of the RAMs. We have introduced these registers in order to prevent situations, where reads and writes to the same address of a RAM are performed during the same cycle[11]. Note that such situations are not problematic in our

---

[11] Our construction guarantees that we never perform accesses to different ports of the same RAM with the same cache line address in a single cycle. As a result,

hardware model, because our RAMs are edge triggered. However, in many technologies RAMs are pulse triggered, and then reads and writes to the same address in the same cycle lead to undefined behaviour. With the auxiliary registers the design of this book is simply implementable in far more technologies, in particular in the FPGA based implementation from [8]. For the purpose of correctness proof we show in Lemma 8.24 that they always have the same data as the current output of the edge triggered RAM. Hence, in the remainder of the book we simplify our reasoning about the data paths by simply replacing these registers with wires.

Data Paths of the Data RAM

The data paths in Fig. 135 support the following operations:

- Local read accesses. This includes read hits and negative CAS hits. The processor addresses port a of the RAM with pa. The hit is signaled by a processor hit signal $phit$. This signal is produced by the data paths for the tag RAM as shown in Fig. 136. Data RAM output $outa$ is routed to the data output $pdout$ at the processor side.
- Local write accesses. This includes write hits to an exclusive state and positive CAS hits to an exclusive state. It requires two cycles which together perform an operation. The cache line addressed by pa is read out and temporarily stored in register $dataouta'$. From there it becomes an input to a $modify$ circuit which computes the modify function

$$byte(i, modify(x, y, bw)) = \begin{cases} byte(i, x) & bw[i] = 1 \\ byte(i, y) & bw[i] = 0 \end{cases}.$$

Simple construction of a modify circuit is given in Sect. 4.2.2. For any kind of write, data to be written y and byte write signals bw come from the processor. The result is written to the data RAM via port a.
- Flushes. Except for times when the cache is filling up, a cache miss access is generally preceded by a flush: a so called $victim$ line with some $eviction$ $line$ $address$ va is evicted from the cache in order to make space for the missing line. In a direct mapped cache the eviction address has cache line address

$$va.c = pa.c .$$

The victim line is taken from output $outa$ of the data RAM and put on the bus via register $bdout$.

---

reads and writes to the same cache line address in a single cycle can only occur through the same port (our RAM construction does allow to read and write the same port in a single cycle). Outputs of port b of data and tag RAMs are never used in cycles when these ports are being written. Hence, we do not introduce auxiliary registers for them.

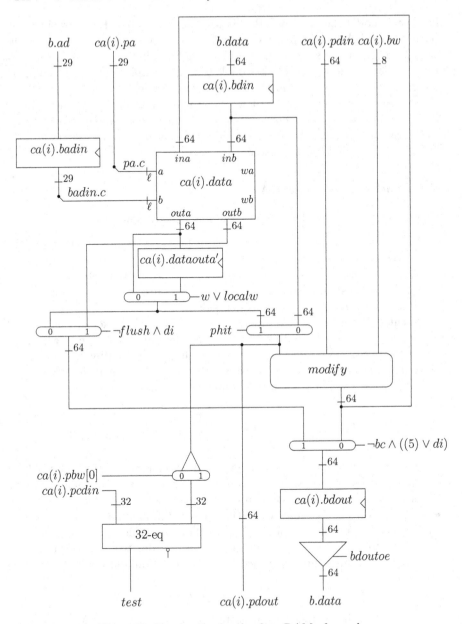

Fig. 135. Data paths for the data RAM of a cache

- Global write accesses. This includes write misses, positive CAS misses, write hits to shared data, and positive CAS hits to shared data. In case of a cache miss, the missing line is clocked from the bus into register *bdin*. From there it becomes an input to the modifier. The output of the modifier is written back to the data RAM at port a. In case of a hit to shared data, the cache line is fetched from port a and stored temporarily in register *dataouta'*. After that it goes to the modify circuit; the output of the modifier is written to the RAM via port a and is broadcast on the bus via register *bdout*.
- Global read accesses. This includes read misses and negative CAS misses. The missing line is clocked from the bus into register *bdin*. The modifier with byte write signals $bw = 0^8$ is used as a data path for the missing cache line. It is output to the processor via signal *pdout* and written into the data RAM via input *ina*.
- Data intervention. The line address is clocked from the bus into register *badin*. The intervention line missing in some other cache is taken from output *outb* of the data RAM and put on the bus via register *bdout*.

Signal *test* is used to denote the result of the CAS test both for local and global accesses:

$$test \equiv pcdin = \begin{cases} data(pa.c)[63:32] & \neg bw[0] \land phit \\ data(pa.c)[31:0] & bw[0] \land phit \\ bdin[63:32] & \neg bw[0] \land \neg phit \\ bdin[31:0] & bw[0] \land \neg phit \ . \end{cases}$$

Data Paths of the Tag RAM

The tag RAM is very much wired like a tag RAM in an ordinary direct mapped cache. It is addressed from the processor side by signal *pa* and from the bus side by register *badin*. We operate the data paths for the tag RAM under the following rules:

- New tags are only written into the tag RAM from the processor side.
- Hit signal *phit* for the processor side is computed from outputs *souta* and *tagouta* of state and tag RAMs respectively or from the outputs of auxiliary registers *souta'* and *tagouta'*, depending on whether port a of these RAMs is written in this cycle or not. Lemma 8.24 allows us to treat these auxiliary registers simply as wires, which results in the desired definition of the *phit* signal:

$$phit \equiv pa.t = tag(pa.c) \land \neg s(pa.c).I \ .$$

Signal *bhit* for the bus side is computed using outputs *soutb* and *tagoutb* directly, because signal *bhit* is never used in cycles when state and tag RAMs are written through port b:

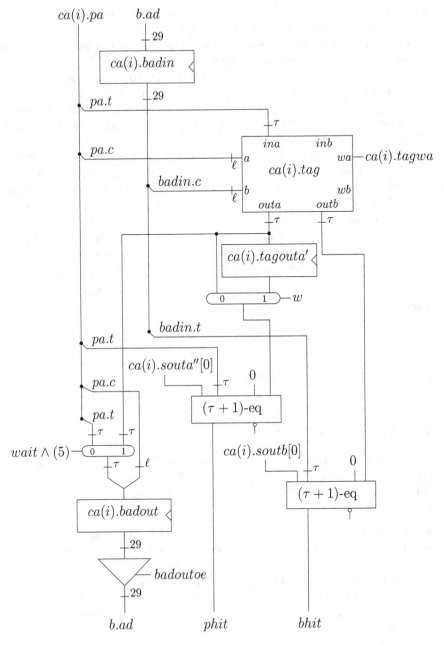

Fig. 136. Data paths for the tag RAM of a cache

$$bhit \equiv badin.t = tag(badin.c) \wedge \neg s(badin.c).I \ .$$

- For global accesses, the processor address can be put on the bus via register *badout*.
- For flushes, the tag of the victim address is taken from output *outa* of the tag RAM. The victim line address is then

$$va = ca(i).tagouta \circ pa.c \ .$$

It is put on the bus via register *badout*.

Data Paths of the State RAM

As before, addressing from the processor side is by signal *pa* and from the bus side by register *badin*. Some control signals come from the control automata and are explained in Sect. 8.4.3. The data paths of the state RAM use the circuits $C1$, $C2$, and $C3$ from Sect. 8.3.3 which compute the memory protocol signals and the next state of cache lines. We operate the data paths for the state RAM under the following rules:

- The current master state is read from output *outa* of the state RAM.
- The new state ps' is computed by circuit $C3$ and is written back to input *ina* of the state RAM. As one of the inputs to $C3$ we provide the type of the access. This type depends not only on the processor request, but also on the current state of the master automaton (Sect. 8.4.3): if the automaton is in state *flush* then we calculate the new state for a flush access (which is I independent of other inputs of $C3$); there is also a case when we perform a flush access while we are still in *wait* without going to state *flush* – this corresponds to an invalidation of a clean line without writing it back to memory. For more explanations refer to the description of states *wait* and *flush* in Sect. 8.4.4.
- For global accesses, the master protocol signals are computed by circuit $C1$ and put on the bus via register *mprotout*. The mux on top of $C1$ provides the invalid state in case if we don't have a processor hit. The mux on top of register *mprotout* is used to clear the master protocol signals after a run of the protocol.
- If the cache works as a slave, it determines the slave response with circuit $C2$ using the state from output *outb* of the state RAM and puts in on the bus via register *sprotout*. The mux on top of circuit $C2$ forwards the effect of local writes whose line address conflicts with the line address of the current global access (so that we don't have to wait 1 cycle until the modified state is written to the RAM in case of a local write). The mux on top of register *sprotout* is used to clear the slave response after a run of the protocol.
- The new state of a slave ss' is computed by circuit $C2$ and is written back to input *inb* of the state RAM.

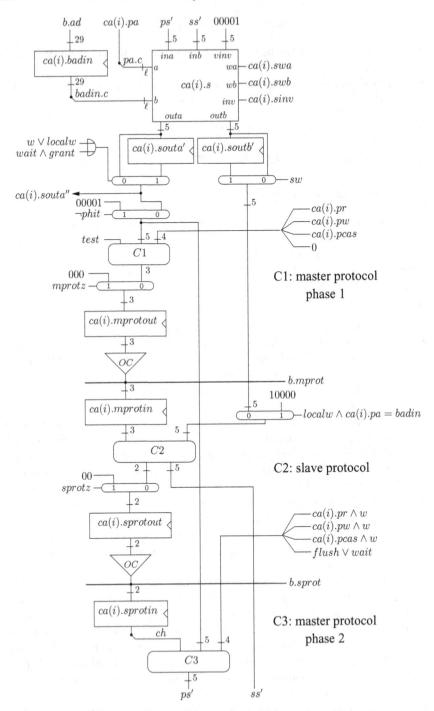

Fig. 137. Data paths for the state RAM of a cache

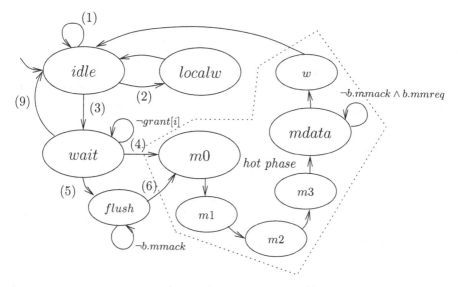

Fig. 138. Master automaton

8.4.3 Cache Protocol Automata

We define state automata for the master and the slave case in order to implement the cache coherency protocol. In general the protocol is divided into 3 phases:

- Master phase 1: Ca, im, bc are computed and put on the bus.
- Slave phase: slave responds by computing and sending ch, di, generating new slave state ss'.
- Master phase 2: master computes new state ps'.

For local accesses, only the last step of the protocol is performed (master phase 2).

The state diagrams for the master and slave automata are presented in Figs. 138 and 139.

Automata States

We define sets of master and slave automata states as

$$M = \{idle, localw, wait, flush, m0, m1, m2, m3, mdata, w\}$$
$$S = \{sidle, sidle', s1, s2, s3, sdata, sw\} \ .$$

The sets of states belonging to local and global transactions are defined as

$$L = \{idle, localw\}$$
$$G = M \setminus L \ .$$

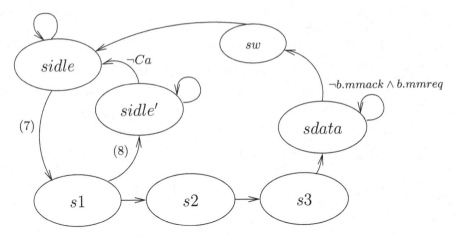

Fig. 139. Slave automaton

We also define sets of states that correspond to warm and hot phases of global transactions:

$$W = G \setminus \{wait\}$$
$$H = W \setminus \{flush\} .$$

The overview on the states is given in Table 12.

We denote by $z(i)$ and $zs(i)$ the state of a master or a slave automaton i respectively.

For states $x \in M$, we mean by $x(i)^t$ the statement that master automaton i is in state x during cycle t. Similarly for $x \in S$ we mean by $x(i)^t$ the statement that slave automaton i is in state x during cycle t.

$$x(i)^t \equiv \begin{cases} z(i)^t = x & x \in M \\ zs(i)^t = x & x \in S . \end{cases}$$

We use the following notation for the set of states $A \in \{M, S, L, G, W, H\}$:

$$A(i)^t \equiv \begin{cases} z(i)^t \in A & A \neq S \\ zs(i)^t \in A & A = S \end{cases}$$
$$A(i)^{[t:t']} \equiv \forall q \in [t : t'] : A(i)^q .$$

Statements without index t are implicitly quantified for all cycles t. For transitions numbered with (n) in Figs. 138 and 139, we mean with $(n)(i)^t$ that the condition holds for the automata of cache i in cycle t.

When talking about automata states and transitions we often omit explicitly specifying index i in case when it is clear from the context or when the statement is implicitly quantified for all cache indices i.

Table 12. An overview on the automata states

#	master state	intended work	slave state	intended work
0	*idle*	local read accesses (unless colliding with global transaction on the bus)	*sidle*	snooping on bus
1	*localw*	local write accesses (unless collision)	-	-
2	*wait*	wait for the arbiter to grant bus access, compute Ca, im, bc	-	-
3	*flush*	write back dirty line to mm, compute Ca, im, bc	-	-
4	$m0$	transmit Ca, im, bc via $b.mprot$	-	-
5	$m1$	wait for slave response	$s1$	check for $bhit$, compute slave response ch, di
6	$m2$	wait for slave response	$s2$	transmit response ch, di on $b.sprot$
6'			*sidle'*	wait until Ca is lowered on the bus (in *sidle* new transaction would start)
7	$m3$	analyze slave signals, prepare memory access or data broadcast (if necessary)	$s3$	prepare data for data intervention (if necessary)
8	*mdata*	wait for memory response (if necessary), read data from the bus (if necessary)	*sdata*	transmit data on the bus or read data from the bus (if necessary)
9	w	write $data$,tag,s	sw	write $data$, s (if necessary)

8.4.4 Automata Transitions and Control Signals

Before we consider the transition and control signals of the master and slave automata we first introduce some auxiliary signals.

Local reads are identified by signal $rlocal$:

$$rlocal = phit \wedge (pr \vee pcas \wedge \neg test) \, .$$

Local writes are indicated by signal $wlocal$:

$$wlocal = phit \wedge s(pa.c) \in \{E, M\} \wedge (pw \vee pcas \wedge test) \, .$$

A local computation is performed if either $rlocal$ or $wlocal$ is active:

$$local = rlocal \vee wlocal \, .$$

If a processor issues a request for data, which are currently being processed in a global transaction, handling the request locally is not possible. In this case the signal $snoopconflict$ is raised:

$$snoopconflict \equiv \neg sidle \wedge pa.c = badin.c \,.$$

Note that a snoop conflict is discovered one cycle after the address is actually on the bus (we have to clock data from the bus to register *badin* first).

A crucial decision on whether to handle an access locally or globally is performed when the master automaton is in state idle and a processor request is active. For decisions to go local, the master additionally has to ensure that no snoop conflict is raised. In case of a global CAS hit we have to reassure that the decision to go global is still correct in the last cycle of stage *wait*.

With these prerequisites at hand, we now continue with the actual state transitions and generated control signals of the automata, starting with state *idle*. For every state we write the generated signals in the form

signal name := condition,

meaning that this signal is raised in the given state if the condition is satisfied. If we omit stating the condition, then the signal is always high in a given state.

State *idle*

In the *idle* state the signal *mbusy* is deactivated if either a local read is performed (which can be finished in one cycle) or there is no processor request at all:

$$\neg mbusy := \neg preq \vee (rlocal \wedge \neg snoopconflict) \,.$$

Note that *mbusy* is a Mealy signal and thus does not need to be precomputed before the clock edges. There are three possible transitions starting from state *idle*.

1. Transition (1): $idle \rightarrow idle$.
   This transition is taken if there is a snoop conflict or if we have a local read or there is no request from the processor to its cache at all:

   $$(1) = \neg preq \vee snoopconflict \vee rlocal \,.$$

2. Transition (2): $idle \rightarrow localw$.
   This transition is taken if there is a local write request and no global transaction currently accesses the respective data (no snoop conflict):

   $$(2) = preq \wedge \neg snoopconflict \wedge wlocal \,.$$

3. Transition (3): $idle \rightarrow wait$.
   This transition is taken if the processor request is not local:

   $$(3) = preq \wedge \neg local \,.$$

In case we go to the *localw* state we clock registers $ca(i).dataouta'$ and $ca(i).souta'$ which will be used in the next cycle in place of outputs of data and state RAMs:

$ca(i).dataouta'ce := (2)$

$ca(i).souta'ce := (2)$.

With the transition into state *wait* we activate signal $ca(i).reqset$ to issue a request for the bus to the arbiter (Sect. 8.4.5). Additionally, we clock register $ca(i).souta'$ which might be used in the next cycle in place of the output of the state RAM:

$ca(i).souta'ce := (3)$

$ca(i).reqset := (3)$.

In *idle* we also transmit the content of $ca(i).data(ca(i).pa.c)$ via $ca(i).pdout$ back to the processor which waits for $\neg mbusy$.

State *localw*

In state *localw* the master changes its state ps' for the given cache line from E to M, see Fig. 137. The activated signals are

$ca(i).swa$

$ca(i).datawa$

$\neg ca(i).mbusy$.

Signal *swa* is used in the state RAM (Fig. 137) and signal *datawa* is used in the data RAM (Fig. 135). In state *localw* we always go back directly to *idle* in the next cycle.

State *wait*

In state *wait*, the processor waits for its request to be granted by the bus arbiter (Sect. 8.4.5.

In the last cycle of *wait* we have to repeat the test for global CAS hits. In case we went from *idle* to *wait* under condition

$$phit \wedge s(pa.c) \in \{S, O\} \wedge pcas \wedge test,$$

it may happen that during the time when we are waiting for the bus our slave automaton updates the cache data or the cache state for address *pa.c*. An update of the state is not a problem, because from S and O the line can go only to S, O, or I, which means that we still need to perform a global transaction. Yet, if the data RAM has been updated, the outcome of the local test might not be the same anymore. In this case we should not start a global transaction at all; instead, we should return to *idle*. We call such an access *delayed local*.

There are four transitions starting from state *wait*:

1. Transition: *wait* → *wait*.
   While ¬*grant*[*i*], the automaton stays in *wait*.
2. Transition (5): *wait* → *flush*.
   When the request is granted, but the cache line is occupied and dirty, the automaton goes to state *flush*:

$$(5) = grant[i] \land \neg phit \land ca(i).souta' \in \{O, M\} .$$

We use the output of the auxiliary register *souta'* instead of the output of port a of the state RAM here because signal (5) is used below to generate the write enable signal to port a of the state RAM. By Lemma 8.24 (auxiliary registers) we always have:

$$wait(i) \land grant[i] \rightarrow ca(i).souta' = ca(i).s(ca(i).pa.c) .$$

3. Transition (9): *wait* → *idle*.
   If the conditions for a local read are satisfied by a CAS access, we go to state *idle* and perform a delayed local access:

$$(9) = grant[i] \land phit \land pcas \land \neg test .$$

4. Transition (4): *wait* → *m0*.
   If the request is granted, there is no cache line to be evicted, and the condition (9) is not satisfied, then we go to *m0* and start a global transaction:

$$(4) = grant[i] \land \neg(5) \land \neg(9) .$$

The following signals are set in state *wait*:

$ca(i).bdoutce := (5)$

$ca(i).badoutce := (5) \lor (4)$

$ca(i).mmreqset := (5)$

$ca(i).mmwset := (5)$

$ca(i).bdoutoeset := (5)$

$ca(i).badoutoeset := (5) \lor (4)$

$ca(i).mmreqoeset := (5)$

$ca(i).mmwoeset := (5)$

$ca(i).mprotoutce := (4)$

$ca(i).reqclr := (9)$

$\neg ca(i).mbusy := (9)$

$ca(i).swa := (4) \land \neg phit \land ca(i).souta' \in \{E, S\}$

$ca(i).souta'ce := \neg((5) \lor (4) \lor (9))$.

Signal $reqclr$ is used to clear the request to the bus arbiter (Sect. 8.4.5) in case of (9). Note that in case of (4) we have to load the master protocol data for transmission on the bus.

There is a case when the cache line is occupied by another line (i.e., the current tag of the cache line does not match to the tag of the processor address) but we still go to state $m0$. This happens when the line is clean; hence, it can be evicted without writing it back to the memory. In this case we write I to the state RAM (as guaranteed by the output of the circuit $C3$ in Fig. 137). This write is not necessary for the correctness of implementation: we could simply "evict" this line later in state w, by overwriting the current tag in the tag RAM with the tag of the processor address (such a write would make the overwritten cache line invalid in the abstract cache). In the proof, however, that would force us to simulate two accesses simultaneously: a global access for the line addressed by pa and a flush access for the evicted line. To avoid this confusion and to (greatly) simplify the proofs, we prefer to do this invalidation explicitly by writing I to the state RAM on a transition from $wait$ to $m0$. Note, that for the generation of signal swa we use the output of the auxiliary register $souta'$ instead of the output of port a of the state RAM. By Lemma 8.24 (auxiliary registers) we have in this case:

$$ca(i).souta' = ca(i).s(ca(i).pa.c) .$$

State $flush$

In state $flush$, we write the cache line that needs to be evicted to memory. The following signals are set:

$ca(i).bdoutoeclr := (6)$

$ca(i).mmreqoeclr := (6)$

$ca(i).mmreqclr := (6)$

$ca(i).mmwoeclr := (6)$

$ca(i).mmwclr := (6)$

$ca(i).badoutce := (6)$

$ca(i).mprotoutce := (6)$

$ca(i).swa := (6)$.

When we leave the state $flush$ we have to load master data for transmission on the bus[12]. After the flush is done, we write I to the state RAM. Just

---

[12] The multiplexer controlled by signal $phit$ on Fig. 137 makes sure that we forward the invalid state as an input to circuit $C1$. Note that for the computations of

as the same kind of write performed in state *wait*, this write is not strictly necessary for the correctness of implementation. Yet it makes the proofs much easier. Particularly, in Lemma 8.64 we can simulate the 1-step flush access immediately when the master automaton leaves the state flush, and do not have to wait until the tag of the evicted line gets overwritten in state w.

There are two transitions starting from state *flush*.

1. Transition: $flush \rightarrow flush$.
   While $\neg b.mmack$, we stay in *flush* since the memory is still busy.
2. Transition (6): $flush \rightarrow m0$.
   When the $b.mmack$ signal gets active, the memory access is finished and the automaton proceeds to state $m0$:

$$(6) = b.mmack \ .$$

States $m0$ and *sidle*

During the $m0$ phase (1 cycle), master protocol data are transmitted on the bus. In the next cycle, master automaton always advances to state $m1$.

The following transitions in the slave automaton start from state *sidle*.

1. Transition (7): $sidle \rightarrow s1$.
   Slave i leaves the *sidle* state iff some master j is in state $m0$ transmitting signal Ca and $j \neq i$:

$$(7) = b.mprot.Ca \wedge \neg grant[i] \ .$$

2. Transition : $sidle \rightarrow sidle$.
   The slave stays in *sidle* if signal Ca is not active on the bus or if its master automaton got control of the bus.

There are no signals raised in the master in state $m0$. The following signals are raised in the slave in state *sidle*:

$ca(i).mprotince := (7)$

$ca(i).badince := (7) \ .$

---

signal *phit* in this case we use the output of port a of the state RAM, rather than the output of the auxiliary register $souta'$, even though port a of the state RAM is written in the same cycle. The reason why this behaviour is acceptable here is simple: we went to state flush because the tag of the line in the cache did not match to the tag of the requested line. In state *flush* the tag RAM is not updated. Hence, the requested line stays invalid in the abstract cache and the output of the state RAM is simply ignored in the computation of signal *phit*.

States $m1$ and $s1$

During these states (1 cycle), the master does nothing and the slave computes response signals. If the slave doesn't have the requested data it goes to state $idle'$, where it waits until signal Ca is removed from the bus. The snoop conflict starts to be visible in this phase.

Two transitions are starting in state $s1$.

1. Transition (8): $s1 \rightarrow sidle'$.
   If the slave does not have an active $bhit$ signal, then it goes to state $sidle'$:

$$(8) = \neg bhit .$$

2. Transition: $s1 \rightarrow s2$.
   If the slave doesn't go to $sidle'$, then it goes to state $s2$.

The following signal is raised in the slave:

$ca(i).sprotoutce := bhit .$

State $sidle'$

The slave waits until Ca is removed from the bus, then moves to $idle$.

States $m2$ and $s2$

During these states (1 cycle), the slave response signals are transmitted on the bus. The following signal is raised in the master:

$ca(i).sprotince .$

States $m3$ and $s3$

Recall, that in a global transaction the master either has to read the data from the memory or from another cache (in case of a cache miss) or has to broadcast the data to other caches (in case of a cache hit in a shared or owned state). In state $m3$ (1 cycle), the master makes a decision whether a memory access must be performed in the $mdata$ phase. This depends on whether di was active on the bus during stage $m2$. In case of a cache hit the master prepares the data for broadcasting. The following signals are raised in the master:

$ca(i).mmreqset := \neg ca(i).mprotout.bc \wedge \neg ca(i).sprotin.di$
$ca(i).mmreqoeset := \neg ca(i).mprotout.bc \wedge \neg ca(i).sprotin.di$
$ca(i).bdoutce := ca(i).mprotout.bc$
$ca(i).bdoutoeset := ca(i).mprotout.bc .$

The following signals are raised in the slave (preparing the data intervention if necessary):

$ca(i).bdoutce := ca(i).sprotout.di$

$ca(i).bdoutoeset := ca(i).sprotout.di$.

States $mdata$ and $sdata$

During this phase the master performs a memory access if necessary and reads the data from the bus. The data are either provided by a slave or are provided by the main memory. In case the data are provided by a slave, the $mdata$ and $sdata$ phases only last for 1 cycle. If the data are provided by the main memory, the automata stay in states $mdata$ and $sdata$ as long as there is an active memory request:

$$\neg b.mmack \land b.mmreq.$$

Leaving this state, the master clears control signals. The following signals are raised in the master:

$ca(i).bdince := b.mmreq \land b.mmack \lor ca(i).sprotin.di$

$ca(i).mmreqclr := b.mmreq \land b.mmack$

$ca(i).mmreqoeclr := b.mmreq \land b.mmack$

$ca(i).badoutoeclr := b.mmack \lor \neg b.mmreq$

$ca(i).bdoutoeclr := b.mmack \lor \neg b.mmreq$

$ca(i).dataouta'ce := b.mmack \lor \neg b.mmreq$

$ca(i).souta'ce := b.mmack \lor \neg b.mmreq$

$ca(i).tagouta'ce := b.mmack \lor \neg b.mmreq$

$ca(i).mprotoutce := b.mmack \lor \neg b.mmreq$

$ca(i).mprotz := b.mmack \lor \neg b.mmreq$.

The slave has to clock the broadcast data or clear the data output enable signal. When leaving state $sdata$, the b output of the state RAM is clocked into register $ca(i).soutb'$, which will be used in the next cycle:

$ca(i).bdince := ca(i).mprotin.bc$

$ca(i).bdoutoeclr := ca(i).sprotout.di$

$ca(i).soutb'ce := b.mmack \lor \neg b.mmreq$.

States w and sw

During this phase (1 cycle) the master and the slave write the results of the transaction into their RAMs (data, tag, and state). The following signals are raised in the master:

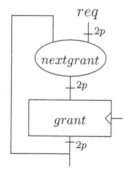

Fig. 140. Arbiter for masters

$ca(i).datawa$

$ca(i).tagwa$

$ca(i).swa$

$ca(i).reqclr$

$\neg ca(i).mbusy$.

The following signals are raised in the slave:

$ca(i).datawb := ca(i).mprotin.bc$

$ca(i).swb$

$ca(i).sprotoutce$

$ca(i).sprotz$.

8.4.5 Bus Arbiter

We need bus arbitration for masters trying to get control of the bus for accessing the main memory or communicating with other caches. We could also do arbitration of slave di signals when they all are in a shared (S) state. Currently we assume that no di signals are raised in this case and the master reads the main memory.

Master Arbitration

In case of *master arbitration* we have to ensure fairness. Fairness means that every request to access the bus is finally granted. The arbiter collects requests $req(i)$ from the caches and chooses exactly one cache that will get the permission to run on the bus. The winner is identified by the active $grant[i]$ signal.

The implementation of a fair arbiter is presented in Fig. 140. For the computation of *nextgrant*, we use circuit $f1$, which finds the first 1 in a bit-string starting from the smallest index:

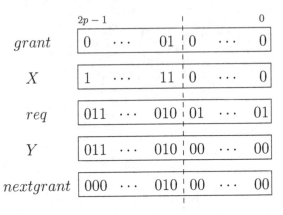

Fig. 141. Computation of signal *nextgrant*

$$f1(X)[i] = 1 \leftrightarrow min\{j \mid X[j] = 1\} = i.$$

Implementation of the $f1$ circuit is done in the following way.

1. Apply parallel prefix OR to input X:

$$Y[i] = \begin{cases} X[0] & i = 0 \\ X[i] \vee Y[i-1] & i \neq 0 . \end{cases}$$

2. Compute the result as follows:

$$f1(X)[i] = \begin{cases} Y[0] & i = 0 \\ Y[i] \wedge \neg Y[i-1] & i \neq 0 . \end{cases}$$

Implementation of the *nextgrant* circuit uses another instance of the parallel prefix and circuit $f1$:

1. We apply parallel prefix OR to input *grant*:

$$X[i] = \begin{cases} grant[0] & i = 0 \\ X[i-1] \vee grant[i] & i \neq 0 . \end{cases}$$

2. We compute conjunction Y, where

$$Y[i] = X[i] \wedge req[i] .$$

3. We apply function $f1$ constructed above to compute *nextgrant*:

$$nextgrant = \begin{cases} f1(Y) & \bigvee_i Y[i] \\ f1(req) & \text{otherwise} . \end{cases}$$

The computation of *nextgrant* is illustrated in Fig. 141.

We clock the *grant* register every cycle when we have an active request:

$$grantce = \bigvee_i req(i) \ .$$

During the initialization phase we set *grant*[0] to 1 and all other grant signals to 0. This guarantees that we always have an active *grant* signal, even if we don't have any active requests.

Note that if cache i gets a permission to run the bus it will maintain this permission until it lowers its *req* signal (it will always be the winner in the $f1$ circuit). A cache may get access to the bus in two consecutive memory accesses, however, *only* if there are no waiting requests from other caches. The master lowers the *req* signal when it leaves stage w. Thus, when the master returns to *idle* a new set of grant signals is computed and another cache may start its bus access in the next cycle.

Fairness of the Master Arbiter

Our construction of the master arbiter guarantees that every request to access the bus is finally granted if the following conditions are satisfied:

1. Without grant, request stays stable:

$$req(i)^t \wedge \neg grant[i]^t \rightarrow req(i)^{t+1} \ .$$

2. Every granted request is eventually taken away:

$$grant[i]^t \rightarrow \exists t' \geq t : \neg req(i)^{t'} \ .$$

The first condition is true, since in state *wait* signal $req(i)$ stays active and we do not leave the state before $grant[i]$ holds. The second condition holds due to system liveness: being in the warm phase, the master automaton will, eventually, always reach state *idle* and lower its request signal.

Lemma 8.13 (arbiter fairness).

$$req(i)^t \rightarrow \exists t' \geq t : grant[i]^{t'}$$

Proof. We only give a sketch of the proof here. In the proof we show that the distance between the index of the current master and the index of any other requesting cache i is *strictly* monotonic, decreasing with each arbitration. Let $one(X)$ be defined as[13]

$$one(X) = i \leftrightarrow X[i] = 1 \ .$$

---

[13] Well-defined only if string X contains exactly one bit that is set.

Then,

$$one(nextgrant) = \begin{cases} min\{j \geq one(grant) \mid req[j] = 1\} & \text{such } j \text{ exists} \\ min\{j \mid req[j]\} & \text{otherwise .} \end{cases}$$

We define the distance measure M:

$$M(i,t) = \begin{cases} i - one(grant^t) & i \geq one(grant^t) \\ i - one(grant^t) + 2p & \text{otherwise} \end{cases}$$
$$= (i - one(grant^t)) \mod 2p .$$

By induction one can show that $M(i,t)$ is decreasing with every new arbitration (i.e., when the *grant* register is clocked with the new value). □

8.4.6 Initialization

We assume the *reset* signal to be active in cycle -1. The following signals are activated during reset:

- Signals $mprotz^{-1}$, $mprotoutce^{-1}$, $sprotz^{-1}$, $sprotoutce^{-1}$. This ensures that master and slave protocols are initialized correctly:

$$\forall i : ca(i).mprotout^0 = 000 \wedge ca(i).sprotout^0 = 00 .$$

- Signal $sinv^{-1}$, which guarantees

$$\forall i, x : ca(i).s(x)^0 = I .$$

- Master and slave automata are initialized with idle states:

$$\forall i : idle(i)^0 \wedge sidle(i)^0 .$$

- Signal $reqclr^{-1}$ guarantees that caches don't request the bus until they get to the *mwait* state.
- Signals $bdoutoeclr^{-1}$, $badoutoeclr^{-1}$ and signals $mmreqclr^{-1}$, $mmwclr^{-1}$, $mmwoeclr^{-1}$, $mmreqoeclr^{-1}$ make sure that no master automaton gets the bus before requesting it.
- The grant signal for the cache 0 is set to 1 and all other grant signals are set to 0:

$$grant[i]^0 = \begin{cases} 1 & i = 0 \\ 0 & \text{otherwise .} \end{cases}$$

8.5 Correctness Proof

Recall that for cache abstraction $aca(i) = aca(ca(i))$ we use the same definition as was introduced for direct mapped caches in Sect. 8.1.2:

$$aca(i).s(a) = \begin{cases} ca(i).s(a.c) & hhit(ca(i), a) \\ I & \text{otherwise} \end{cases}$$

$$aca(i).data(a) = \begin{cases} ca(i).data(a.c) & hhit(ca(i), a) \\ * & \text{otherwise} . \end{cases}$$

We proceed with the correctness proof of the shared memory system in the following order:

1. We show properties of the bus arbitration guaranteeing that the warm phases of global transactions don't overlap.
2. We show that caches not involved in global accesses output ones to the open collector buses, i.e., they do not disturb signal transmission by other caches.
3. We show that control automata run in sync during global accesses.
4. This permits to show that tristate buses are properly controlled.
5. We show that protocol data are exchanged in the intended way.
6. This permits to show that data are exchanged in the intended way.
7. Aiming at a simulation between hardware and the atomic MOESI cache system, we identify the accesses of the hardware computation.
8. We prove a technical lemma stating that accesses $acc(i, k)$ of the atomic protocol only depend on cache lines with line address $acc(i, k).a$ and only modify such cache lines.
9. In Lemma 8.64 we show simulation between the hardware model executing a given access and the atomic model executing the same access.
10. We order hardware accesses by their end cycle and relate the hardware computation with the computation of the atomic protocol in Lemma 8.65. Moreover, we show that the state invariants are maintained by the hardware computation.
11. In Lemma 8.67 we show that our hardware memory system is a sequentially consistent shared memory.

In lemmas and theorems given in this section we abbreviate

- (A) – automata construction,
- (HW) – hardware construction,
- (IH) – induction hypothesis.

8.5.1 Arbitration

We start with showing very basic properties of the bus arbitration.

Lemma 8.14 (grant unique).

$$grant[i] \land grant[j] \to i = j$$

Proof. Trivial by construction of the arbiter. The output has the form $f1(x)$.
□

Lemma 8.15 (grant stable). During an active request a grant is not taken away:

$$grant[i]^t \land req(i)^t \to grant[i]^{t+1} .$$

Proof. By construction of the arbiter.
□

Lemma 8.16 (request at global). Automata in a global phase request access to the bus:

$$G(i)^t \to req(i)^t .$$

Proof. By induction $t - 1 \to t$. Trivially true for $t = 0$ because $idle(i)^0$, and thus, $\neg G(i)^0$.

In the induction step we consider cycles t satisfying $G(i)^t$ (because otherwise there is nothing to show) and argue here - and many times later - with a very typical case distinction:

- $\neg G(i)^{t-1}$. By (A) we conclude

$$idle(i)^{t-1} \land (3)(i)^{t-1} \land wait(i)^t \land reqset(i)^{t-1} .$$

  By hardware construction of set/clear flip-flops we conclude

$$req(i)^t .$$

- $G(i)^{t-1}$. Then by (A) we have $\neg w(i)^{t-1}$, and hence, $\neg reqclr(i)^{t-1}$. Using (IH) and (HW) we conclude,

$$req(i)^t = req(i)^{t-1} \quad (HW)$$
$$= 1 . \quad (IH)$$
□

Lemma 8.17 (grant at warm). A master can only be in the warm phase if he is granted access to the bus:

$$W(i)^t \to grant[i]^t .$$

Proof. By induction $t - 1 \to t$. Nothing to show for $t = 0$. For the induction step, consider t such that $W(i)^t$:

- $\neg W(i)^{t-1}$. By automata construction we conclude

$$wait(i)^{t-1} \land \neg wait(i)^t .$$

  By (A) this implies $grant[i]^{t-1}$ and by Lemma 8.16 (request at global) we get $req(i)^{t-1}$. By Lemma 8.15 (grant stable) we conclude $grant[i]^t$.

- $W(i)^{t-1}$. By Lemma 8.16 (request at global) we get $req(i)^{t-1}$. By (IH) we get $grant[i]^{t-1}$ and by Lemma 8.15 (grant stable) we get $grant[i]^t$.

$\square$

Now we state the very crucial lemma about the uniqueness of the automaton in the warm phase.

Lemma 8.18 (warm unique). Only one processor at a time can be in a warm phase:

$$W(i) \wedge W(j) \rightarrow i = j .$$

Proof. $W(i) \wedge W(j)$ implies $grant[i] \wedge grant[j]$ by Lemma 8.17 (grant at warm). By Lemma 8.14 (grant unique) one concludes $i = j$.

$\square$

8.5.2 Silent Slaves and Silent Masters

Since the signals between caches are transmitted via an open collector bus, we want both slaves and masters to stay silent when they do not participate in a global transaction.

Lemma 8.19 (silent slaves). When a slave is not participating in the protocol, it puts slave response 00 on the control bus:

$$zs(i)^t \in \{sidle, sidle', s1\} \rightarrow sprotout(i)^t = 00 .$$

Proof. Proof by induction $t - 1 \rightarrow t$. Reset ensures $sidle^0$ and activates signal $sprotz$ which by (HW) clears the register. Thus, we have $sprotout(i)^0 = 00$ and the lemma holds for $t = 0$.

Let $t > 0$ and $zs(i)^t \in \{sidle, sidle', s1\}$. We consider two cases:

- $zs(i)^{t-1} \notin \{sidle, sidle', s1\}$. Then, by automata construction,

$$zs(i)^{t-1} = sw \wedge sprotz(i)^{t-1} \wedge sprotce(i)^{t-1} .$$

Thus, the lemma holds by (HW).

- $zs(i)^{t-1} \in \{sidle, sidle', s1\}$. Thus, we have $\neg(s1(i)^{t-1} \wedge s2(i)^t)$. Therefore, $sprotout$ is not clocked ($\neg sprotoutce(i)^{t-1}$) (HW) and we get by (IH) and register semantics

$$sprotout(i)^t = sprotout(i)^{t-1} \quad (HW)$$
$$= 00 . \quad (I)$$

$\square$

In exactly the same way one shows the next lemma.

Lemma 8.20 (silent master).

$$\neg H(i) \rightarrow mprotout(i) = 000$$

8.5.3 Automata Synchronization

This section contains two lemmas. We prove both of them simultaneously by induction on the number of cycles t. Thus, the statements of both lemmas in this section form together a single induction hypothesis.

Lemma 8.21 (idle slaves). If no automaton is in a hot phase, then all slaves are idle:
$$(\forall i : \neg H(i)^t) \rightarrow \forall j : sidle(j)^t .$$

Proof. For all i, we have after reset $idle(i)^0 \notin H$ and $sidle(i)^0$. Thus, the lemma holds initially. The induction step requires to argue about all states and can only be completed at the end of the section.   □

The next lemma explains how in a hot phase the master and the slave states are synchronized.

Lemma 8.22 (sync). Consider a hot phase of master i lasting from cycles t to t', i.e we have
$$\neg H(i)^{t-1} \wedge H(i)^{[t:t']} \wedge \neg H(i)^{t'+1} .$$

Then,

1. For the master i we have
$$m0(i)^t \wedge m1(i)^{t+1} \wedge m2(i)^{t+2} \wedge m3(i)^{t+3} \wedge$$
$$mdata(i)^{[t+4:t'-1]} \wedge w(i)^{t'} \wedge idle(i)^{t'+1} .$$

2. The slave automaton of cache i doesn't leave state $sidle$:
$$sidle(i)^{[t:t'+1]} .$$

3. For not affected slaves, i.e., for slaves j with $j \neq i$ and $\neg bhit(j)^{t+1}$, we have
$$sidle(j)^t \wedge s1(j)^{t+1} \wedge sidle'(j)^{[t+2:t']} \wedge sidle(j)^{t'+1} .$$

4. The affected slaves, i.e the slaves j with $j \neq i$ and $bhit(i)^{t+1}$, run in sync with the master of the transaction:
$$sidle(j)^t \wedge s1(j)^{t+1} \wedge s2(j)^{t+2} \wedge s3(j)^{t+3} \wedge$$
$$sdata(j)^{[t+4:t'-1]} \wedge sw(j)^{t'} \wedge sidle(j)^{t'+1} ,$$

Proof. Part (1) follows directly by (A). For the proof of parts (2), (3), and (4), recall that we are proving both lemmas together by induction on t[14]. Our induction hypothesis is stated for all cycles $q \leq t$ and consists of two parts:

- $\forall q \leq t : \forall t' : \neg H(i)^{q-1} \wedge H(i)^{[q:t']} \wedge \neg H(i)^{t'+1} \rightarrow (2), (3), (4),$ (sync)
- $\forall q \leq t : (\forall i : \neg H(i)^q) \rightarrow \forall j : sidle(j)^q.$ (idle slaves)

---

[14] Observe that for Lemma (sync) t is the start time of the hot phase.

The base case $(t = 0)$ is trivial by (A). In the proof of the induction step from $t - 1$ to t, the induction hypothesis trivially implies both statements in case $q < t$. Hence, we only need to do the proof for the case $q = t$.

For the induction step of (sync), we have

$$\neg H(i)^{t-1} \wedge H(i)^{t} \wedge H(i)^{[t:t']} \wedge \neg H(i)^{t'+1}$$

and conclude

$$(wait(i)^{t-1} \vee flush(i)^{t-1}) \wedge grant[i]^{t-1} .$$

By Lemma 8.14 (grant unique) it follows that

$$\forall j \neq i : \neg grant[j]^{t-1} .$$

By Lemma 8.17 (grant at warm) we have $\neg W(j)^{t-1}$ and $\neg H(j)^{t-1}$. Hence,

$$\forall j : \neg H(j)^{t-1} .$$

Using (idle slaves) as part of the induction hypothesis for cycle $t - 1$ we get

$$\forall j : sidle(j)^{t-1} .$$

Using Lemma 8.20 (silent master), part (1) of Lemma (sync), (A), and (HW) we then conclude for the cycles $s \in [t - 1 : t']$:

$$b.mprot.Ca^s = \bigvee_j mprotout(j).Ca^s = \begin{cases} 0 & s \in \{t - 1, t'\} \\ 1 & s \in [t : t' - 1] \end{cases} .$$

By Lemmas 8.17, 8.14 (grant at warm, grant unique) we know that the grant signals are stable during cycles $s \in [t - 1 : t']$:

$$grant[i]^s \wedge \forall j \neq i : \neg grant[j]^s.$$

Parts (2), (3), and (4) follow now by construction of the slave automata and observing that the exit conditions for states $mdata$ and $sdata$ are identical.

For the induction step of (idle slaves), we consider a cycle t such that $\forall i : \neg H(i)^t$. We make the usual case distinction:

- $\forall i : \neg H(i)^{t-1}$. By (IH) we have

$$\forall (j) : sidle(j)^{t-1}.$$

By Lemma 8.20 (silent master) we get

$$b.mprot.Ca^{t-1} = 0$$

and the lemma follows by construction of the slave automata.

- $\exists i : H(i)^{t-1}$. By Lemma 8.18 (warm unique) this i is unique. By construction of the master automaton we conclude $w(i)^{t-1}$. This is the end of a hot phase which started before cycle t. Therefore, we can apply parts (2), (3), and (4) of (sync) as part of (IH) to conclude

$$\forall(j) : sidle(j)^t .$$

$\square$

Now we are able to argue about the uniqueness of the di signal put on the bus by the slaves.

Recall, that the predicate $SINV(t)$, introduced in Sect. 8.3.1, denotes that the state invariants hold for the memory system $ms(h)$ for all cycles $t' \le t$:

$$SINV(t) \equiv \forall t' \le t : sinv(ms(h^{t'})) .$$

In the following lemma and in many other lemmas in this chapter we assume that the predicate $SINV(t)$ holds. Later, we apply these lemmas in the proof of a very important Lemma 8.64 (1 step). Then we use Lemma (1 step) as the main argument in the induction step of Lemma 8.65 (relating hardware with atomic protocol), where we in turn make sure that the predicate $SINV(t)$ actually holds.

Lemma 8.23 (di unique).

$$SINV(t) \wedge sprotout(i).di^t \wedge sprotout(j).di^t \to i = j$$

Proof. Proof by induction $t - 1 \to t$. We make the usual case distinction:

- $\neg di^{t-1}$. This implies $s2(i)^t$ (from (A)). Applying Lemma 8.22 (sync) we get that all other slaves are either in $s2$ or are in $sidle'$. If a slave j is in $sidle'$, it doesn't have active di (from (A) and (HW)). If a slave is in $s2(j)^t$, that means it was in $s1(j)^{t-1}$ (from (A)). From $SINV(t)$ we get $sinv(ms(h^{t-1}))$. Hence, we can conclude that only one cache was in cycle $t - 1$ in O, E, or M state. Since we know $di^t(i)$ holds, then by (A)

$$aca(i).s^{t-1}(ca(i).badin^{t-1}) \in \{O, E, M\} .$$

From (HW) we also know that $ca(j).badin^{t-1} = ca(i).badin^{t-1}$. From $SINV(t)$ and (A) it follows

$$\forall j \ne i : aca(j).s^{t-1}(ca(i).badin^{t-1}) \notin \{O, E, M\} .$$

And thus, from construction of circuit $C2$ we get

$$\forall j \ne i : C2(aca(j).s^{t-1}(ca(j).badin^{t-1}), ca(j).mprotin^{t-1}).di = 0.$$

- di^{t-1}. Trivial using (IH) and Lemma 8.22 (sync).

$\square$

We can now also prove a technical lemma about auxiliary registers $ca(i).dataouta'$, $ca(i).tagouta'$, $ca(i).souta'$, and $ca(i).soutb'$. This lemma guarantees that the content of the registers in the cycles when they are used is the same as the corresponding output values of the edge-triggered RAMs. Hence, we can simplify our reasoning about the data paths by simply replacing these registers with wires.

Lemma 8.24 (auxiliary registers). Output of registers $tagouta'$, $dataouta'$, $souta'$, and $soutb'$ in cycles when they are used is the same as the corresponding output values of the RAMs:

1. $w(i)^t \vee localw(i)^t \rightarrow dataouta'(i)^t = dataouta(i)^t$,
2. $w(i)^t \rightarrow tagouta'(i)^t = tagout(i)^t$,
3. $w(i)^t \vee localw(i)^t \vee (wait(i)^t \wedge grant[i]^t) \rightarrow souta'(i)^t = souta(i)^t$,
4. $sw(i)^t \rightarrow soutb'(i)^t = soutb(i)^t$.

Proof. By a case split on the state of master and slave automata in cycle t:

- Let $w(i)^t$ hold. By (A) we have $mdata(i)^{t-1}$, which implies for $X \in \{dataouta, tagouta, souta\}$

$$X'(i)^t = X(i)^{t-1} .$$

Applying Lemma 8.22 (sync) we know that the slave automaton of cache i is in state $sidle$ in cycle $t - 1$:

$$sidle(i)^{t-1} .$$

Since we don't activate write enable signals for the RAMs in states $sidle$ and $mdata$, we know that the content of RAMs doesn't change from $t - 1$ to t. By Lemma 8.16 (request at global), definition of $mbusy$, and stability of processor inputs we get

$$pa(i)^t = pa(i)^{t-1} .$$

Hence,

$$X'(t)^t = X(i)^{t-1} = X(i)^t .$$

- Let $localw(i)^t$ hold. As in the previous case we conclude $idle(i)^{t-1}$ and for $X \in \{dataouta, souta\}$

$$X'(i)^t = X(i)^{t-1} .$$

Because transition (2) was taken in cycle $t-1$, we know that signals $preq(i)$ and $mbusy(i)$ were high in cycle $t - 1$. Hence, from stability of processor inputs we get

$$pa(i)^t = pa(i)^{t-1} .$$

In cycle $t - 1$ there was no snoop conflict:

$$sidle(i)^{t-1} \vee pa(i)^{t-1}.c \neq badin(i)^{t-1}.c ,$$

which implies that ports b of RAMs were either not written, or were written with a cache line address different from $pa(i)^t.c$. The a ports of RAMs are not clocked in state $idle$ at all. Hence, for all outputs X we get

$$X(i)^t = X(i)^{t-1}$$

and conclude the proof.

- Let $sw(i)^t$ hold. This implies $sdata(i)^{t-1}$ and

$$soutb'(i)^t = soutb(i)^{t-1} .$$

Moreover, we can conclude by (A):

$$sdata(i)^{t-2} \vee s3(i)^{t-2} .$$

In states $sdata$ and $s3$ register $badin$ is not clocked. Hence,

$$badin(i)^t = badin(i)^{t-1} = badin(i)^{t-2} .$$

Port b of the state RAM is never written in $sdata$. Port a is written only in states w, $flush$, and $localw$. By Lemmas 8.22 and 8.18 (sync, warm unique) we conclude that the master automaton of cache i can not be in states w or $flush$ in cycle $t - 1$. In case $localw(i)^{t-1}$ holds, we know that in cycle $t - 2$ there was no snoop conflict on the bus:

$$pa(i)^{t-2}.c \neq badin(i)^{t-2}.c ,$$

From stability of processor inputs we get

$$pa(i)^{t-2} = pa(i)^{t-1} ,$$

which implies

$$pa(i)^{t-1}.c \neq badin(i)^{t-1}.c .$$

Hence, port a of the state RAM could only be written with a different cache line address and we get

$$soutb'(i)^t = soutb(i)^{t-1} = soutb(i)^t .$$

- Let $wait(i)^t \wedge grant[i]^t$ hold. In the previous cycle the master automaton of cache i was in state $wait$ or $idle$. Hence, the register $souta'$ was clocked:

$$souta'(i)^t = souta(i)^{t-1} .$$

By (A) we know that port a of the state RAM was not clocked in cycle $t-1$. We show by contradiction that port b of the RAM is also not clocked in cycle $t - 1$. Let $swb(i)^{t-1}$. Then by (A) we have $sw(i)^{t-1}$ and by Lemma 8.22 (sync) there exists master $j \neq i$, s.t., $w(j)^{t-1}$ holds. By Lemmas 8.17, 8.16, and 8.15 (grant at warm, request at global, grant stable) we conclude[15]

$$grant[j]^t.$$

This contradicts to $grant[i]^t$ by Lemma 8.14 (grant unique). Hence, using stability of processor inputs, we conclude

$$souta'(i)^t = souta(i)^{t-1} = souta(i)^t .$$

□

8.5.4 Control of Tristate Drivers

Recall that in Sect. 3.5 we defined a discipline for the clean operation of the tristate bus with and without the main memory. This discipline guaranteed the absence of bus contention and the absence of glitches on the bus during the transmission interval.

For the control of the tristate bus without the main memory we introduced the function $send(i) = j$ and the time intervals $T_i = [a_i : b_i]$ when unit j is transmitting the data on the bus. We allowed unit j to transmit in two consecutive time intervals T_i and T_{i+1} where $a_{i+1} = b_i$ without disabling and re-enabling the driver. If this is not the case, i.e., the driver of unit j is disabled in cycle b_i, then there must be at least one cycle between two consecutive time intervals:

$$b_i + 1 < a_{i+1} .$$

The sending register X is always clocked in cycle $a_i - 1$ and must not be clocked in the time interval $[a_i : b_i - 1]$. The flip-flop controlling the output enable signal Xoe must be set in cycle $a_i - 1$ (unless the same unit is sending in the consecutive time interval, i.e., only if $a_i - 1 \neq b_{i-1}$) and must be cleared in cycle b_i (again, only if $b_i + 1 \neq a_{i+1}$).

A tristate bus with the main memory is controlled in the same way. The start of the time interval $T_i = [a_i : b_i]$ of the memory access is identified by an activation of signal $mmreq(j)$ and the end of the time interval is determined by the memory acknowledge signal. Note that for other inputs to the main memory the time intervals are allowed to be larger than the time interval for $mmreq$.

---

[15] Observe, that this proof works only because we have a one cycle delay in the generation of the grant signal: master j still has the request to the arbiter high in state $w(j)^q$. Hence, in cycle $q + 1$ the signal $grant[j]$ is high, even though cache j is already is state $idle$. This proof is the only place where we rely on this one cycle delay in the generation of grant signals. With a more agressive arbitration, i.e., if request to the arbiter was lowered one cycle earlier, one would have to forward the value written to the state RAM as an input to register $souta'$ in cycle q.

In this section we show that the construction of our control automata does adhere to this control discipline. For all signals with the exception of signal *badout* we always leave at least one cycle between two consecutive transmissions. Signal *badout* is treated in a somewhat special manner:

- In case the automaton does not go to state *flush*, the signal *badout* is transmitted on the bus starting from state $m0$ and up to state w. If later on, a memory access starts in state *mdata*, then the time interval for *badout* happens to start earlier than the time interval for signal *mmreq* (in *mdata* we can have only a read access to the main memory).
- In case the automaton goes to state flush, the signal *badout* is transmitted on the bus starting from the first cycle in *flush* and up to state w. Moreover, in the last cycle of flush, the sending register *badout* is clocked and is overwritten with the new value (without disabling and then re-enabling the driver). Hence, for *badout* in this case we have two time intervals $T_i = [a_i : b_i]$ and $T_{i+1} = [a_i + 1 : b_{i+1}]$. The first memory access (i.e., the one performed in state *flush*), is performed during interval T_i. The second memory access, if performed in state *mdata*, lasts during $[a_i + 4 : b_{i+1}]$. Hence, the time interval for *badout* simply starts earlier then the interval for signals *mmreq*, *mmw*, and *bdout*.

We start with characterising for each register $X(i)$ connected via a tristate driver to a component $b.Y$ of the bus the cycles t during which the driver for register $X(i)$ is enabled:

$$Cy(X, i) = \{t \mid Xoe(i)^t\} \ .$$

For each of the signals X concerned, we will formulate Lemma (X) characterizing the set $Cy(X, i)$ (Lemmas 8.28, 8.29, 8.30, 8.31). Clearly, the flip-flop controlling the output enable driver of register X is set in cycle t if

$$t \notin Cy(X, i) \wedge t + 1 \in Cy(X, i)$$

and is cleared in cycle t if

$$t \in Cy(X, i) \wedge t + 1 \notin Cy(X, i) \ .$$

To make sure that out construction satisfies the control discipline we show the following properties:

- sets $Cy(X, i)$ and $Cy(X, j)$ are disjoint for $i \neq j$ and there is at least one cycle in between cycles $t \in Cy(X, i)$ and $t' \in Cy(X, j)$; hence, there can be no bus contention (as guaranteed by Lemma 3.9 (tristate bus control),
- for cycles $t \in Cy(X, i)$ registers $X(i)$ can be clocked in cycle t only if cycle $t + 1$ does not belong to $Cy(X, i)$ (with the exception of the signal *badout*, as discussed above); the set-clear flip-flops controlling the drivers obey the same rules; thus, the enabled drivers do not produce glitches on the bus,

- we show that the disabled drivers are not redundantly cleared; thus, the disabled drivers do not produce glitches on the bus,
- one could also show that register X is always clocked in cycle $t \notin Cy(X,i)$ if $t+1 \in Cy(X,i)$; yet, the absence of bus contention and the absence of glitches does not really depend on this condition, so we do not bother.

Our next goal is to show the absence of bus contention. This involves a case distinction. The easy case deals with signals which are active only during the warm phases of master states, i.e., satisfying

$$\forall t : t \in Cy(X,i) \rightarrow W(i)^t .$$

It will turn out that these are all signals except $bdout$. We deal with bus contention for the latter signal at the end of the next section in Lemma 8.39. For the easy case we formulate the following lemma.

Lemma 8.25 (no contention). Assume signal X satisfies

$$\forall i,t : t \in Cy(X,i) \rightarrow W(i)^t .$$

Then,

$$i \neq j \wedge t \in Cy(X,i) \rightarrow \{t,t+1\} \cap Cy(X,j) = \emptyset .$$

Proof. By contradiction. For $i \neq j$, first assume $t \in Cy(X,i) \cap Cy(X,j)$. By hypothesis we have $t \in W(i)^t \cap W(j)^t$. By Lemma 8.18 (warm unique) we conclude $i = j$.

Now let $t \in Cy(X,i) \wedge t+1 \notin Cy(X,i)$. Assume $t+1 \in Cy(X,j)$. The only way for the automaton i to leave the warm phase is to go from w to $idle$. Hence, we have $w(i)^t$. By Lemmas 8.16, 8.17, and 8.15 (request at global, grant at warm, grant stable) this implies $grant[i]^{t+1}$ and gives a contradiction by Lemmas 8.17 and 8.14 (grant at warm, grant unique). □

Showing absence of glitches for signals of the form $mmreq(i)$, $mmw(i)$, $bdout(i)$, and $badout(i)$ involves two statements: one for enabled and one for disabled drivers.

Lemma 8.26 (no glitches, enabled). Let

$$X \in \{mmreq, mmw, bdout, badout\}$$

and let t, $t+1$ be consecutive cycles in $Cy(X,i)$. Then in the first of these cycles registers X and Xoe are not clocked:

$$t \in Cy(X,i) \wedge t+1 \in Cy(X,i) \rightarrow \neg Xce(i)^t \wedge \neg Xoeclr(i)^t \wedge \neg Xoeset(i)^t .$$

The only exception is the $badoutce(i)$, which might be clocked when $flush(i)^t \wedge m0(i)^{t+1}$ holds.

Proof. For each of the signals X concerned, this lemma follows directly from Lemmas 8.28, 8.29, 8.30, and 8.31 characterizing $Cy(X,i)$ and (A). □

A glitch on the output enable signal Xoe of a disabled driver might propagate to the output of the driver and thus on the bus.

Lemma 8.27 (no glitches, disabled). Let

$$X \in \{mmreq, mmw, bdout, badout\}$$

and let $t, t+1$ be consecutive cycles not in $Cy(X, i)$. Then the output enable signal Xoe is not redundantly cleared:

$$t \notin Cy(X, i) \wedge t+1 \notin Cy(X, i) \rightarrow \neg Xoeclr(i)^t .$$

Proof. For each signal concerned, the proof follows again directly from Lemmas 8.28, 8.29, 8.30, and 8.31 and automata construction.   □

The next few lemmas are characterizing the sets $Cy(X, i)$.

Lemma 8.28 (mmw). We write to the main memory only in state $flush$:

$$t \in Cy(mmw, i) \leftrightarrow flush(i)^t .$$

Proof. We first show

$$t \in Cy(mmw, i) \rightarrow flush(i)^t .$$

Consider any maximal interval $[t : t'] \subset Cy(mmw, i)$, i.e.,

$$\neg mmwoe(i)^{t-1} \wedge \forall q \in [t : t'] : mmwoe(i)^q \wedge \neg mmwoe(i)^{t'+1} .$$

By hardware construction we have $mmwoeset(i)^{t-1}$. By (A) we have

$$wait(i)^{t-1} \wedge (5)(i)^{t-1} \wedge flush(i)^t .$$

For $q \in [t : t']$ we show by induction on $q - 1 \rightarrow q$ that $flush(i)^q$ holds. For $q > t$, we have $flush(i)^{q-1}$ by induction hypothesis and $mmwoe(i)^q$. Hence,

$$\neg b.mmack^{q-1} \wedge flush(i)^q$$

by automata construction.
    Finally, we conclude from

$$flush(i)^{t'} \wedge \neg mmwoe(i)^{t'+1}$$

by automata construction

$$mmwoeclr(i)^{t'} \wedge m0(i)^{t'+1} .$$

This shows that $t \in Cy(mmw, i) \rightarrow flush(i)^t$. The inverse direction

$$flush(i)^t \rightarrow t \in Cy(mmw, i)$$

follows by automata construction with a trivial induction on t.   □

The proofs of all other lemmas characterizing sets $Cy(X, i)$ follow very similar patterns and we, therefore, just formulate the lemmas without proofs. For many of the following lemmas it is convenient to define for each cycle t and cache i the cycle $ez(t, i)$ when the master automaton did the most recent change of states, i.e., the cycle when the master left the previous state before entering the current state $z(i)^t$:

$$z(i)^t \neq idle \rightarrow ez(t, i) = \max\{t' \mid t' < t \land z(i)^{t'} \neq z(i)^t\} .$$

Lemma 8.29 ($mmreq$). We request a memory access when we flush or after a miss of the master with no data intervention from any of the slaves:

$$t \in Cy(mmreq, i) \leftrightarrow mdata(i)^t \land \neg(mprotout(i).bc^{ez(t,i)} \lor sprotin(i).di^{ez(t,i)})$$
$$\lor flush(i)^t .$$

Lemma 8.30 ($badout$). The bus address always comes from the master during the entire warm phase:

$$t \in Cy(badout, i) \leftrightarrow W(i)^t .$$

Observe that the output enable signal $badoutoe$ for this signal stays constantly 1 during the entire warm phase, the content of the address register $badout$ changes after $flush$. The last signal $bdout$ treated here can be activated both by masters and by slaves.

Lemma 8.31 ($bdout$). Signal $bdout(i)$ is put on the bus by the master in state $mdata$ in case of a global write access, by the slave in state $sdata$ if it intervenes after a miss, or by a master in case of a flush access:

$$t \in Cy(bdout, i) \leftrightarrow mdata(i)^t \land mprotout(i).bc^{ez(t,i)}$$
$$\lor sdata(i)^t \land sprotout(i).di^{ez(t,i)}$$
$$\lor flush(i)^t .$$

We see that, with the exception of $X = bdout$, all signals satisfy the hypothesis of Lemma 8.25 (no contention), thus we can summarize in

Lemma 8.32 (no contention 2).

$$i \neq j \land t \in Cy(X, i) \rightarrow \{t, t+1\} \cap Cy(X, j) = \emptyset$$

The corresponding result for $X = bdout$ happens to depend on certain data transmitted during the operation of the MOESI protocol. As these data are not transmitted over the bus $b.d$, we can show the correct transmission of the protocol data using the lemmas we already have.

8.5.5 Protocol Data Transmission

For states $z \in \{m0, m1, m2\}$, we identify what data are processed and transmitted during state z.

Lemma 8.33 (before $m0$). In the cycle before entering $m0$ registers $badout$ and $mprotout$ are loaded with the processor address and the output of circuit $C1$. Let $m0(i)^t \wedge \neg m0(i)^{t-1}$ and let us abbreviate

$$ptype(i)^t = (ca(i).prt, ca(i).pw(i)^t, ca(i).pcas^t, 0) .$$

Then,

$$badout(i)^t = pa(i)^{t-1}$$
$$mprotout(i)^t = C1(aca(i).s^{t-1}(pa(i)^{t-1}), ptype(i)^{t-1}) .$$

Proof. If in cycle $t-1$ we don't have an active *phit* signal, then we obviously have

$$aca(i).s^{t-1}(pa(i)^{t-1}) = I .$$

The mux on top of circuit $C1$ guarantees that the invalid state is provided as an input to the circuit. If *phit* is on then it holds

$$ca(i).s^{t-1}(pa(i)^{t-1}) = aca(i).s^{t-1}(pa(i)^{t-1})$$

and we use the output of the state RAM as an input to $C1$. The lemma now follows directly by automata and hardware construction and from stability of processor inputs.   □

Lemma 8.34 ($m0$). During $m0$ the content of registers $mprotout$ and $badout$ does not change and the protocol data and the bus address of the master are broadcast. Let $m0(i)^t$ hold. Then for all $j \neq i$:

$$mprotout(i)^{t+1} = mprotout(i)^t$$
$$badout(i)^{t+1} = badout(i)^t$$
$$mprotin(j)^{t+1} = mprotout(i)^t$$
$$badin(j)^{t+1} = badout(i)^t .$$

Proof. For *mprotout* this follows directly from automata and hardware construction. For the *mprotin*, we have by Lemma 8.22 (sync) for all $j \neq i$:

$$sidle(j)^t \wedge (7)(j)^t .$$

By (A), Lemma 8.18 (warm unique), and Lemma 8.20 (silent master) we conclude:

$$mprotin(j)^{t+1} = b.mprot^t$$
$$= \bigvee_k mprotout(k)^t$$
$$= mprotout(i)^t .$$

For the bus address data $b.ad$, we have by (HW), (A), and Lemmas 8.30 and 8.32 ($badout$, no contention 2):

$$badin(j)^{t+1} = b.ad^t$$
$$= badout(i)^t .$$

□

Lemma 8.35 ($m1$). During $m1$ the affected slaves load their answer $sprotout$ with the output of circuit $C2$. The content of registers $X \in \{badout, mprotout\}$ of the master and registers $Y \in \{badin, mprotin\}$ of the slaves is unchanged. Let $m1(i)^t$. Then for all j, s.t., $s1(j)^t \wedge \neg(8)(j)^t$:

$$X(i)^{t+1} = X(i)^t$$
$$Y(j)^{t+1} = Y(j)^t$$
$$sprotout(j)^{t+1} = C2(soutb(j)^t, mprotin(j)^t)$$
$$= C2(aca(j).s^t(badin(j)^t), mprotin(j)^t) .$$

Proof. Proof analogous to Lemma 8.33 (before $m0$). □

Lemma 8.36 ($m2$). During $m2$ the protocol answer of the slaves is broadcast. The content of registers $X \in \{badout, mprotout\}$ of the master and registers $Y \in \{badin, mprotin, sprotout\}$ of the slaves is unchanged. Let $m2(i)^t$. Then,

$$X(i)^{t+1} = X(i)^t$$
$$Y(j)^{t+1} = Y(j)^t$$
$$sprotin(i)^{t+1} = \bigvee_j sprotout(j)^t .$$

Proof. Proof analogous to Lemma 8.34 ($m0$). □

Lemma 8.37 (after $m2$). Let $m3(i)^t$ and $t' = min\{q \mid q > t \wedge w(i)^q\}$, then for all cycles $q \in [t+1, t']$ the content of registers $X \in \{badout, mprotout, sprotin\}$ of the master and registers $Y \in \{badin, mprotin, sprotout\}$ of the slaves is unchanged:

$$X(i)^q = X(i)^t$$
$$Y(j)^q = Y(j)^t .$$

Proof. Trivial by (A). □

With the above lemmas we can conclude a crucial lemma about the data intervention signals.

Lemma 8.38 (no DI after BC). If the master signals a write hit during $m2(i)$ with $mprotout(i).bc$, then no slave signals data intervention. Let $m2(i)^t$. Then for all j:

$$mprotout(i).bc^t \rightarrow \neg sprotout(j).di^t .$$

Proof. $m2(i)^t$ implies $m0(i)^{t-2}$ by automata construction. By Lemma 8.22 (sync) we know that slave automaton of cache i remains in state $sidle$ during the whole hot phase and for $j \neq i$ we have

$$sidle(j)^{t-2} \wedge s1(j)^{t-1}.$$

By Lemma 8.19 (silent slaves) we get:

$$sprotout(i).di^t = 0.$$

For all $j \neq i$ we can conclude:

$$
\begin{aligned}
mprotout(i).bc^t &= mprotout(i).bc^{t-2} \quad (m0, m1) \\
&= mprotin(j).bc^{t-1}. \quad (m0)
\end{aligned}
$$

By Lemma 8.22 (sync), if slave j does not have a hit (i.e., $\neg bhit(j)^{t-1}$), then it goes to state $sidle'(j)^t$ and by Lemma 8.19 (silent slaves) we have for all such j:

$$sprotout(j).di^t = 0.$$

If slave j does have a hit, then we have $s1(j)^{t-1} \wedge \neg(8)(j)^{t-1}$. From the protocol and its correct implementation in circuit $C2$ we conclude using Lemma 8.35 $(m1)$:

$$sprotout(j).di^t = C2(soutb(j)^{t-1}, mprotin(j)^{t-1}).di = 0.$$

$\square$

We are now able to show the absence of contention for $bdout$.

Lemma 8.39 ($bdout$ contention). Assume $SINV(t)$. Then,

$$\forall q \leq t : \forall j \neq i : q \in Cy(bdout, i) \rightarrow \{q, q+1\} \cap Cy(bdout, j) = \emptyset.$$

Proof. Let $q \in Cy(bdout, i)$. By Lemma 8.31 we conclude

$$flush(i)^q \vee mdata(i)^q \vee sdata(i)^q.$$

Assume for some $t \in \{q, q+1\}$ we have $bdoutoe(j)^t$ for a different cache j. By (A) this implies

$$flush(j)^t \vee sdata(j)^t \vee mdata(j)^t.$$

We split cases:

- $flush(i)^q$. By (A) we conclude

$$flush(i)^{q+1} \vee m0(i)^{q+1}.$$

By Lemma 8.18 (warm unique) $flush(j)^t \vee mdata(j)^t$ is impossible. By Lemmas 8.21 and 8.22 (idle slaves, sync) $sdata(j)^t$ is impossible too.

- $mdata(i)^q$. By (A) we conclude

$$w(i)^{q+1} \wedge m3(i)^{q-1} \wedge m2(i)^{q-2} \wedge mprotout(i).bc^{q-1} .$$

By Lemma 8.18 (warm unique) $flush(j)^t \vee mdata(j)^t$ is impossible. The case $sdata(j)^{q+1}$ is impossible by Lemma 8.22 (sync). The case $sdata(j)^q$ implies $s3(j)^{t-1}$ and $sprotout(j).di^{t-1}$. By Lemma 8.36 $(m2)$, we conclude

$$mprotout(i).bc^{q-2} \wedge sprotout(j).di^{q-2} .$$

and get a contradiction by Lemma 8.38 (no DI after BC).
- $sdata(i)^q$. By (A) this implies $sw(i)^{q+1}$. The case for $mdata(j)^q$ has been already ruled out in the proof for the previous case (with the reversed indices). The cases

$$flush(j)^t \vee mdata(j)^{q+1} \vee sdata(j)^{q+1}$$

are not possible by Lemmas 8.21 and 8.22 (idle slaves, sync). Finally, the case $sdata(j)^q$ is ruled out by Lemma 8.23 (di unique).

$\square$

8.5.6 Data Transmission

Now that we know that the tristate drivers are properly controlled, it is very easy to state the effect of data transferred via the buses.

Lemma 8.40 (*flush* transfer). Assume $SINV(t)$ and consider a maximal time interval $[s:t]$ when master i is in state flush:

$$\neg flush(i)^{s-1} \wedge \forall q \in [s:t] : flush(i)^q \wedge \neg flush(i)^{t+1} .$$

Then $bdout(i)^s$ is written to line $badout(i)^s$ of the main memory:

$$mm^{t+1}(badout(i)^s) = bdout(i)^s ,$$

and all other memory cells are left unchanged:

$$\forall a \neq badout(i)^s : mm^{t+1}(a) = mm^q .$$

Proof. By (A) and (HW) we have for the start cycle s of the time interval:

$$wait(i)^{s-1} \wedge (5)(i)^{s-1} \wedge mmreq(i)^s \wedge mmw(i)^s .$$

Let $X \in \{mmreq, mmw, badout, bdout\}$. Then we have by Lemma 8.26 (no glitches, enabled):

$$\forall q \in [s:t-1] : X(i)^q = X(i)^{q+1} .$$

By Lemmas 8.32 (no contention 2), 8.39 (*bdout* contention) and Lemmas 8.28, 8.29, 8.30, 8.31 characterising $Cy(X, i)$, we get for the bus component $b.X$:

$$\forall q \in [s, t] : b.X^q = X(i)^q .$$

By Lemmas 8.26 (no glitches, enabled) and 8.27 (no glitches, disabled) we can conclude that the rules for operations with the main memory defined in Sect. 3.5.7 are fulfilled. Hence, by Lemma 3.10 we have absence of glitches in the main memory inputs. The lemma follows now from the specification of the main memory[16]. □

Lemma 8.41 (*m3*). Let $m3(i)^t$. Then,

1. $mprotout(i).bc^t \rightarrow bdout(i)^{t+1} = modify(aca(i).data^t(a), pdin(i)^t, bw(i)^t)$,
2. $sprotout(j).di^t \rightarrow bdout(j)^{t+1} = aca(j).data^t(a)$.

Proof. Proof analogous to Lemma 8.34 (*m0*). □

Lemma 8.42 (*mdata* **write hit**). Assume $SINV(t)$. Let

$$mprotout(i).bc^{t-1} \wedge mdata(i)^t.$$

Then $bdout(i)^t$ is broadcast to all slaves which are in state *sdata*:

$$\forall j : sdata(j)^t \rightarrow bdin(j)^{t+1} = bdout(i)^t .$$

Proof. By Lemma 8.31 (*bdout*) we have

$$bdoutoe(i)^t .$$

By Lemma 8.39 (*bdout* contention) we conclude

$$b.d^t = bdout(i)^t .$$

By automata construction and hardware construction we conclude

$$\forall j : sdata(j)^t \rightarrow bdin(j)^{t+1} = b.d^t .$$

□

---

[16] Additionally, one has to argue here that the memory write is not performed to an address in ROM, i.e., that $badout(i)^s[28 : r] \neq 0^{29-r}$. Intuitively this is true, because the software condition introduced in Sect. 8.4.1 guarantees that processors never issue write or CAS requests to such addresses. Hence, a cache line with the line address less or equal to $0^{29-r}1^r$ can not be in states M or O. Formally, one can prove this by maintaining a simple invariant for such addresses and we leave that as an easy exercise for the reader.

Lemma 8.43 (*mdata* **data intervention**). Assume $SINV(t)$. Let

$$mdata(i)^t \wedge sprotout(j).di^{t-1} .$$

Then $ca(j).bdout^t$ is transferred to the master

$$bdin(i)^{t+1} = bdout(j)^t .$$

Proof. Proof along the lines of the previous two lemmas.   □

Lemma 8.44 (*mdata* **miss no intervention**). Assume $SINV(t)$ and consider a maximal time interval $[s : t]$ when the master is in state *mdata*:

$$\neg mdata(i)^{s-1} \wedge mdata(i)^{[s:t]} \wedge \neg mdata(i)^{t+1} .$$

Assume the absence of a write hit and of data intervention in cycle $s - 1$:

$$\neg mprotout(i).bc^{s-1} \wedge \neg sprotin(i).di^{s-1} .$$

Then line $mm^s(badout(i)^s)$ is sent to the master:

$$bdin(i)^{t+1} = mm^s(badout(i)^s) .$$

Proof. This lemma is proven along the lines of Lemma 8.40 (*flush* transfer).
   □

8.5.7 Accesses of the Hardware Computation

In this section we construct a series of accesses $acc(i, k)$ from a given hardware computation and prove a number of properties for these accesses depending on their type. We start by defining the hardware cycle $e(i, k)$ when the hardware access corresponding to $acc(i, k)$ ends. A read, write, or CAS access to cache i ends in cycle t when the processor request signal $preq(i)^t$ is on and the busy signal $mbusy(i)^t$ is off. A flush access ends in cycle t when the master leaves state *flush* or when the master writes I to the state RAM while leaving state *wait* and going to $m0$ (this corresponds to invalidation of a clean line):

$$flushend(i, t) = flush(i)^t \wedge \neg flush(i)^{t+1} \vee wait(i)^t \wedge swa(i)^t$$
$$someend(i, t) = preq(i)^t \wedge \neg mbusy(i)^t \vee flushend(i, t) .$$

The definition of the end cycles $e(i, k)$ for cache i is obviously

$$e(i, k) = \begin{cases} min\{t \mid someend(i, t)\} & k = 0 \\ min\{t \mid t > e(i, k - 1) \wedge someend(i, t)\} & k > 0 . \end{cases}$$

Note that from (A) and stability of processor inputs it follows that

$$idle(i)^{e(i,k)} \vee wait(i)^{e(i,k)} \vee localw(i)^{e(i,k)} \vee flush(i)^{e(i,k)} \vee w(i)^{e(i,k)} .$$

Table 13. Classification of accesses

Classification of accesses		
by hardware execution	by atomic execution	by operation type
local read	local read	read, negative CAS
delayed local read	local read	negative CAS
local write	local write	write, positive CAS
global access	global access	write, read, CAS
flush access	flush access	flush access

Thus far we have introduced two classifications of accesses. In Sect. 8.2.3 we distinguished accesses by the type of their operation: read accesses, write accesses, CAS accesses, and flushes. In Sect. 8.3.4 we grouped all accesses depending on the way they are treated in the atomic protocol. There we had local reads, local writes, global accesses, and flushes. Now we have to introduce a third classification of accesses depending on the way they are treated by the hardware. This classification is very close to the one we had for the atomic protocol and considers the following types of accesses:

- An access (i, k) is a local read if it ends in state *idle*:

$$idle(i)^{e(i,k)} .$$

- An access (i, k) is a delayed local read if it ends in state *wait* and is not a flush access:

$$wait(i)^{e(i,k)} \wedge \neg flushend(i, e(i, k)) .$$

- An access (i, k) is a local write if it ends in state *localw*:

$$localw(i)^{e(i,k)} .$$

- An access (i, k) is a global access if it ends in state *w*:

$$w(i)^{e(i,k)} .$$

- An access (i, k) is a flush if the condition for the end of a flush access is satisfied:

$$flushend(i, e(i, k)) .$$

A local access is either a local read, a local write, or a delayed local read. The correspondence between three introduced classifications of accesses is shown in Table 13.

Start cycles $s(i, k)$ of accesses are defined in the following way. Local reads start and end in the same cycle. Delayed local reads also start and end in the same cycle. Local writes start 1 cycle before they end. Global accesses start in the cycle when their hot phase begins. Flushes ending is state *flush* start when the master enters state *flush*. Flushes ending in state *wait* start in the same cycle.

Let $t = e(i,k)$. Then,

$$s(i,k) = \begin{cases} t & idle(i)^t \vee wait(i)^t \\ t-1 & localw(i)^t \\ max\{q \mid q < t \wedge wait(i)^q\} + 1 & flush(i)^t \\ max\{q \mid q < t \wedge m0(i)^q\} & \text{otherwise} . \end{cases}$$

From (A) we conclude

$$idle(i)^{s(i,k)} \vee wait(i)^{s(i,k)} \vee flush(i)^{s(i,k)} \vee m0(i)^{s(i,k)} .$$

One easily shows the following lemma.

Lemma 8.45 (local order).

$$\forall k : s(i,k) \leq e(i,k) < s(i,k+1)$$

With the help of the end cycles $e(i,k)$ alone we define the parameters of the $acc(i,k)$ of the sequential computation. We start with flush accesses ending in state $flush$, i.e., with the case

$$flush(i)^{e(i,k)}.$$

The address comes from $badout$ at the end of the access. The rest is obvious:

$$acc(i,k).a = badout(i)^{e(i,k)}$$
$$acc(i,k).f = 1$$
$$acc(i,k).r = acc(i,k).w = acc(i,k).cas = 0 .$$

For flush accesses ending in state $wait$, i.e., for the case

$$wait(i)^{e(i,k)} \wedge flushend(i, e(i,k)) ,$$

the tag of the address is taken from the tag RAM in cycle $e(i,k)$ while the cache line address is copied from the processor input. Let $pa = pa(i)^{e(i,k)}$, then:

$$acc(i,k).a = ca(i).tag(pa.c)^{e(i,k)} \circ pa.c$$
$$acc(i,k).f = 1$$
$$acc(i,k).r = acc(i,k).w = acc(i,k).cas = 0 .$$

For all other accesses, we construct $acc(i,k)$ from the processor input at the end of the access $t = e(i,k)$ (note that the processor inputs don't change during the access):

$$acc(i,k).a = pa(i)^t$$
$$acc(i,k).data = pdin(i)^t$$
$$acc(i,k).cdata = pcdin(i)^t$$
$$acc(i,k).bw = pbw(i)^t$$
$$acc(i,k).w = pw(i)^t$$
$$acc(i,k).r = pr(i)^t$$
$$acc(i,k).cas = pcas(i)^t$$
$$acc(i,k).f = 0 .$$

For accesses $acc(i,k)$ which are not flushes, we also define the last cycle $d(i,k)$ before or during (in case of a local operation) the access, when master i was making a decision to go either global or local. For all CAS accesses which end in stage w (i.e., global CAS accesses) and for those CAS accesses which end in stage $wait$ (i.e., delayed local reads), this will be the last cycle of wait. For all other accesses, this is the last cycle when master automaton i was in state $idle$:

$$d(i,k) = \begin{cases} \max\{q \mid q \le s(i,k) \wedge wait(i)^q\} & acc(i,k).cas \wedge (w(i)^{e(i,k)} \\ & \vee \ wait(i)^{e(i,k)}) \\ \max\{q \mid q \le s(i,k) \wedge idle(i)^q\} & \text{otherwise} . \end{cases}$$

Note that for global CAS accesses and for delayed local reads we actually do tests two times: the first time when we leave state $idle$ and the second time when we leave state $wait$. For these accesses we take into consideration only the results of the second case. However, we also partially depend on the results of the first test, because only the first test guarantees us that we do not have a positive CAS hit in an exclusive state. In the proof of Lemma 8.46 we show that if a positive exclusive CAS hit was not signalled at the time of the first test, then it would also not be signalled at the time of the second test.

Further we aim at lemmas stating that the conditions for local and global accesses are stable during an access: if we would make the decision based on the cache content later during the access we would get the same result.

We now show some crucial lemmas for these accesses. For the predicates defined in Sect. 8.3.4, we use the following shorthands:

$$global(i,k,aca) = global(aca, acc(i,k), i)$$
$$local(i,k,aca) = local(aca, acc(i,k), i)$$
$$rlocal(i,k,aca) = rlocal(aca, acc(i,k), i)$$
$$wlocal(i,k,aca) = wlocal(aca, acc(i,k), i) .$$

Lemma 8.46 (global end cycle). Let $acc(i,k)$ be an access. Then the global test is successful in state $d(i,k)$ iff the access ends in stage w:

$$global(i,k,aca^{d(i,k)}) \leftrightarrow w(i)^{e(i,k)} .$$

Proof. We first prove the direction from left to right. We show $w(i)^{e(i,k)}$ by contradiction. Let

$$idle(i)^{e(i,k)} \vee wait(i)^{e(i,k)} \vee localw(i)^{e(i,k)} .$$

By definition of *global* we get $\neg acc(i,k).f$. This implies

$$\neg flush(i)^{e(i,k)} .$$

We consider two cases:

- Let (i,k) be a delayed local read:

$$acc(i,k).cas \wedge wait(i)^{e(i,k)} .$$

Then we have $s(i,k) = e(i,k) = d(i,k)$. By automata construction we get $(9)(i)^{d(i,k)}$, which implies $rlocal(i)^{d(i,k)}$. This contradicts

$$global(i,k,aca^{d(i,k)}) .$$

- If (i,k) is not a delayed local read, we have $idle(i)^{s(i,k)}$ and

$$s(i,k) = d(i,k) \in \{e(i,k), e(i,k) - 1\} .$$

This implies by (A) that condition (3) for the master automaton did not hold in cycle $d(i,k)$, which contradicts $global(i,k,aca^{d(i,k)})$.

For the direction from right to left, we have $\neg acc(i,k).f$ by definition of $e(i,k)$. By automata construction we find cycles t, t', and t'', such that

$$t = max\{q \mid q < e(i,k) \wedge m0(i)^q\}$$
$$t' = max\{q \mid q < t \wedge wait(i)^q\}$$
$$t'' = max\{q \mid q < t' \wedge idle(i)^q\} .$$

By definition we have $t = s(i,k)$. We again consider two cases:

- $acc(i,k).cas$. Then by definition we have $t' = d(i,k)$. From hardware and automata construction we get

$$grant[i]^{t'} \wedge \neg(9)(i)^{t'} ,$$

which implies

$$\neg phit(i)^{t'} \vee test(i)^{t'} .$$

In case $\neg phit(i)^{t'}$ holds we obviously have $global(i,k,aca^{t'})$. For case $phit(i)^{t'} \wedge test(i)^{t'}$, we still have to show $aca(i).s^{t'}(a) \in \{O, S\}$. Let this be not true, i.e.,

$$aca(i).s^{t'}(a) \in \{E, M\} .$$

During cycles $q \in [t'' : t']$ the master automaton was in state *wait* or in state *idle*. The tag RAM of cache i during these cycles is not updated. If in any such cycle the state RAM of cache i gets updated with address $a.c$ (this can only happen at cycle q if $sw(i)^q$ holds), then we can conclude by (HW) and the construction of circuit $C2$:

$$aca(i).s^{q+1}(a) \in \{I, S, O\} .$$

Hence, the only possible case for line a to be in one of the exclusive states in t' is to be in the same state in cycle t'':

$$aca(i).s^{t''}(a) \in \{E, M\} .$$

But this by (A) and (HW) contradicts the fact that we moved from state $idle$ to state $wait$ in cycle t''.

- $\neg acc(i, k).cas$. By definition we have $t'' = d(i, k)$. Since we have moved to state $wait$ in this cycle, we have $(3)(i)^{d(i,k)}$ and the lemma follows by (HW) and (A).

$\square$

In the very same way we show a lemma for the local accesses.

Lemma 8.47 (local end cycle). Let $acc(i, k)$ be an access. Then

1. the test for a local read is successful in cycle $d(i, k)$ iff the access ends in stage $idle$ or in stage $wait$:

$$rlocal(i, k, aca^{d(i,k)}) \leftrightarrow (idle(i)^{e(i,k)} \vee (wait(i)^{e(i,k)} \wedge \neg acc(i, k).f)) ,$$

2. the test for a local write is successful in cycle $d(i, k)$ iff the access ends in stage $localw$:

$$wlocal(i, k, aca^{d(i,k)}) \leftrightarrow localw(i)^{e(i,k)} .$$

Proof. We first show the direction from right to left for both statements. By definition of $e(i, k)$ we have

$$preq(i)^{e(i,k)} \wedge \neg mbusy(i)^{e(i,k)} .$$

We do an obvious case split. If $idle(i)^{e(i,k)}$, then $d(i, k) = e(i, k)$ and by (A) we get

$$rlocal(i)^{d(i,k)} ,$$

which implies $rlocal(i, k, aca^{d(i,k)})$. If $wait(i)^{e(i,k)} \wedge \neg acc(i, k).f$, then again $d(i, k) = e(i, k)$ and by (A) we get

$$(9)(i)^{e(i,k)} ,$$

which also implies $rlocal(i, k, aca^{d(i,k)})$. Finally, if $localw(i)^{e(i,k)}$, then $d(i, k) = e(i, k) - 1$ and by (A) we have

$$(2)(i)^{d(i,k)}.$$

This implies $wlocal(i, k, aca^{d(i,k)})$.

For the direction from left to right, we have $\neg acc(i, k).f$ from the definition of $rlocal$ and $wlocal$. From Lemma 8.46 (global end cycle) we get $\neg w(i)^{e(i,k)}$. Hence, we have

$$idle(i)^{e(i,k)} \vee wait(i)^{e(i,k)} \vee localw(i)^{e(i,k)} .$$

Observing that $rlocal(i, k, aca^{d(i,k)})$ and $wlocal(i, k, aca^{d(i,k)})$ are mutually exclusive and applying the (already proven) direction from right to left of both statements, we conclude the proof. $\qquad\square$

The lemmas global/local end cycle are (sometimes implicitly) applied in the proofs of almost all the lemmas given below.

Lemma 8.48 (slave write at hot). For all $X \in \{data, tag, s\}$:

$$grant[i]^t \wedge \neg H(i)^t \rightarrow Xwb(i)^t = 0 .$$

Proof. By Lemma 8.14 (grant unique) we get $\forall j \neq i : \neg grant[j]^t$. Applying Lemma 8.17 (grant at warm) again we get

$$\forall j : \neg H(j)^t .$$

Hence, by Lemma 8.21 (idle slaves) we know that all slaves are idle (including slave i):

$$\forall j : sidle(j)^t .$$

By (A) we get $Xwb(i)^t = 0$ and the lemma holds. $\qquad\square$

Lemma 8.49 (stable master). Assume $acc(i, k).f \vee global(i, k, aca^{d(i,k)})$, i.e., $acc(i, k)$ is a flush or a global access. Then, during the entire access, abstract cache i does not change:

$$\forall q \in [s(i, k) : e(i, k)] : aca(i)^q = aca(i)^{s(i,k)} .$$

Proof. For $X \in \{data, tag, s\}$ the master automaton activates write signals Xwa only in cycle $q = e(i, k)$. These writes update the cache only after the end of the access.

If access $acc(i, k)$ is a flush, then for any cycle q under consideration we have

$$wait(i)^q \wedge grant[i]^q \vee W(i)^q$$

and conclude the statement by Lemmas 8.17 and 8.48 (grant at warm, slave write at hot). If access $acc(i, k)$ is a global read or write, then by Lemma 8.22 (sync) for the slave automaton of cache i we have $sidle(i)^q$. In this state the slave automaton does not activate a write signal Xwb. $\qquad\square$

The following lemma states that in the last cycle of $wait$ the RAMs of a waiting cache are not updated, unless a flush access is performed on a transition from $wait$ to $m0$.

Lemma 8.50 (last cycle of wait). Let $wait(i)^q \wedge \neg wait(i)^{q+1}$. Then

1. $\neg swa(i)^q \rightarrow aca(i)^q = aca(i)^{q+1}$,
2. $swa(i)^q \rightarrow aca(i).s^q(pa(i)^q) = aca(i).s^{q+1}(pa(i)^q) = I$.

Proof. For $X \in \{data, tag, s\}$ we have $Xwb(i)^q = 0$ by Lemma 8.48 (slave write at hot). We do an obvious case split:

- $\neg swa(i)^q$. Then the RAMs are not updated via port a and we conclude

$$aca(i)^q = aca(i)^{q+1} .$$

- $swa(i)^q$. By (A) and (HW) this implies

$$ca(i).tag^q(pa(i)^q.c) \neq pa(i)^q.t .$$

Hence, in the abstract cache the line addressed by $pa(i)$ is invalid:

$$aca(i).s^q(pa(i)^q) = I.$$

Since we do not update the tag RAM, the line stays invalid in cycle $q+1$.
$\square$

Another lemma argues that in the last cycle of *flush* the state of the abstract cache line addressed by pa is not changed. As a result, the output of circuit $C1$ is the same as if it was computed one cycle later.

Lemma 8.51 (last cycle of flush). Let $flush(i)^t \wedge \neg flush(i)^{t+1}$. Then

$$aca(i).s^t(pa(i)^t) = aca(i).s^{t+1}(pa(i)^t) = I .$$

Proof. The idea behind the proof is simple: when we made a decision to go to state *flush*, the cache line addressed by pa had a different tag. Hence, in the abstract cache this line was invalid. Since we do not write the tag RAM in the cycles under consideration, the line stays invalid when we leave the state *flush*.

Formally, let q be the last cycle when we were in state *wait* before the flush:

$$q = max\{t' \mid wait(i)^{t'} \wedge t' < q\} .$$

Since in cycle q we made a decision to go to state *flush*, it holds that

$$pa(i)^q.t \neq ca(i).tag^q(pa(i)^q.c) .$$

Lemma 8.48 (slave write at hot) guarantees that in between cycles q and t we don't activate signal $tagwb(i)$. Since we also don't write the tag RAM from the master side in states *wait* and *flush*, and the processor inputs are stable we get

$$pa(i)^q.t = pa(i)^t.t$$
$$= pa(i)^{t+1}.t$$
$$ca(i).tag^q(pa(i)^q.c) = ca(i).tag^t(pa(i)^t.c)$$
$$= ca(i).tag^{t+1}(pa(i)^{t+1}.c) .$$

Hence, we conclude

$$aca(i).s^t(pa(i)^t) = aca(i).s^{t+1}(pa(i)^t) = I .$$

$\square$

Lemma 8.52 (overlapping accesses with global). Let $acc(i,k)$ be a global access with address $a = acc(i,k).a$ ending in cycle $e(i,k) = t$. Let $acc(r,s)$ be an access with address a that is not a flush access and that is overlapping with $acc(i,k)$. Then $acc(r,s)$ is a local write and the overlap is in cycle $\{s(i,k), s(i,k)+1\}$ or $acc(r,s)$ is a local read and the overlap is in cycle $s(i,k)$:

$$w(i)^{e(i,k)} \wedge (i,k) \neq (r,s) \wedge \neg acc(r,s).f$$
$$\wedge\ acc(i,k).a = acc(r,s).a \wedge u \in [s(i,k) : e(i,k)] \cap [s(r,s) : e(r,s)]$$
$$\rightarrow localw(r)^{e(r,s)} \wedge u \in \{s(i,k), s(i,k)+1\}$$
$$\vee\ idle(r)^{e(r,s)} \wedge u = s(i,k) = s(r,s) .$$

Proof. Access $acc(r,s)$ cannot be on the same master by Lemma 8.45 (local order) and it cannot be global by Lemma 8.18 (warm unique). Thus, it is a local access. It cannot be a delayed local read because that would imply $grant[r]^{s(r,s)}$ which gives a contradiction by Lemmas 8.17 and 8.14 (grant at warm, grant unique). Hence, the decision to go local is made in stage *idle*:

$$idle(r)^{d(r,s)} \wedge d(r,s) = s(r,s) \in \{e(r,s), e(r,s)-1\} .$$

$acc(r,s)$ cannot start later than $s(i,k)$ because by Lemma 8.34 ($m0$) in cycle $s(i,k)+1$ slave r has already clocked in address a:

$$badin(r)^{s(i,k)+1} = a .$$

This gives a snoop conflict for address a in cache r in cycle $s(i,k)+1$ and the access $acc(r,s)$ cannot start. $\square$

Lemma 8.53 (stable local). Let $acc(i,k)$ be a local access. Then during the access abstract cache i does not change:

$$local(i,k,aca^{d(i,k)}) \rightarrow aca(i)^{s(i,k)} = aca(i)^{s(i,k)+1} .$$

Proof. By Lemma 8.47 (local end cycle), by the definition of $s(i,k)$, and by (A) we have

$$idle(i)^{s(i,k)} \lor (wait(i)^{s(i,k)} \land idle(i)^{s(i,k)+1}) .$$

For $X \in \{data, tag, s\}$ we have to show $Xwa(i)^{s(i,k)} = Xwb(i)^{s(i,k)} = 0$. This is trivial for signals $Xwa(i)$ because they are not activated in state $idle$ and on a transition from $wait$ to $idle$. Signals $Xwb(i)^{s(i,k)}$ are active if slave automaton i is in state sw, i.e., $sw(i)^{s(i,k)}$. In this case by Lemma 8.22 (sync) there is a master $r \neq i$ and an access $acc(r,s)$ such that $w(r)^{s(i,k)}$. Thus, the accesses overlap while the master is in state w. But this contradicts Lemma 8.52 (overlapping accesses with global): the accesses can only overlap when the master is in states $m0$ or $m1$. $\qquad\square$

Lemma 8.54 (overlapping accesses with flush). Assume $SINV(t)$. Let $acc(i,k)$ be a flush with address $a = acc(i,k).a$ ending in cycle $e(i,k) = t$. Let $acc(r,s)$ be any access to address a except a local read. Then the time intervals of the two accesses are disjoint. Thus, only local reads can overlap with flushes:

$$(i,k) \neq (r,s) \land acc(i,k).f \land e(i,k) = t$$
$$\land \ \neg idle(r)^{e(r,s)} \land acc(r,s).a = acc(i,k).a$$
$$\rightarrow [s(i,k) : e(i,k)] \cap [s(r,s) : e(r,s)] = \emptyset .$$

Proof. Proof by contradiction. Assume

$$(r,s) \neq (i,k) \land q \in [s(i,k) : e(i,k)] \cap [s(r,s) : e(r,s)] .$$

The case $r = i$ is impossible by Lemma 8.45 (local order). Hence, $r \neq i$. For cycle q we have

$$grant[i]^q .$$

Hence, $acc(r,s)$ can not be a flush, a global access or a delayed local read by (A) and by Lemmas 8.17 and 8.14 (grant at warm, grant unique). Thus, access $acc(r,s)$ is a local write access at cache r and it consists of 2 cycles:

$$e(r,s) = s(r,s) + 1 .$$

Hence, access $acc(r,s)$ has started in cycle q or in cycle $q - 1$ with a cache hit in an exclusive state:

$$s(r,s) \in \{q-1,q\} \land aca(r).s^{s(r,s)}(a) \in \{E, M\} .$$

By Lemma 8.53 (stable local) we get

$$aca(r).s^q(a) \in \{E, M\} .$$

On the other hand, flush accesses like $acc(i,k)$ are preceded by a cache hit in state $wait$ at the eviction address in cycle $s(i,k) - 1$ or $s(i,k)$. We split cases:

- $flush(i)^{s(i,k)}$. This implies

$$wait(i)^{s(i,k)-1} \wedge aca(i).s^{s(i,k)-1}(a) \neq I \ .$$

By (A) and by Lemmas 8.49, 8.50 (stable master, last cycle of wait) we get

$$\forall u \in [s(i,k) - 1 : e(i,k)] : aca(i).s^u(a) \neq I \ .$$

For $u = q$ this contradicts the state invariants.

- $wait(i)^{s(i,k)}$. This implies $s(i,k) = e(i,k) = q$ and

$$aca(i).s^q(a) \neq I \ .$$

Again, this contradicts the state invariants.

$\square$

Lemma 8.55 (overlapping accesses with local write). Assume $SINV(t)$. Let $acc(i,k)$ be a local write access with address $a = acc(i,k).a$ ending in cycle $e(i,k) = t$. Let $acc(r,s)$ be another local access with address a. Then it cannot overlap with $acc(i,k)$:

$$(i,k) \neq (r,s) \wedge e(i,k) = t \wedge localw(i)^{e(i,k)}$$
$$\wedge \ acc(i,k).a = acc(r,s).a \wedge local(r,s,aca^{d(r,s)})$$
$$\rightarrow [s(i,k) : e(i,k)] \cap [s(r,s) : e(r,s)] = \emptyset \ .$$

Proof. Assume intervals overlap in cycle q. We have $i \neq r$ by Lemma 8.45 (local order). For $acc(i,k)$ we have $d(i,k) = s(i,k)$. For $acc(r,s)$ we have by Lemma 8.47 (local end cycle), by the definition of $s(r,s)$, and by (A):

$$idle(r)^{s(r,s)} \vee (wait(r)^{s(r,s)} \wedge idle(r)^{s(r,s)+1})$$

and

$$d(r,s) = s(r,s).$$

By (A) and by Lemmas 8.53, 8.50 (stable local, last cycle of wait) we conclude

$$aca(i).s^{d(i,k)}(a) = aca(i).s^q(a)$$
$$aca(r).s^{d(r,s)}(a) = aca(r).s^q(a) \ .$$

By Lemma 8.47 (local end cycle) we get

$$wlocal(i,k,aca^{d(i,k)}).$$

Together with $local(r,s,aca^{d(r,s)})$, this gives us

$$aca(i).s^{d(i,k)}(a) \in \{E, M\}$$
$$aca(r).s^{d(r,s)}(a) \neq I \ .$$

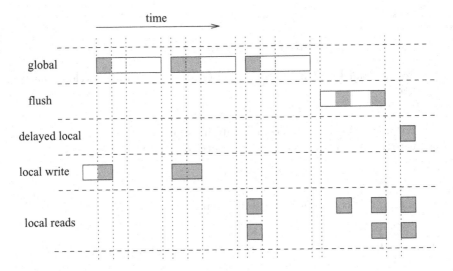

Fig. 142. Possible overlaps between accesses to the same cache address a

Thus,

$$aca(i).s^q(a) \in \{E, M\}$$
$$aca(r).s^q(a) \neq I \,,$$

which contradicts the state invariants.   □

The last three lemmas can be summarized as follows. The only possible overlaps between accesses to the same cache address a are (see Fig. 142):

1. a flush with local reads,
2. a global access with local reads or local writes; in this case a local access ends at most 1 cycle after the start of the global access,
3. a local read with other local reads and with delayed local reads.

If we are interested in accesses to the same address a and ending at the same cycle t we are left only with the first and the third cases. Formally, let

$$E(a,t) = \{(i,k) \mid e(i,k) = t \wedge acc(i,k).a = a\}$$

be the set of accesses with address a ending in cycle t. Then we have

Lemma 8.56 (simultaneously ending accesses). Assume $SINV(t)$. For any a and t, either set $E(a,t)$ contains at most one element, or all accesses in $E(a,t)$ are local reads and delayed local reads, or one access in $E(a,t)$ is a flush and all other accesses are local reads:

$$\#E(a,t) \le 1$$
$$\lor \; (\forall(i,k) \in E(a,t) : idle(i)^{e(i,k)} \lor (wait(i)^{e(i,k)} \land \neg acc(i,k).g))$$
$$\lor \; (\exists(i,k) \in E(a,t) : acc(i,k).f \land \forall(r,s) \in E(a,t) :$$
$$(r,s) \ne (i,k) \rightarrow idle(r)^{e(r,s)}) \; .$$

Proof. Trivial by using Lemmas 8.47, 8.46 (local end cycle, global end cycle) and overlapping lemmas.   □

Let predicate $P(i,k,a,t)$ be true if access (i,k) ends in cycle t, accesses address a, and is not a local read or a delayed local read:

$$P(i,k,a,t) \equiv e(i,k) = t \land acc(i,k).a = a$$
$$\land \neg(idle(i)^{e(i,k)} \lor wait(i)^{e(i,k)} \land \neg acc(i,k).f) \; .$$

There is an obvious correspondence between $P(i,k,a,t)$ and set $E(a,t)$:

$$P(i,k,a,t) = 1 \leftrightarrow (i,k) \in E(a,t) \land \neg(idle(i)^{e(i,k)} \lor wait(i)^{e(i,k)} \land \neg acc(i,k).f) \; .$$

By Lemma 8.47 (local end cycle) this is equivalent to

$$P(i,k,a,t) = 1 \leftrightarrow (i,k) \in E(a,t) \land \neg rlocal(i,k,aca^{d(i,k)}) \; .$$

We can now identify all cache lines that get modified in cycle t.

Lemma 8.57 (unchanged cache lines). Let $X \in \{s, data\}$, then

$$aca(i).X^{t+1}(a) \ne aca(i).X^t(a) \rightarrow$$
$$\exists k, j : P(i,k,a,t) \lor j \ne i \land P(j,k,a,t) \land w(j)^t \; .$$

Proof. On cache i ports a of RAMs are updated only when

$$w(i)^t \lor localw(i)^t \lor ((flush(i)^t \lor wait(i)^t) \land m0(i)^{t+1}) \; .$$

Ports b of state and data RAMs are updated only when the slave automaton of cache i is in state $sw(i)^t$. Port b of the tag RAM is never written.

A write to a state or a data RAM can modify at most one line in the abstract cache. A write to a tag RAM can modify at most 2 lines. We do the proof by considering all possibly updates to cache RAMs.

- $w(i)^t$. In this state all the RAMs are updated via ports a with the address $pa(i)^t$. In the abstract cache i this update can possibly modify the lines

$$a = pa(i)^t \quad \text{and} \quad b = ca(i).tag^t(pa(i)^t.c) \circ pa(i)^t.c \; .$$

By definition we obviously have

$$acc(i,k).a = pa(i)^t \; .$$

By Lemma 8.46 (global end cycle) we get

$$global(i, k, aca^{d(i,k)})$$

and conclude

$$P(i, k, aca(i, k).a, t) .$$

Hence, for line address $a = acc(i, k).a$ we are done. The line b can possibly be affected by the update only if

$$ca(i).tag^t(a.c) \neq a.t ,$$

i.e., if we are overwriting the tag with the new value. In that case the cache line addressed by b becomes invalid:

$$aca(i).s^{t+1}(b) = I .$$

Our goal is to show that (in this case) this line was already invalid in cycle t and, hence, no change to the memory slice b in cache i has occured. By Lemma 8.49 (stable master) we have

$$aca(i)^t = aca(i)^{s(i,k)} .$$

In cycle $s(i, k)$, the automaton of cache i was in state $m0$. Hence, in the previous cycle we had:

$$wait(i)^{s(i,k)-1} \wedge (4)(i)^{s(i,k)-1} \vee flush(i)^{s(i,k)-1} .$$

The tag RAMs are not updated on both of these transitions, as well as in the time interval $[s(i, k) : t - 1]$. Hence,

$$ca(i).tag^{s(i,k)-1} = ca(i).tag^{s(i,k)} = ca(i).tag^t .$$

Thus, if the tags did not match in cycle t, then they also did not match in cycle $s(i, k) - 1$:

$$ca(i).tag^{s(i,k)-1}(a.c) \neq a.t .$$

Hence, independently of whether the automaton of cache i was in state $wait$ or in state $flush$ in cycle $s(i, k)$, we get by (A) and (HW):

$$ca(i).s^{s(i,k)}(a.c) = I .$$

This, in turn, implies

$$aca(i).s^{s(i,k)}(b) = I .$$

- $sw(i)^t$. In this state ports b of state and data RAMs are updated with the address $badin(i)^t$. In the abstract cache i this update can only modify the line

$$a = ca(i).tag^t(badin(i)^t.c) \circ badin(i)^t.c .$$

By Lemmas 8.22, 8.46 (sync, global end cycle) there exists cache j and access (j, k), s.t., $w(j)^t$ and

$$P(j, k, pa(j)^t, t) .$$

Hence, we only need to show that

$$a = pa(j)^t$$

and we are done. For slave i we get by the data transfer lemmas:

$$badin(i)^t = pa(j)^t.$$

By Lemma 8.22 (sync), we know that there was a bus hit on slave i in cycle $s(j, k) + 1$:

$$bhit(i)^{s(j,k)+1} .$$

Applying data transfer lemmas again this gives us

$$ca(i).tag^{s(j,k)+1}(pa(j)^t.c) = pa(j)^t.t .$$

Since local write accesses never overwrite tags (global and flush accesses in the interval $[s(j, k) : t]$ can not occur at cache j by Lemmas 8.17 and 8.14 (grant at warm, grant unique)), we conclude

$$ca(i).tag^t(pa(j)^t.c) = pa(j)^t.t .$$

- $localw(i)^t$. In this state ports a of data and state RAMs are updated with the address $pa(i)^t$. In the abstract cache i this update can only modify the line

$$a = ca(i).tag^t(pa(i)^t.c) \circ pa(i)^t.c .$$

By Lemma 8.47 (local end cycle) there must be an access $acc(i, k)$ ending in cycle t:

$$P(i, k, pa(i)^t, t) .$$

Hence, we only have to show that

$$a = pa(i)^t .$$

This is very easy. By Lemma 8.53 (stable local) and by (A) we get

$$aca(i).s^t(pa(i)^t) \neq I .$$

Hence,

$$ca(i).tag^t(pa(i)^t.c) = pa(i)^t.t .$$

- $flush(i)^t \wedge m0(i)^{t+1}$. In this case port a of the state RAM is updated with the address $pa(i)^t$. In the abstract cache i this update can only modify the line

$$a = ca(i).tag^t(pa(i)^t.c) \circ pa(i)^t.c .$$

By definition, there is a flush access $acc(i, k)$ ending in cycle t:

$$P(i, k, badout(i)^t, t) .$$

By (A), (HW), and by Lemma 8.49 (stable master) we conclude

$$badout(i)^t.c = pa(i)^t.c$$
$$badout(i)^t.t = ca(i).tag^t(pa(i)^t.c) .$$

Hence,

$$a = badout(i)^t .$$

- $wait(i)^t \wedge m0(i)^{t+1} \wedge swa(i)^t$. Port a of the state RAM is updated with the address $pa(i)^t.c$. In the abstract cache i this update can only modify the line

$$a = ca(i).tag^t(pa(i)^t.c) \circ pa(i)^t.c .$$

By definition, there is a flush access (i, k) to address a ending in cycle t

$$P(i, k, a, t) .$$

$\square$

The next two lemmas make sure that (i) the state of a slave does not change after it computes its response and until the global access ends and (ii) that the slave decision to participate or not participate in the transaction stays stable during the entire access.

Lemma 8.58 (stable slaves). Assume $SINV(t)$. Let $acc(i, k)$ be an access to address $a = acc(i, k).a$ ending in cycle $t = e(i, k)$ in state $w(i)^t$. Let $X \in \{s, data\}$ and $q \in [s(i, k) + 2 : t]$ then

$$\forall j \neq i : aca(j).X^q(a) = aca(j).X^t(a) .$$

Proof. By Lemmas 8.52 and 8.54 (overlapping accesses with global, overlapping accesses with flush) we know that no local write or flush access to address a can end in slave j in cycles $q \in [s(i, k) + 2 : t]$. Hence, we conclude the proof by Lemma 8.57 (unchanged cache lines). $\square$

Lemma 8.59 (stable slave decision). Assume $SINV(t)$. Let $acc(i, k)$ be an access to address $a = acc(i, k).a$ ending in cycle $t = e(i, k)$ in state $w(i)^t$. Then

$$\forall j \neq i : bhit(j)^{s(i,k)+1} = bhit(j)^t .$$

Proof. By Lemma 8.30 (*badout*), we know that the address is put on the bus by the master during the entire hot phase. By (A), we know that the register *badout*(i) is not clocked during the hot phase. Hence, for all $q \in [s(i,k):t]$

$$b.ad^q = a .$$

By Lemma 8.22 (sync) for all slaves $j \neq i$ we have

$$s1(j)^{s(i,k)+1} .$$

By Lemma 8.58 (stable slaves) we get for cycle $q \in [s(i,k)+2:t]$ and RAMs $X \in \{s, data\}$:

$$aca(j).X^q(a) = aca(j).X^t(a) .$$

Now, we consider cases on whether there is a bus hit in state $s(i,k)+1$ or not:

- $\neg bhit(j)^{s(i,k)+1}$. Hence,

$$aca(j).s^{s(i,k)+1}(a) = I .$$

  As a result, there can be no local write access to address a on cache j ending at cycle $s(i,k)+1$ (that would give a contradiction by (A) and by Lemmas 8.47 and 8.53 (local end cycle, stable local)). Hence, with the help of Lemma 8.57 (unchanged cache lines) we conclude

$$aca(j).s^{s(i,k)+1}(a) = aca(j).s^{s(i,k)+2}(a)$$
$$= aca(j).s^t(a)$$
$$= I .$$

  This implies $\neg bhit(j)^t$.
- $bhit(j)^{s(i,k)+1}$. Hence,

$$aca(j).s^{s(i,k)+1}(a) \neq I .$$

  If there is no access to address a on cache j ending at cycle $s(i,k)+1$, then we again apply Lemma 8.57 (unchanged cache lines) to get

$$aca(j).s^{s(i,k)+2}(a) = aca(j).s^{s(i,k)+1}(a) .$$

  If there is such access, then by (A) and (HW) we conclude

$$aca(j).s^{s(i,k)+2}(a) = M$$

  and

$$aca(j).s^t(a) = M$$
$$\neq I .$$

  This implies $bhit(j)^t$.

$\square$

Now we can state the crucial lemmas that guarantee stability of decisions to go for a global or a local transaction.

Lemma 8.60 (stable local decision). Let access $acc(i, k)$ end in cycle $t = e(i, k)$. Let in cycle $d(i, k)$ the decision for a local read or a local write hold. Then the same decision holds in cycle t:

$$\forall x \in \{r, w\} : xlocal(i, k, aca^{d(i,k)}) \rightarrow xlocal(i, k, aca^t).$$

Proof. Expand the definition of *rlocal* or *wlocal* and apply Lemma 8.53 (stable local). □

Lemma 8.61 (stable global decision). Assume $SINV(t)$. Let $acc(i, k)$ be a global access, i.e., in cycle $d(i, k)$ we have $global(i, k, aca^{d(i,k)})$. Then we could have reached the same decision in cycle $t = e(i, k)$:

$$global(i, k, aca^{d(i,k)}) \rightarrow global(i, k, aca^t) .$$

Proof. Assume $global(i, k, aca^{d(i,k)})$ and let $a = acc(i, k).a$. We expand the definition of *global* and observe

$$global(i, k, aca) \equiv \neg acc(i, k).f \wedge (aca(i).s(a) = I \vee aca(i).s(a) \in \{S, O\}$$
$$\wedge (acc(i, k).w \vee acc(i, k).cas \wedge test(acc(i, k), aca(i).data(a)))) .$$

By Lemma 8.49 (stable master) we have

$$aca(i)^{s(i,k)} = aca(i)^{e(i,k)} .$$

Hence, all we need to show is

$$global(i, k, aca^{s(i,k)}) .$$

By Lemma 8.46 (global end cycle) and the definition of $s(i, k)$, we have

$$m0(i)^{s(i,k)} \wedge w(i)^{e(i,k)} .$$

If a flush access ends in cycle $s(i, k) - 1$:

$$flush(i)^{s(i,k)-1} \vee wait(i)^{s(i,k)-1} \wedge swa(i)^{s(i,k)-1} ,$$

then we have by (A) and (HW)

$$aca(i).s^{s(i,k)}(a) = I ,$$

which obviously implies $global(i, k, aca^{s(i,k)})$.
   If in cycle $s(i, k) - 1$ no flush access ends, then we have

$$ca(i).tag^{s(i,k)-1}(a.c) = a.t .$$

We consider cycles $q \in [d(i,k) : s(i,k) - 1]$ when the master is in state *idle* or *wait*:

$$idle(i)^q \vee wait(i)^q .$$

The tag RAM of cache i is not updated during these cycles:

$$\begin{aligned} ca(i).tag^q(a.c) &= ca(i).tag^{s(i,k)-1}(a.c) \\ &= ca(i).tag^{s(i,k)}(a.c) \\ &= ca(i).tag^{d(i,k)}(a.c) . \end{aligned}$$

The state RAM of cache i is updated only if there is another global access ending in q and if cache i is participating in that access, i.e., if $sw(i)^q$ holds. We split cases on the state of line a in cycle $d(i,k)$:

- $ca(i).s^{d(i,k)}(a.c) = I$. Hence, line a is invalid in $aca(i)$. We show by contradiction that this line stays invalid until $s(i,k)$. Let q be the first cycle when line a gets updated:

$$q = min\{t \mid t \geq d(i,k) \wedge t < s(i,k) \wedge sw(i)^t \wedge badin(i)^t.c = a.c\} .$$

Then by (A) there exists cache j with $w(j)^q$ and there exists an access (j,k') ending at cycle q. Applying data transfer lemmas and Lemma 8.30 (*badout*) we get

$$acc(j,k').c = pa(j)^q.c = a.c = b.ad^q.c = b.ad^{s(j,k')+1}.c .$$

By (A), slave i had a bus hit in state $s(j,k') + 1$. Hence, by Lemma 8.59 (stable slave decision) it also has a bus hit in state q. This implies

$$ca(i).s^q(a.c) \neq I$$

and gives a contradiction. Hence, we can conclude for this case

$$aca(i).s^{s(i,k)}(a) = I .$$

- $ca(i).s^{d(i,k)}(a.c) \in \{S, O\}$. In this case, by (HW) and by the construction of circuit $C2$, any update to the state RAM can only change the state of the line to S, O, or I. Hence, we can conclude for this case

$$aca(i).s^{s(i,k)}(a) \in \{S, O, I\} .$$

If $acc(i,k)$ is not a CAS access, then this already gives us

$$global(i, k, aca^{s(i,k)}) .$$

If $acc(i,k)$ is a CAS access and we are not in *flush* in cycle $s(i,k) - 1$, then we have

$$wait(i)^{d(i,k)} \wedge s(i,k) = d(i,k) + 1 .$$

By Lemma 8.50 (last cycle of wait) we get

$$aca(i)^{d(i,k)} = aca(i)^{s(i,k)} ,$$

which implies

$$global(i, k, aca^{s(i,k)}) .$$

□

An important consequence is a reformulation of predicate $P(i, k, a, t)$.

Lemma 8.62 (reformulation of P). Assume $SINV(t)$. Then,

$$P(i, k, a, t) \equiv e(i, k) = t \wedge acc(i, k).a = a \wedge \neg rlocal(i, k, aca^t) .$$

Proof. We have to show that

$$rlocal(i, k, aca^{d(i,k)}) \leftrightarrow rlocal(i, k, aca^t) .$$

For the implication from left to right, we apply Lemma 8.60 (stable local decision) and get the proof.

For the other direction, we prove by contradiction. Let

$$rlocal(i, k, aca^t) \wedge \neg rlocal(i, k, aca^{d(i,k)}) .$$

Then we have

$$wlocal(i, k, aca^{d(i,k)}) \vee global(i, k, aca^{d(i,k)}) .$$

By Lemmas 8.60 and 8.61 (stable local decision, stable global decision) we get

$$wlocal(i, k, aca^t) \vee global(i, k, aca^t) ,$$

which gives a contradiction to $rlocal(i, k, aca^t)$.

□

With this definition at hand, we conclude a carefully phrased technical lemma.

Lemma 8.63 (unchanged memory slices).
Let $SINV(t)$ hold. Then the following is true:

1. Memory system slice a is only changed in cycle t if $P(i, k, a, t)$ holds for some (i, k):

$$(\forall (i, k) : \neg P(i, k, a, t)) \rightarrow \Pi(ms(h^{t+1}), a) = \Pi(ms(h^t), a) .$$

2. If access (i, k) ends in t and $P(i, k, a, t)$ does not hold, then in the atomic protocol access $acc(i, k)$ applied to port i does not change slice a of memory system $ms(h^t)$:

$$t = e(i, k) \wedge \neg P(i, k, a, t) \rightarrow \Pi(\delta_1(ms(h^t), acc(i, k), i), a) = \Pi(ms(h^t), a) .$$

3. At most one access ending in cycle t can change slice a both in the hardware computation and in the atomic protocol:

$$P(i, k, a, t) \wedge P(r, s, a, t) \rightarrow (i, k) = (r, s) .$$

4. If $P(i, k, a, t)$ holds and access (i, k) is not a global access, then content of abstract cache $j \neq i$ for address a is not changed at cycle t. Let $X \in \{data, s\}$, then

$$j \neq i \wedge P(i, k, a, t) \wedge \neg w(i)^t \rightarrow aca(j).X^{t+1}(a) = aca(j).X^t(a) .$$

5. If $P(i, k, a, t)$ holds and access (i, k) does not end in state $flush$, then the content of the main memory for address a is not changed at cycle t:

$$P(i, k, a, t) \wedge \neg flush(i)^t \rightarrow mm^{t+1}(a) = mm^t(a) .$$

Proof. We prove the statements one by one.

1. By contradiction. Assume for some a

$$\Pi(ms(h^{t+1}), a) \neq \Pi(ms(h^t), a).$$

There are two cases possible:
- $\exists i : aca(i).X^{t+1}(a) \neq aca(i).X^t(a)$. Then we get a contradiction by Lemma 8.57 (unchanged cache lines).
- $mm^{t+1}(a) \neq mm^t(a)$. By (A) and (HW) this is only possibly when there exists cache i such that

$$flush(i)^t \wedge m0(i)^{t+1} .$$

Hence, there is a flush access ending in cycle t:

$$P(i, k, badout(i)^t, t) .$$

By Lemma 8.40 (flush transfer) we conclude that the only address a that is modified in the memory is $a = badout(i)^t$, and get a contradiction.

2. If access (i, k) ends in cycle t but the predicate $P(i, k, a, t)$ does not hold, then we have two options:
- access (i, k) is either a local read or a delayed local read. By Lemma 8.62 (reformulation of P) we get

$$rlocal(i, k, aca^t) .$$

By part 1 of Lemma 8.12 (properties one step), this implies

$$\delta_1(ms(h^t), acc(i, k), i) = ms(h^t) .$$

- access (i, k) is performed to an address different from a:

$$acc(i, k).a \neq a.$$

By part 2 of Lemma 8.12, we conclude

$$\Pi(\delta_1(ms(h^t), acc(i, k), i), a) = \Pi(ms(h^t), a) .$$

3. The proof immediately follows by Lemma 8.56 (simultaneously ending accesses).
4. By contradiction. Let

$$P(i, k, a, t) \wedge \neg w(i)^t,$$

and let for some $j \neq i$ and for some a

$$aca(j).X^{t+1}(a) \neq aca(j).X^t(a) .$$

By Lemma 8.57 (unchanged cache lines), a cache line can change in cycle t only in two cases:

$$\exists k' : P(j, k', a, t) \vee \exists r \neq j : P(r, k', a, t) \wedge w(r)^t . \tag{19}$$

By part 3 of the lemma we are now proving, we conclude that there are no other accesses to address a ending in cycle t:

$$\forall r \neq i : \forall k' : \neg P(r, k', a, t) .$$

Hence, for cache $j \neq i$ we get

$$\forall k' : \neg P(j, k', a, t) .$$

Since (i, k) is the only access to address a ending in cycle t and it does not end in state w, we conclude

$$\forall r, k' : \neg(P(r, k', a, t) \wedge w(r)^t) .$$

and get a contradiction to (19).
5. By contradiction. Let $mm^{t+1}(a) \neq mm^t(a)$. By (A) and (HW) this is only possibly when there exists cache $j \neq i$ such that

$$flush(j)^t \wedge m0(j)^{t+1} .$$

Hence, there is a flush access ending in cycle t:

$$P(j, k', badout(j)^t, t) .$$

By Lemma 8.40 (flush transfer) we conclude that the only address a that is modified in the memory is $a = badout(i)^t$, and get a contradiction by part 3 of the lemma we are now proving.

8.5.8 Relation with the Atomic Protocol

We are now ready to establish a crucial simulation result between the sequential computation of the atomic protocol and the hardware computation. Essentially it states that an access $acc(i,k)$ of the hardware computation ending in cycle t has the same effect as the same access $acc(i,k)$ applied to port i and memory system $ms(h^t)$ of the atomic protocol.

Lemma 8.64 (1 step). Assume $SINV(t)$. Then

1. $\Pi(ms(h^{t+1}),a) = \begin{cases} \Pi(\delta_1(ms(h^t),acc(i,k),i),a) & P(i,k,a,t) \\ \Pi(ms(h^t),a) & \text{otherwise}, \end{cases}$
2. let $acc(i,k).r \lor acc(i,k).cas$ and $e(i,k)=t$ then

$$pdout(i)^t = pdout1(ms(h^t),acc(i,k),i).$$

Proof. The second statement is trivial for local reads and delayed local reads. We will show the second statement for other accesses together with the first statement.

By part 1 of Lemma 8.63 (unchanged memory slices) $\Pi(ms(h^t),a)$ only changes in cycles $t+1$ following cycles t when a flush, a local write access, or a global access with address a ends. Thus, for $\neg\exists(i,k) : P(i,k,a,t)$ there is nothing left to show.

Next, we observe by part 3 of Lemma 8.63 (unchanged memory slices) that in any cycle t there is at most one access $acc(i,k)$ satisfying the conditions of the predicate $P(i,k,a,t)$ for any given address a. Thus, the statement of the lemma is well defined. By definition of $e(i,k)$ and automata construction we have

$$localw(i)^t \lor w(i)^t \lor ((flush(i)^t \lor wait(i)^t) \land m0(i)^{t+1}).$$

Now we split cases on the kind of access to address a ending in cycle t:

- Access $acc(i,k)$ ends in state $localw$. Hence, $s(i,k)+1=t$ and by Lemmas 8.47, 8.60 (local end cycle, stable local decision) we have

$$local(i,k,aca^t).$$

By Lemma 8.53 (stable local) we have

$$aca(i)^{s(i,k)} = aca(i)^{s(i,k)+1}.$$

By part 4 of Lemma 8.63 (unchanged memory slices) we get for $X \in \{s,data\}$:

$$\forall j \neq i : aca(j).X^{t+1}(a) = aca(j).X^t(a)$$

and by part 5 of the same lemma we get

$$mm^{t+1}(a) = mm^t(a).$$

In state *localw* we write to cache address $pa(i).c$ via ports a of the data and the state RAMs. The tag RAM is not updated. The writes via port a always have precedence over the writes via port b. Hence, even if there was a write to $pa(i).c$ via port b of the data or the state RAM, it would not have any effect (below, in the proof for the global accesses, we show that simultaneous writes via ports a and b to the same address never occur). Hence, by (A), (HW), and the definition of the one step protocol we can conclude:

$$\Pi(ms(h^{t+1}), a) = \Pi(\delta_1(ms(h^t), acc(i,k), i), a) .$$

In case of a CAS access we also have by automata and hardware construction:

$$pdout(i)^t = aca(i).data^t(a) = pdout1(ms(h^t), acc(i,k), i) .$$

- Access $acc(i,k)$ ends in state w. By Lemmas 8.46 and 8.61 (global end cycle, stable global decision) we have

$$global(aca^t, acc(i,k), i) .$$

By part 5 of Lemma 8.63 (unchanged memory slices) we know that the memory content for address a is unchanged:

$$mm^{t+1}(a) = mm^t(a) .$$

Using Lemma 8.49 (stable master) we get

$$\forall q \in [s(i,k) : t] : aca(i)^q = aca(i)^t .$$

Moreover, by Lemmas 8.50 and 8.51 (last cycle of wait, last cycle of flush) we have

$$aca(i).s^{s(i,k)-1}(a) = aca(i).s^t(a) .$$

By Lemma 8.58 (stable slaves) we get for slaves $j \neq i$, cycle $q \in [s(i,k)+2 : t]$, and RAMs $X \in \{s, data\}$:

$$aca(j).X^q(a) = aca(j).X^t(a) .$$

Using the protocol transfer lemmas and the stability of processor inputs we get for all slaves $j \neq i$:

$$
\begin{aligned}
mprotin(j)^{s(i,k)+1} &= mprotout(i)^{s(i,k)} \\
&= C1(aca(i).s(a)^{s(i,k)-1}, ptype(i)^{s(i,k)-1}) \\
&= C1(aca(i).s(a)^t, ptype(i)^t) \\
sprotout(j)^{s(i,k)+2} &= C2(aca(j).s^{s(i,k)+2}(a), mprotin(j)^{s(i,k)+1}).(ch, di) \\
&= C2(aca(j).s^t(a), mprotout(i)^t).(ch, di) \\
sprotin(i)^{s(i,k)+3} &= \bigvee_j sprotout(j)^{s(i,k)+2} \\
&= \bigvee_j C2(aca(j).s^t(a), mprotout(i)^t).(ch, di) .
\end{aligned}
$$

By Lemma 8.22 (sync) all slaves in cycle t are either in state $sidle'$ (if they do not participate in the transaction) or are in state sw (if they participate in the transaction). For participating slaves we have by Lemmas 8.22 and 8.59 (sync, stable slave decision):

$$bhit(j)^t .$$

Hence,

$$ca(j).tag^t(a.c) = a.t .$$

For not participating slaves by the same arguments we get

$$\neg bhit(j)^t$$

and

$$aca(j).s^t(a) = I .$$

By part 3 of Lemma 8.63 (unchanged memory slices) we know that no other global, flush or local write accesses to address a end in cycle t. If some access to address $b \neq a$, where $b.c = a.c$, on cache j ends in cycle t, then this access cannot be a flush or a global access by Lemmas 8.17 and 8.14 (grant at warm, grant unique). If it is a local write, then by Lemmas 8.47 and 8.53 (local end cycle, stable local) and by (A) we get:

$$\begin{aligned} ca(j).tag^{t+1}(b.c) &= ca(j).tag^t(a.c) \\ &= b.t \\ &\neq a.t . \end{aligned}$$

Hence, such an access can occur only on a not participating cache j and for such cache it then holds:

$$aca(j).s^{t+1}(a) = I .$$

For participating slaves j, possible updates to port a of state RAMs (ports a of other RAMs are not clocked at all) can only be done to cache addresses different from $a.c$. Hence, they do not interfere with the updates performed through ports b by the slave automata. The statement

$$\Pi(ms(h^{t+1}), a) = \Pi(\delta_1(ms(h^t), acc(i,k), i), a)$$

now follows from the data transfer lemmas. If $acc(i,k)$ is a read or a CAS access, the statement

$$pdout(i)^t = pdout1(ms(h^t), acc(i,k), i)$$

also follows from the data transfer lemmas.

- If a flush access $acc(i,k)$ ends in cycle $t = e(i,k)$ then we have

$$flush(i)^t \vee wait(i)^t .$$

In cycle t we write to cache address $pa(i).c$ via port a of the state RAM. Ports a of the data and the tag RAMs are not updated. By Lemmas 8.17 and 8.14 (grant at warm, grant unique) we know that no global access can end in cycle t. Hence, ports b of the RAMs are also not updated in cycle t. We now split cases on whether the access ends in state $flush$ or in state $wait$:

- $flush(i)^t$. By (A) and (HW) we have

$$aca(i).s^{s(i,k)-1}(a) \in \{M, O\} \wedge aca(i).s^{t+1}(a) = I.$$

By (A), by (HW), and by Lemma 8.40 (flush transfer) we conclude

$$
\begin{aligned}
mm^{t+1}(a) &= mm^{t+1}(badout(i)^{e(i,k)}) \\
&= mm^{t+1}(badout(i)^{s(i,k)}) \\
&= bdout(i)^{s(i,k)} \\
&= ca(i).data^{s(i,k)-1}(a.c) \\
&= aca(i).data^{s(i,k)-1}(a) .
\end{aligned}
$$

By (A) and by Lemmas 8.50, 8.49 (last cycle of wait, stable master) we conclude:

$$\forall q \in [s(i,k) - 1 : e(i,k)] : aca(i)^q = aca(i)^t .$$

Hence, we have

$$
\begin{aligned}
aca(i).s^t(a) &\in \{M, O\} \\
aca(i).s^{t+1}(a) &= I \\
mm^{t+1}(a) &= aca(i).data^t(a)
\end{aligned}
$$

and conclude the statement

$$\Pi(ms(h^{t+1}), a) = \Pi(\delta_1(ms(h^t), acc(i,k), i), a)$$

by part 4 of Lemma 8.63 (unchanged memory slices).

- $wait(i)^t$. By (A) and (HW) we have

$$aca(i).s^t(a) \in \{E, S\} \wedge aca(i).s^{t+1}(a) = I .$$

The memory content for address a is unchanged by part 5 of Lemma 8.63 (unchanged memory slices):

$$mm^{t+1}(a) = mm^t(a) .$$

Again, by part 4 of Lemma 8.63 (unchanged memory slices) we conclude

$$\Pi(ms(h^{t+1}), a) = \Pi(\delta_1(ms(h^t), acc(i,k), i), a) .$$

$\square$

8.5.9 Ordering Hardware Accesses Sequentially

Recall that the set of accesses to address a ending in cycle t is denoted by

$$E(a,t) = \{(i,k) \mid e(i,k) = t \wedge acc(i,k).a = a\} \ .$$

The set $E(t)$ of all accesses ending in cycle t we define as

$$E(t) = \{(i,k) \mid e(i,k) = t\} = \bigcup_a E(a,t) \ .$$

Then $\#E(t)$ is the number of accesses ending in cycle t, and the number $NE(t)$ of accesses that have ended *before* cycle t is defined by

$$NE(0) = 0$$
$$NE(t+1) = NE(t) + \#E(t) \ .$$

We number accesses $acc(i,j)$ according to their end time and accesses with the same end time arbitrarily. Thus, accesses ending before t get sequential numbers $[0 : NE(t) - 1]$ and accesses ending at t get numbers from set $Q(t) = [NE(t) : NE(t+1) - 1]$. Thus,

$$seq(E(0)) = [0 : NE(1) - 1]$$
$$seq(E(t)) = [NE(t) : NE(t+1) - 1] \ .$$

If a flush access and one or more local reads to the same address end in cycle t, we order the flush access last:

$$(i,k), (i',k') \in E(a,t) \wedge acc(i,k).f \rightarrow seq(i',k') < seq(i,k) \ . \tag{20}$$

The resulting sequentialized access sequence acc' is defined by

$$acc'[seq(i,k)] = acc(i,k) \ .$$

The sequence is of corresponding port indices is defined by

$$is[seq(i,k)] = i \ .$$

We can now relate the hardware computation with the computation of the atomic protocol and show that the state invariants hold for the hardware computation.

Lemma 8.65 (relating hardware with atomic protocol). The following statements hold for cycle t and hardware configuration h^t:

1. The first $NE(t)$ sequential atomic accesses lead exactly to the same abstract memory system configuration ms as the first t cycles of the hardware computation:

$$ms(h^t) = \Delta_1^{NE(t)}(ms(h^0), acc'[0 : NE(t) - 1], is[0 : NE(t) - 1]) \ .$$

2. The state invariants hold until cycle t:

$$SINV(t) .$$

3. The memory abstraction after the first t cycles equals the memory abstraction after $NE(t)$ sequential atomic memory accesses:

$$m(h^t) = \Delta_M^{NE(t)}(m(h^0), acc'[0 : NE(t) - 1]) .$$

Proof. By induction $t \to t + 1$. For $t = 0$ the first statement is trivial. After reset, we have for all a and i:

$$aca(i).s^0(a) = I$$

and we have $sinv(ms(h^0))$ by Lemma 8.7.

For the induction step, we assume that the lemma holds for t and consider accesses ending in cycle t. For $x \in [1 : \#E(t)]$ we set

$$n_x = NE(t) + x - 1 .$$

Then we have

$$seq(E(t)) = [NE(t) : NE(t + 1) - 1] = \{n_x \mid x \in [1 : \#E(t)]\} .$$

For $x \in [1 : \#E(t)]$ we define the pair (i_x, k_x) of indices by

$$seq(i_x, k_x) = n_x .$$

Then,

$$acc(i_x, k_x) = acc'[n_x] \quad \text{and} \quad i_x = is[n_x] .$$

We also define a sequence of memory system configurations ms_x by

$$ms_0 = ms(h^t)$$
$$x > 0 \to ms_x = \delta_1(ms_{x-1}, acc'[n_x], i_x) .$$

Using the induction hypothesis and Lemma 8.8 we get

$$
\begin{aligned}
ms_x &= \Delta_1^x(ms_0, acc'[NE(t) : n_x], is[NE(t) : n_x]) \\
&= \Delta_1^x(ms(h^t), acc'[NE(t) : n_x], is[NE(t) : n_x]) \\
&= \Delta_1^x(\Delta_1^{NE(t)}(ms(h^0), acc'[0 : NE(t) - 1], is[0 : NE(t) - 1]), \\
&\quad acc'[NE(t) : n_x], is[NE(t) : n_x]) \\
&= \Delta_1^{NE(t)+x}(ms(h^0), acc'[0 : n_x], is[0 : n_x]) .
\end{aligned}
\tag{21}
$$

For $x = \#E(t)$ this gives

$$ms_{\#E(t)} = \Delta_1^{NE(t+1)}(ms(h^0), acc'[0 : NE(t + 1) - 1], is[0 : NE(t + 1) - 1]) .$$

By part 2 of the induction hypothesis the state invariants hold for ms_0:

$$SINV(t) \rightarrow sinv(ms_0) \ .$$

Using Lemma 8.9 we conclude by induction that the state invariants hold for all memory systems ms_x under consideration:

$$\forall x \in [1 : \#E(t)] : sinv(ms_x) \ .$$

We proceed to characterize the slices $\Pi(ms_x, a)$ as a function of a and x. We split cases:

- $\forall x : \neg P(i_x, k_x, a, t)$. Then by part 1 of Lemma 8.63 (unchanged memory slices), slice a does not change:

$$\Pi(ms_{\#E(t)}, a) = \Pi(ms_x, a) = \Pi(ms_0, a) \ .$$

- $\exists x : P(i_x, k_x, a, t)$. By part 3 of Lemma 8.63 index x is unique:

$$\forall y \neq x : \neg P(i_y, k_y, a, t) \ .$$

By part 2 of Lemma 8.63, no other access $acc'[n_y]$ with $y \neq x$ ending in cycle t changes slice a in the atomic protocol:

$$\Pi(ms_{x-1}, a) = \Pi(ms_0, a)$$
$$\Pi(ms_{\#E(t)}, a) = \Pi(ms_x, a) \ .$$

Using part 3 of Lemma 8.12 we conclude

$$\begin{aligned}
\Pi(ms_{\#E(t)}, a) &= \Pi(ms_x, a) \\
&= \Pi(\delta_1(ms_{x-1}, acc'[n_x], i_x), a) \\
&= \Pi(\delta_1(ms_0, acc'[n_x], i_x), a) \ .
\end{aligned}$$

Using the definition of ms_0 this can be summarized in

$$\Pi(ms_{\#E(t)}, a) = \begin{cases} \Pi(\delta_1(ms(h^t), acc'[n_x], i_x), a) & \exists x : P(i_x, k_x, a, t) \\ \Pi(ms(h^t), a) & \text{otherwise} \ . \end{cases}$$

Using the definition of $acc'[n_x]$ and part 1 of Lemma 8.64 (1 step) we conclude

$$\begin{aligned}
\Pi(ms_{\#E(t)}, a) &= \begin{cases} \Pi(\delta_1(ms(h^t), acc(i_x, k_x), i_x), a) & \exists x : P(i_x, k_x, a, t) \\ \Pi(ms(h^t), a) & \text{otherwise} \end{cases} \\
&= \Pi(ms(h^{t+1}), a) \ .
\end{aligned}$$

Hence,

$$ms_{\#E(t)} = ms(h^{t+1}) \ .$$

This concludes the first and the second statements.

For the third statement, we conclude by Lemma 8.11 and by (21):

$$
\begin{aligned}
m(h^{t+1}) &= m(ms(h^{t+1})) \\
&= m(ms_{\#E(t)}) \\
&= m(\Delta_1^{NE(t+1)}(ms(h^0), acc'[0:NE(t+1)-1], is)) \\
&= \Delta_M^{NE(t+1)}(m(h^0), acc'[0:NE(t+1)-1]) .
\end{aligned}
$$

$\square$

8.5.10 Sequential Consistency

In Sect. 8.2.5 we claimed that a memory system is sequentially consistent if for read or CAS accesses (i, k) we have

$$
msdout(ms, acc, i, k) = \Delta_M^{seq(i,k)}(m(ms), acc')(acc(i, k).a) .
$$

In our construction the answer of a memory system to a read or a CAS access is defined as

$$
acc(i, k).r \vee acc(i, k).cas \rightarrow msdout(ms(h^0), acc, i, k) = pdout(i)^{e(i,k)} .
$$

Hence, we can rewrite the definition of sequential consistency as

$$
\begin{aligned}
acc(i, k).r \vee acc(i, k).cas &\rightarrow \\
pdout(i)^{e(i,k)} &= \Delta_M^{seq(i,k)}(m(ms(h^0)), acc')(acc(i, k).a) \\
&= \Delta_M^{seq(i,k)}(m(h^0), acc')(acc(i, k).a) .
\end{aligned}
$$

With the notation from the proof of Lemma 8.65 (relating hardware with atomic protocol) this is transformed to

$$
\begin{aligned}
acc(i_x, k_x).r \vee acc(i_x, k_x).cas &\rightarrow \\
pdout(i_x)^t &= \Delta_M^{n_x}(m(h^0), acc')(acc(i_x, k_x).a) .
\end{aligned}
$$

In the next lemma we show that the answer of the memory system produced by the hardware at port i_x is the content of the memory system ms_{x-1}. We use this result in Lemma 8.67 which asserts sequential consistency of the hardware memory. In both lemmas we stick to the notation from Lemma 8.65 (relating hardware with atomic protocol).

Lemma 8.66 (almost sequentially consistent). Let $acc(i_x, k_x)$ be a read or a CAS access with address a ending in cycle t, i.e., we have $acc(i_x, k_x).r \vee acc(i_x, k_x).cas$ and $acc(i_x, k_x).a = a$. Then the answer $pdout$ produced by the hardware at port i_x in cycle t is the content of the memory system ms_{x-1} at address a:

$$
pdout(i_x)^t = m(ms_{x-1})(a) .
$$

Proof. By Lemma 8.65 (relating hardware with atomic protocol) we know that the state invariants hold up to cycle t:

$$SINV(t).$$

We consider two cases:

- $\#E(a, t) = 1$. No other access with address a ends at t. Hence,

$$\forall y \neq x : \neg P(i_y, k_y, a, t) .$$

- $\#E(a, t) \geq 2$. By Lemma 8.56 (simultaneously ending accesses) access $acc(i_x, k_x)$ is a local read or a delayed local read. By the ordering seq as specified in (20) we get

$$\forall y < x : \neg P(i_y, k_y, a, t) .$$

As in the proof of Lemma 8.65 (relating hardware with atomic protocol) we conclude

$$\Pi(ms_0, a) = \Pi(ms_{x-1}, a) .$$

Using part 4 of Lemma 8.12, part 2 of Lemma 8.10, and Lemma 8.64 (1 step) we get

$$\begin{aligned}
pdout(i_x)^t &= pdout1(ms_0, acc(i_x, k_x), i_x) & \text{(Lemma 8.64)} \\
&= pdout1(ms_{x-1}, acc(i_x, k_x), i_x) & \text{(Lemma 8.12)} \\
&= m(ms_{x-1})(a) . & \text{(Lemma 8.10)}
\end{aligned}$$

□

Lemma 8.67 (sequential consistency). The hardware memory is sequentially consistent. Let $e(i_x, k_x) = t$ and $acc(i_x, k_x).r \lor acc(i_x, k_x).cas$. Then

$$pdout(i_x)^t = \Delta_M^{n_x}(m(h^0), acc')(acc(i_x, k_x).a) .$$

Proof. Using Lemma 8.66, (21), Lemma 8.11, and recalling the definition $m(h) = m(ms(h))$ of the hardware memory we get

$$\begin{aligned}
pdout(i_x)^t &= m(ms_{x-1})(acc(i_x, k_x).a) \\
&= m(\Delta_1^{NE(t)+x-1}(ms(h^0), acc', is))(acc(i_x, k_x).a) \\
&= m(\Delta_1^{n_x}(ms(h^0), acc', is))(acc(i_x, k_x).a) \\
&= \Delta_M^{n_x}(m(ms(h^0)), acc')(acc(i_x, k_x).a) \\
&= \Delta_M^{n_x}(m(h^0), acc')(acc(i_x, k_x).a) .
\end{aligned}$$

□

8.5.11 Liveness

Having fairness of the bus arbiter (Lemma 8.13) and liveness of the main memory (Sect. 3.5.6), the liveness proof of the shared memory construction becomes trivial. Assuming stability of processor inputs defined in Sect. 8.4.1, we can also guarantee that signal *mbusy* is off when there is no processor request. This simple but important property of the memory system is very helpful when we show liveness of the multi-core processor in Sect. 9.3.9. We state the desired properties in the following lemma and leave the proof of the lemma as an easy exercise for the reader.

Lemma 8.68 (liveness of shared memory).

1. $preq(i)^t \rightarrow \exists t' \geq t : \neg mbusy(i)^{t'}$,
2. $\neg preq(i)^t \rightarrow \neg mbusy(i)^t$.

Note, that the *mbusy* signal from cache i is guaranteed to eventually go away even if for some cache $j \neq i$ signal $preq(j)$ always stays high. This is the case because the master automaton of cache j, if it is in the hot phase, eventually reaches state *idle* where it lowers its request to the arbiter and gives up ownership of the bus (Sect. 8.4.5). This property of the shared memory system is very important for us, since in the next section we construct a processor where the *preq* signal to the instruction cache can possibly stay high until the *mbusy* signal for the data cache goes away. As a result, when proving liveness of that construction (Lemma 9.18) we heavily rely on the fact that a memory access to the data cache eventually ends (i.e, the *mbusy* signal from the data cache goes away), even if the processor request to the instruction cache stays high for the duration of the entire access to the data memory.

A Multi-core Processor

We finally are able to specify a multi-core MIPS machine, build it, and show that it works. Clearly the plan is to take pipelined MIPS machines from Chap. 7 and connect them to the shared memory system from Chap. 8. Before we can do this, however, we have to address a small technical problem: the pipelined machine was obtained by a transformation from a sequential reference implementation, and that machine does not have a compare-and-swap operation. Thus, we have to add an introductory Sect. 9.1, where we augment the sequential instruction set with a compare-and-swap instruction. This turns out to be an instruction with 4 register addresses, where we accommodate the fourth address in the sa field of an R-type instruction. In order to process such instructions in a pipelined fashion we now also need in the sequential reference implementation the ability to read three register operands and to write one register operand in a single hardware cycle. If we would have treated interrupts here, we would have a special purpose register file as in [12], and we could take the third read operand from there. Here, we simply add a third read port to the general purpose register file using technology from Chap. 4.

In Sect. 9.2 we specify the ISA of multi-core MIPS and give a reference implementation with sequential processors. Like the hardware, ISA and reference implementation can be made completely deterministic, but in order to hide implementation details they are modelled for the user in a nondeterministic way: processors execute instructions one at a time; there is a stepping function s specifying for each time n the processor $s(n)$ executing an instruction at step n. We later derive this function from the implementation, but the user does not know it; thus, programs have to work for any such stepping function. Specifying multi-core ISA turns out to be very easy: we split the sequential MIPS configuration into i) memory and ii) processor (everything else). A multi-core configuration has a single (shared) memory component and multiple processor components. In step n an ordinary sequential MIPS step is executed with processor $s(n)$ and the shared memory.

In the multi-core reference implementation, we hook the sequential reference processors to a memory (which now has to be able to execute compare-

M. Kovalev et al.: A Pipelined Multi-core MIPS Machine, LNCS 9000, pp. 311–344, 2014.

and-swap operations). We do not bother to give a hardware construction for this memory; it suffices to use the specification from Sect. 8.2. Note, however, that for this reference implementation of multi-core MIPS we have to generalize the hardware model: we have to partition hardware into portions which are selectively clocked under the control of a stepping function s.

In Sect. 9.3 we "simply" hook pipelined implementations of the sequential MIPS processors into the shared memory system from Sect. 8. The generation of processor inputs to the caches and the consumption of the answers of the memory system are completely straightforward to implement. Unifying the correctness proofs for pipelined processors from Chap. 7 with the lemmas about the shared memory system from Chap. 8 is not terribly difficult any more. It *does* however require the development of some technical machinery permitting to couple local scheduling functions for the pipelined processors with local instruction numbers of the multi-core reference implementation. Liveness is finally shown using the machinery from Sect. 7.4.

9.1 Compare-and-Swap Instruction

9.1.1 Introducing CAS to the ISA

We start with extending the MIPS ISA from Sect. 6.2 with the compare-and-swap operation. We define it as an R-type instruction with the function bits being all ones:

$$cas(c) \equiv opc(c) = 0^6 \wedge fun(c) = 1^6 .$$

Recall that previously we defined the effective address of load and store instructions as

$$ea(c) = c.gpr(rs(c)) +_{32} sxt(imm(c)) .$$

In R-type instructions we do not have an immediate constant. So for the effective memory address of a CAS instruction we simply take the value from the GPR file addressed by the rs field:

$$cas(c) \rightarrow ea(c) = c.gpr(rs(c)) .$$

All CAS operations are assumed to be word accesses:

$$cas(c) \rightarrow d(c) = 4 .$$

The comparison data for a CAS operation is taken from a GPR specified by field sa of the instruction[1]:

$$cas(c) \rightarrow cdata(c) = c.gpr(sa(c)) .$$

---

[1] An alternative would be to take this value from a dedicated SPR (special purpose register file), but we do not consider SPRs in this book.

The result of the CAS data test is then defined as

$$castest(c) \equiv cdata(c) = c.m_4(ea(c)) \; .$$

The data to be stored in the memory is obtained from the GPR specified by rt. Field rd is used to specify a destination register. The resulting configuration c' after executing a CAS instruction is obtained in an obvious way:

$cas(c) \rightarrow$

$$c'.m(x) = \begin{cases} byte(i, c.gpr(rt(c))) & x = ea(c) +_{32} i_{32} \wedge i < 4 \wedge castest(c) \\ c.m(x) & \text{otherwise} \end{cases}$$

$$c'.gpr(x) = \begin{cases} c.m_4(ea(c)) & x = rd(c) \\ c.gpr(x) & \text{otherwise} \; . \end{cases}$$

The GPR write predicate is now defined as

$$gprw(c) = alu(c) \vee su(c) \vee l(c) \vee jal(c) \vee jalr(c) \vee cas(c) \; .$$

9.1.2 Introducing CAS to the Sequential Processor

For implementing CAS instructions, a couple of modifications have to be applied to the construction of a sequential reference machine.

A schematic view of the reference hardware machine with support for CAS operations is shown in Fig. 143. The 3-port GPR RAM used in previous designs is replaced with a 4-port GPR RAM, where ports a, b, and d are used for reading:

$$A(h) = h.gpr(rs(h))$$
$$B(h) = h.gpr(rt(h))$$
$$D(h) = h.gpr(sa(h))$$

and port c is used for writing:

$$gprin(h) = \begin{cases} lres(h) & l(h) \vee cas(h) \\ C(h) & \text{otherwise} \; . \end{cases}$$

The circuit computing the input for the GPR register file is shown in Fig. 144. Construction of a 4-port GPR RAM is done in the very same manner as the construction of a 3-port GPR RAM and we omit it here.

Figure 145 shows a simple modification which has to be done to the effective address computation. The load mask is now computed as

$$lmask(h) = \begin{cases} I(h)[27]^{16}I(h)[26]^8 1^8 & l(h) \\ 1^{32} & cas(h) \\ 0^{32} & \text{otherwise} \end{cases}$$

$$= l(h) \wedge I(h)[27]^{16}I(h)[26]^8 1^8 \vee cas(h) \wedge 1^{32} \; .$$

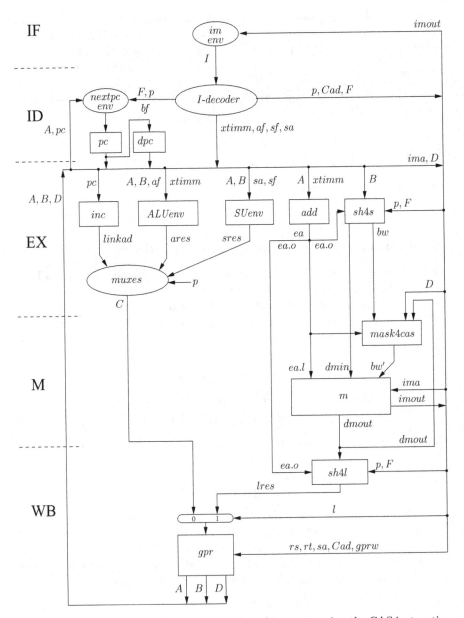

Fig. 143. Schematic view of a simple MIPS machine supporting the CAS instruction

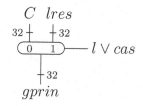

Fig. 144. Computing the data input of the GPR

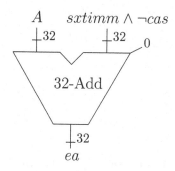

Fig. 145. Effective address computation

For computing the memory byte write signals in case of CAS accesses, we have to take into consideration the result of the CAS test. Hence, we first have to read the data from the hardware memory and only then decide whether we need to perform a write. This is possible, because the construction of a 2-port multi-bank RAM-ROM from Sect. 4.3.3 allows reading and writing the same address through port b in a single cycle[2].

We now split the computation of byte write signals into two parts. First, the environment $sh4s$ computes the byte write signals assuming that the result of the CAS test has succeeded. The construction of the circuit stays the same as in the previous designs shown in Fig. 110, but the initial $smask$ signals are now calculated as

$$smask(h)[3:0] = \begin{cases} I(h)[27]^2 I(h)[26]1 & s(h) \\ 1^4 & cas(h) \\ 0^4 & \text{otherwise} \end{cases}$$
$$= s(h) \wedge I(h)[27]^2 I(h)[26]1 \vee cas(h) \wedge 1^4 \ .$$

For the shifted version of the byte write signals, this gives us

$$\neg(cas(h) \vee s(h)) \rightarrow bw(h) = 0^8 \ .$$

---

[2] For practical reasons, such a construction would be inefficient. We use it here just to construct a "reference" machine which we use for the simulation proof of the multi-core processor with a shared memory system.

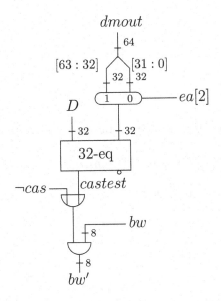

Fig. 146. Implementation of circuit *mask4cas*

Circuit *mask4cas* shown in Fig. 146 first computes the signal *castest*, where

$$castest(h) \equiv \begin{cases} D(h) = dmout(h)[63:32] & ea(h)[2] = 1 \\ D(h) = dmout(h)[31:0] & ea(h)[2] = 0 \,, \end{cases}$$

and then uses this signal to mask all active byte write signals in case the CAS test was not successful.

These are all modification one has to make to the sequential reference hardware implementation to introduce support for the CAS instruction. Additionally, we extend the software condition on disjoint code and data regions to handle the CAS instructions:

$$ls(c) \vee cas(c) \rightarrow ea(c).l \in DR.$$

Correctness of the construction is stated in

Lemma 9.1 (MIPS with CAS correct). Let alignment hold and let code and data regions be disjoint. Then

$$sim(c, h) \rightarrow sim(c', h') \,.$$

Proof. For the case when we don't execute a CAS instruction, i.e., $\neg cas(c)$, we observe that the signals generated by the hardware are the same as in the sequential MIPS machine from Chap. 6. Hence, we simply use Lemma 6.8 and we are done.

If $cas(c)$ holds, then we consider the cases when the CAS test succeeds and when it fails. In both cases the proof is completely analogous to the proofs from Chap. 6 and we omit it here.   □

9.2 Multi-core ISA and Reference Implementation

9.2.1 Multi-core ISA Specification

Recall that MIPS configurations c have components $c.pc$, $c.dpc$, $c.gpr$, and $c.m$. For the purpose of defining the programmer's view of the multi-core MIPS machine, we collect the first three components of c into a processor configuration:

$$c.p = (c.p.pc, c.p.dpc, c.p.gpr) .$$

We denote by K_p the set of processor configurations. A MIPS configuration now consists of a processor configuration and memory configuration:

$$c = (c.p, c.m) .$$

The next state function $c' = \delta(c)$ is split into a next processor component δ_p and a next memory component δ_m:

$$\begin{aligned}
c' &= \delta(c) \\
&= (c'.p, c'.m) \\
&= (\delta_p(c.p, c.m), \delta_m(c.p, c.m)) .
\end{aligned}$$

A multi-core MIPS configuration mc with P processors consists of the following components:

- $mc.p : [0 : P - 1] \to K_p$. The configuration of processor $q \in [0 : P - 1]$ in configuration mc is $mc.p(q)$.
- $mc.m$ is the memory shared by all processors.

We introduce a step function $s : \mathbb{N} \to [0 : P - 1]$, which maps step numbers n of the multi-core configuration to the ID $s(n)$ of the processor making a step in configuration mc^n. We require the step function to be *fair* in the sense that every processor q is stepped infinitely often:

$$\forall n, q : \exists m > n : s(m) = q .$$

Note that this step function is unknown to the programmer; we will eventually construct it from the hardware. Programs, thus, have to perform well for all fair step functions.

Initially, we require

$$mc^0.p(q).pc = 4_{32}$$
$$mc^0.p(q).dpc = 0_{32} .$$

We now define the multi-core computation (mc^n) where mc^n is the configuration before step n:

$$mc^{n+1}.p(x) = \begin{cases} \delta_p(mc^n.p(x), mc^n.m) & x = s(n) \\ mc^n.p(x) & x \neq s(n) \end{cases}$$

$$mc^{n+1}.m = \delta_m(mc^n.p(s(n)), mc^n.m) .$$

An equivalent definition is given in the following lemma.

Lemma 9.2 (multi-core computation).

$$(mc^{n+1}.p(s(n)), mc^{n+1}.m) = \delta(mc^n.p(s(n)), mc^n.m)$$
$$q \neq s(n) \rightarrow mc^{n+1}.p(q) = mc^n.p(q)$$

9.2.2 Sequential Reference Implementation

We define a sequential multi-core reference "implementation". It is almost hardware and it could easily be turned into hardware, but we don't bother[3]. Recall that a hardware configuration h of the sequential processor had components

$$h = (h.pc, h.dpc, h.gpr, h.m) .$$

In case the *reset* signal is off, the hardware construction of the sequential processor defines a hardware transition function

$$h' = \delta_H(h) .$$

We collect components pc, dpc, gpr into a processor component:

$$h.p = (h.pc, h.dpc, h.gpr) .$$

and rewrite the hardware transition function as

$$h' = (h'.p, h'.m) = \delta_H(h.p, h.m) .$$

We define the data access $acc = dacc(h)$ in the hardware configuration h as

$$acc.a = ea(h).l$$
$$acc.f = 0$$
$$acc.r = l(h)$$
$$(acc.w, acc.cas) = \begin{cases} (s(h), cas(h)) & ea(h).l[28:r] \neq 0^r \\ (0,0) & \text{otherwise} \end{cases}$$
$$acc.data = dmin(h)$$
$$acc.cdata = D(h)$$
$$acc.bw = bw(h) .$$

---

[3] Turning our construction into a real sequential implementation would require a scheduler and a number of multiplexors connecting the shared memory to the processors.

In case instruction $I(h)$ is neither a load, a store, nor a CAS instruction, all bits f,w, r, and cas of access $dacc(h)$ are off and we have a void access. Recall that a void access does not update memory and does not produce an answer. In case a write or a CAS is performed to an address in the ROM region we also have a void access[4].

In the same way we construct instruction fetch access $acc = iacc(h)$ as

$$acc.a = ima(h)$$
$$acc.r = 1$$
$$acc.w = 0$$
$$acc.cas = 0$$
$$acc.f = 0 \, .$$

We observe that our hardware memory of the reference implementation together with the control logic matches the specification of the sequential memory introduced in Sect. 8.2.2.

Lemma 9.3 (hardware memory is sequential). Hardware memory of the sequential reference machine follows the semantics of the sequential memory:

1. $cas(h) \vee r(h) \rightarrow dmout(h) = dataout(h.m, dacc(h))$,
2. $imout(h) = dataout(h.m, iacc(h))$,
3. $h'.m = \delta_M(h.m, dacc(h))$.

Proof. The first and the second statements we simply get by unfolding the definitions and applying the semantics of the 2-port multi-bank RAM-ROM:

$$dmout(h) = h.m(ea(h).l)$$
$$= dataout(h.m, dacc(h))$$
$$imout(h) = h.m(ima(h))$$
$$= dataout(h.m, iacc(h)) \, .$$

For the third statement we have by the hardware construction and the semantics of the 2-port multi-bank RAM-ROM:

$$h.m(b) = \begin{cases} modify(h.m(b), dmin(h), bw'(h)) & b = ea(h).l \wedge (s(h) \vee \\ & cas(h) \wedge castest(h)) \\ h.m(b) & \text{otherwise} \end{cases}$$

---

[4] Note that this situation never occurs if the reference hardware computation is simulated by an ISA computation and disjointness of data and code regions holds. The only reason why we consider it possible here, is because we want to specify the multi-core reference hardware *before* we show that it is simulated by a multi-core ISA. Hence, at that point we cannot yet assume that there are no writes to the ROM portion of the hardware memory.

$$= \begin{cases} modify(h.m(b), dmin(h), bw(h)) & b = ea(h).l \wedge (s(h) \vee \\ & cas(h) \wedge castest(h)) \\ h.m(b) & \text{otherwise} . \end{cases}$$

For the original byte write signals generated by $sh4s$ environment, in case of a CAS access we have

$$cas(h) \rightarrow bw(h) = \begin{cases} 0^4 1^4 & ea(h)[2] = 0 \\ 1^4 0^4 & ea(h)[2] = 1 , \end{cases}$$

which gives us

$$cas(h) \rightarrow bw(h)[0] = \neg ea(h)[2] .$$

For the result of the CAS test, we have by construction of circuit $mask4cas$:

$$castest(h) = \begin{cases} D(h) = dmout(h)[63:32] & ea(h)[2] = 1 \\ D(h) = dmout(h)[31:0] & ea(h)[2] = 0 \end{cases}$$

$$= \begin{cases} D(h) = h.m(ea(h).l)[63:32] & \neg bw(h)[0] \\ D(h) = h.m(ea(h).l)[31:0] & bw(h)[0] \end{cases}$$

$$= test(dacc(h), h.m(ea(h).l)) .$$

Hence,

$$h.m(b)$$

$$= \begin{cases} modify(h.m(b), dmin(h), bw(h)) & b = ea(h).l \wedge (s(h) \vee \\ & cas(h) \wedge castest(h)) \\ h.m(b) & \text{otherwise} \end{cases}$$

$$= \begin{cases} modify(h.m(b), dmin(h), bw(h)) & b = ea(h).l \wedge (s(h) \vee cas(h) \wedge \\ & test(dacc(h), h.m(ea(h).l)) \\ h.m(b) & \text{otherwise} \end{cases}$$

$$= \delta_M(h.m, dacc(h)) .$$

$\square$

As a result of Lemma 9.3 we can rewrite the hardware transition function as

$$h' = \delta_H(h.p, h.m)$$
$$= (\delta_{hp}(h.p, h.m), \delta_{hm}(h.m, dacc(h)))$$
$$= (\delta_{hp}(h.p, h.m), \delta_M(h.m, dacc(h))) .$$

For the definition of the multi-core reference implementation, we duplicate the processor component $h.p$ of the hardware for every processor ID. Thus, the new hardware has components $h.m$ and $h.p(q)$ for each processor ID q.

For the case the *reset* signal is off, the computation (h^n) of the multi-core reference implementation is simply defined by

$$h^{n+1}.p(s(n)) = \delta_{hp}(h^n.p(s(n)), h^n.m)$$
$$h^{n+1}.m = \delta_M(h^n.m, dacc((h^n.p(s(n)), h^n.m)))$$

and

$$h^{n+1}.p(q) = h^n.p(q) \quad \text{for} \quad q \neq s(n) .$$

An equivalent definition we state in the following lemma.

Lemma 9.4 (computation of the reference machine). Assume $reset^n = 0$, then

$$(h^{n+1}.p(s(n)), h^{n+1}.m) = \delta_H(h^n.p(s(n)), h^n.m)$$
$$q \neq s(n) \rightarrow h^{n+1}.p(q) = h^n.p(q) .$$

Recall that we assume the *reset* signal to be on in cycle $n = -1$ and to be off afterwards. For the case when the reset signal is on, we initialize processor components the same way as in the case of a single-core implementation:

$$h^0.p(q).dpc = 0_{32}$$
$$h^0.p(q).pc = 4_{32} .$$

9.2.3 Simulation Relation

As in Chap. 6 we assume alignment, disjointness of code and data regions, and, hence, no self modifying code. The basic sequential simulation relation $sim(c, h)$ is extended to multi-core machines by

$$msim(mc, h) \equiv$$

1. $(\forall q : mc.p(q).pc = h.p(q).pc) \wedge$
2. $(\forall q : mc.p(q).dpc = h.p(q).dpc) \wedge$
3. $(\forall q : mc.p(q).gpr = h.p(q).gpr) \wedge$
4. $mc.m \sim_{CR} h.m \wedge$
5. $mc.m \sim_{DR} h.m .$

The correctness of the reference implementation is asserted in the following lemma.

Lemma 9.5 (correctness of the reference implementation). There is an initial multi-core ISA configuration mc^0 such that

$$\forall n : msim(mc^n, h^n) .$$

Proof. This is a straightforward bookkeeping exercise using Lemmas 9.2, 9.4 and the correctness of the basic MIPS processor. Assuming reset to be on in cycle $n = -1$ we set

$$mc^0.p(q).gpr = h^0.p(q).gpr$$

and

$$\forall a \in CR \cup DR : mc^0.m_8(a000) = h^0.m(a)$$

and obtain

$$msim(mc^0, h^0) \, .$$

For the induction step, we conclude for processor $s(n)$ from the induction hypothesis

$$sim((mc^n.p(s(n)), mc^n.m), (h^n.p(s(n)), h^n.m)) \, .$$

By Lemma 9.1 , i.e., the correctness of the basic sequential hardware for one step, we conclude

$$sim((mc^{n+1}.p(s(n)), mc^{n+1}.m), (h^{n+1}.p(s(n)), h^{n+1}.m)) \, .$$

For processors $q \neq (s(n))$ that are not stepped, we have by induction hypothesis

$$mc^n.p(q).pc = h^n.p(q).pc$$
$$mc^n.p(q).dpc = h^n.p(q).dpc$$
$$mc^n.p(q).gpr = h^n.p(q).gpr \, .$$

By the definitions of the multi-core ISA and the reference implementation program counters, delayed program counters, and general purpose register files do not change for the processors which are not stepped, so we have

$$X \in \{pc, dpc, gpr\} \rightarrow mc^{n+1}.p(q).X = h^{n+1}.p(q).X \, .$$

$\square$

Lemma 9.5 obviously implies that write or CAS accesses to the ROM portion of $h.m$ never occur. Hence, we have

$$cas(h) \equiv dacc(h).cas$$
$$s(h) \equiv dacc(h).w.$$

From now on we argue only about cycles $n \geq 0$ and assume $reset^n = 0$.

9.2.4 Local Configurations and Computations

For processor IDs q and local step numbers i, we define the step numbers $pseq(q, i)$ when local step i is executed on processor q:

$$pseq(q, 0) = \min\{n \mid s(n) = q\}$$
$$pseq(q, i) = \min\{n \mid n > pseq(q, i - 1) \wedge s(n) = q\} \ .$$

Configuration $h^{pseq(q,i)}$ is the hardware configuration directly before local step i of processor q.

We also define a function $ic(q, n)$ which counts how often processor q was stepped before step n resp. the number of instructions completed on processor q before step n by

$$ic(q, 0) = 0$$
$$ic(q, n + 1) = \begin{cases} ic(q, n) + 1 & s(n) = q \\ ic(q, n) & \text{otherwise} \ . \end{cases}$$

An easy induction on n shows the following lemma.

Lemma 9.6 (instruction count).

$$ic(q, n) = \#\{j \mid j < n \wedge s(j) = q\}$$

We also establish a simple relation between functions $pseq$ and ic.

Lemma 9.7 (instruction count and step numbers).

$$ic(q, n) = i \wedge s(n) = q \rightarrow pseq(q, i) = n$$

Proof. In case $i = 0$ we have by definition

$$pseq(q, 0) = min\{n \mid s(n) = q\} \ .$$

Because $ic(q, n) = 0$, we conclude

$$\forall m \in [0 : n - 1] : s(m) \neq q \ .$$

Hence,

$$pseq(q, 0) = n \ .$$

In case $i > 0$, let

$$\{j_0, \ldots j_{i-1}\} = \{j \mid j < n \wedge s(j) = q\}$$

and

$$j_0 < \ldots < j_{i-1} \ .$$

A trivial induction shows

$$\forall x \le i - 1 : j_x = pseq(q, x) \ .$$

Because

$$\forall m \in [j_{i-1} + 1 : n - 1] : s(m) \ne q \ ,$$

we conclude

$$n = \min\{m \mid m > pseq(q, i - 1) \wedge s(m) = q\} = pseq(q, i) \ .$$

$\square$

Hence, up to configuration $h^{pseq(q,i)}$, processor q has already been stepped i times. The next step to be executed in $h^{pseq(q,i)}$ is step number i of processor q, which is the $(i + 1)$-st local step of this processor.

For processor IDs q and step numbers i, we define the local hardware configurations $h^{q,i}$ of processor q before local step i. We start with the multiprocessor hardware configuration $h^{pseq(q,i)}$ in which processor q makes step i; then we construct a single processor configuration $h^{q,i}$ by taking the processor component of the processor that is stepped, i.e., q, and the memory component from the shared memory:

$$h^{q,i} = (h^{pseq(q,i)}.p(q), h^{pseq(q,i)}.m) \ .$$

The following lemma asserts, for every q that, as far as the processor components are concerned, the local configurations $h^{q,i}$ behave as in an ordinary single processor hardware computation; the shared memory of course can change between steps i and $i + 1$ of the same processor.

Lemma 9.8 (local computations).

$$h^{q,0}.p = h^0.p(q)$$
$$h^{q,i+1}.p = \delta_H(h^{q,i}.p, h^{pseq(q,i)}.m).p$$

Proof. By the definition of $pseq(q, 0)$ processor q is not stepped before step $pseq(q, 0)$:

$$n < pseq(q, 0) \to s(n) \ne q \ .$$

Thus, the configuration of processor q is not changed in these steps and we get

$$h^{q,0}.p = h^{pseq(q,0)}.p(q)$$
$$= h^0.p(q) \ .$$

By the definition of $pseq(q, i+1)$ processor q is also not stepped between steps $pseq(q, i)$ and $pseq(q, i + 1)$:

$$n \in [pseq(q, i) + 1 : pseq(q, i + 1) - 1] \to s(n) \ne q \ .$$

As above we conclude that the configuration of processor q does not change in these steps:

$$h^{q,i+1}.p = h^{pseq(q,i+1)}.p(q)$$
$$= h^{pseq(q,i)+1}.p(q)$$
$$= \delta_H(h^{pseq(q,i)}.p(q), h^{pseq(q,i)}.m).p$$
$$= \delta_H(h^{q,i}.p, h^{pseq(q,i)}.m).p .$$

$\square$

Next we show a technical result relating the local computations with the overall computation.

Lemma 9.9 (relating local and overall computations).

$$h^n.p(q) = h^{q,ic(q,n)}.p$$

Proof. By induction on n. For $n=0$ we have

$$h^0.p(q) = h^{q,0}.p = h^{q,ic(q,0)}.p .$$

For the induction step assume the lemma holds for n. Let $i = ic(q,n)$. We distinguish two cases:

- $q = s(n)$. Then,

$$ic(q, n+1) = i+1 .$$

  By induction hypothesis, Lemma 9.7, and Lemma 9.8 we get

$$h^{n+1}.p(q) = \delta_H(h^n.p(q), h^n.m).p$$
$$= \delta_H(h^{q,i}.p, h^{pseq(q,i)}.m).p$$
$$= h^{q,i+1}.p$$
$$= h^{q,ic(q,n+1)}.p .$$

- $q \neq s(n)$. Then,

$$ic(q, n+1) = ic(q, n) = i$$

  and by induction hypothesis and Lemma 9.7 we get

$$h^{n+1}.p(q) = h^n.p(q)$$
$$= h^{q,i}.p$$
$$= h^{q,ic(q,n+1)}.p .$$

$\square$

9.2.5 Accesses of the Reference Computation

We define the instruction fetch access $iacc(q, i)$ and the data access $dacc(q, i)$ in local step i of processor q as

$$iacc(q, i) = iacc(h^{q,i})$$
$$dacc(q, i) = dacc(h^{q,i}) .$$

Lemma 9.10 (accesses of reference computation). The hardware memory of the multi-core reference machine follows semantics of the sequential memory:

1. For fetch accesses it holds

$$imout(h^{q,i}) = dataout(h^{pseq(q,i)}.m, iacc(q,i)) = dataout(h^0.m, iacc(q,i)) .$$

2. For loads or CAS accesses it holds

$$l(h^{q,i}) \vee cas(h^{q,i}) \rightarrow dmout(h^{q,i}) = dataout(h^{pseq(q,i)}.m, dacc(q,i)) .$$

3. For updates of $h.m$ it holds

$$h^{pseq(q,i)+1}.m = \delta_M(h^{pseq(q,i)}.m, dacc(q,i)) .$$

Proof. Assuming disjointness of data and code region and correctness of the multi-core reference implementation (Lemma 9.5) we can easily show

$$iacc(q,i).a \in CR$$

and

$$\forall a \in CR : h^{pseq(q,i)}.m(a) = h^0.m(a).$$

The statement of the lemma now follows by simple unfolding of definitions and applying Lemma 9.3.   □

9.3 Shared Memory in the Multi-core System

We proceed with constructing a pipelined multi-core MIPS processor, where a single hardware memory is replaced with caches *ica* and *dca* of the shared memory system constructed in Chap. 8. The hardware memory is replaced together with the circuit *mask4cas*. Schematic view of a single core of the pipelined MIPS processor is shown in Fig. 147.

9.3.1 Notation

As we did in the correctness proof of the single-core pipelined processor, we denote the multi-core sequential reference implementation by h_σ and the pipelined multi-core implementation with the shared memory system by h_π.

For registers, memories, or circuit signals X in the reference machine, processor IDs q, and instruction numbers i, we abbreviate

$$
X_\sigma^{q,i} =
\begin{cases}
h_\sigma^{q,i}.X & X \in \{pc, dpc, gpr, m\} \\
X(h_\sigma^{q,i}) & \text{otherwise}
\end{cases}
$$

$$
=
\begin{cases}
h_\sigma^{pseq(q,i)}.p(q).X & X \in \{pc, dpc, gpr, m\} \\
X((h_\sigma^{pseq(q,i)}.p(q), h_\sigma^{pseq(q,i)}.m)) & \text{otherwise} .
\end{cases}
$$

Values of registers R and circuit signals X during cycle t in processor q of the multi-core hardware machine we abbreviate resp. by

$$R_\pi^{q,t} \quad \text{and} \quad X_\pi^{q,t} .$$

As before, for signals or registers only occurring in the pipelined design we drop the subscript π. If an equations holds for all cycles or for all processors (like equations describing hardware construction) we drop the indices t and q respectively.

We denote the instruction cache of processor q by $ica = ca(2q)$ and the data cache of processor q by $dca = ca(2q + 1)$. For inputs and outputs X of a data cache or an instruction cache of processor q we write respectively

$$ica.X = X(2q)$$
$$dca.X = X(2q + 1) .$$

9.3.2 Invisible Registers and Hazard Signals

In order to implement CAS instructions in the pipelined design we add invisible registers $D.2$ and $D.3$ into the pipeline.

The *used* predicates from Sect. 7.2.3 are adapted for CAS operations, which are treated as loads and stores at the same time:

$$\forall X \in \{C.3, C.4\} : used(X, I) = gprw'(I) \wedge \neg(l'(I) \vee cas'(I))$$
$$\forall X \in \{ea.3, ea.4\} : used(X, I) = l'(I) \vee s'(I) \vee cas'(I)$$
$$\forall X \in \{dmin\} : used(X, I) = s'(I) \vee cas'(I)$$
$$used(dmout, I) = l'(I) \vee cas'(I) .$$

Registers $D.2$ and $D.3$ are used only for CAS instructions:

$$D\text{-}used(I) = cas'(I)$$
$$\forall X \in \{D.2, D.3\} : used(X, I) = D\text{-}used(I) .$$

The forwarding engine is extended to forward the data into $D.2$ during the instruction decode stage:

$$hit_D[k] \equiv full_k \wedge Cad.k = sa_\pi \wedge gprw.k \wedge cas_\pi$$
$$top_D[k] = hit_D[k] \wedge \bigwedge_{j<k} \neg hit_D[j]$$

$$D.2in_\pi = \begin{cases} C.3in_\pi & top_D[2] \\ C.4in_\pi & top_D[3] \\ gprin_\pi & top_D[4] \\ gproutD_\pi & \text{otherwise} . \end{cases}$$

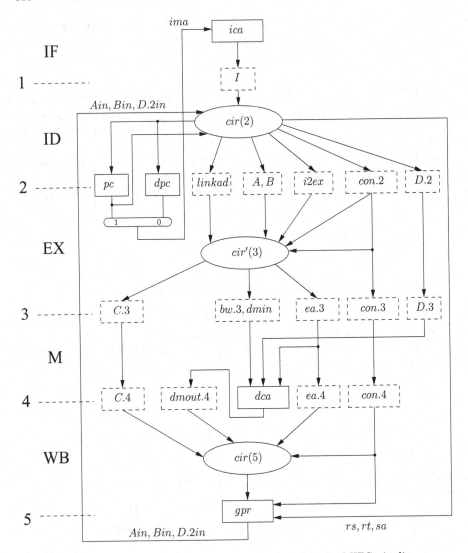

Fig. 147. Schematic view of the pipelined multi-core MIPS pipeline

CAS instructions load data from the memory just as regular loads do. Hence, we have to update the hazard signals:

$$haz_A = A\text{-}used \wedge \bigvee_{k\in[2,3]} (top_A[k] \wedge (con.k.l \vee con.k.cas))$$

$$haz_B = B\text{-}used \wedge \bigvee_{k\in[2,3]} (top_B[k] \wedge (con.k.l \vee con.k.cas)) .$$

The stall engine has to additionally generate a hazard signal when the D data can not be forwarded:

$$haz_2 = haz_A \lor haz_B \lor haz_D$$
$$haz_D = D\text{-}used \land \bigvee_{k \in [2,3]} (top_D[k] \land (con.k.l \lor con.k.cas)) .$$

9.3.3 Connecting Interfaces

Every MIPS processor in the multi-core system has an instruction cache and a data cache. We connect the instruction cache $ica = ca(2q)$ to MIPS processor q in the following way:

$$ica.pa = ima_\pi$$
$$ica.pw = 0$$
$$ica.pr = 1$$
$$ica.pcas = 0$$
$$ica.preq = 1$$
$$Iin_\pi = ica.pdout$$
$$haz_1 = ica.mbusy .$$

The data cache $dca = ca(2q + 1)$ is connected to processor q in the following way:

$$dca.pa = ea.3.l_\pi$$
$$dca.pw = con.3.s_\pi$$
$$dca.pr = con.3.l_\pi$$
$$dca.pcas = con.3.cas_\pi$$
$$dca.bw = bw.3_\pi$$
$$dca.pdin = dmin_\pi$$
$$dca.pcdin = D.3_\pi$$
$$dca.preq = full_3 \land (con.3.s_\pi \lor con.3.l_\pi \lor con.3.cas_\pi)$$
$$dmout_\pi = dca.dout$$
$$haz_4 = dca.mbusy .$$

Recall that the stall engine is defined as

$$stall_k = full_{k-1} \land (haz_k \lor stall_{k+1})$$
$$ue_k = full_{k-1} \land \neg stall_k$$
$$full_k^{t+1} = ue_k^t \lor stall_{k+1}^t .$$

In stage 1 we always perform a memory access, but we clock the results of the access to the registers only if we don't have a $stall_2$ signal coming from the stage below. As a result, we might perform the same access to the instruction cache several times, until we are actually able to update the register stage below. In Sect. 9.3.9 we show that this kind of behaviour does not produce any deadlocks.

9.3.4 Stability of Inputs of Accesses

Lemma 9.11 (stable inputs of accesses). Inputs for the data and instruction caches are stable:

- For data cache $2q + 1$, if the request signal $preq(2q + 1)$ and the memory busy signal $mbusy(2q+1)$ are both on, register stage 3 of processor q which contains the inputs of the access is not updated:

$$preq(2q + 1)^t \wedge mbusy(2q + 1)^t \rightarrow ue_3^{q,t} = 0 \ .$$

- For instruction cache $2q$, if the request signal $preq(2q)$ and the memory busy signal $mbusy(2q)$ are both on, the inputs to the instruction cache remain stable:

$$preq(2q)^t \wedge mbusy(2q)^t \rightarrow preq(2q)^{t+1} \wedge ima_\pi^{q,t+1} = ima_\pi^{q,t} \ .$$

Proof. For data caches we have

$$haz_4^{q,t} = mbusy(2q + 1)^t = 1$$

and

$$preq(2q + 1)^t \rightarrow full_3^{q,t} \ .$$

Hence,

$$\begin{aligned} stall_4^{q,t} &= full_3^{q,t} \wedge haz_4^{q,t} \\ &= 1 \ . \end{aligned}$$

Thus,

$$\begin{aligned} ue_3^{q,t} &= full_2^{q,t} \wedge \neg stall_4^{q,t} \\ &= 0 \ . \end{aligned}$$

For instruction caches we have

$$ima_\pi^{q,t} = \begin{cases} pc_\pi^{q,t}.l & full_1^{q,t} \\ dpc_\pi^{q,t}.l & \neg full_1^{q,t} \end{cases}$$

$$haz_1^{q,t} = mbusy(2q)^t = 1$$

$$\begin{aligned} stall_1^{q,t} &= full_0^{q,t} \wedge (haz_1^{q,t} \vee stall_2^{q,t}) \\ &= 1 \end{aligned}$$

$$\begin{aligned} ue_1^{q,t} &= full_0^{q,t} \wedge \neg stall_1^{q,t} \\ &= 0 \end{aligned}$$

$$\begin{aligned} full_1^{q,t+1} &= ue_1^{q,t} \vee stall_2^{q,t} \\ &= stall_2^{q,t} \ . \end{aligned}$$

The instruction address is taken either from the PC or from the DPC register depending on whether stage 1 is full or not. Hence, we split cases on values of $full_1^{q,t}$ and $full_1^{q,t+1}$:

- if $\neg full_1^{q,t}$ we have

$$ue_2^{q,t} = full_1^{q,t} \wedge \neg stall_2^{q,t}$$
$$= 0$$
$$stall_2^{q,t} = full_1^{q,t} \wedge (haz_2^{q,t} \vee stall_3^{q,t})$$
$$= 0$$
$$full_1^{q,t+1} = stall_2^{q,t}$$
$$= 0$$
$$ima_\pi^{q,t+1} = dpc_\pi^{q,t+1}.l$$
$$= dpc_\pi^{q,t}.l$$
$$= ima_\pi^{q,t} ,$$

- if $full_1^{q,t} \wedge full_1^{q,t+1}$ we have

$$ue_2^{q,t} = full_1^{q,t} \wedge \neg stall_2^{q,t}$$
$$= 0$$
$$ima_\pi^{q,t+1} = pc_\pi^{q,t+1}.l$$
$$= pc_\pi^{q,t}.l$$
$$= ima_\pi^{q,t} ,$$

- if $full_1^{q,t} \wedge \neg full_1^{q,t+1}$ we have

$$ue_2^{q,t} = full_1^{q,t} \wedge \neg stall_2^{q,t}$$
$$= 1$$
$$ima_\pi^{q,t+1} = dpc_\pi^{q,t+1}.l$$
$$= pc_\pi^{q,t}.l$$
$$= ima_\pi^{q,t} .$$

$\square$

9.3.5 Relating Update Enable Signals and Ends of Accesses

By the definition of function $someend(i,t)$ read, write, or CAS accesses to cache i end in cycles t when $preq(i)^t \wedge \neg mbusy(i)^t$. In this section we relate ends of memory accesses with the update enable signals of the processors.

Lemma 9.12 (update enable implies access end). An active update enable signal denotes the end of a memory access:

1. For data cache $2q + 1$, if the update enable signal of stage 4 is activated and stage 3 contains a memory request, then a read, write, or CAS access ends:

$$ue_4^{q,t} \wedge preq(2q + 1)^t \rightarrow \exists k : e(2q + 1, k) = t \wedge \neg acc(2q + 1, k).f \ .$$

2. For instruction cache $2q$, if the update enable signal of stage 1 is activated, then a read access ends:

$$ue_1^{q,t} \rightarrow \exists k : e(2q, k) = t \wedge acc(2q, k).r \ .$$

Proof. For data caches we have by hypothesis

$$ue_4^{q,t} = full_3^{q,t} \wedge \neg stall_4^{q,t}$$
$$= 1 \ .$$

Also by hypothesis we have

$$preq(2q + 1)^t = full_3^{q,t} \wedge (con.3.s_\pi^{q,t} \vee con.3.l_\pi^{q,t} \vee con.3.cas_\pi^{q,t})$$
$$= 1 \ .$$

Hence,

$$con.3.s_\pi^{q,t} \vee con.3.l_\pi^{q,t} \vee con.3.cas_\pi^{q,t} \ .$$

Thus, the update is due to a memory access and does not come from an instruction that does not require accessing the memory. Because $ue_4^{q,t}$ holds, we have

$$stall_4^{q,t} = full_3^{q,t} \wedge (haz_4^{q,t} \vee stall_5^{q,t})$$
$$= 0 \ .$$

Because $stall_5^{q,t} = 0$ and $full_3^{q,t} = 1$ we conclude

$$haz_4^{q,t} = mbusy(2q + 1)^t = 0 \ .$$

Thus, we have $someend(2q+1, t)$. The ending access cannot be a flush access, because by the construction of the control automata of the caches the $mbusy$ signal stays active during flush accesses.

For instruction caches we have by hypothesis

$$ue_1^{q,t} = full_0^{q,t} \wedge \neg stall_1^{q,t}$$
$$= 1 \ .$$

Hence,

$$stall_1^{q,t} = 0 \ .$$

Because

$$stall_1^{q,t} = full_0^{q,t} \wedge (haz_1^{q,t} \vee stall_2^{q,t})$$

and $full_0^{q,t} = 1$, we conclude

$$haz_1^{q,t} = mbusy(2q)^t = 0$$
$$preq(2q)^t = 1 \ .$$

Thus, we have $someend(2q, t)$. We argue as above that the ending access is not a flush access. Moreover, we know that write and CAS accesses do not occur at instruction caches and conclude the proof.   □

We come to a subtle point which is crucial for the liveness of the system.

Lemma 9.13 (access end implies update enable). When a read, write, or CAS access ends, the corresponding stage is updated, unless there is a stall signal coming from the stage below:

1. For data cache $2q + 1$, we have

$$\neg acc(2q + 1, k).f \wedge e(2q + 1, k) = t \rightarrow ue_4^{q,t} \ .$$

2. For instruction cache $2q$, we have

$$acc(2q, k).r \wedge e(2q, k) = t \wedge \neg stall_2^{q,t} \rightarrow ue_1^{q,t} \ .$$

Proof. For the data cache we have by hypothesis

$$preq(2q + 1)^t \wedge \neg mbusy(2q + 1)^t \ .$$

Because

$$preq(2q + 1)^t = full_3^{q,t} \wedge (con.3.l^{q,t} \vee con.3.s^{q,t} \vee con.3.cas^{q,t}) \ ,$$

we conclude

$$full_3^{q,t} = 1 \ .$$

Because

$$\begin{aligned}
stall_4^{q,t} &= full_3^{q,t} \wedge (haz_4^{q,t} \vee stall_5^{q,t}) \\
&= haz_4^{q,t} \\
&= mbusy(2q + 1)^t \\
&= 0 \ ,
\end{aligned}$$

we conclude

$$\begin{aligned}
ue_4^{q,t} &= full_3^{q,t} \wedge \neg stall_4^{q,t} \\
&= 1 \ .
\end{aligned}$$

For the instruction cache we conclude in a similar manner:

$$stall_2^{q,t} = 0$$
$$haz_1^{q,t} = mbusy(2q)^t$$
$$= 0$$
$$stall_1^{q,t} = full_0 \wedge (haz_1^{q,t} \vee stall_2^{q,t})$$
$$= 0$$
$$ue_1^{q,t} = full_0 \wedge \neg stall_1^{q,t}$$
$$= 1 .$$

$\qquad\qquad\qquad\qquad\qquad\qquad\qquad\qquad\qquad\qquad\qquad\qquad$ □

9.3.6 Scheduling Functions

The scheduling functions for a processor q of the pipelined multi-core system are defined analogous to the single-core processor. $I(q, k, t) = i$ means that instruction i^5 is in circuit stage k of processor q in cycle t:

$$I(q, k, 0) = 0$$

$$I(q, 1, t+1) = \begin{cases} I(q, 1, t) + 1 & ue_1^{q,t} \\ I(q, 1, t) & \text{otherwise} \end{cases}$$

$$I(q, k, t+1) = \begin{cases} I(q, k-1, t) & ue_k^{q,t} \\ I(q, k, t) & \text{otherwise} . \end{cases}$$

For the scheduling functions of the multi-core system, we state the counterpart of Lemma 7.14.

Lemma 9.14 (scheduling functions difference multi-core). Let $k \geq 2$. Then for all q:
$$I(q, k-1, t) = I(q, k, t) + full_{k-1}^{q,t} .$$

Proof. Completely analogous to the proof of Lemma 7.14. $\qquad\qquad$ □

9.3.7 Stepping Function

In what follows we distinguish, as in the sequential case, between the pipelined machine π and the sequential reference implementations σ. For every hardware cycle t of the multi-core pipelined machine π, we define the set $PS(t)$ of processors stepped at cycle t by

$$PS(t) = \{q \mid ue_4^{q,t} = 1\} ,$$

i.e., a processor q of the multi-core reference implementation σ is stepped whenever an instruction is clocked out of the memory stage of processor q of

---
^{5} Here, i is the local index of the instruction.

the pipelined machine. The number NS of processors stepped before cycle t is defined as

$$NS(0) = 0$$
$$NS(t + 1) = NS(t) + \#PS(t) .$$

Thus, in every cycle t we step $\#PS(t)$ processors. For every t we will define the values $s(m)$ of the step function s for $m \in [NS(t) : NS(t + 1) - 1]$ such that

$$s([NS(t) : NS(t + 1) - 1]) = PS(t) .$$

Any step function with this property would work, but we will later choose a particular function which makes the proof (slightly) easier. For any function with the above property the following easy lemma holds.

Lemma 9.15 (relating instruction count with scheduling functions).
For every processor q the scheduling function $I(q, 4, t)$ of the pipelined machine at time t counts the instructions completed $ic(q, t)$ on the sequential reference implementation:

$$ic(q, NS(t)) = I(q, 4, t) .$$

Proof. By induction on t. For $t = 0$ both sides of the equation are 0. For the induction step we assume

$$ic(q, NS(t)) = I(q, 4, t)$$

and split cases:

- $q \in PS(t)$. This implies

$$ic(q, NS(t + 1)) = ic(q, NS(t)) + 1.$$

  Since processor q is stepped in cycle t, we have $ue_4^{q,t}$ and, hence, $full_3^{q,t}$. By definition of the scheduling functions and Lemma 9.14 we conclude

$$I(q, 4, t + 1) = I(q, 3, t)$$
$$= I(q, 4, t) + 1.$$

- $q \notin PS(t)$. This implies

$$ic(q, NS(t + 1)) = ic(q, NS(t)).$$

  Since processor q is not stepped in cycle t, we have $\neg ue_4^{q,t}$ and by definition of the scheduling functions:

$$I(q, 4, t + 1) = I(q, 4, t).$$

$\square$

For $y \in [1 : \#PS(t)]$ we define step numbers m_y of steps performed during cycle t and processor IDs q_y, identifying the processors which perform these steps:

$$m_y = NS(t) + y - 1$$
$$q_y = s(m_y) .$$

In cycle t every processor is stepped at most once

$$z \neq y \rightarrow q_z \neq q_y ,$$

and hence, processor q_y cannot be stepped in between step numbers $NS(t)$ and m_y:

$$ic(q_y, m_y) = ic(q_y, NS(t)) . \tag{22}$$

By Lemmas 9.15, 9.7, and (22) we get

$$pseq(q_y, I(q_y, 4, t)) = pseq(q_y, ic(q_y, NS(t))) = m_y . \tag{23}$$

Thus,

$$pseq(q_1, I(q_1, 4, t)) = m_1 = NS(t)$$

and

$$pseq(q_{\#PS(t)}, I(q_{\#PS(t)}, 4, t)) = NS(t+1) - 1 .$$

We define the linear data access sequence $dacc'$ by

$$dacc'[m_y] = dacc(q_y, I(q_y, 4, t))$$

and conclude with part 3 of Lemma 9.10:

$$\begin{aligned}
h_\sigma^{m_y+1}.m &= h_\sigma^{pseq(q_y, I(q_y, 4, t))+1}.m \\
&= \delta_M(h_\sigma^{pseq(q_y, I(q_y, 4, t))}.m, dacc(q_y, I(q_y, 4, t))) \\
&= \delta_M(h_\sigma^{m_y}.m, dacc'[m_y]) .
\end{aligned}$$

By Lemma 8.6 we get the following relation for the hardware memory of the reference machine.

Lemma 9.16 (hardware memory of the reference computation).

$$h_\sigma^{NS(t+1)}.m = \Delta_M^{\#PS(t)}(h_\sigma^{NS(t)}.m, dacc'[NS(t) : NS(t+1) - 1])$$

9.3.8 Correctness Proof

For the correctness result of the multi-core system, we assume as before alignment and the absence of self modifying code. Recall that for $R \in reg(k)$ the single-core system simulation (correctness) theorem had the form

$$R_\pi^t = \begin{cases} R_\sigma^{I(k,t)} & vis(R) \\ R_\sigma^{I(k,t)-1} & full_k^t \wedge \neg vis(R) \wedge used(R, I_\sigma^{I(k,t)-1}) \end{cases}.$$

For the multi-core machine we aim at a theorem of the same kind. We have, however, to couple it with an additional statement correlating the memory abstraction $m(h_\pi^t)$ of the pipelined machine with the hardware memory $h_\sigma.m$ of the sequential reference implementation. We correlate the memory $m(h_\pi^t)$ of the pipelined machine π with the memory of the sequential machine σ after $NS(t)$ sequential steps:

$$a \in CR \cup DR \rightarrow m(h_\pi^t)(a) = h_\sigma^{NS(t)}.m(a) .$$

The main result of this book asserts the simulation of the pipelined multi-core machine π by the sequential multi-core reference implementation σ.

Lemma 9.17 (pipelined multi-core MIPS correctness). For $a \in CR \cup DR$ there are initial values $h_\sigma^0.m(a)$ and for every t there is a step function

$$s : [0 : NS(t) - 1] \rightarrow [0 : P - 1] ,$$

such that

- for all stages k, registers $R \in reg(k)$, and all processor IDs q, let

$$I(q, k, t) = i ,$$

then

$$R_\pi^{q,t} = \begin{cases} R_\sigma^{q,i} & vis(R) \\ R_\sigma^{q,i-1} & full_k^t \wedge \neg vis(R) \wedge used(R, I_\sigma^{q,i-1}) , \end{cases}$$

-

$$a \in CR \cup DR \rightarrow m(h_\pi^t)(a) = h_\sigma^{NS(t)}.m(a) .$$

Proof. By induction on t. For $t = 0$ all cache lines of π are invalid, as specified in Sect. 8.4.6. Thus, the memory abstraction of π is defined by the main memory:

$$m(h_\pi^0(a)) = h_\pi^0.mm(a) .$$

For $a \in CR \cup DR$ we choose initial values of the memory of σ by

$$h_\sigma^0.m(a) = h_\pi^0.mm(a) .$$

A meaningful initial program can only be guaranteed if the initial code region CR is realized in the main memory as a ROM. We choose the size of the ROM in $h_\sigma.m(a)$ to be the same as the size of the read only region in $h_\pi.mm$.

Compared to the proof for a single pipelined processor, the proof of the induction step changes only for the instruction and memory stages, i.e., for $k = 1$ and $k = 4$, and only for the memory components and their outputs. In what follows, we only present these parts of the proof. We first consider stage $k = 4$ and consider processors q with $ue_4^{q,t} = 1$ resp. with $q \in PS(t)$.

Using the formalism from Sect. 9.3.7, we have for $y \in [1 : \#PS(t)]$, step numbers m_y of steps performed during cycle t, and processor IDs q_y of processors that perform these steps:

$$m_y = NS(t) + y - 1$$
$$q_y = s(m_y) .$$

Since in cycle t every processor is stepped at most once, we have

$$\forall y_1, y_2 \in [1 : \#PS(t)] : y_1 = y_2 \leftrightarrow q_{y_1} = q_{y_2} .$$

The linear sequence of hardware data accesses $dacc'$ is defined as

$$dacc'[m_y] = dacc(q_y, I(q_y, 4, t)) .$$

Now, let $i_y = I(q_y, 4, t)$. From $ue_4^{q_y,t}$ we get $full_3^{q_y,t}$. By Lemmas 9.14 and 9.15 we get

$$I(q_y, 3, t) = I(q_y, 4, t) + 1$$
$$= i_y + 1$$
$$= ic(q_y, NS(t)) + 1 .$$

All registers R of register stage 3 are invisible. From the induction hypothesis we get

$$used(R, I_\sigma^{q,i_y}) \rightarrow R_\pi^{q_y,t} = R_\sigma^{q_y, I(q_y,3,t)-1}$$
$$= R_\sigma^{q_y, i_y}$$
$$= R_\sigma^{q_y, ic(q_y, NS(t))} .$$

We split cases on the value $preq(2q_y + 1)^t$ of the memory request signal of the data cache of processor q_y. Recall that it is defined as

$$preq(2q_y + 1)^t = (con.3.l^{q_y,t} \vee con.3.s^{q_y,t} \vee con.3.cas^{q_y,t}) \wedge full_3^{q_y,t}$$
$$= con.3.l^{q_y,t} \vee con.3.s^{q_y,t} \vee con.3.cas^{q_y,t} .$$

- If $preq(2q_y + 1)^t = 0$, instruction i_y is not accessing the memory. Since the register $con.3$ is always used, we can conclude that data access

$$dacc(q_y, i_y) = dacc'[m_y]$$

  is a void access.
- If $preq(2q_y + 1)^t = 1$, we conclude with part 1 of Lemma 9.12 that there exists a number k_y, such that a data access $acc(2q_y + 1, k_y)$ ends in cycle t. Because for the input registers R of the memory stage we have shown

$$used(R, I_\sigma^{q,i_y}) \rightarrow R_\pi^{q_y,t} = R_\sigma^{q_y,ic(q_y,NS(t))} ,$$

we can conclude by an easy case split on the type of instruction i_y:

$$acc(2q_y + 1, k_y) = dacc(q_y, ic(q_y, NS(t))) = dacc(q_y, i_y) = dacc'[m_y] .$$

Now things are easy. By induction hypothesis we have

$$a \in CR \cup DR \rightarrow m(h_\pi^t)(a) = h_\sigma^{NS(t)}.m(a) .$$

What we aim at showing is

$$a \in CR \cup DR \rightarrow m(h_\pi^{t+1})(a) = h_\sigma^{NS(t+1)}.m(a) .$$

Recall that in Sect. 8.5.9 we have numbered accesses $acc(i, k)$ according to their end time:

$$seq(E(0)) = [0 : NE(1) - 1]$$
$$seq(E(t)) = [NE(t) : NE(t+1) - 1] ,$$

and have defined sequentialized access sequence acc' as

$$acc'[seq(i, k)] = acc(i, k) .$$

By Lemma 8.65 we get for $a \in CR \cup DR$

$$m(h_\pi^{t+1})(a) = \Delta_M^{\#E(t)}(m(h_\pi^t), acc'[NE(t) : NE(t+1) - 1])(a)$$
$$= \Delta_M^{\#E(t)}(h_\sigma^{NS(t)}.m, acc'[NE(t) : NE(t+1) - 1])(a) .$$

The sequence $acc'[NE(t) : NE(t+1) - 1]$ of memory accesses ending in cycle t consists of read, write, CAS, and flush accesses. Let $acc''[0 : u - 1]$ be the subsequence of $acc'[NE(t) : NE(t+1) - 1]$ consisting exactly of the write and CAS accesses. Because reads and flushes don't change the memory abstraction we get

$$m(h_\pi^{t+1})(a) = \Delta_M^u(h_\sigma^{NS(t)}.m, acc'')(a) .$$

By Lemma 9.16 we have

$$h_\sigma^{NS(t+1)}.m = \Delta_M^{\#PS(t)}(h_\sigma^{NS(t)}.m, dacc'[NS(t) : NS(t+1) - 1]) .$$

Let $dacc''[0 : v-1]$ be the subsequence of the data access sequence $dacc'[NS(t) : NS(t+1) - 1]$ consisting only of the write and CAS accesses. Because reads and void accesses don't change the memory abstraction we get

$$h_\sigma^{NS(t+1)}.m = \Delta_M^v(h_\sigma^{NS(t)}.m, dacc'') .$$

Lemmas 9.13 and 9.12 guarantee that, if a write or a CAS memory access ends in a cache of processor q in cycle t, then it is an access to the data cache and the memory stage of processor q is updated. Thus, we have $q \in PS(t)$. Hence, all accesses from acc'' are included in the sequence $dacc''$. From the other side, Lemma 9.12 also implies that all accesses from $dacc''$ are included in the sequence acc''. Hence, sequences acc'' and $dacc''$ consist of exactly the same (write or CAS) accesses $acc(2q_y + 1, k_y)$, ending at cycle t.

From the definition of the end of a memory access, we know that there can be only one access to the data cache of processor q_y ending at cycle t:

$$\forall k, k' : e(2q_y + 1, k) = e(2q_y + 1, k') \rightarrow k = k' .$$

For every such access, we step the processor q_y exactly once. Hence, the lengths of sequences acc'' and $dacc''$ are the same:

$$u = v .$$

The order of accesses in these sequences might be different but by Lemma 8.56 write and CAS accesses ending in the same cycle have different addresses. Thus, the two access sequences have the same effect on memory. For $a \in DR \cup CR$ this gives us

$$\Delta_M^u(h_\sigma^{NS(t)}.m, acc'')(a) = \Delta_M^u(h_\sigma^{NS(t)}.m, dacc'')(a) ,$$

which implies

$$m(h_\pi^{t+1})(a) = h_\sigma^{NS(t+1)}.m(a) .$$

This shows the second statement of the lemma.

Next, for the data outputs of data caches of π we consider read and CAS accesses

$$acc(2q_y + 1, k_y) = dacc(q_y, I(q_y, 4, t)) = dacc(q_y, i_y) = dacc'[m_y] .$$

Let

$$a = acc(2q_y + 1, k_y).a .$$

By Lemma 8.56 read accesses and write accesses ending in the same cycle have different addresses. Hence,

$$h_\sigma^{NS(t)}.m(a) = h_\sigma^{NS(t)+y-1}.m(a) = h_\sigma^{m_v}.m(a) .$$

By Lemma 8.64 (1 step), part 2 of Lemma 8.10, (23), and part 2 of Lemma 9.10 we get

$$
\begin{aligned}
pdout_\pi(2q_y + 1)^t &= pdout1(ms(h_\pi^t), dacc'[m_y], 2q_y + 1) \quad \text{(Lemma 8.64)} \\
&= m(h_\pi^t)(a) \quad \text{(Lemma 8.10)} \\
&= h_\sigma^{NS(t)}.m(a) \\
&= h_\sigma^{m_v}.m(a) \\
&= h_\sigma^{pseq(q_y,i)}.m(a) \quad \text{(23)} \\
&= dataout(h_\sigma^{pseq(q_y,i)}.m, dacc(q_y, i)) \\
&= dmout_\sigma^{q_y,i} . \quad \text{(Lemma 9.10)}
\end{aligned}
$$

Finally, for the outputs of instruction caches $2q$ in stage $k = 1$ we consider processors q with $ue_1^{q,t} = 1$. Then by part 2 of Lemma 9.12 a read access $acc(2q, r)$ ends in cycle t, i.e., $(2q, r) \in E(t)$. Let

$$a = acc(2q, r).a \quad \text{and} \quad i = I(q, 1, t) \, .$$

By the same argument as for single-core pipelined processors we conclude

$$a = ima_\pi^{q,t} = ima_\sigma^{q,i} \in CR \, .$$

Thus, the access ending at the instruction cache of processor q in cycle t is a fetch access $iacc(q, i)$[6]:

$$acc(2q, r) = iacc(q, i) \, .$$

By Lemma 8.64 (1 step), part 2 of Lemma 8.10, and part 1 of Lemma 9.10 we get

$$
\begin{aligned}
pdout_\pi(2q)^t &= pdout1(ms(h_\pi^t), acc(2q, r), 2q) \qquad \text{(Lemma 8.64)} \\
&= m(h_\pi^t)(a) \qquad \text{(Lemma 8.10)} \\
&= h_\sigma^{NS(t)}.m(a) \\
&= h_\sigma^0.m(a) \\
&= dataout(h_\sigma^0.m, iacc(q, i)) \\
&= imout_\sigma^{q,i} \, . \qquad \text{(Lemma 9.10)}
\end{aligned}
$$

$\square$

9.3.9 Liveness

In the liveness proof of the multi-core processor we argue that every stage which is being stalled is eventually updated.

Lemma 9.18 (multi-core liveness).

$$stall_k^t \to \exists t' > t : ue_k^{t'}$$

Proof. The order of stages for which we prove the statement of the lemma is important. For liveness of the upper stages, we use liveness of the lower stages.

Recall that the signals in the stall engine are defined as

---

[6] Note that, due to the fact that we keep the request signal to the instruction cache active until the stall signal from the previous stage is removed, there may be several accesses $acc(2q, r_1)$, $acc(2q, r_2)$, ... corresponding to the access $iacc(q, i)$. Fortunately, all these accesses are reads which don't modify the state of the memory abstraction. As a result, we don't care about the exact reconstruction of the access sequence to the instruction cache and talk only about the existence of an access, which ends in the same cycle when we activate signal ue_1.

$$stall_k = full_{k-1} \wedge (haz_k \vee stall_{k+1})$$
$$full_k^{t+1} = ue_k^t \vee stall_{k+1}^t$$
$$ue_k = full_{k-1} \wedge \neg stall_k .$$

- For $k \in [5,6]$ we always have $stall_k = 0$ and there is nothing to show.
- For $k = 4$ we have

$$stall_4^t = full_3^t \wedge haz_4^t$$
$$= full_3^t \wedge dca.mbusy^t .$$

From Lemma 8.68 (liveness of shared memory) we know that the processor request to the data cache must be active in cycle t if the $mbusy$ signal is high:

$$dca.mbusy^t \rightarrow dca.preq^t .$$

Moreover, there exists a cycle $t' > t$ such that

$$\neg dca.mbusy^{t'} \wedge \forall t'' \in [t : t') : dca.mbusy^{t''}$$

holds. From Lemma 9.11 (stable inputs of accesses) we get that the registers of stage 3 are not updated:

$$\forall t'' \in [t : t') : \neg ue_3^{t''} ,$$

which implies

$$\forall t'' \in [t : t'] : dca.preq^{t'} .$$

Hence, there is a data access to the data cache ending in cycle t', which implies $ue_4^{t'}$ by Lemma 9.13.
- For $k = 3$ we have

$$stall_3^t = full_2^t \wedge stall_4^t$$

and conclude the statement by applying liveness of stage 4.
- For $k = 2$ we assume

$$\forall t' > t : \neg ue_2^{t'}$$

and prove the lemma by contradiction. From $stall_2^t$ we get $full_1^t$ and, hence,

$$\forall t' \geq t : full_1^{t'} \wedge stall_2^{t'} .$$

The stall signal for stage 2 is defined as

$$stall_2^t = full_1^t \wedge (haz_2^t \vee stall_3^t) .$$

If we have haz_2^t, we do a case split depending on the top-most stage when we have a hit. If for some $X \in \{A, B, D\}$ we have

$$top_X[2]^t \wedge (con.2.l_\pi^t \vee con.2.cas_\pi^t) ,$$

then by the liveness of stage 3 we find the smallest $t' > t$ such that $ue_3^{t'}$ holds, which implies $\neg stall_3^{t'}$. Since stage 2 is not updated in cycle t', we have

$$full_2^{t'+1} = (ue_2^{t'} \vee stall_3^{t'}) = 0 \, ,$$

which means that in cycle $t' + 1$ we do not have a hit in stage 2 anymore and have a top-most hit in stage 3:

$$top_X[3]^{t'+1} \wedge (con.3.l_\pi^{t'+1} \vee con.3.cas_\pi^{t'+1}) \, .$$

Moreover, for all cycles $t^* \geq t' + 1$ we also have

$$ue_3^{t^*} = full_2^{t^*} = 0 \, .$$

Using liveness of stage 4, we find the smallest cycle $t'' > t'$ such that $\neg stall_4^{t''}$ holds and get

$$full_3^{t''+1} = (ue_3^{t''} \vee stall_4^{t''}) = 0 \, .$$

Hence, at cycle $t'' + 1$ both stages 2 and 3 are not full. This implies

$$\neg haz_2^{t''+1} \wedge \neg stall_3^{t''+1}.$$

Thus, we have $\neg stall_2^{t''+1}$ and get a contradiction.

The case when we have $haz_2^t \wedge top_X[3]^t$ is proven in the same way using liveness of stage 4. For the last case we have

$$stall_3^t \wedge \neg haz_2^t \, ,$$

which also gives a contradiction by liveness of stage 3.

- For $k = 1$ we again assume

$$\forall t' > t : \neg ue_1^{t'}$$

and prove by contradiction. We have

$$\forall t' \geq t : haz_1^{t'} \vee stall_2^{t'}.$$

The hazard signal in stage 1 is generated by the instruction cache:

$$haz_1 = ica.mbusy \, .$$

We consider two cases. If

$$stall_2^t$$

holds, then we use liveness of stage 2 to find the smallest $t' > t$, such that

$$ue_2^{t'} \wedge \neg stall_2^{t'} \, .$$

Together with assumption $\forall t' > t : \neg ue_1^{t'}$ this implies for all cycles $t^* \geq t' + 1$

$$\neg full_1^{t^*} \wedge \neg stall_2^{t^*} .$$

If $\neg haz_1^{t'}$, we are done. If $haz_1^{t'}$, then using Lemma 8.68 (liveness of shared memory) we find $t'' > t'$, such that $\neg mbusy^{t''}$ holds, which implies $\neg haz_1^{t''}$ and gives a contradiction.

In the second case we have

$$haz_1^t \wedge \neg stall_2^t .$$

In the proof of the first case we have already considered the same situation for cycle t'.

$\square$

References

1. Beyer, S., Jacobi, C., Kroning, D., Leinenbach, D., Paul, W.: Instantiating un-interpreted functional units and memory system: Functional verification of the VAMP. In: Geist, D., Tronci, E. (eds.) CHARME 2003. LNCS, vol. 2860, pp. 51–65. Springer, Heidelberg (2003)
2. Cohen, E., Paul, W., Schmaltz, S.: Theory of multi core hypervisor verification. In: Emde Boas, P., Groen, F.C.A., Italiano, G.F., Nawrocki, J., Sack, H. (eds.) SOFSEM 2013: Theory and Practice of Computer Science. LNCS, vol. 7741, pp. 1–27. Springer, Heidelberg (2013)
3. Dalinger, I., Hillebrand, M.A., Paul, W.J.: On the verification of memory management mechanisms. In: Borrione, D., Paul, W. (eds.) CHARME 2005. LNCS, vol. 3725, pp. 301–316. Springer, Heidelberg (2005)
4. Emerson, E.A., Kahlon, V.: Rapid parameterized model checking of snoopy cache coherence protocols. In: Garavel, H., Hatcliff, J. (eds.) TACAS 2003. LNCS, vol. 2619, pp. 144–159. Springer, Heidelberg (2003)
5. Keller, J., Paul, W.J.: Hardware Design. Teubner-Texte zur Informatik. Teubner, Stuttgart (1995)
6. Kröning, D.: Formal Verification of Pipelined Microprocessors. PhD thesis, Saarland University (2001)
7. Lamport, L.: How to make a multiprocessor computer that correctly executes multiprocess programs. IEEE Trans. Comput. 28(9), 690–691 (1979)
8. Maisuradze, G.: Implementing and debugging a pipelined multi-core MIPS machine. Master's thesis, Saarland University (2014)
9. MIPS Technologies, Inc. MIPS32 Architecture For Programmers – Volume 2 (March 2001)
10. Müller, C., Paul, W.: Complete formal hardware verification of interfaces for a FlexRay-like bus. In: Gopalakrishnan, G., Qadeer, S. (eds.) CAV 2011. LNCS, vol. 6806, Springer, Heidelberg (2011)
11. Müller, S.M., Paul, W.J.: On the correctness of hardware scheduling mechanisms for out-of-order execution. Journal of Circuits, Systems, and Computers 8(02), 301–314 (1998)
12. Müller, S.M., Paul, W.J.: Computer Architecture, Complexity and Correctness. Springer, Heidelberg (2000)
13. Pong, F., Dubois, M.: A survey of verification techniques for cache coherence protocols (1996)

14. Schmaltz, J.: A formal model of clock domain crossing and automated verification of time-triggered hardware. In: FMCAD, pp. 223–230. IEEE Computer Society, Los Alamitos (2007)

15. Schmaltz, S.: Towards the Pervasive Formal Verification of Multi-Core Operating Systems and Hypervisors Implemented in C. PhD thesis, Saarland University, Saarbrücken (2013)

16. Sweazey, P., Smith, A.J.: A class of compatible cache consistency protocols and their support by the IEEE futurebus. SIGARCH Computer Architecture News 14(2), 414–423 (1986)

17. Weaver, D.L.: OpenSPARC internals. Sun Microsystems (2008)

Index